Making the Connections

Using Internal Communication to Turn Strategy into Action

SECOND EDITION

BILL QUIRKE

GOWER

Published by
Gower Publishing Limited
Gower House
Croft Road
Aldershot
Hampshire
GU11 3HR
England

Gower Publishing Company
Suite 420
101 Cherry Street
Burlington
VT 05401-4405
USA

Bill Quirke has asserted his moral right under the Copyright, Designs and Patents Act, 1988, to be identified as the author of this work.

British Library Cataloguing in Publication Data
Quirke, Bill, 1954–
  Making the connections : using internal communication to
  turn strategy into action
  1. Communication in management 2. Communication in
  organizations 3. Information resources management
  4. Organizational change
  I. Title
  658.4'5

  ISBN-13: 9780566087806

Library of Congress Control Number: 2007931876

Printed and bound in Great Britain by MPG Books Ltd, Bodmin, Cornwall.

Contents

List of Figures and Tables

Acknowledgements

I would like to thank the following people for their help and contributions towards this book: Richard Bloomfield, Josef Goetz, James Greathouse, Sabine Jaccaud, Alex Kalombaris, Charlotte Knight, Jane Lebeau, Helena Norman, David Norton, Paul Santamaria, Jane Sparrow, Jacqueline Wallach, Dominic Walters, Mark Watkins, Elli Xuereb, Per Zetterquist.

Preface

This new edition reflects a number of changes that have happened over the last 5 years.

Internal communication has gone further up chief executives' agendas. They know that it is important, and understand that engaging their people is all the more crucial, and more difficult to achieve, in a world of joint ventures, outsourcing and partnering.

Perhaps as a result, chief executives are demanding greater professionalism from internal communicators, with tougher questioning on what value they add. A Deloitte and Touche Human Capital Survey asked which HR issues were very important to the success of an organization. The good news is that 95 per cent of chief executives said 'effective internal communication'. The bad news is that only 22 per cent thought it was being delivered effectively.

Internal communication has been driven up the agenda by external forces such as greater regulation and the need for compliance with financial regulations. Just when it seems harder to keep secrets and respect confidentiality, regulations like Sarbanes Oxley are changing what you can tell people, and when. Chief executives have to balance when and how they will share market sensitive information so that they can meet their regulatory duties, and ensure they bring their employees into the picture as quickly as possible.

Organizations want to be employers of choice, to tap into emotional commitment and discretionary overtime by creating more engaged employees.

The impact of poor industrial relations, the rise of employee representative forums and the complexities of different national labour laws means organizations know they need to take greater care over their communication.

Globalization means that organizations are playing on a global chessboard, to take advantage of their scope and scale. This means they face greater complexity of cultural differences, need international collaboration and have to balance global and local communication.

The blurring of boundaries between what's inside and outside an organization, where outsourced employees disappear off the organization chart but stay in the same office, means that 'internal' communication has to cover more than those who are inside. Outsourced partners, offshore call centres, joint ventures and supply chain partnerships are increasingly within the remit of internal communicators who aim to harmonize the different voices customers hear from an organization, and protect the values of its brand.

Integration and interdependency

Organizations are increasingly sensitive to the importance of their reputation and their vulnerability to their own employees' behaviour. They understand both the risk of not communicating with their people, and the need for communicating well.

As reputation becomes important to maintaining a 'licence to operate', and the vulnerability of that reputation increases, organizations are having to take an integrated approach to communicating with all their stakeholders. It is no longer possible to box off audiences and keep them hermetically sealed from each other.

There is no longer such a thing as a local story. A story happening, say, in Hong Kong, can be accessible online. For example, British newspaper *The Guardian* has as many online readers as print readers, with a great deal of those on the West Coast of the US. Now what happens in one part of the globe is rapidly communicated in another.

People are our voice

More industries are finding that their licence to operate is being challenged. Companies are expected to deliver more by a broader range of stakeholders, who are more likely to blame businesses for problems. One example of this is the riots in India, provoked by India's health ministry's rejection of the findings of an environmental group which had reported high levels of pesticides in Coca Cola and Pepsi.

It is all the more important then for employees to act as advocates for their organization, to tell its story and argue its case, especially since employees are so influential.

The Edelman Annual Trust Barometer tracks 2000 opinion leaders' trust of institutions, companies and information source's credibility. Opinion leaders consider rank-and-file employees more credible spokespersons than corporate CEOs, and information conveyed by regular company employees have the same credibility as articles in newspapers (2007 Annual Edelman Trust Barometer).

As employees become more influential, they may also become less cooperative. Employees' deference to institutions has decreased, and their trust in management has eroded. The promise of a stable career ladder, in exchange for following the rules and being a good corporate citizen, has all but disappeared. Organizations ask their people to give their engagement, enthusiasm and passion, while simultaneously reminding them that they're responsible for their own employability, and that there are no jobs for life.

Impact of technology

The rise of open networking is increasing the power of employees to inform themselves and network directly with each other. At the time of writing there are 20 million blogs worldwide, 75 000 new blogs every day and 11 000 blog updates per hour. MySpace is adding 250 000 users a day.

This means organizations will realize they don't have a captive audience, that they are competing for time and attention and may not be very competitive.

A 2006 study of 119 chief information officers (CIOs) in mid size and larger US companies by Forrester Research, indicated that Web 2.0 developments are being widely introduced into companies, with 90 per cent of respondents having adopted at least one of six prominent Web 2.0 tools – blogs, wikis, podcasts, RSS, social networking and content tagging – with over a third already using all six of them. CIOs saw 'relatively high business value' in RSS (the syndication systems used in the blogging world), wikis (user-editable websites) and tagging, but relatively low value in social networking and blogging.

A 2007 McKinsey survey of 2800 executives looked at six Web 2.0 tools and found that social networking was the most popular, with 19 per cent of companies having invested in it (John Naughton, *The Observer*, Sunday 1st April 2007).

In the old world of 'command and control' and 'information is power', information was held at the top by the leadership and was cascaded sparingly. In a world where it is now hard to control where information may emerge, and the means of sharing it are so widespread, the balance between information 'haves' and 'have-nots' shifts dramatically. This means leaders have to rethink what they should tell their people, and when.

Consumers are no longer passive receivers of information

The impact of new media means employees can bypass censorship and are less easy to control. Individuals can generate their own news content. News pictures are now regularly provided by members of the public on telephones and digital cameras. This means that an employee can easily become a journalist. There are 12 million bloggers in the US, and 4 million of those describe themselves as journalists.

People are becoming more selective, using search engines to filter and select the kind of content they want, subscribing to the information they want and stripping out stuff they see as irrelevant. News is becoming a consumer item, and people will increasingly select what news they want, how they want it and when they want it.

Employees are more media literate, more active and less passive. This means damaging allegations and bad news – such as Coca Cola in India, Apple's battery problems and McDonalds Super Size Me – travel faster and hit you quicker.

In the old days, organizations had to worry about the threat of the news crew at the factory gates. As employees emerged, and were quizzed by reporters, what would they say? This drove the need for effective communication, if only to reduce the chance of a bad quote. Now with access to a camera phone and an Internet connection, employees can become journalists themselves and what employees used to write as graffiti, they can now post to the web.

Making the connections

Companies know that communication with their people is important. They know that the energies and the enthusiasm of their employees need to point in the same direction. However, in the enthusiastic rush to plug together different components of communication best practice, many organizations are short-circuiting their own efforts. There is no shortage of good intentions and no shortfall in professionalism and good ideas. However, the road to incoherence is paved with good communications. Often, internal communication is less than the sum of its parts, because those parts do not fit together effectively. Organizations concentrate on getting the right individual parts and then merely cobble them together – the recipe for Frankenstein's monster.

What's the problem?

Too often, those on the front line report that there are fatal disconnects between the business strategy and the communication strategy. There is no clear link between information that is sent to employees and what they are supposed to understand from it. The small detail, carefully crafted in the boardroom, makes no sense when it is divorced from its context. Meanwhile, companies are keen to find new technological approaches to communication, which, in fact, only exacerbate the problem.

Life is moving too fast to rely on the inadequate way we currently communicate in organizations. Today's best practice hero too easily becomes tomorrow's financial zero. Employees who thought their company was doing well and their future was secure can suddenly discover that events on the other side of the globe can put them out of a job.

In a world of tighter interdependencies, where fortunes are so closely linked, people need a better understanding of the connections. Internal communication has absorbed too well the lesson that the medium is the message. The message is often failing to get through because the medium eats the message. Never has so much been communicated by so many, and meant so little. We need to move from the message and media business to that of creating meaning and understanding.

What needs to change?

In an information age, internal communication is what enables businesses to engage their people's intellectual and creative assets to produce value. Despite the increasing complexity of the world, people still want to know some simple truths about what is going on, and they want to be treated as if they matter.

We have to make two changes simultaneously – identify what is the intended business value in communicating and design a better process to deliver that value. We have to shift from seeing internal communication as a process of distribution, to using it as a process of conversion. Just as an assembly line worker converts, or adds value to, a component he receives from up the line, so we have to convert information we receive into meaning in order to help employees make the right decisions.

The role of internal communication is to illuminate the connections between different pieces of information, to shine a light on the web of interdependencies and to show the links between one area and another. Its job is to provide employees with the information they need to do their work, and to paint the bigger picture and tell the fuller story that puts that information into context.

How this book will help

This book looks at what a successful business needs from its people, what gets in the way and the role of communication in helping to bridge the gap. It is designed to help companies link together the disparate components of their internal communication for a more effective result. It describes the why, the what and the how of internal communication – why business needs better

communication to achieve its objectives, what internal communication
needs to deliver to add value and how organizations need to manage their
communication for best results.

Its aims are fivefold:

- to focus communication on creating business value;

- to make the connection between business strategy and communication
  strategy;

- to alert leaders to their impact, influence and responsibility;

- to show how better internal communication engages employees;

- to show how to integrate communication for greater coherence.

The book is organized into three parts. Part I, 'Turning Communication to
Advantage', shows how organizations need better communication to deliver
results and how the management and practice of internal communication
need to be improved in order to meet business needs.

It examines how good communication can produce greater value by
addressing key issues at the top of business agendas. It focuses on the
key concerns of chief executives – creating competitive differentiation,
developing new markets and products, reducing cost, streamlining processes,
and restructuring. It highlights how internal communication can help
organizations achieve their strategic objectives enabling employees to deliver
a brand promise to customers; making restructuring work, or increasing cross-
business collaboration and innovation.

Change is a significant feature of today's business world and Part II, 'Leading
Change', looks at how to use communication to make more effective change
and how to create greater responsiveness and agility within the organization.
It gives specific recommendations for communicating change, driving change
initiatives and projects, promoting internal campaigns and sustaining greater
responsiveness.

In terms of their internal communication, organizations first have to do
the right thing by connecting communication strategy to their business
strategy and, second, do things right – have efficient and effective processes.
Part III, 'Pulling it Together', shows how to structure and manage internal
communication to deliver the business agenda and closely details the links in
the communication chain.

Satellite broadcasts alienate the middle managers they were designed to
inspire, e-mail clutters and voicemail frustrates instead of helping. Face-to-face
meetings force managers to undermine their own credibility by presenting
irrelevant and tedious corporate information. Then, after all the effort and

the investment involved in communicating, the finance director asks the inevitable questions about how much this will all cost, and if it is worthwhile.

As the quantity of information increases, the quality decreases. Although employees are sent more and more pieces of the jigsaw, they are unable to put them together to form a coherent picture. Organizations indulge in 'flat pack communication' – sending out the components of the picture and relying on the recipient to assemble them, with the inevitable result that the end-product has a few screws loose or missing.

None of this is inevitable. Some simple links and connections can be made to ensure that communication helps, rather than hinders, the business. This book is about making those connections. It explains how businesses can use better internal communication to achieve differentiation from their competition, to improve their quality, customer service and innovation, and to manage change more effectively. It shows how organizations need to use their best 'joined up' communication if they want to be successful.

REFERENCES

Deloitte and Touche (2003), Human Capital Survey, *Personnel Today*, January.
Edelman (2007), *Edelman Trust Baromoter.*
Forrester Research (2006), *Q4 CIO Confidence Poll.*
Naughton, J. (2007), McKinsey Survey, *The Observer*, 1 April.

I Turning Communication to Advantage

1 Getting More Value From Internal Communication

Business today faces a torrent of changes that redefines what is required of employees. Organizations are quickly discovering that they need more than simple compliance from their staff: they need – now more than ever – to engage their minds, creativity, energy and commitment. A business can only achieve its best when everyone's energies point in the same direction.

This changes not only the assumptions on which internal communication is based, but also the job it is intended to do. Traditionally, internal communication has focused on the announcement of management conclusions and the packaging of management thinking into messages for mass distribution to the 'troops'. However, its real place is at the leading edge of change. The value that it can add is immense – faster change, more flexibility and innovation, better quality decisions, better knowledge sharing and a more motivated workforce. Although, as a whole, leaders believe in the power of communication, even leading companies fail to harness that power to deliver the necessary results. Internal communication is vital to success and when done well can provide strategic advantage through aligning employee efforts, sharing knowledge and engaging their passion.

The purpose of this chapter is to lay the foundations for the remainder of the book. It highlights the urgent need to improve communication, the business pay-off for doing so and the gap that needs to be closed between aspirations and day-to-day practice. It also makes the connection between the business issues that senior management see as priorities and the importance of good communication in achieving them. It describes how successful organizations see the value of internal communication and highlights those areas in which outdated approaches have created toxic complexity.

TRAPPED IN A TIME WARP

The problem is very simple – although success depends on a new approach to internal communication, organizations are spending all their time and effort on an outdated one. Failure to change in organizations is due to the disconnect between the communication that the business needs and the communication it receives. In other words, internal communication is trapped in a time warp. 'If cars had improved at the same rate as computers,' says Bill Gates, 'we'd have $25 cars achieving 1000 miles to the gallon.' But if cars had improved at the same rate as internal communication, we'd still be walking in front of them with a red flag!

The way in which organizations have traditionally approached communication has been based on applying outdated rules – with disappointing and frustrating results. Companies are falling into a vicious circle. By failing to make a strong enough connection between business strategy and internal communication, they fail to plan and monitor progress appropriately. They then become increasingly frustrated by the failure of communication to deliver results. Organizations are short-changing themselves by not seeing communication through to the end – converting awareness into action. The real value of internal communication is to help deliver business ends by enabling employees to turn strategy into action. However, getting there means draining a swamp of communication confusion and complexity to create a path of coherence and consistency.

WHAT IS CHANGING?

The job which internal communication has to do has changed because organizations are facing unprecedented pressures to deliver in a rapidly changing environment. Research consistently shows that senior managers have five principal concerns:

- creating competitive differentiation;

- developing new markets and products;

- reducing cost and streamlining processes;

- restructuring, integrating an acquisition, making a merger work or divesting a non-core business;

- redefining the roles of the corporate centre and the divisions.

Organizations are discovering that business challenges like these can all be affected by the clear targeting and management of internal communication.

However, a 'one size fits all' approach will not work. Internal communication needs to be aligned specifically with the organization's individual business strategy. Discussed below are four examples of how different strategies demand different internal communication approaches and how successful companies take the role of internal communication seriously.

Using internal communication to create competitive differentiation

Tesco, the UK supermarket chain, aims to create greater loyalty among its customers and to increase the average size of their shopping basket. One enjoyable personal contact with staff per trip, their research shows, can earn lifetime loyalty from a customer.

Tesco employs 150 000 staff in 560 stores who need to deliver this experience to its customers. Since personal contact plays such a key role in customer retention, employees must understand Tesco's brand promise. The job of internal communication is to create a deeper understanding of the brand promise among employees, and to help them translate it into specific actions for customers – opening up checkouts when queues get long, packing bags, helping shoppers take their shopping out to the car park and even providing jump leads when their car batteries go flat. Internal communication's value lies in helping differentiate Tesco from its competitors and creating higher customer loyalty for higher profitability.

In the world of professional services, the big accountancy and consulting firms are federations which share a name and a culture. Now they want to build distinctive brands. Ernst & Young, KPMG, PricewaterhouseCoopers and Accenture are spending significantly on building global brands. Their investment is aimed at differentiating themselves and reassuring their clients worldwide, who feel branding is increasingly important in helping them choose from whom to buy a service.

These firms sell a diverse set of sophisticated services worldwide, but global clients expect consistent delivery throughout the world, wherever offices are located. Global branding carries with it the promise of global consistency.

Professional service firms have to develop a portfolio of standard processes differentiated by strong brand values, thought leadership and the ability to develop solutions for clients. These ambitions demand not only better management of the knowledge and learning within the firm, but also greater collaboration between employees. Creating value therefore demands that employees have an external focus, since it is knowledge of their clients' industry issues which demonstrates a real familiarity with the business and helps win contracts. The challenge is for employees to combine knowledge and understanding of the client's problems with the knowledge of the consultancy's worldwide capabilities that could help solve them.

Ernst & Young, for example, uses internal communication to help them do just that. Its role is to help create an organization which is increasingly comfortable with continuous change, has higher levels of staff retention, increased project efficiency and knowledge management, and thus greater client value.

Using internal communication to develop new products and markets

GlaxoSmithKline (GSK) is a successful company in a very successful sector, with spectacular growth figures. Within the consumer healthcare organization, internal communication is clearly linked to creating shareholder value.

The company's strategy is to exploit its portfolio of brands as effectively as possible. To do that, GSK applies global processes with a local face in individual markets. The aim is to drive greater innovation and creativity across the business, to reduce costs and to reduce duplication by sharing services. They also aim to standardize processes where possible, because it makes it easier to improve them and focuses time and effort on innovation in new areas, rather than on reinventing wheels that exist elsewhere in the business.

To GSK the importance of internal communication lies in helping develop a global business in which managers from each country understand and support a global approach and have stronger local ownership of global processes.

Using internal communication to reduce cost and streamline processes

Unipart manufactures and distributes auto parts to car manufacturers and a large supply chain for the replacement market. In terms of quality and productivity it is now a world leader. It has three key objectives – remove cost and waste, improve productivity and deliver outstanding customer service.

Unipart's aim is for its 4000 employees to help achieve those objectives, as well as pursuing its core crusade of achieving 50 per cent more for 50 per cent less cost. Its key to achieving this is to target the supply chain.

The organization recognizes that there is a close interdependence between the suppliers in the chain. If there are inefficiencies, duplication and waste in the supplier at the bottom of the chain, these are inevitably passed upwards. Waste is then multiplied at each successive link, saddling the ultimate customer with disproportionately high costs. Beating the competition therefore requires a much tighter management of the supply chain.

Unipart has developed its own approach to supply chain management which involves working in project teams with suppliers to identify the hidden cost of transactions which benefit nobody and eliminate them, thereby reducing cost and inconvenience to both parties. This approach is in stark contrast to the traditional one of using purchasing power to browbeat suppliers into offering better deals.

However, to make this partnership approach work, attitudes and behaviours needed to shift within the Unipart workforce; they had to understand and buy into the ethos of partnership and let go of the browbeating approach.

For Unipart the importance of internal communication lies in providing employees with the knowledge to do the job, the will to identify and make change, and the licence and permission to get on and do it.

All these organizations have adopted a similar approach to internal communication. They have approached it as a means to an end, rather than an end in itself, and they have:

- clearly identified their strategy;

- made the connection between the strategy and the specific attitudes and behaviours they need from their people;

- focused their communication on helping achieve those attitudes and behaviours.

USING INTERNAL COMMUNICATION TO GAIN PEOPLE'S SUPPORT FOR THE BUSINESS STRATEGY

Organizations are keen for their employees to understand the business strategy but, more importantly, they want their people to help turn this strategy into reality by providing excellent customer service, continuous improvement and innovation.

A company thrives by offering customers something different and more valuable than its competitors can. It then has to ensure that its employees deliver on the promise it makes to customers and that employee values, loyalty and behaviour are all connected. Building an internal culture that creates unity and pride among employees acts as a competitive edge that is difficult for competitors to copy.

Indifference, however, can kill differentiation. Customers' satisfaction is affected by their experience of the entire organization's performance, so employee attitudes and behaviour are critical to retaining them. The Journal of Marketing cites the main reasons for customer defection as being employee-related. While only 9 per cent of customers are lured away by the competition, 68 per cent are turned away by an employee's indifferent attitude.

Providing a quality service or product to the customer and good communication are inextricably linked. Research shows that good internal communication fosters increased employee satisfaction. Better satisfaction reduces staff turnover, and higher staff retention is linked with higher customer satisfaction. Research carried out by the management consultancy, Bain and Co, reveals that satisfied customers are more likely to stay loyal, and that higher customer retention leads to higher profitability.

Organizations are eager to make the customer's voice heard within the organization, to challenge internal viewpoints, create a greater sense of commercialism and re-educate employees about customers' priorities. Yet, too often, the way in which they manage communication does not fit these aspirations but, instead, causes resistance and misunderstanding.

In one organization, senior management were frustrated at the failure of production workers to appreciate the true level of market competitiveness. While only 25 per cent of the board believed that customers were satisfied, nearly 50 per cent of first-line supervisors believed that they were satisfying customers. Worse, supervisors then reassured their team members that everything was fine – defeating the board's efforts to sound a wake-up call to the workforce.

This disconnect between top management and those at the sharp end was due to a breakdown in the management chain and a failure to educate employees. This company is not alone: 80 per cent of companies reviewed by continuous improvement consultancy Peter Chadwick in the UK, France and Germany monitored customer satisfaction, but only 20 per cent made the information available below middle management. Information about customers and what they value is typically only circulated to 35 per cent of staff. Without such knowledge, how can those dealing with customers be expected to understand them and add value?

INNOVATION IS CRUCIAL TO STRATEGY

Research by KPMG suggests that most of the UK's largest businesses believe innovation to be crucial in creating an enduring and successful strategy. Management seems convinced that successfully introducing new products and ideas can help even mature companies revive their fortunes. This is borne out by a PricewaterhouseCoopers study of 800 large companies. The most innovative 20 per cent had generated 75 per cent of their turnover from new products and services in the previous 5 years. The least effective 20 per cent gained only 10 per cent of their turnover in that way.

Today's pace of technological advance means that any gain in superior performance will be brief. Points of competitive differentiation – such as price, quality and distribution – are soon matched. No single innovation will yield a sustainable competitive advantage. The competitive advantage of companies such as General Electric grows out of the company's culture – a climate that fosters continual innovations and keeps searching for competitive advantage. The question marks that have appeared over Marks and Spencer would have been unthinkable at almost any previous point in the company's history and show that no competitive advantage can be taken for granted. However, if you get the culture right, sustainable competitive advantage by innovation and other means can follow. Good internal communication is key to getting the culture right.

CONTINUOUS IMPROVEMENT

A KPMG study of a cross-section of 135 manufacturers worldwide over a 15-year period highlighted lack of quality as the single most important source of weakness in Western industry. It concluded that the most significant cost reductions are realized by improved cooperation and communication between the marketing and research and development departments. This approach leads to the reduction of waste through better process control, reduced engineering changes and improved product design. Creating this sort of continuous improvement culture requires better communication, for well informed and more widely educated employees.

Lack of attention to communication and involvement has undermined improvement programmes. Western manufacturing still lags behind due to the very limited success of its improvement programmes, most of which start with a bang, become bogged down and finally fizzle out. They fail principally because project leaders take too narrow a view and do not communicate with, and involve, enough other disciplines and departments – particularly the shopfloor.

All the changes described make great demands on employees. They have to understand what's happening, deal with change, form new relationships, play by new rules and make new decisions faster and in cooperation with colleagues, all with one end in mind – creating greater value. Creating that value depends upon giving them internal communication which is itself valuable.

HOW CAN COMMUNICATION CREATE VALUE?

The first step to realizing the value of internal communication is to expect it to have some.

Competition has forced companies to compete more fiercely and prompted consumers to ask for more for their money. To compete through greater innovation, better quality, cost-effectiveness and customer service, organizations need motivated and committed employees.

As things now stand, organizations are unlikely to achieve the objectives of engaging and informing their employees. There are two reasons for this. First, communication strategies are too often based on keeping people informed in a stable, 'jobs-for-life' hierarchical organization with a dominant market position. These are useless in a fast-changing, insecure organization fighting for market share and trying to innovate and develop new products. Second, organizations are not applying the lessons which they have learned in other areas of the business – that value is created through careful management of assets, efficiencies in supply chain management, applying a customer focus and continuous process improvement.

Communication is vital to creating value. Its importance lies in turning strategy into action. For strategies to succeed people need to understand what the strategy is, the context to the strategy and the rationale behind it. They need to know their own role and the specific actions they should take. Unfortunately, organizations often do not treat communication as a value-adding business discipline but as a branch of welfare, and, when necessary, a means of management propaganda.

Internal communication is so critical to business success that it cannot be approached as a cottage industry, or left to 'gifted amateurs'.

HELPING MANAGE COMPLEXITY

Flatter structures are devolving decision making to lower levels in the organization, creating the need for more information to ensure high-quality decisions. Employees expect to be treated as adults and want to know the 'why' as well as the 'what' behind management decisions. All this means a geometric increase in the amount and complexity of information being circulated.

Change now means being in a state of almost constant flux. Winning organizations are those which are most fluid, anticipate change and adapt quickly. Businesses which are able to make constant changes quickly and effectively are more competitive. This means that agility, learning and adaptation are key to competitive advantage. Speed of implementation is more important than brilliance of strategy. However, speeding up the change process is a tall order; in effect, organizations have to change the gearbox while keeping the car on the road. They have to win the support and participation of their employees, manage change while maintaining normal activities and ensure that the changes they introduce stay in place. Effective internal communication facilitates change. Handled correctly, it makes implementation easier and faster, reduces resistance to change and provides clearer leadership.

TOXIC COMMUNICATION

Although internal communication can provide greater value for organizations, there are some improvements which have to be made first.

Business leaders are failing to convey their objectives to their staff. Trust inside organizations is low, and some employees are happy to be ignorant of what is going on around them. While change is constant, it is communicated poorly, and the volume of information overloads limited employee 'brain space'. Finally, organizations are confusing volume and value, and producing 'toxic communication' which consumes employees' time while creating confusion.

Research among employees over the last 10 years shows the impact of the disconnect between the thinking of the leaders and the attitudes of the led. Understanding what leads to success creates the motivation to achieve it; 84 per cent of employees who understand what makes their business successful want to help create that success, whereas only 46 per cent of those who don't understand share that feeling. When employees understand their overall role in the business, 91 per cent will work towards that success, but the number plummets to 23 per cent if they don't. The message is clear – employees who understand the big picture are more likely to play their part to help their company succeed.

To succeed, companies need employees who are clear about the overall direction and the part they need to play. They also need their employees to be willing to follow the lead and play their part.

When it comes to being clear and willing, employees fall into four categories (see Figure 1.1):

Unclear what the strategy is, but willing to help

Fifty per cent of employees typically do not know what the strategy is and only 25 per cent ever get feedback on progress. This 25 per cent tends to be positioned near the top of the organization, so those on the front line, with customer contact, have the least idea. Willing, but unclear about direction, they are 'unguided missiles'. These represent the greatest opportunity for organizations. They have good will towards the organization, and usually a desire for greater involvement. If people are a company's greatest asset, these people represent assets which are seriously underperforming.

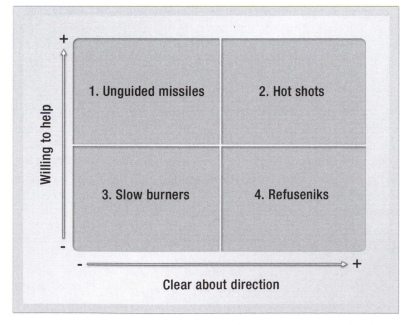

Figure 1.1   The different degrees of employees clarity and willingness

Employees rarely operate in a 'strategy vacuum'. Even when they are completely misguided or out-of-date, they usually believe that they have some idea of what's going on in the business and fill in the vacuum for themselves. In other words, a lack of direction from the leadership leaves these people to find their own way. At best, this robs the company of their true efforts; at worst, it turns them into 'unguided missiles'.

When organizations are shifting strategy – responding to change in markets and among competitors, and looking for new ways of adding value – they are very likely to leave their employees behind. These employees will continue to pursue a vague notion of a strategy based on past glories and outdated definitions of value and service.

Employees who insist on providing Rolls Royce solutions to Mini-sized problems are often working from a keen sense of heritage and pride based on their past product leadership. Their enthusiasm creates unnecessary cost, complexity and confusion.

Clear and willing

These employees know the company's direction, understand the broader context, know their part, and get feedback on both the company's progress and on their own performance. They are the 'hot shots', warming to the company's aspirations and fired up to help achieve them.

Unclear and unwilling

These employees are the 'slow burners' who are not sure where the company is heading, but drag their feet anyway. They are usually characterized as not knowing and not caring. However, they are in fact a mixture of sheep and goats – those who feel unmotivated because they lack a sense of direction and those who are happy to continue going their own way.

Companies tend to become fixated both with this group – because they are perceived not to care – and with the next group, the 'refuseniks', because they seem actively to oppose change. However, their real focus should be on the 'unguided missiles', who represent huge untapped potential, and on providing them with clear goals and direction. Similarly, clearer direction will raise the motivation and desire to contribute of significant numbers of 'the slow burners'.

Clear but disagree

People resist doing anything which violates their sense of professionalism. They may try to continue with an old strategy because they believe that it makes better sense. Where they disagree with the direction of the company, these 'refuseniks' may actively resist or undermine it.

COMMUNICATION AS A WAY OF MAKING CONNECTIONS

If companies want high performance, leaders must demonstrate the connection between the company's success and that of its employees. There has to be a link between the leader, who can see what needs to be done, and the doers, who have their hands on the levers of change but who may not see the big picture. Communication should provide that link, connecting those who know what needs to change to those who have the power to make change happen.

Making the connection means providing everyone with a shared understanding of the organization's strategic business issues and ensuring that they understand the 'whys' as well as the 'whats'. As reasonable as this sounds, that connection is not being made strongly or consistently enough.

A survey by Albert Karr of the chief executives of 164 large companies showed that most of them believed that personal communication increases workers' job satisfaction and commitment and results in improved earnings. However, most of the chief executives questioned also said that, because of other demands, they couldn't afford to give more time to communicating with their people.

A survey carried out by Forum Corporation found that 82 per cent of Fortune 50 executives believed that their corporate strategy is understood by 'everyone who needs to know'. This suggests that there is a limited number of people who need to know, and that the majority of employees are not among that number. A Louis Harris study concludes that, 'less than a third of employees say management provides clear goals and direction', pointing to a large gap between perception and reality. Further evidence comes from Professor Robert Kelley of Carnegie Mellon University who found that nearly 70 per cent of the 400 corporate executives he asked believed that business leaders fail adequately to communicate their goals to employees.

TRUST IS LOW

Employee attitude surveys typically show that most of the information employees receive is via the grapevine, and they have a healthy scepticism about the information they receive through formal channels. Often they believe management has a hidden agenda, and feel that saying what they really think would be a career-limiting move. At the same time, managers think that they are good at communicating, are cynical about their leadership's ability, and are overloaded with information they can make little sense of, but still won't share.

IGNORANCE IS BLISS

Employee research consistently shows that only 50 per cent of employees know where their companies are going or what they are trying to achieve.

Despite this level of ignorance, managers think they are doing a good job in communicating. The lower you go down the organization – that is, closer to the customer – the less clear the business's objectives become. Where people do know the objectives, they rarely get feedback on progress, making the business's objectives academic and detached from day-to-day work.

Almost 100 per cent of employees are convinced that they themselves are already doing a good job; they are helping their company reach its destination even when they don't know what that destination is. Where understanding of business strategy is restricted to a few senior managers, implementing that strategy successfully will be all the more unlikely.

THE ROLE OF LEADERSHIP IN COMMUNICATION

Senior business leaders are under pressure. The stakes are high, both for the business and for them personally – between 35–50 per cent of CEOs are replaced within 5 years.

In today's turbulent environment, business needs leadership from managers – people who don't just execute the rules but understand the principle behind them, so they can deal with the changing demands of the business. Jack Welch, former CEO of General Electric, recognized this:

> '...yesterday's idea of the boss, who became the boss because he or she knew one more fact than the person working for them, is yesterday's manager. Tomorrow's person leads through a vision, a shared set of values, a shared objective.'

Within organizations, structures are flatter, staff are more mobile and power and authority are vested in the person, not in the position. It is the job of leaders to navigate the inevitable turbulence of change. In today's world, business is driven by knowledge, networks and relationships.

A key issue for internal communicators is building stronger relationships between management and staff, especially at times of change, when the staff's trust in senior management usually declines. This needs the commitment from senior management to invest time in face-to-face communication, despite apparently always having more urgent things to do.

Communication is not the responsibility of a single charismatic leader, but of all managers. Peter Drucker estimated that '60 per cent of all management problems result from faulty communication'. Creating a customer- and quality-focused culture requires strong and clear leadership from a committed senior management, because lack of commitment is transparent and readily detected.

POOR COMMUNICATION OF CHANGE

Employees report that they want to perform well at work, but are often prevented from doing so by a limited understanding of what is required. This is compounded by communication with unclear meaning and which does not specify what, if any, action is required, and by information which is poorly presented and difficult to use.

Management credibility and trust are assets under attack from confused and poorly integrated communication. Such complexity and confusion is being driven by competing communicators within the organization, by a proliferation of messages and a multiplicity of channels. A report by Synopsis which examined practice in internal communication within 123 organizations in the UK, Europe and North America found that well intentioned communication is generating more heat than light. It is raising both senior management and employee frustrations and wasting the considerable investment that organizations make in communication. Senior management's frustration at the slow pace of change is matched by employees' frustration at information overload and the continuous waves of change initiatives. Employees' horizons and tolerance thresholds are sinking and their willingness to listen and engage is diminishing.

The speed of organizational change is hindered by:

- initiative indigestion – the number of initiatives exceed people's ability to digest change;

- change initiatives that confuse employees and clamour for their time and attention;

- dissonance between the strategic thinking of senior leaders and the perceptions of those at the sharp end;

- a disconnect between the leaders and the change strategists and the professional communicators whose function is to facilitate change within the rest of the organization.

This failure to make communication clear and simple is creating resistance and contributing to the high failure rate of initiatives. The growing volume of information competing for employees' attention is confusing rather than helpful, and frustration with how communication is managed is rising. A survey by Pitney Bowes (2000) revealed that, 'Communication tools are being adopted by Fortune 1000 companies at a stunning pace, with little sensitivity to cost or the overall effect of the communications glut upon workers'.

EMPLOYEE OVERLOAD

Organizations are beginning to realize that information overkill is consuming precious time, creating mixed messages and exacerbating the media onslaught on the individual. However, people in organizations do not passively swallow all the information they receive. Because they only have a limited capacity, they develop coping strategies to deal with information overload – deleting e-mails unread, waiting until messages are sent many times as a test of their urgency or assuming that anything really important will be repeated around the coffee machine.

The limit to communication is not the number of trees left standing from which to make newsletters, but the extent to which people have the inclination, time and goodwill to engage with the communicator.

Employees' 'brain space' – the time and attention they are willing to give to messages aimed at them – is shrinking. Their capacity to process the information they receive is also under attack. With more work being done by fewer people, there is less time for chatting and for the social interactions that used to diffuse communication around organizations. An international engineering company that reduced its headcount and closed the staff restaurant to save costs discovered that its employees' understanding of the business direction plummeted.

As companies outsource, use flexible workforces, use third party telephone call centres and mix and match full- and part-timers, this erosion of understanding threatens to get worse. Part-timers may see the job as only a part of their lives and as something that has to fit in with other commitments. They will be working short and irregular hours, and may rarely come together in one place as a group. Yet they will increasingly come to represent their company to the customer, and the impression they give will depend on the communication they get.

CONFUSING VOLUME AND VALUE

Organizations are crippling themselves by distributing large amounts of meaningless information, and technology is exacerbating existing bad habits. The information flow inside the typical company is increasing at about 2 per cent per month, yet a recent survey showed that 75 per cent of people were not getting the relevant information that they needed. Just over half said that technology had increased the quantity, but not the quality, of internal communication.

As organizations distribute more, but lower-quality, information, raw information that is not refined into meaning threatens to become deadweight. One company, for example, issued frequent newsletters describing, in great detail, the workings of the distribution process. It used words suitable for a graduate-level reading ability – despite the fact that the average reading level among employees was that of a 9-year-old.

People who do not understand what's happening do not feel in control of their own destiny. Failure to make communication simpler increases resistance to change initiatives. These can range from business process re-engineering, with a failure rate of around 70 per cent, to the 70 per cent of mergers which do not realize their promise due to human resource issues.

In a world of constant change, demanding quantum leaps in performance, communication can be a powerful means of making change happen. To do that it must be well managed. Continuing as it is, undisciplined and unmanaged, it will clutter the organization, spreading greater complexity and confusion. Poorly disciplined communication will prove a roadblock to the very change that's needed.

The traditional approach to internal communication is that of the production line. The most efficient communication is that at the lowest unit cost, exposing the greatest number of eyeballs, in the largest sized groups, to the greatest number of slides in the shortest amount of time. This may be efficient, but it certainly is not effective. While some organizations continue to view internal communication as the dissemination of information or messages, others are starting to use it as a key means of engaging and directing their people.

Having laid out all the problems, we are forced to ask, 'Where's the solution?'. The rest of this chapter lays out a model for the way forward, which subsequent chapters unpack in detail.

IMPROVING INTERNAL COMMUNICATION

In the restless quest for value, organizations will turn out every cupboard in the business to find underperforming assets which they can turn to their advantage. Increased competition, rapid product development cycles, faster innovation, more sophisticated supply partners and more demanding customers can mean that sustainable advantage cannot depend on product, brands and services alone. Companies must use all their assets, business processes and relationships to compete successfully.

In our information age, an organization's assets include the knowledge and interrelationships of its people. Businesses take the input of information, and use the creative and intellectual assets of their people to produce value. Internal communication is one of the core processes by which business can create value. Managing communication as a core process requires the adoption of some established business principles.

This section describes an integrated approach which will turn communication to business advantage. It highlights the typical flaws in traditional approaches to communication and identifies some of the key elements of succesful internal communication. It argues that to gain the greatest value from communication, the process must be better managed, and provides a framework for integrating communication more effectively. Finally, it shows how to reconnect broken communication links to form a virtuous circle.

As organizations reorganize around greater customer focus, supply chain management and key processes, functional departments have reinvented themselves to redefine how they can be valuable to the business. Traditional business functions have transformed themselves as they sought to demonstrate the relevance of their role. Manufacturing has been reborn as logistics, order fulfillment and supply chain management. Purchasing has become the more strategic-sounding 'procurement and supplier partnership'. Born-again finance departments have transformed themselves from accounts and spreadsheet producers to 'decision supporters', providing management with information, interpretation and strategic options.

These functions have focused on creating value, reducing duplication, increasing cooperation and managing end-to-end processes. Their reinvention has been driven by the need to create greater customer and shareholder value.

Internal communication has joined the party as a function which is trying to apply the same principles. This is being driven by companies demanding a better return from their investment in communication, and a realization that internal communication has a more significant task in the business.

For an organization's communication to be a strategic tool, it must be able to help employees share knowledge and information, extract meaning from them and make decisions that add value. This demands internal communication that helps people convert information into action in a four-step process:

1. Providing content – providing people with data, information, ideas and concepts.

2. Putting it in context – people need to be able to process that information, and to make it relevant to their situation. They need to be able to put it into a context – to add a new piece to the jigsaw of what they already know.

    Putting information in context is important because meaning depends on shared context. Seeing the bigger picture also helps people navigate through information sources and communication channels. After all, if you know where you are trying to get to, and you know where you are, reading the map is easier.

3. Having conversations – people need to explore, test and understand the implications of what they are doing. This is best done through conversation – a process that enables them to develop a shared understanding through sharing views and perceptions.

4. Gathering feedback – ensuring that communication has been understood as intended, to see what has been added to it and what has resulted from it.

The problem is that organizations typically concentrate on the first element of this four-step process – delivering content and creating awareness. Their first step should be to shift from seeing communication as providing input, to seeing it also as producing outcome. Without checking the outcome of communication – that the information has been received, that it has been understood correctly, how it has been interpreted and whether it has been translated into action – there is no true communication, just the distribution of information and the broadcasting of messages.

MANAGING COMMUNICATION AS A CYCLE

While it is politically correct among senior managers to say that internal communication is important, several problems typically accompany such a claim. Business leaders do not give communications priority, and it is not seen as a key part of leadership. A vicious circle therefore turns into a downward spiral. For example, a lack of time invested in communicating strategy leads to a lack of understanding at all levels of the organization.

Behaviours do not change, so actions do not match the strategy, so frustration sets in and less time is invested in communication. Business priorities continue to squeeze out communication time and local management do not make communication a priority. The communication function is inadequately resourced, and there is insufficient business support for skills development. Finally, regular measurement and accountability are avoided, so there is no evidence of change or return on investment.

Meanwhile, those who are keen to improve internal communication inside the organization become increasingly concerned. They want to link communication to the business strategy, but may have managers or internal clients who perceive communication as being largely about distributing newsletters. Communicators – that is those whose primary job is to support communication within the organization – will see senior management commitment as crucial to building stronger relationships between the leaders and employees. They want senior managers to participate actively in internal communication, but managers may already feel they are committed enough.

Communicators understand that forward planning is critical to avoiding information overload, to making the best use of communication channels and to targeting the information to the right people. However, simply getting the communication infrastructure in place to get the right information, to the right people, at the right time is often enough of a challenge. Whether they can become involved in planning will depend on the organization's perception and role of the internal communication department, and of them personally.

Almost all of them will want to develop a vibrant two-way communication process that adds value to the business. In this they will be hampered by a lack of time and by the apparent reluctance of senior management to buy in to two-way communication on matters which are important to staff.

Finally, they will yearn for valid measurement of internal communication, to help accelerate the rate of improvement, demonstrate the value they add, and to defend their budgets in lean times. They will understand that the true cost of communication lies in the line manager and employee time it takes up, not only in their production budgets.

While they are there to support the line managers in fulfilling their duty to communicate, they will know that the best way to achieve a return on investment is to make managers accountable, and to measure them regularly. However, it may be only the communication department, not the managers who are held to account.

Communicators will be all the more frustrated, seeing how internal communication can add value, while the rest of the business seems blind to the possibilities.

Many organizations have already improved their communication in a first phase of greater professionalism, better standards and consistency of presentation. This has taken them some distance toward their goals.

Now they need to move to the second phase – using internal communication to create understanding that can be turned into valuable action. This requires better communication integration and management, and greater employee involvement and dialogue.

While no company gets everything right, there are some simple reasons why some get it so wrong. At the heart of their failure is a series of broken connections in the communication circuit. Communication strategy is not connected to business strategy; measurement is not connected to business outcomes; face-to-face communication is not connected to creating understanding and engagement.

In most organizations different responsibilities are placed in different departments – planning in Strategy, internal communication in Corporate Affairs, measurement in Human Resources – and are not integrated or connected to each other. This is like setting different builders to work on different parts of a house, with different plans and hoping the individual parts will come together harmoniously.

Organizations therefore first need to make the connections between departments that own parts of internal communication and then make the connections between the separate elements of internal communication that each department owns. The key is to view communication as a process and to manage it as a cycle. Based on work with leading companies over the last

15 years, and drawing on Synopsis' research into best practice in over 120 UK and US organizations, outlined below is a framework for integrating communication more effectively.

INTEGRATING COMMUNICATION EFFECTIVELY

Many organizations are doing good things in individual parts of their internal communication processes, but lose the benefit by not linking them together. Problems in one part of the corporate body show up as symptoms in a different area, in the same way that referred pain in the leg can point to a problem in the back. For example, the team meeting process in an organization may constantly be reviewed in the face of continual complaints from employees. Yet despite continually retraining managers and team leaders to improve their interpersonal skills, they still fail to turn the sow's ear of poorly produced and irrelevant information into the silk purse of enthused and engaged employees. The root problem may simply be that the corporate information supplied is so boring and irrelevant that it discourages local managers from holding meetings at all. The fact that the information is so poor may be due to the lack of forward planning, resulting in a last minute scramble for content, whatever its relevance.

To get a better return from their investment in internal communication, organizations need to use the principles of linkage and mutual reinforcement, to form a virtuous circle of communication, with the following seven links (see Figure 1.2):

- strategy
- leadership
- planning and prioritization
- channel management and content development
- role of the internal communication function
- face-to-face communication
- impact measurement

The first three links focus on doing the right thing, and making the connection between the business strategy and the communication strategy. The next four links focus on doing things right – having efficient and effective processes. When activity in all the links is aligned, internal communication brings a real business pay-off.

While this framework is based on experience of the best internal communication practice in leading companies, it is not offered as a prescription of 'best practice'. It is good practice which has to be tailored to an organization's individual business needs. Organizations can make the

Figure 1.2   **Seven links of communication**

mistake of 'cherry-picking' apparent 'best practices' and adopting them without considering their unique needs – a strategy rather like taking someone else's medication just because it seems to have done them good

Thus, the challenge for internal communicators is twofold: to develop and implement good practice in each of these areas, and to link them together so they are mutually reinforcing.

Strategy

The purpose of internal communication is not just to keep employees happy. It should be business-focused and help employees understand the business' competitive strategy and how to deliver on it to produce profit.

There are three steps to achieving this. Organizations should clearly identify their strategy, identify the attitudes and behaviours they need from their people and then target their communication towards helping achieve those attitudes and behaviours. The focus is on closing a performance gap – identifying the roadblocks to adding value and then using communication to help remove them.

Successful companies do not start to communicate when some change is needed, they already have the understanding of the bigger picture in place to allow for rapid response. Succesful communicators forge strong links with those who drive strategy and change – the strategy, planning, marketing and IT functions.

Leadership

Leadership involves setting the agenda and then taking others with you. To do this effectively leaders have to communicate in a way that inspires others and builds a sense of commitment to shared goals.

Leaders may have different styles, ranging from big picture to small detail, and from entrepreneurial to controlling. Whatever their style, communication remains central to their leadership role, the critical success factors being:

- **Consistency of message.** The leadership team must be seen to be in agreement and consistent in purpose.

- **Clarity of purpose.** The top team should define the direction of the organization, state it clearly and simply, and then make sure it is distilled into a few unambiguous targets.

- **Clarity of principles.** People should understand the way in which their leader would apply the organization's values, so that they can make decisions on the ground according to these principles.

- **Focus.** Very few priorities should be set, and they should be emphasized repeatedly.

Successful leaders understand the importance of good communication and plan time to make themselves visible to their people. For example, Jim Burke, the CEO of Johnson & Johnson, spent 40 per cent of his time communicating the organization's credo. The fact that the board allocates time for communicating sends a message to leaders at all levels that they too are expected to make such time available.

To have full impact on the organization, internal communication and its strategy must have the full endorsement of the board. This will make finances and resources for communication more readily available and keep communication on the board's agenda since they will want to see a return on investment.

Leaders need to sponsor and review the internal communication strategy and plan, and agree and stick to key messages. They should show the way by having specific communication targets which are publicly measured.

Business is complex, yet strategy needs to be simplified if it is to connect to those at the front line. Successful leadership is directly rooted in effective communication which is kept simple. This means presenting the case clearly, in a way that is compelling and allows people to take action. Too often, leaders create difficulties by communicating a million complicated things rather than a few, significant ones. Organizations should therefore be able to express plainly the business strategy in a one-page summary, with the top five priorities clearly described. There should be clear goals linked directly to the strategy of the business and a clear link to what the customer wants and needs. Performance information should be communicated as a series of simple, 'Are we winning?' measures, not as a raft of ratios and percentages.

Planning and prioritization

The disconnection between leaders and their organization is reflected in the fact that, although 55 per cent of companies surveyed in the UK have board-level representation of internal communication, only one-third of boards actually approve the communication strategy and plan. To make matters worse, internal communicators are not being involved closely enough with the functions which typically plan and drive change – strategy and planning, marketing and IT.

Without planning, organizations cannot hope to manage people's reactions to change. Instead, they are forever 'catching up', so reducing the speed with which change can be brought about. If communicators do not have sufficient contact with those directing change in the business, they can be forced into setting the wrong priorities and end up announcing the 'what' of change rather than sharing the 'why'. Communication plans need to be reviewed quarterly to help the business respond quickly to change. Most communication plans tend to be set annually and are rarely revisited by the leadership team. Small wonder then that businesses struggle to make change happen; one of the most powerful weapons in the change armoury – communication – is firing blanks.

For example, the objective of most mega mergers is to increase market share while making substantial cost savings via economies of scale. This usually involves merging functions or organizations, removing duplication and increasing operating efficiencies. The end result is fewer employees who then have to operate in new environments, roles and locations. Achieving this involves the careful communication of redundancies, training, cultural change and relocation. However, although communicating to employees is a critical part of achieving the benefits of a merger, 75 per cent of acquirers reviewed in one survey had given the communication plan very little consideration before acquisition. Employees typically do not receive information in a timely manner and become disaffected when they hear of key decisions through the grapevine. The outcome can be a host of 'people problems' that leads to poor productivity, lower employee commitment and, ultimately, an exodus of disgruntled employees. From the leadership's viewpoint, therefore, failure to plan communication means failing to achieve the full benefits of the merger.

Programmes of change are a fact of modern business life. Yet research shows that over a quarter of those managing change initiatives do not produce communication plans. Without these it is harder clearly to coordinate how and when different change initiatives will affect people in the organization. This leads to change managers competing for communication time and resources, with the risk that change fails through initiative overload – too many changes hitting people too quickly. This may explain why employees keep seeing sudden, unexpected and uncoordinated changes, which only serve to increase their anxiety and frustration. It may also reinforce employees' perception that the management team does not have its collective act together.

Too few businesses involve their top team in approving the internal communication strategy and plan. Businesses may say they want their people to sing from the same songsheet, but they fail to ensure that the top team agrees the words – small wonder, then, that the result is a cacophony of mixed messages.

Organizations need to think ahead, show clear linkages between different initiatives and give people the bigger picture of change. Those leading change initiatives are risking failure by not planning communication and not coordinating it with other initiatives.

If communicators are to help the business achieve its objectives, they must be involved earlier in the planning process and involve senior management in the planning. They need to ensure they focus on business objectives, not communication objectives, and identify issues from the employees' viewpoint, not just the organization's. Communicators can help by being explicit and specific about what decisions must be made, and what people need to do differently.

Developing an annual calendar of communication events and milestones, explicitly linked to the business plan, is a good first step. The focus should be on educating people about the rationale for change, rather than simply announcing conclusions. This will require involving communicators earlier in the planning, rather than at the end when implementation looms.

Channel management and content development

Communication is about the transfer of meaning from person to person, not simply the passing on of messages. The more chaotic, new or interconnected change becomes, the more employees are forced to make choices and prioritize. Helping them find their way through the maze of change depends on making information meaningful and highlighting its point. In other words, companies who want to create understanding need to make meaning not messages.

Employees' mental capacity to absorb and process information should be treated as a strategic resource. The success of the business depends on employees being able to use information well to make good decisions. The average professional worker receives 178 messages per day by email and voicemail. In a world that automatically increases employees' information load by 2 per cent per month, communication reducers, not producers, are needed.

Communication channels need to be better managed to target information, reduce interruptions by irrelevant messages, and liberate employees' time and 'brain space'. Organizations need the right mix of communication channels, and to be able to use the right channel for the right type of information. Equally, organizations need to target their audiences more closely and tailor messages more relevantly to address their people's interests and concerns.

Reducing information overload requires organizations to shift from the 'oil refinery' model of communication, in which more messages are pumped down communication pipelines. They need to shift instead towards a model of 'air traffic control', which has an overview of communication activities and plans and coordinates communication to avoid overload and communication collisions. This means that organizations will have to work harder to make communication simpler, translating 'management-speak' into 'plain talking'.

Supply partnerships are well established in virtually every industrial sector. To become more valuable, internal communication has to follow the same route. Internal communication needs to be treated as an end-to-end process, with greater partnership and cooperation among all the different communicators within an organization.

The role of the internal communication function

Most businesses want a great deal from their internal communication function, ranging from the strategic to the tactical. Internal communicators are typically overloaded and frustrated as they try to focus on the strategic, while having to devote most of their time to dealing with the tactical.

The obstacle to internal communication departments adding value is often a lack of access to decision makers and being trapped in their internal customers' perception of them as messengers. This is made worse by their own narrow focus on internal communication objectives rather than on business objectives.

For internal communication to deliver value it has to be located close to the heart of the business – somewhere it can support the ways in which value is created for customers and close to where the money is made.

Communication professionals should be of high standard, with the skills and experience to understand business strategy. Clearly, if part of their job is to express strategy in words that can be turned into action, it helps if they understand it first themselves. Furthermore, clarifying the role of the internal communications department forces the top team to clarify what it wants its internal communication to achieve. In doing so, the top team is more likely to realize that internal communication needs to be more than a production department.

Face-to-face communication

By distributing information in the belief that they are communicating, organizations are deluding themselves. They are confusing information with communication. The distribution of information is the first, but not the last step in the communication process. Information can travel over wires, but communication happens between the ears.

Communication combines two strands – information and interaction. Information refers to the delivery and receipt of data, concepts and messages, and involves issues of how best to share, structure and extract meaning. Interaction refers to how people perceive and relate to each other, and involves issues of relationships, familiarity, credibility, trust and collaboration. Both strands needs to be intertwined for success.

Despite the availability of technology, effective communication is as much about interaction as information. Technology may get information to people more quickly, but it is not a substitute for face-to-face communication.

Face-to-face contact – or 'talking' to use the full technical term – is still employees' preferred method of communication, and organizations need to do more to exploit its full value. Time is the most limited resource in most organizations, and better use can be made of precious face-to-face time which is too often used for the wrong purposes – to tell people things they could more easily read about, in meetings which are badly run and boring.

As mentioned earlier, effective face-to-face communication depends on conversation that allows information to be put in context. The moment of truth for communication is in conversation, which depends on how well people relate to each other – the quality of interaction. Since local relevance emerges from discussion with colleagues, organizations need more opportunities for dialogue and conversation between their people. People need to be given time to think through information, react to it and discuss it. The more they are force-fed with information, the less they digest it.

Face-to-face communication sessions often happen in teams, so teams need to be provided with tools and techniques to get the most value out of the time they spend together. Those who lead sessions should be trained in facilitation and interpersonal skills and in understanding how people relate and respond to each other. Briefing and presentation skills are not enough.

Turning information into knowledge depends on people's ability to process and apply it. The value of information is down to the individuals who bring their experience and knowledge to interpreting it. This is turn depends on the relationship between members of the team, as they pool experience and spark ideas off each other.

Organizations are increasingly investing time in coaching their people in how to understand and deal with each other, to increase communication, collaboration and innovation.

Middle managers can add more value not by acting as a mere conduit for messages, but by putting information into context and painting the bigger picture. However, to do this, they must be given a clear understanding themselves of what the issues and implications are likely to be for their people.

Actions speak louder than words, and how managers behave is the most powerful communication. Managers need to be trained in the skills of building relationships with people, in presenting information clearly and in eliciting feedback to discover how they have been heard. Presentation skills are only the starting point.

Impact measurement

The goal of any communication programme is to have impact but this can only be established by measuring results against the original intention. Measurement is the only way to ensure that what was planned has actually happened, and to show a return on investment.

Businesses are not doing enough to measure and track the progress and impact of their communication efforts, principally because they rarely specify the intended outcome of their communication. Although many senior managers now have specific communication targets and are measured against them, their achievement is usually kept private. In measuring how communication is performing, there are two options – keep the measurement private, so that only the guilty managers know how badly they have performed, or make it public by publishing the scores.

Embarrassment is more effective than guilt in motivating managers to change. Good companies do regular surveys, include communication competencies in appraisals, track managers' performance via research and publish the results.

Communication standards make it clear what employees have a right to expect in terms of communication, and also establish what is expected from them. By setting standards, the boundaries of communication are less open to interpretation, and people know what to expect. The organization needs to establish clear principles, and then measure performance against standards regularly.

MAKING MEANING: THE BUSINESS OF UNDERSTANDING

The seven links in the communication chain described above are designed to reconnect an organization's people to its business agenda. However, this is based not just on repairing broken links but on redefining the role of internal communication.

Companies need to create understanding for their people, to bring clear meaning to their information and to simplify the complex. Communication is about creating and sharing meaning, not simply about sending messages. It is not enough to tell employees that you have a strategy, and not enough for them to be able to repeat the corporate values or recite the mission statement.

Communication will continue to be viewed as a soft area until leaders are harder on themselves. Unless business leaders insist on early planning, well coordinated communication and clear and consistent messages with specific actions, communication will fail to deliver the changed attitudes and behaviour they need.

A one-off road show by the chief executive may give employees a temporary awareness of the strategy, but the next day, their re-entry into the pressures of the workplace will reduce the presentation to a distant and fuzzy memory.

Organizations therefore need to move from this traditional view of communication – 'telling the troops' – towards engaging with their people and helping them understand what change means for them. Rather than simply adding new pieces to the jigsaw puzzle, management must explain the picture on the box, so that staff can work out where their contribution fits in.

To summarize, organizations must first do the right thing – connect communication to achieving their business strategy – and second, do things right – have efficient and effective processes. How to do both of these is explored further in the following chapters.

REFERENCES AND FURTHER READING

Deloitte and Touche (1996), *Information Management Survey* (London: Deloitte and Touche).

Deekeling, E. and Fiebig, N. (1999), *Interne Kommunikation* (Frankfurt: Frankfurter Allgemeine Zeitung Gabler).

Hopton, C., Bain and Co. (1994), *'Measuring and Maximising Customer Retention'* Conference.

KPMG (2002/2003), *European Knowledge Management Survey*.

Oliver, R. (1999), Whence consumer loyalty, *Journal of Marketing*, Vol. 63 No. 4.

Pitney Bowes (2000), *'Managing Corporate Communications Study'*, conducted by the Institute for the Future (IFTF), with research from the Gallup Organization and San Jose State University, 2 March.

2 Turning Strategy into Action

Internal communication is a means to an end, not an end in itself – and part of its rationale is to help turn strategy into action by engaging, informing and directing employees. This chapter looks at developing an internal communications strategy that is rooted in business, contributes to the business, and makes the connection between the strategy of the organization and its employees' contribution. It also looks at what prevents employees following strategy, and what causes the mismatches between organizations' strategies and employees' actions.

Organizations are having to pay more attention to their competitive strategies in an attempt to differentiate themselves. This is not easy. In a quickly changing world, what was distinctive yesterday comes as standard today. One way of being distinctive is to build a powerful brand, even if what you actually provide is unremarkable. Another is to increase the value of what you provide, or to change the way you deliver a service to your customers.

Whatever the strategy for differentiation, internal communication has a key role. The promise that the business makes to the customer – accessibility, respect, friendliness, helpfulness – has to be reflected by its employees, or the gap between the claim and reality will be all too clear. Unless the culture and the promise to the customer are completely in step, neither will be differentiating or competitive. As well as fulfilling the promise made by marketing, employees need to understand how they can add value by understanding the typical problems facing the customer and how they can help solve them.

The job that communication has to do will differ according to which strategy an organization chooses to follow. Communication must be based squarely upon the business's strategy or it will unknowingly work against it. It is not enough to tell employees what the strategy is, you have to equip them to deliver on it. Existing communication practices are usually based on the old, implicit, strategy and will work against the new one if not realigned.

Businesses have to maintain a balancing act between external and internal markets, as they attract and retain customers, and attract and retain employees. Differentiation is important in both. As the market shifts, and as customer expectations grow, the business has to stay ahead of the game by finding new ways to add value while protecting and building the equity of its brands. The ability of employees to meet customer expectations depends on their managers realizing that communication with their people is vital.

This chapter first looks at aligning employees' efforts with the strategy, and at the central role of internal communication in converting employees' understanding of the strategy into action. It then provides an approach to developing an internal communication strategy that is linked to the business strategy.

SUCCEEDING BY STANDING OUT?

Faced with a competitive market, price sensitivity and customers' perceptions of them as 'me-too' suppliers of a commodity, companies have to fight harder. They look for an offer which the customer will value, which will set the supplier apart from the competition and which will create customer satisfaction and loyalty.

Customers expect some basic things as a matter of course, and the supplier has to provide these simply to be a credible option. These may include providing the basic service or product in a timely and professional manner, with prompt follow-up and servicing plus efficient back-up. These are things that the customer expects and only really notices if they are not there. They are not seen as remarkable, nor do they earn the supplier any brownie points with the customer.

There are, though, those 'X' factors that customers may not at first think of, or expect, but which are more valuable to them and which they appreciate. These include such things as advice, creative ideas and problem solving. These do provide competitive differentiation and can justify higher pricing to reflect extra value.

All businesses adopt a competitive strategy in terms of the value they offer for the money they charge. Companies focus on how they will compete, what they will offer and how they will go about providing it. They will have to meet industry standards in each of the three following categories, but differentiate themselves in one. The job that communication has to do will differ according to which of these routes to differentiation an organization chooses.

Operational efficiency

Operational efficiency means providing customers with reliable products or services at competitive prices and delivered with minimum difficulty or inconvenience. DHL and FedEx are good examples of this kind of company.

Closeness to the customer

Closeness to the customer means segmenting and targeting markets precisely and then tailoring offerings to match them. Knowledge of the customer and flexibility in their operations allows organizations to meet individual needs, or to tailor individual products. A merchant bank or an IT consultancy would be a good example.

Product leadership

Sony, Apple and Microsoft are good examples of these kind of companies, who compete by offering leading edge products, and who aim to produce a continuous stream of innovative products and services.

The different competitive strategies can be seen, for example, in the airline industry. Ryanair has positioned itself as a 'no frills' airline, selling cheap travel by reducing its costs through less baggage handling, faster turnaround times and getting passengers to help clean up after themselves. British Airways positions itself as being closer to its customers and Virgin claims product leadership through its innovations such as the in-flight lounge and door to door limousine service.

However, nothing is forever, and companies often shift their competitive strategy, or rebalance their mix of operational efficiency, closeness to the customer and product leadership.

To have employees deliver any change in differentiation requires the realignment of internal communication. Playing the game by new rules moves the communication goalposts.

The following case study shows how shifting the strategy redefines what internal communication is needed.

CASE STUDY: FRATERNAL FINANCE

Fraternal Finance is a fictitious, though not untypical, financial services company whose internal communication strategy is out of line with its business strategy. It has decided that, in its marketplace, it will differentiate itself through closeness to the customer. It will be distinctive in its ability to understand intimately its customers' needs as they move through different stages of their lives. From childhood, to young married, to empty nester, they will provide them with appropriate financial solutions tailored to their changing needs, via staff in their branch network.

The new strategy requires branch staff to understand customers more deeply and also to have good in-depth knowledge of a wider range of products. This means they must receive and digest a greater amount of information and understand how to apply it.

Consequently, branch staff find themselves increasingly under pressure: more responsibilities and tasks are devolved to the branch network, resulting in increased workloads. A tighter regulatory environment means that they have to qualify as advisers and master competitors' product knowledge as more sophisticated customers increasingly shop around to get the best rates.

The pressure of time and workload drives staff to set their own priorities, and to focus only on the information that is of immediate use in completing their tasks on deadline. Staff feel there is simply no time to assimilate information for anything other than the immediate job at hand.

Briefing sheets containing procedural changes and regulation changes – such as alerts to lost cards and stolen cheques – are circulated regularly, and in great numbers, to the branches. Everyone is supposed to read, assimilate, tick and then file the briefing sheets. To save time, however, the sheets are circulated and ticked off without anyone actually reading or understanding their contents. So, even for those tasks which are perceived as most important, there is a growing danger that staff are not up-to-date with crucial operational procedures.

Time pressure on staff means that they also have to be more selective in the information they use. Operational procedures are read first and, then, because there is commission to be earned, sales messages are studied next. Information about customers, though central to the strategy, is relegated to last place and is the first to be discarded if time is scarce. In other words, staff have developed coping strategies for selecting and prioritizing information from all the competing communication aimed at them. This is based on how they themselves believe they are supposed to be serving the customer – which may be at odds with the actual strategy.

The net result is that the business's strategy of closeness to the customer is undermined by its internal communication practices. Fraternal Finance has, in effect, three internal communication strategies which are simultaneously at work. Each is designed to support a different competitive strategy, and each works against the other. They are as follows:

1. The efficient distribution of information to allow compliance with operational procedures, and to ensure the best operational efficiency.

2. The distribution of sales information to maximize the sales of distinctive and well designed products.

3. The education about customers, the different stages of their life cycle and relevant needs, to enable staff to provide service to customers and colleagues.

Each is the legacy of a different strategy for competitive differentiation, which the organization has followed in succession over the years. Each is championed by a different department, each of which has access to the branches, each with a finger in the communication pie.

The Fraternal Finance case study illustrates a number of issues that have to be addressed if its strategy is not to be undermined. Trying to educate staff about the new strategy will not be successful without addressing how they select and prioritize information, or without better coordinating the departments who communicate with the branches. For both producers and consumers of information, existing habits of communication are based on the past. While competitive strategy points to the future, communication habits, if unchanged, imprison the organization in its past.

MOMENTS OF TRUTH

Lack of coordination in internal communication is a problem because it undermines the consistency on which a brand depends. There are certain critical points of contact between the customer and company. These include reception, telephone, meetings, PR, point of sale, advertising, mailings and so on. These points of contact are 'moments of truth' because, at each one, the company and its promises are tested and judged.

Because organizations often do not clearly communicate their point of differentiation to their employees, it is not unusual to find different departments focusing on different differentiators. The sales department might act on the basis that differentiation comes from building close relationships with customers. The production department might believe that excellent products confer differentiation. The marketing department might believe in the distinctiveness of a trusted brand.

The greater the number of moments of truth, the greater the danger of inconsistency. Since a number of the moments can be owned and managed by different departments who may not share the same views and priorities, the danger grows. This means that there has to be tighter management of internal communicators. This is discussed further in Chapter 9, 'Repositioning the Role of the Internal Communication Function', and Chapter 8 'Planning and Managing Communication'.

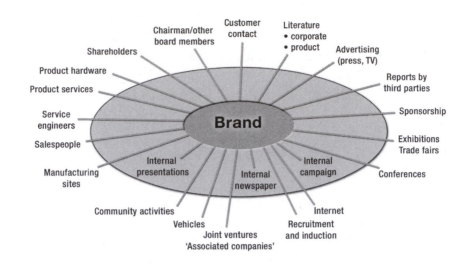

Figure 2.1   Moments of truth: points of contact with an organization's stakeholders

BRAND AND BEHAVIOUR

Brands are valuable to their owners because they can differentiate products and services from the competition, 'In a world of constant change, a strong corporate brand is one of the few sources of competitive differentiation' (RSA Inquiry). Companies are recognizing that their brands are an asset, which can command premium prices.

In acquisitions in the consumer goods business, as much as 85 per cent of the acquisition price is attributable to goodwill – the difference between the acquired company's net asset value and the price paid. Despite the huge premium paid for goodwill, this is still seen as a more effective means of growing than trying to imitate the acquired company's brands. For example, Grand Metropolitan, which merged with Guinness to form Diageo, became the first large brand-based company to capitalize their brand assets and declare the value attached to its brands on its balance sheet.

Brands are seen as valuable, often expensive, assets and as passports to market growth. However, obtaining a return on these assets depends on aligning employee values with the brand's values. For brand owners, business success depends on employees translating brand values into appropriate behaviour. That is not always straightforward. One of the ways in which customers build up a sense of a brand is by their daily interaction with the organization, especially its people. This means that customers' experience of employees can undermine the brand, when employees do not behave in line with the implicit promise, especially when employees in what were traditionally backroom jobs suddenly find themselves having front line contact with customers.

Everyone has to be involved in delivering on the promise marketed to the customer. As Lew Platt, former Chief Executive of Hewlett Packard, put it in an interview with P. Doyle, 'Marketing is too important to leave to the marketing department.' The scope of this challenge, and the risk of not achieving it, has grown. Nowadays, customers have more contacts with a wider range of employees, from front line sales and service to backroom warehousing and distribution. As they deal with customers on this broader front, businesses have to be able to translate the brand approach to a wider range of areas. For example, it is easier to identify an appropriately branded way of recruiting people, than how a credit control department would behave in an "on brand" way.

For brand owners that manufacture products, the more frequent contact of the customer with different parts of the organization puts them on their mettle. For service businesses, however, there's often no place to hide, since the customer is right there with the employees, looking over their shoulders as the service is delivered.

Two factors play a principal role in keeping employees aligned to new aims and objectives; the brand – which embodies the organization's shared culture and values – and internal communication.

As one of the strongest brands in the technology industry, Hewlett Packard takes seriously the link between the competitive advantage of a strong corporate brand and ensuring employees deliver on the brand promise. The organization has always had a reputation for product quality, especially in their business-to-business relationships. As they have moved increasingly into consumer markets, selling peripherals and printers for home use, they used the strength of their brand in consumer, as well as in business-to-business, marketing. They believe that creating customer loyalty comes from moments of truth, delivering brand values, through people.

Hewlett Packard sees one role of internal communication as getting every employee to understand what their brand value promise is, how they individually might affect it, which moment of truth they own and how they are expected to deliver on the promise to the customer. Internal communication therefore has to:

- get all their people to understand their role in moments of truth;

- provide employees with the information they need to fulfil their role;

- educate them in the processes they will need to solve problems.

Many companies, in contrast to Hewlett Packard, believe that circulating a lavishly produced glossy booklet evoking the brand values will light the blue touchpaper of employees' enthusiasm and ignite their passion to deliver. Such high-gloss communication (all too often) turns out to be a damp squib.

Even for those companies who feel that they have clearly articulated their brand promise, and have their people firmly behind it, there are further complications.

Consumers want to have a relationship with suppliers beyond purchasing the basic product or service and are looking for more than brand image and product quality. They want a deeper relationship and to be confident that suppliers can maintain commitments over time. Brand owners are building such relationships with their consumers, based on their corporate values. Virgin, Marks & Spencer and Tesco are all examples of strongly trusted organizations extending their influence into new areas, based on the strength of their brand. Their reputation is not just based on their products but on all their activities and values. Virgin, for example, sells its personality and characteristic approach more than its individual products.

The offer to the customer of a deeper relationship and a link between brand values and the customer's values raises the stakes for companies. It increases the risk to the organization of its employees not delivering on a now greater promise. If, for example, you are selling yourself as a trusted adviser, you have to live up to a wider range of more demanding values throughout the organization. Furthermore, if you fail it is much more damaging, since, having put yourself on a pedestal, there is further to fall.

Avoiding a fall requires strong coordination between a range of departments. Brand values are normally the province of the marketing department, corporate values are often developed by the corporate affairs or corporate communications department, and employee values and managerial behaviours are often developed by the human resources department. Each of these departments often takes a different approach, with a different emphasis, so that there is little match and an apparent confusion between the different values they promote.

Managers' personal style and skills often have the most powerful impact on communication, so there has to be a strong link between managerial values, corporate values, brand values and employee values to make sure they are all consistent.

Employees are more likely to deliver on the promise effectively if they feel a sense of ownership of, and pride in, what the company stands for. Employees gain status from being associated with strong well known brands when they wear the employer's badge. Badged employees with aligned values make effective brand ambassadors.

Organizations which seem exciting in the external market also seem to attract and motivate employees. Innocent, Virgin and Pret a Manger are all entrepreneurial start-ups which have grown by responding to the needs of customers. However, they are perceived as focusing not solely on profit but as having a wider vision of what can be achieved through doing business. In all these companies a strong external profile feeds back into the organization and gives a greater sense of worth to employees. In the future, then, creating a strong internal sense of mission is likely to require companies to adopt a high external profile, and a greater demonstration of a contribution to society.

COMMUNICATION CREATES PROFIT

There is a strong link between the quality of internal communication and greater profitability. While greater customer loyalty has been shown to produce greater profit, it depends on employee loyalty and satisfaction. According to Frederich Reicheld, author of 'The Loyalty Effect', employee and customer loyalty are very closely related. On average, US companies lose 50 per cent of their customers every 5 years and 50 per cent of their employees every 4 years, but the most successful US companies hold on to their employees and customers much longer.

Employee attitude research over the last 15 years shows that better communication creates more employee satisfaction and improves employee's perception of their line manager. Higher satisfaction reduces staff turnover and higher retention of staff creates higher customer satisfaction and more customer retention. Finally, according to management consultancy Bain and Co. (Hopton, 2004), higher customer retention equals higher profitability (see Figure 2.2).

Using better communication to improve profit is easier to achieve if people have a strong identification with the product and with the values behind

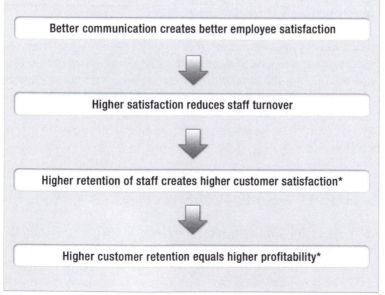

* Source : Bain and Co

Figure 2.2   Better communication means higher profit

it. In response to external and internal pressures, organizations are having to pay far more attention to creating shared values among their employees. Externally, customers are more interested in the values behind their suppliers; internally, shared values help create consistent employee behaviour.

The more organizations use their brands as an entry into new markets, the more they reach into different areas of their customers' lives asking for a much bigger 'share of life'. The greater the influence of a brand or organization on our lives through the extent of its operations, the greater the need for a new level of trust and the warier people will be about organizations' values and motivations. This is illustrated by the antagonism directed towards Microsoft and the suspicion of the dominance of its technology and its increasing spread into so many areas of our lives.

Organizations' increasing focus on corporate values is not an irrelevant exercise of dreaming up value statements for display in the corporate lobby – it is about risk management. The organization wants to protect its corporate reputation from the inappropriate behaviour of its own people; customers want to protect themselves from the power and influence of their suppliers. Internally, in times of change, shared values act as corporate glue. As organizations devolve authority to the front line, common approaches and consistent decisions cannot be achieved simply by providing more rules and procedures. It is shared values and beliefs that help ensure common approaches.

In terms of employees, companies increasingly realize you only get so much productivity out of reorganizations, systems and policies. It is by reaching the hearts and minds of employees and getting them involved that you gain surges of productivity and leaps of imagination.

To keep customers, companies have to continually improve the product and the service they supply. Service and customer satisfaction depend on the commitment and 'emotional labour' of employees. Companies with high-profile values attract and retain people who give high productivity, and high-quality work. Employees do not give that emotional labour to an organization that does not share their values and which seems to focus only on increasing shareholder value.

CASE STUDY: 'STORE WARS'

For employees' enthusiasm and emotional labour to be channelled in the best way, employees have to fully understand how they are supposed to be serving the customer and to be able to convert that understanding into action (see Figure 2.3). The importance of converting awareness into action can be seen in the 'store wars' between the giant UK food retailers.

Food retailing is highly competitive, and how staff serve customers is vital to the differentiation that competing food retailers are trying to establish. Over the past 15–20 years grocery retailers such as Sainsbury's and Tesco have invested in better stores, new 'convenience stores', employee training, consumer helplines and supply chain efficiency. This has yielded good results, giving own-label brands a market share of just under 40 per cent, despite competition from branded products, advertising, image, packaging and line extensions.

Sainsbury's also set out to change the way in which its staff work and manage. While store location and product range are key to attracting and keeping customers, the way in which people deal with customers is also a differentiator. The company wanted to alter the style of service its customers experienced. It believed that the way to achieve this was to change the way in which it managed. Store managers aimed to involve their people more so that, in turn, staff would treat customers more personally.

Over 3 years, Justin King, Chief Executive of Sainsbury's, arrested the supermarket company's perilous decline and headed it back towards its former glory.

He inherited stores that had lost their way. The IT system was not up to the job, supply lines were always breaking down and shelves that should have been full were empty. Research said their 14 million customers weren't spending enough and couldn't find the items they wanted. As they went elsewhere to find the items Sainsbury's lacked, they found Sainsbury's was more expensive than its competitors.

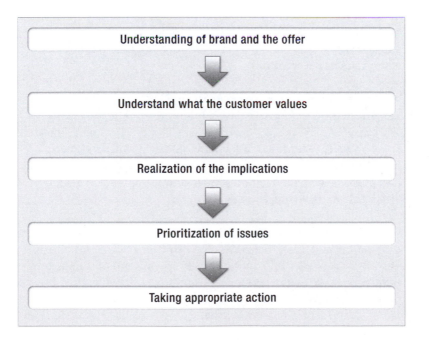

Figure 2.3   Converting awareness into action

Sainsbury's had hidden strengths – good locations, a great heritage and a reputation for good, healthy food. King restored Sainsbury's emphasis on quality, product development and advertising.

How, overall, has he done it? King says:

> *'By re-engaging and re-motivating our staff – they're the difference between success and failure.'*

(*London Evening Standard*, 7 February 2007)

Tesco aimed to create greater loyalty among its customers and to increase their average number of purchases, as keys to increased profit. They have recognized that the customer wants more help and advice from staff in order to make shopping a more personal experience.

However, with 150 000 employees making contact with customers, the business has to treat its people as ambassadors or risk them becoming liabilities. To achieve its aim Tesco gave its staff a wider understanding of the brand, so that each employee could translate it into appropriate actions locally. The organization translated marketing-speak into everyday language, avoiding the use of the word 'brand' and using instead the phrase 'every little helps'. The greater the level of understanding and translation to specifics, the greater is the likelihood of everyone taking the right action.

Tesco is a good example of an organization serving customers by educating staff in brand values and helping them express them. However, this is not just an issue for front line staff. Value for the customer has to be delivered by the whole organization, from supply chain, product design and manufacturing, through to sales and servicing.

Rolls-Royce, for example, aims to create the greatest value by getting colleagues from different functional disciplines to work together as a team from the outset of a project. Specialists with a manufacturing background who know about the latest technologies work closely with designers, who have an intimate understanding of how the product works and with purchasing people who understand sourcing and supply management, to improve speed, effectiveness and quality.

This kind of teamwork brings a significant benefit in terms of reducing cost, over-engineering and time. It also calls for a shift in attitude, knowledge sharing and cooperation. Trade-offs between volume and customization now have to be made by the whole team working closely together. Because they can no longer concentrate exclusively on their individual specialized requirements, and take decisions as a team, each member has to share an understanding of customers and their priorities.

MOVING FROM THE CORE

The above are all examples of companies using communication to create greater differentiation and profitability through product leadership, operational excellence and closeness to the customer. However, the real pressure on their success depends on continually improving the value they offer to their customers. This, in turn, depends on understanding how customers' definition of value shifts over time. Services may have become more important to customers, as the importance of the 'core' product the company has historically provided has changed. A company's 'core' product – be it computer, telephone, bank account or copier – may no longer be enough to provide a competitive edge.

During the 1980s and early 1990s, marketing's way of trying to differentiate its offerings was by adding services to their products, such as financing, transportation and insurance (see Figure 2.4).

These add-on services, originally conceived as promotional tools, then became the principal differentiation. Customers could, in theory, obtain the 'core' items anywhere – although specifications and price would always be a major competitive factor – so, ironically, they came to place more value on the add-ons. Customers were more interested in what they could achieve by applying products to their problems than the detail of the product itself. Thus, for example, British Airways are less interested in all the technical details of an aero-engine, and more interested in having 'power by the hour' to ensure smooth operating of their planes.

Thus, the value added had less to do with the 'core' – be it a product or a service – and more to do with how it would be applied. Companies have had to become as good at providing new value-added services and solutions as they previously were at producing their core product. Encouraging employees to make that mental shift, however, is not easy, and demands a change in the approach to internal communication.

THE IMPLICATION FOR INTERNAL COMMUNICATION

As a business redefines its value to the customer, it risks getting out of step with its people. Employees will still define themselves in terms of what used to lie at the core of their business, whether that is excellence in engineering or providing a good telephone service. However, the value of those traditional strengths, in which they take so much pride, may have evaporated. Redefining what's valuable to the customer, redefines what's needed from employees. This includes the kind of service they provide and the knowledge they need to gather and keep. Employees need to be reeducated about how to provide new value for the customer. Employees who take pride in providing excellent customer service are not necessarily providing great customer value. In one

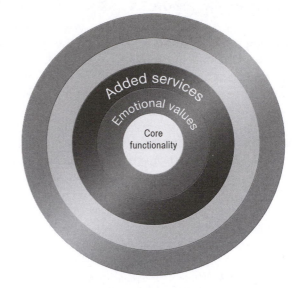

Figure 2.4   Adding value to the core product

organization, for example, tens of millions of pounds were spent on a process improvement programme speeding up the processes needed to create bank accounts for customers. While everyone worked their hardest to halve the time it took to process the necessary documents, their research showed that customers barely noticed the change and, where they did, did not value it.

SHIFTING THE VALUE PROPOSITION MEANS EMPHASIZING DIFFERENT VALUES

Organizations are trying to use the strength of their brands to extend their activities into areas not traditionally theirs – examples are Virgin and Tesco which are entering the financial services market. This means that companies with good brands and good reputations, currently in very different markets, will find themselves competing with each other in new markets.

Such organizations, with trusted and innovative brands, must be certain that their employees' core competencies are closely matched to their brand values. As the brand is the passport to extending beyond the organization's traditional core, it needs protection. The customers' relationship is with the brand, so, at the very least, employees' behaviour must not damage that relationship. Where a company uses other partners or providers to deliver the new proposition, customers must perceive that the values and the people match.

Employees who cling to the past, or to corporate values which have become disconnected from a value proposition to customers, endanger this process. If a company redefines what it offers to customers, employees have to redefine the importance and value of what they do and how they behave.

What customers valued in the past is likely to be different to what they value in the future. For example, customer contact staff typically get high job satisfaction from providing good service to appreciative customers. Such staff are often disappointed to discover that shifts in customers' expectations now mean that service is important but no longer valuable or exclusive. Appreciative customers still go and buy from competitors. Companies therefore need to explain to their people that they have to find other ways to provide value if they are to have a successful future. Being proud of what no longer differentiates you can be frustrating and is often the cause of a perceived values clash between employees and their leadership.

One of the key reasons for lost productivity is that employees are working hard doing something their company no longer needs them to do.

Internal communication is essential to connecting employees' pride in the past with the company's potential for the future. Its role is to provide the necessary re-education and to bring the voice of the customer into the organization, in order to:

- ensure consistency between the promise being made to customers and customers' experience;

- ensure that the promise being made to the customer market and to employer markets are consistent and reinforce each other;

- provide information to employees on their core products and services;

- provide information about customers, their different requirements and what they value

Internal communication is needed to bring employees out of the past and into the present and is vital to preparing them for the future. Employees have to be educated about changing definitions of value to prepare them for fresh surprises ahead. Both companies and their employees need to understand how technology will change their relationship with customers and with each other.

During the 1960s and 1970s managers had one of two options – either produce products en masse for the generic end of the market or customize offerings for smaller selective niches. Then, as targeting became a more common approach during the 1980s, managers began to tailor their offerings to different segments of their mass markets. By the 1990s, thanks to technology, they could both have their cake and eat it. Mass customization meant that large numbers of customers could enjoy the benefits of mass-produced items with customized features to suit some of their individual needs. Dell's tailoring of laptops to individual customers is a good example of this.

In addition to mass customization, technology now also allows a shift towards 'one-to-one' marketing. Firms can track what their best customers buy, talk to them and tailor products especially for them. With each transaction, the customer's needs and tastes are defined in increasing detail, and computers and databases allow every preference to be registered. British Airways assigns frequent flyers their favourite seats based on previous choices. Amazon.com recommends books to customers based on past choices.

Most enterprises will not be able to treat all their customers so well; it is too expensive. Nevertheless the move from mass marketing to more targeted individual marketing via finer targeting and better data inevitably means that all customers are not treated the same. While the ultimate aim is to treat each customer as an individual, the flip side of the coin of individuality is selectivity. Companies are able to identify valuable customers and to concentrate on them, while holding back on, or even shedding, less profitable ones.

This segmentation of customers, and the culling of less profitable or more troublesome customers can lead to a clash of values with employees. They may have bought into the concept of providing customer service to their customers – all customers – and believe in fair treatment for all. In their eyes any selectivity should favour the more deserving, rather than more profitable, customers for whom life is probably good enough already.

A healthcare organization introduced a 'club class' hospital bedroom for example, in a bid to attract more corporate patients. As part of this offer, they included a basket of fruit and a copy of the Financial Times. However, the nurses, whose vocation was to serve the sick irrespective of their class or wealth, sabotaged what they perceived as the inequity of creating first- and second-class patients. They redistributed the fruit baskets and newspapers among all patients, thereby defeating the purpose of the exercise.

One financial services organization found that the 80/20 rule applied: 20 per cent of accounts absorbed 80 per cent of resources. The remaining 80 per cent of accounts had higher balances, more products, were less costly in terms of service and support and thus were more profitable. The business strategy devised was to shift towards offering more investment-related products, such as bonds. Customer research showed that the customers for these tended to be middle-class and fairly sophisticated and selective investors. This did not fit employees' traditional, and largely mythical, picture of the typical customer as a thrifty saver who had to count pennies carefully. This outdated perception of the average customer, and the mismatch between those customers from whom the organization wanted to withdraw and those that employees wanted to serve, caused confusion.

The company had two communication tasks: first, it had to explain why it had to move away from the minority of customers who took up the majority of resources; and, second, it had to update its employees on the company's typical customer profile.

The possibilities of using technology for greater personalization means employees have to learn to respond to customers as individuals rather than as part of an undifferentiated mass. The more a business tries to respond to customers individually, the more its employees must be able to relate to customers differently, and understand the variations to processes needed to serve them. They have to understand that customers want different kinds of information, tailored to their needs, and delivered differently.

The issue, internally, is trying to explain to employees *why* there is this selectivity and difference among customers – especially where the staff hold a customer service ethic that involves treating customers equitably, if not identically. Improved customer information drives an organization towards selectivity, and towards increasing the staff's empathy with the customer as an individual.

Research shows that service workers most value having the ability and the authority to solve problems and provide value to customers. They require high levels of information to be able to take action and prioritize demands. They also need to understand why things are happening, both for their own peace of mind, and to answer customers' questions. This means that the internal communication system needs to distribute a wider range of information, and to ensure that it is put in context.

First Direct is a prime example of an organization that established not only its own differentiation but a new approach to an industry. It was conceived as a way of providing banking by telephone, avoiding the need for a branch network, and gaining market share by doing it differently enough to attract new customers. Although it pioneered telephone banking, the telephone has now become an accepted means of doing business, as the growth of call centres testifies. Telephone customer service is still important but is not unique to First Direct any more. It is no longer quite so novel to, or valued by, its customers.

First Direct is a business that established a differentiating customer proposition and realized it was not enough to do it once. Differentiation must be redefined as the market changes, rather than resting on past laurels. The launch of Internet banking rival Egg added to the competition it faced from new sources such as Virgin, Sainsbury's and Tesco.

First Direct had three trends snapping at its heels. First, its differentiation was eroding, as customers become used to what was once unique and competitors entered the market with new offerings. Second, technology opened new possibilities not just for banking but for providing customers with useful and valuable information. Third, customers change and the problems they face in organizing their lives are no longer the ones that First Direct was created to address. Life moves on, and the business has to move too, making sure that it takes its people along with it.

With its moves into direct banking via personal computers (PC banking), and its use of mobile technology, First Direct extended from its original core of telephone service-based banking to broader problem-solving. The company's basic strategy evolved: it still aimed to remove hassle from people's lives. At the outset, customer service was one way of reducing hassle; now it aimed to remove more hassle from more people in more ways.

It aimed to anticipate what customers' problems are likely to be in the future, rather than reacting only to those problems it was set up to tackle in the past. New technology made it possible to move from telephone banking to banking via other channels such as PC banking, small messaging system, palm top computing and digital television. PC banking and mobile phone banking means that customers have greater control about where and when they want to do their banking. This shifted the traditional balance of the business, and redefined activities and priorities. For employees it meant doing new and different things with their core skills – enquiry, exploration of needs, active service and anticipation – and keeping those skills relevant for the future.

HOW SHIFTING THE STRATEGY AFFECTS INTERNAL COMMUNICATION

As a business redefines how it wants to serve its selected customers, its internal communication has to ensure that it educates employees in the following:

1. **Understanding the brand.** Employees need to understand the brand, the offer it makes to the customer and the values it represents. They should be able to translate that into specific behaviours in their own area and to have a clear sense of what would be appropriate and inappropriate to the brand.

2. **Understanding the real competition.** As a business builds on its core business and moves into what used to be peripheral areas in order to provide value to customers, it can find itself competing with new competitors. For First Direct, for example, the real competition is not high street banks, but brands such as Orange and Microsoft who could move into areas similar to theirs.

3. **Understanding customers and their changing needs.** While it is important for all employees to know their company's objectives, for a business focused on the customer, it is vital that they also know their customers' objectives and priorities. This is a significant issue in organizations which have decided to target new groups of customers.

The traditional picture of the former customer can live on within a business long after the strategy has begun to focus on a quite different sector of the market.

4. **Redefining value and service.** How people define the nature and importance of service and value has to alter. Employees need to understand that good customer service is still a basic requirement, but that they have to take a further step to create value both for the customer and the company.

5. **Reappraising their role.** Employees have to redefine their own roles and the importance of what they do. The way to add value in the future is to be relevant and valuable to what the customer wants to achieve. Since the customer defines value, organizations need people who can respond to different kinds of customer in different kinds of ways.

6. **Withstanding uncertainty.** Employees who have been successful in providing one product or service can feel wrong-footed and vulnerable when they suspect that it is no longer valued. There is a delicate balance to be struck between educating employees in the need to follow customers up the value chain and telling them that the great job they are proud of having done in the past is no longer valued.

7. **Staying connected to the organization.** As a business's definition of value changes, what were previously fringe departments move to centre-stage. When car manufacturers began to make more money from servicing a car than they did from selling it, for example, service departments became more important. Resentment between old-style departments and new-style departments can emerge as arguments over where money is best invested arise. Is money better invested in the increasingly outdated core, which nevertheless still brings in the most money, or should it be invested more in new areas which are going to be more relevant for the future? Departments or business units which feel they are being milked to fund the future begin to feel doubly neglected. They have lost their star status, and now investment is being diverted away from them to a newly favoured child.

Such a situation calls for internal communication to educate each department or business unit about the other in order to create a feeling of common interest and thereby minimize resentment. It also calls for education about what new areas are doing to avoid the 'unknown incompetent' syndrome. Research shows that where a department's activities are unfamiliar, colleagues in other departments rate its effectiveness poorly. In other words, if people do not know what their colleagues are doing, they think they are doing it badly.

DEVELOPING STRATEGY

So far, we have discussed how good internal communication is important to turning strategy into action. We have also seen how a shift in business strategy requires a shift in internal communication. The following section looks at developing an internal communication strategy that supports the business strategy.

There may be a number of communication strategies that internal communicators need to develop:

- for their department. Here they may be trying to identify what the focus of their department should be, what value it should add to their business, what their priorities and core activities should be;

- for a project or an initiative, for example the group IT change initiative, or Sustainable Development;

- for a function – such as HR, IT or Finance – and its role and projects;

- for a campaign, or promoting a specific issue such as corporate social responsibility, or diversity;

- for a particular key process – logistics or supply chain management, for example;

- for product launches, sales campaigns or marketing programmes.

While the principles in the following section may be useful, developing these types of strategies are discussed in later chapters.

WHAT IS THE PROBLEM?

A typical communication strategy is usually a summary of what management wants to say, and a list of ways it intends to say it. Rather than seeing communication as a means to an end, it treats communication as an end in itself. More importantly it demonstrates a naive belief that if we simply tell employees what we want, they will go off and do it.

For example, the leaders of one financial services company wanted to increase the number of products its employees sold to customers. They had initially communicated to their employees that they should, 'become brand ambassadors and advocates of world class products and services'.

Employees were cheered to hear this , because they firmly believed that this was what they were already doing. They continued what they had been doing, basking in the apparent praise of their leadership and looking forward to healthy year-end bonuses.

The leaders' intended wake-up call had employees continuing to snooze. There were a number of lessons this taught the leaders:

1. They hadn't based their communication approach on the key business challenges facing the organization. Their business was part of a larger group whose new chief executive had promised to double the share price. They had committed to do this through organic growth, which meant they needed more sales fast. Selling more services was not a nice option, it was vital to success.

2. They hadn't considered what they needed their people to think, feel and do. The leadership communicated their strategy at too abstract a level and did not translate rhetoric into specifics about what they wanted to happen. They were more focused on what they wanted to say, not what they wanted done.

Their business objectives were first expressed in Anglo Saxon words – 'make more money, serve more customers, make cheaper products'. Then they expressed communication objectives in Latin words – 'increase market penetration, enhance customer satisfaction, optimize manufacturing efficiencies'.

At their off-site meeting, the board considered its strategy. In the discussion there was a mix of aspiration and exasperation. 'We could be number one by share in our market if call centre employees would simply deal with customers more promptly, sell them more and then could just let the customer service department know accurately what they've promised.'

From that first clear expression of the specific, the message is generalized and turned into an abstraction. The point is expressed as, 'Employees must become more proactively oriented at the telephonic customer interface.'

This will end up eventually as a bullet point in a PowerPoint presentation, at an executive road show, that employees may briefly register before their eyes glaze over.

While it may have involved employees becoming, 'brand ambassadors and advocates of world class products and services', what the company actually wanted was employees to sell more. They wanted employees to suggest additional products and services to customers when they spoke to them. They wanted their people to understand how competitive the market was, how urgent the need for growth was and how influential the role of the front line employees talking to the customer.

They wanted their people to feel they were helping customers by anticipating their needs, and to feel proud enough about the company and its range of leading products to recommend products with confidence.

3. They hadn't thought through what they needed from which people.

Communication can often become 'one size fits all' – generic messages addressed to all employees when we need different things from different groups of employees.

This company needed different things from different employees in different functions. Customer contact staff in the contact centres needed to change the way they dealt with customers. Marketing and sales people needed to understand changes in regulations and the entry of new competitors into the market, and feed competitive information back up the line. IT and systems people needed to accelerate the rate at which they were rolling out the integrated Customer Relationship Management system to the contact centres. Finally, contact centre managers needed to invest more time in sales and service training for their people.

4. They did not consider people's current attitudes and behaviour, and what might be holding people back. Leadership can believe that if only employees were aware what was required of them, they would do it. Awareness is rarely enough. Employees continue on their way if it seems right to them.

Asking why they are doing one thing and not another is a good question. If customer contact people are not selling additional products – why not? Is it that they don't know they are supposed to talk to customers? Do they fear jeopardizing their call answering targets by chatting too long? Are they penalized for calls which customers abandon?

Why don't customer contact people update customer service people? Is it that they don't like each other or that they lack the channels to talk to each other?

Later investigation among customer contact staff about their attitudes to selling more brought some interesting issues to light.

They lacked information about what their company's products and services actually were. They didn't know many examples of where products and services had been successfully adopted, or for what types of customers they suited. They didn't get any feedback on how well products and services were received and used by customers – except for the complaints that came through to them. They suspected that the management was only interested in making more money out of the customers and not providing them with good enough service. Finally, they thought that – wrongly as it turned out – competitors' services were superior and cheaper.

5. They did not focus on where their internal communication could make the greatest impact. With these factors holding back their enthusiasm and cooperation, it was no surprise in retrospect that

employees were cool to leaders' urgings. Since the company did not initially know what its employees' attitudes and behaviour were, it could not have identified where best to target its communication efforts to make the greatest impact.

With limited time and increasing urgency, any organization needs to decide where to invest limited resources for the greatest impact. In this example, there are a number of choices – shifting employees' scepticism about their leaders' motives; educating employees about customers' positive experiences with services; increasing collaboration between contact centres and customer service departments.

6. They did not identify which communication activities were needed to have the desired impact. The company initially invested its time and effort in executive road shows, employee meetings and local town hall meetings. It also introduced a campaign entitled 'Twenty-First Century Service' which used plasma screens, posters, display boards and the Intranet to promote the brand ambassador/customer advocate message. The chief executive filmed a short video segment which was shown to customer contact staff as a 'picture in picture' display on their terminals' screens so they would not lose time dealing with customers while they were also watching.

However, following further research into employees' attitudes and reactions, the internal communication team regrouped and focused their efforts on solutions to the problems they had identified:

*   Small group sessions allowed customer contact staff to meet members of the leadership team and quiz them about the balance they were striking between sales and service – and the sense it made for the organization. Honest feedback from the leaders convinced employees that they could happily reconcile the interests of both the customer and the company.

*   Product guides in simple language provided easily accessible information about products and services, what they did – and when to suggest them.

*   The 'Twenty-First Century Service' campaign was replaced by profiles and stories of customers who were happily using the products and services which were suggested to them.

*   Product 'taste tests' – like Coca Cola versus Pepsi – pitted competitors' products and services against homegrown ones. The results showed where competitors' were sometimes better, but more often where they fell far short of the company's own products and services.

The net result of all this was employees who were more confident in their leaders, more aware of the urgency to sell, and better equipped and more willing to make recommendations to customers.

The whole point in developing internal communication strategy is to support the business and help turn the business strategy into reality. However, the business strategy itself doesn't exist within a vacuum. An organization typically has a number of things which set the context for its business strategy:

- Its vision – this is usually a description of what an organization aspires to be, and a picture of its desired end state.

- Its mission – the direction it will take in order to achieve the vision, together with the broad business goals it will need to achieve to get there.

- Corporate reputation and brand values – this is a description of the kind of organization it wants to be, what it wants to be known and respected for, what it values and what will underlie its behaviour towards its various stakeholders.

All of these provide an important context within which the internal communications strategy needs to be developed.

Communication is a means to an end, and to arrive at the best communication strategy, you first have to start with the business strategy and define the end. Any organization wants to succeed in what it sets out to do. It needs its employees engaged to help it deliver on the promise it makes to its various stakeholders. An organization usually has a strategy for how it is going to achieve this.

It will be operating in a fairly complex environment – facing competitive threats, regulatory change, shifts in consumer preferences, technology developments, restructuring, mergers and acquisitions.

A company's strategy should make some sense of the environment within which it is operating, and clearly outline the strategic choices it has made.

It is a key part of the communicator's job to engage employees in turning strategy into action. When an organization is sailing through troubled waters it needs to have its employees as crew members not passengers.

The following section provides a step by step approach that provides a clear "line of sight" between business strategy and communication activities:

1. What are the key business challenges facing the organization, and what's our strategy for addressing them?

2. What do we need our people to think, feel and do in order to make the strategy a reality?

3. Which people do we need what from? How does this differ for different audiences and stakeholders?

Figure 2.5   Developing internal communication strategy

4.   What's stopping people? How big is the gap between people's current attitudes and behaviour and what we need from them?

5.   Where should internal communication focus to make the greatest impact on shifting people's attitudes and behaviour?

6.   What communication activities are needed to have the desired impact?

1. What are the key business challenges facing the organization?

A good example of an idustry with challenges is the IT industry, which has seen considerable change over the last few years. Let's take a fictitious company, Techco, which can fairly represent some of the changes within the industry, and their implications.

Techco grew quickly on the basis of its technology and its engineering ability. It specializes in providing clients not just with hardware, but also with applications which have been tailored to suit different industries.

The last few years have been hard on Techco. Rising competition, and increasing price resistance from customers, have forced it to compete more on price as its products are commoditized. It can no longer make the margins it needs, nor support the large cost base that it has grown during its 6 years of success.

During its history of developing clever but stand alone boxes it has grown an organizational structure of individual product divisions, with a small part of the service force acting as industry specialists.

Techco has realized it is in deep trouble. It cannot get the margins it needs, it has a cost base it cannot sustain. Worse, it has organized itself to push unremarkable boxes at the customer via siloed product divisions which are too focused on their technology and out of touch with market needs.

After a period of analysis and reflection, Techco's leadership decides to reposition the business radically from being a technology focused, product pushing, seller of boxes. It intends, rather, to shift its focus to the customers, to become their trusted business partner in developing IT solutions to business problems. It will be the ringmaster on the customer's behalf, assembling the various components from its product divisions to provide an end to end solution.

The strategic direction of Techco is now to move away from selling 'boxes', to become instead its customers' preferred business partner. This implies a different way of working with customers and demands a competence shift within the company.

Open systems are driving the commoditization of both Techco's and its competitors' traditional products. Customers are becoming adept at 'cherry-picking' from their offerings – getting technical expertise from one vendor, then buying the hardware from another. Techco's sales strategy therefore is to become its customers' 'trusted adviser', moving upstream from commodity supplier to partner.

The aim is to get customers to appreciate the value of dealing with the Techco organization as a whole and to charge for those services that they used to give for free. Customers will have an opportunity to configure for themselves the best mix of core and peripheral services, such as technical support. By acting as a systems integrator – the ringmaster who understand all the clients' needs, and can artfully assemble a complex and comprehensive solution – Techco aims to move up the value chain. As a valued business partner it will charge higher prices, consultancy fees and support contracts and get much richer margins.

However, simply growing the business will not be enough. The other side of the coin is reducing costs, and Techco knows that if it's going to cope with price pressure, it will have to reduce its cost base to hang on to those improved margins.

Techco summarizes its strategy in the following way:

- We will be more ambitious in creating strategic relationships with customers, focusing on those segments that deliver most value to our business. Working as trusted business partners with customers, we will provide them with comprehensive end-to-end technology solutions that deliver their business objectives.

- We will radically reduce our costs by adopting best, or in-class processes, and radically improving our operational excellence to increase efficiency, deliver better service and reduce cost.

- We will be customer led, not technology driven, and our people will build deep relationships with customers, diagnose their business problems, and use all our capabilities to provide relevant and business value-adding solutions.

- We will provide all our people with an engaging, demanding and satisfying work environment in which they can realize their full potential, and contribute fully to the business.

2. What do we need our people to think, feel and do in order to make the strategy a reality?

In the conversations that led to the development of the strategy, Techco's leadership discussed what would be required of their people to make this work, and what their likely reaction to the strategy might be.

Techco's internal communicators' first job is to take the strategy and identify what is going to be needed from employees, and what employees need to think, feel and do:

- Techco will want its people to focus more on the customer, understand the industry that each customer is in, and understand some of the issues confronting the customers in their industry.

- Employees will need to understand Techco's new business priorities so they can re-prioritize what they have been doing. They will need more context for some of the individual initiatives which are likely to hit them, and a sense of urgency to make the changes happen.

- Techco wants its people to feel part of 'one Techco'. Employees have traditionally worked in their product divisions, and one of the problems besetting the organization is its siloed nature. There will be a need for greater collaboration and cooperation across the silos, the adoption of consistent best practice standards and the eradication of duplicated costs. Employees therefore have to feel part of one organization, rather than members of one of the range of warring tribes.

- Employees will need to feel greater pride in the organization, and be more ambitious if Techco is to sell more comprehensive solutions, develop more innovative products and deliver better customer service.

3. Which people do we need what from? How does this differ for audiences and stakeholders?

While some things will be needed from all Techco's employees, there will be different audiences from whom Techco will need different things. Sales people will need to become more knowledgeable about the market in which their clients operate; project leaders will need to work with team members across each of the project divisions to assemble more comprehensive solutions, and marketing people will need to work more closely with product development to feed in information about customer requirements, market trends and competitor activity.

Therefore the next step in developing the communication strategy is to map out the different internal audiences, and identify what each needs to think, feel and do.

Since there are very few initiatives which are exclusively focused on employees, communicators need to look more widely at key stakeholders. For example how should customers view what Techco is doing, how should suppliers be involved? What impression is Techco trying to create among shareholders and how should the communities in which it operates think and feel about the organization?

4. What's stopping people? How big is the gap between people's current attitudes and behaviour and what we need from them?

It's important to have a reality check to identify what the current perceptions held by employees are. This in turn will identify any gap between employee's current attitudes and behaviours, and what's needed from them in the future to make the strategy succeed.

The information for this can be gathered from a number of different sources – the formal employee survey, communication champions or listening posts throughout the organization, 'meet the boss' lunches, focus groups, telephone sampling and 'appreciative inquiry' sessions.

This highlights why it's important to establish a continual stream of feedback from employees. Internal communicators can keep their finger on the pulse, and remain constantly attuned to attitudes, concerns and issues among employees.

In Techco's case, there is an annual survey, which is supplemented by a quarterly qualitative feedback process through focus groups.

The survey shows that at exactly the time that Techco is setting more ambitious targets, motivation amongst employees has declined since last year. The tough times the business has been through have left their mark, and employees report that their understanding of the overall strategy, their confidence in leadership and their faith in the future of the organization have all declined.

What has increased, on the other hand, is the pride that individual business units feel in their own achievements, and their confidence that what they are doing is right for the business as a whole.

Employees report that their knowledge and understanding of other parts of the business is low, and they don't believe there is good cooperation or collaboration between different parts of the business. They feel leadership is not in touch with what is happening at the sharp end, and they feel the business is not paying enough attention to its traditional strengths.

Feedback from focus groups shows people are proud of their history of technological development, with engineers in particular believing that they should be investing more money in developing and perfecting a broader range of products.

The survey results highlight a lack of understanding of how the market is changing and why competitors are doing better than Techco. A continual theme is engineers' frustration that customers are not specific enough in detailing what products they want and specifying in what configuration.

Research shows a number of worrying indications:

- Employees are no longer proud of, or confident in, the organization.

- They feel that the company has become fragmented.

- There is increasing competition between different parts of the business for recognition and for resources.

- Employees are still focused on technology and production.

- Employees are disconnected from what is changing in the market and customers' priorities.

- Employees believe that Techco is a success and do not see the erosion of its market share as a real problem.

- They do not understand why there have been such severe cost reductions, especially in their part of the business.

- Their confidence in leadership is decreasing, as is their clarity about the direction of the organization.

- Employees are bewildered by a wide range of change initiatives which they see as a continual stream of 'flavours of the month'.

5. Where internal communication should focus to make the greatest impact on shifting people's attitudes and behaviour

Knowing, on one hand, what the business needs from its different employees and on the other what different audiences think highlights the gap that needs to be closed.

The question then is how does internal communication close the gap? What are the key jobs for internal communication, and where should communicators focus?

Setting some priorities means defining what is most important. Is the most important factor urgency, that there's a limited timescale in which to make change? Is there a product launch looming which simply must be successful for the future? Are key customers likely to be reviewing their accounts with the company soon? Are regulators setting deadlines for compliance?

Is the most important factor credibility? Is there a yawning credibility gap between the claims of the leadership and the lack of confidence that employees have in their ability? Is a spreading concern about job security increasing employee turnover dangerously?

Is the most important factor the relative importance of different audiences? Not all audiences are vital to the strategy and some will be more important than others. For example, increasing Techco's closeness to the customers, becoming their trusted counsellor, and cross selling more services will demand that sales and marketing people are in the forefront of those who need good communication. If the drive for differentiation depends upon product leadership and innovation then research and development people are going to be in the forefront. If the strategy depends on greater operating efficiency and reducing operating costs, then those employees in logistics and supply chain management will be at the top of the list of important audiences.

Whatever the focus, Techco needs to be able to summarize the four or five key thrusts of internal communication which will help turn the business strategy into reality. This is, of course, in addition to the internal communications department's continuing to operate a reliable mix of communication channels, to support business as usual and to provide employees with the information they need to do the day-to-day job.

Techco's communicators decide that the key jobs for internal communication are to:

- educate all employees about the shift in business strategy, and how each employee can contribute;

- increase employees' understanding of changes in the market place, the growing threat of competition and the changing needs of customers;

- shift the focus of research and development people from pride in technology to understanding how it could be applied more commercially to customers' problems;

- generate a greater sense of pride and excitement about achievements across the company;

- create greater cross divisional collaboration to stimulate innovation;

- improve operational efficiency to reduce cost.

6. What communication activities are needed to have the desired impact?

Techco wants to get closer to the customer, invest to build long term customer loyalty, and look at the customer's life-time value to the company, not the value of any single transaction.

Moving employees' focus from producing the best products to understanding and solving customers' problems means employees need information on typical customer problems, and how to address them.

Internal communication's job is to link people so that knowledge can be shared. Internal information, in directories and on screen, quickly shows who can provide expert advice, in which area, to speed problem solving. 'Learning lunches' give departments the chance to showcase their experience and abilities and market themselves to colleagues.

'Meet the Customer' forums expose employees to the views of the customer. Team meetings focus on customer feedback, complaints and commendations. Customers are brought in regularly to provide feedback directly. Upward feedback sessions are run at which front line staff update senior management on customer reactions, needs and requests. Stories are circulated of employees who put themselves out to help customers and their ingenuity in solving problems, culminating in the annual 'Heroes' award ceremonies for customer service.

Now that Techco's core products are simply part of a much broader offer, more information will be needed by the sales force and customer service staff about what else is available from third-party partners. The Intranet provides profiles of partners and products, but customer contact staff also attend partner sales conferences and report back to colleagues on developments.

For Techco, improving operational efficiency means eliminating steps in the service and production processes. This reduces the cost of duplication, and avoids having to train employees in different systems and approaches. Employees will have to stick consistently to specified approaches. Standardizing processes is a fine thing to the individual whose method becomes the standard, but to others it can be dismissed as 'not invented here'. Internal communication has to encourage a sense of community and common interest. 'Cross-team' meetings are used to create greater understanding of roles and priorities across departments, and build stronger personal relationships between colleagues in different silos. Colleagues from other departments are invited to discuss ways of eliminating snags in processes, to improve efficiency and reduce costs. They alert each other's teams to upcoming changes, listen to problems that have been caused by their areas and feed back on actions they have taken to fix problems.

Techco's aim to compete as a product leader means getting a continuous stream of innovative products and services into the market. Innovation demands creativity, which in turn means recognizing and embracing ideas that originate outside the company.

Internal communication focuses on feeding in ideas from elsewhere, and keeping track of competitors' activity. Employees need both information and insight to innovate, so 'Innovation Exchanges' provide forums in which colleagues can discuss market and technological trends.

Research and Development's team meetings include feedback on customer experiences and problems, competitors' advances and brainstorming exercises on improving products and processes. To increase the speed of getting innovations to market, Marketing and Research and Development combine their team meetings to identify ways to accelerate the development process. Internal seminars on technical developments provide overviews of social trends, and reports by subject experts are circulated.

MEASURING THE MATCH BETWEEN BUSINESS STRATEGY AND COMMUNICATION STRATEGY

Techco provides a useful example of a company using its business strategy as a starting point for its communication strategy. How successfully its communication activities meet its business ends will depend on whether Techco gets the attitudes and actions from its employees that it needs.

No strategy is forever, and a beautifully crafted and executed communication strategy can be undermined by changes in the market, sudden departures of chief executives and unexpected mergers and acquisitions. Communication strategies, like everything else, have to adapt and change.

Assessing whether you got the outcomes you needed, or identifying what changes are needed both depend upon good measurement and tracking. The final chapter looks at how to add this final step to your strategy development.

MATCHING INTERNAL COMMUNICATION TO BUSINESS STRATEGY

This chapter has argued that it is important to link communication strategy to business strategy. It is important to match how we're communicating with employees with what the business needs from them.

The job that communication has to do will differ according to which competitive route an organization chooses to follow. The rule is, if you shift your strategy, shift the focus of your communication. If a company shifts business strategy, for example, from product leadership to operational efficiency, or from operational efficiency to customer closeness, the range of information that has to be captured and exchanged will also shift.

However, strategy is not the only thing that shifts. Increasingly, an organization's structure can also shift. An organization's strategy and its structure go hand in hand. An organization's structure has to support its strategy or it will work against it.

For example, if your strategy is to be a low cost provider, and to compete on operational efficiency, it may not make sense to have a number of different manufacturing plants all producing only slightly different products in very different ways. All that may do is breed complexity, duplication and unnecessary cost.

Conversely, if your strategy is to compete by being close to your customer, and by responding to the vagaries of your different customers' individual markets, it may not make sense to run your customer services operation from a single global outsourced call centre.

The next chapter looks further at the linkage of strategy and structure; getting a better fit between them and the communication implications.

REFERENCES AND FURTHER READING

Hopton, C., Bain and Co. (1994), *'Measuring and Maximising Customer Retention'* Conference.

London Evening Standard (2007), 7 February.

Reicheld, F. (1996), *The Loyalty Effect – The Hidden Force Behind Growth, Profits and Lasting Value (*Boston: Harvard Business School Press).

3 Going Global and Restructuring

This chapter looks at some of the communication implications of shifting organizational structure and becoming more global. In a world where employees are asked to 'think globally, act locally', this chapter adds the warning 'and communicate coherently'.

It highlights the role of communication in creating global attitudes, underlines the need to rewire lines of communication and defines the role of internal communication in a global business. Finally, the chapter outlines how the management of communication has to change if companies are to realize the business benefits that their structure and brands are intended to deliver.

Organizations increasingly want to get the advantages of scale, and of greater 'oneness', whether it's 'One Vodafone' integrating its acquisitions under one global brand, 'One Diageo', creating a single corporate brand from Guinness, UDV and Seagrams, 'One Ericsson' unifying its research, production and market units, 'One Hewlett Packard' or 'One GM' unifying its various manufacturing sites and product brands.

Organizations are shifting to increase innovation and creativity across the business, reduce costs and duplication by sharing services and using their combined purchasing power. The spread of global brands demands common worldwide approaches and consistency in marketing and manufacturing. Global clients want a consistent approach across all their markets.

The pressure to release shareholder value is driving organizations to reduce the range of different, costly and incompatible approaches to information technology, human resource policies, purchasing and marketing that have evolved across their business units.

They want to get advantages of size, reduce cost structures and avoid stretching investment too thinly over too many products. They want to establish consistency in manufacturing, supply chain and logistics, and stop the costly reinvention of too many similar wheels.

EMPLOYEES ARE BEING HIT FROM ALL OVER

These shifts within organizations have a direct impact on employees. Global manufacturing strategies hit them, regulation changes their day-to-day jobs, and compliance creates more work. Offshoring and outsourcing mean they could lose their jobs, change their employer or shift their location. Rebranding may lose them a familiar trusted name. They may lose support services they have relied on locally, and they may be asked to adopt global processes and standards which are definitely 'not invented here'.

As organizations globalize, global changes have a greater impact on individuals. For example, benchmarking and competition between manufacturing sites increase as manufacturing capacity is reviewed by companies on a global, not a country, basis. Employees who read about the colourful activities of colleagues on the other side of the world in the company newsletter can feel very differently about them when a product is switched from their factory to their colleagues', thereby effectively exporting their jobs.

IDENTIFYING HOW THE STRUCTURE/BRAND BALANCE MIGHT CHANGE

Organizations rarely stand still. They seem to swing like a pendulum from decentralized federation to monolithic global network and back. So how should their communication structure mirror the organization's shifts?

HSBC, originally the Hong Kong and Shanghai Banking Corporation, used to be a federation of banks and financial services companies, located and managed within the communities they served. Managers were asked to focus on the local rather than the global, and operated with minimal involvement from head office. However, the global nature of its competition and the need to produce greater value for customers and shareholders alike has meant a move towards central coordination and the adoption of a single global identity.

To present itself more coherently to customers, employees, shareholders and the financial community, HSBC clearly believes that it needs to adopt one single unified brand and to be much more disciplined and focused in the way it presents itself and communicates. This has involved, for example, changing the long established and well respected names of Marine Midland in the USA and Midland Bank in the UK to a single name, used worldwide – HSBC.

This unified brand is intended to help the customer understand what the organization as a whole can offer, making cross-selling easier. Cross-selling also requires that employees know and understand what different parts of the organization are, feel that they are part of the same organization and owe each other some allegiance and cooperation. HSBC's name change shows a clear link between how it presents itself, with whom it wants employees to identify, its business rationale and what behaviours it wants from employees as a result.

Another organization to move around the chessboard of structure and identity is Hanson. Once a traditional federation, Hanson owned a range of businesses and added value in ways which meant more to the City than to the customer. For example, it could immediately reduce acquired companies' cost of capital, since it had a strong credit rating and could get money more cheaply. It could also extend to acquired companies the low rate of tax that it had achieved and also add value through its management techniques. These strategies worked well for low-technology businesses or those with several factories making the same things, since it was then possible to rationalize the number of factories, and squeeze more from the assets.

Hanson shifted from a diverse conglomerate to a focused building materials producer as investors began to look to companies focused on single sectors. It has 'Hansonized' its three operating companies. Cornerstone, the largest business, became Hanson Building Materials America, ARC became Hanson Quarry Products Europe and what was Hanson Brick became Hanson Brick Europe. This entailed rebalancing employees' identification with the Hanson name and style.

Further shifts in shape and structure happened in the early 2000s. Acquisitions, particularly in the US, developed the company into a global player. Hanson continued streamlining administration, reducing overheads and creating a more integrated building materials business. Then it restructured from business units into regions: Hanson North America, Hanson UK, Hanson Australia and Asia, and Hanson Continental Europe.

Organizations are recognizing the desirability of operating on a global basis. Their customers and specifiers can be given the reassurance of international quality standards. Global brands allow the company a greater return on its marketing spend. Costs can be reduced by efficiencies on a global scale. Heinz, for example, is shifting from being a traditional federation of virtually autonomous businesses in various countries, to becoming a global business, with local accountability, via the creation of eight global categories.

Unilever's culture is one of decentralized local companies and local trading. Business units have a high degree of autonomy, and historically they have acted as mini-businesses doing their own manufacturing, sourcing and marketing.

Now Unilever is pursuing 'Unileverage', gaining the advantages of size and leverage as a global organization, while allowing its decentralized companies the freedom to respond to their local markets. This is being achieved by greater coordination across its business groups to gain the advantages of leverage in areas such as research and development, food science, advertising and marketing, innovation centres and centres of manufacturing excellence.

These increasingly common efforts to gain advantage via restructuring or through a matrix of responsibilities differ from the traditional pendulum swing from decentralization to recentralization. This is more of a 'push and pull' approach, where some responsibilities are pushed out and decentralized, while others are pulled in towards the centre. This can mean decentralizing in operational areas to be more responsive to markets and centralizing in 'back office' support services to regain the benefits of scale and synergies.

These push and pull approaches are easier to achieve on paper than with people. A report by the Institute of Management said of restructuring that there was no end in sight to a relentless cycle of change; 62 per cent of managers who they surveyed said that their organizations had restructured during the preceding year. The frequency of restructuring is increasing with the average time between new structures now down to 18 months. A slight majority believes restructuring has increased profitability but more think it has harmed morale, loyalty and security and led to a loss of essential skills and experience.

In addition, mega mergers are becoming more frequent and increasingly large. All of them are accompanied by job losses – usually 5–10 per cent of the combined workforce. The merger of Deutsche Bank and Bankers' Trust is a good example, involving restructuring charges of $1 billion and $400 million spent on 'golden handcuffs' to retain key people in the new organization. Meanwhile, Exxon and Mobil initially expected to lose 12 000 people – 10 per cent of their workforce – to make annual cost savings of up to $5 billion.

Research has highlighted the frequent failures to deal adequately with the people dimensions of mergers. While most mergers apparently make sound commercial sense, they generally fail to produce the promised benefits.

Germany's Daimler Benz merged with the third of America's big three car makers, Chrysler, in 1998. The deal was designed to create an automotive powerhouse, capable of matching the international reach of General Motors and Ford and confronting the emerging challenge from Japan. In its turbulent nine-year existence the company failed to become the profit-making multinational it was intended to be, and in 2007 it de-merged.

Mark Sirower, of The Boston Consulting Group and New York University's Stern School of Business, says in 'The Synergy Trap: How Companies Lose the Acquisition Game' that two-thirds of deals destroy shareholder value. His findings are echoed by a survey from KPMG which claims that about 65 per cent of acquirers fail to realize their synergy targets.

A study by McKinsey of 100 mergers in Britain and the US in the 1990s found that only a quarter of acquisitions recovered the cost of the deal and achieved synergies promised by management. The most infamous example was the much trumpeted merger between AOL and Time Warner in 2001, heralded as the 'deal of the century', marrying Time Warner's content with the Internet, represented by AOL. But it was a dismal failure, never yielding the synergies the companies promised (*The Observer*, 2007).

These mega mergers mean that, with the move to globalization, organizations risk alienating their people. However, even where restructuring is less dramatic, changing from a 'tribal' organization to a global one is difficult. Shifting structure, changing the relationship between the centre and business units, altering national perspectives to global ones and trying to create global outlooks from tribal loyalties all require more sophisticated internal communication.

Operating on a global scale involves difficult and often unpopular decisions on phasing out local brands, harmonizing standards across countries and dealing with the self-interest and prejudices of local managers. This requires a fundamental change in organization, ways of working and cooperation.

Multinationals tend to have a history of establishing operations in individual countries in an opportunistic and often ad-hoc way. In the past these businesses tended to be run independently, since different local market conditions, distance and slow communications made control from head office impractical. Country managers used their initiative to develop their markets, creating their own brand names, developing their own products and quality standards and pricing to suit the local market. This created a wide variety of products, brands, pricing and manufacturing processes, with little standardization from market to market. Acquisitions and joint ventures exacerbated the problems by bringing in new brands with local strength and familiarity that overlapped and duplicated brands in neighbouring markets. The results were a lack of strong global brands, inefficient cost structures and inadequate investment stretched too thinly over too many new products. Decisions taken too far from the centre resulted in the costly reinvention of too many similar wheels.

Now the barriers to greater cooperation across markets are falling. Deregulation and reductions in tariffs are reducing the idiosyncrasies of local markets. Telecommunication allows direct contact between the centre and local manager, and between colleagues in separate markets across the world. Levi Strauss Europe, for example, has moved to three regions within Europe in a bid to achieve greater standardization and consistency of products. While there are some variations between those regions, within each of them the fashion tastes are broadly the same.

Similarly, car manufacturers are, for example, pressing for worldwide purchasing of oils and lubricants from a single point of contact, and for a consistent product wherever it is produced in the world. The drive for greater consistency of product has led to similar production practices and processes worldwide and a decrease in the autonomy of local management. Because the organization wants to manufacture in a few central locations, rather than having different factories in each country, local managing directors tend to lose their autonomy in production, development and distribution. Their sovereign power is diminished, and they have to focus on implementing approaches and frameworks which have been developed elsewhere.

Organizations are intent on taking better advantage of economies of scale and shared resources through better coordination. This involves moving away from local decisions taken only for local good to more decisions taken centrally for the good of the business as a whole. All this requires different attitudes and behaviours from employees.

Although an organization may operate worldwide, it often comprises a federation of subsidiaries which operate under different brand names and even joint ventures with competitors, which results in a very national focus. Each market tends to be self-contained, with little cross-border product development, manufacturing and distribution. This discourages a global view and encourages the maintenance of national fiefdoms. It also means that employees identify with their local company name and local product brands. Any attempt to change structure inevitably leads to issues of corporate identity, branding, and employees' identification and loyalty.

Employees see themselves increasingly as members of different teams and tribes. In organizations, whether global or parochial, the challenge is to eliminate competition between different loyalties and, instead, to have them coexist and fit together like 'Russian dolls', one within the other.

A study by Frost and Sullivan of 2000 companies in the US, Europe and Asia-Pacific, identified collaboration as a key driver of overall performance. Its impact is twice as significant as a company's aggressiveness in pursuing new market opportunities and five times as significant as the external market environment. Global companies that collaborate better, perform better.

Professional service firms are in the vanguard of fostering collaboration. The professional service firm, says the management guru Tom Peters (*Financial Times*), is 'the best model for tomorrow's organization in any industry'. These firms – consultants, auditors, civil engineers, IT professionals and lawyers – are typically good at teamwork and knowledge sharing.

These professional firms are trying to master the lessons of global networking, project coordination and matrix management.

The lesson that professional services firms learned first was the importance of communication and teamwork. They have had to carry off the neat trick of continually creating new teams to work on assignments, while ensuring that those newly created 'tribes' also felt part of wider national, regional and global organizations. Operating in a matrix structure, they have understood the importance of balancing different employee loyalties to the client, industry, firm, specialization and geography. They also realized that there are some inherent tensions in the structure of a matrix that need careful communication. Objectives that should be complementary can become competitive.

The shift to a matrix organization often leads to an explosion in communication activity. Newsletters, road shows and websites proliferate, as does the number of Christmas parties people attend as members of different teams.

Operating in a matrix poses real challenges for internal communication. Decision making is often by consensus, and implementation is via influencing colleagues and subordinates rather than by diktat. Professional and functional responsibilities have to be balanced with line responsibilities. Each employee can have two or more managers, each with different priorities and performance measurements. All managers are free to communicate, and all lines of the matrix may have their own professional communicators competing for employees' time and attention.

The matrix approach drives consensus seeking but can slow down decision making – a real concern during times of change. The complexities of the matrix can obscure where accountability lies and hinder change. Because of this, good communications and a shared understanding of direction and priorities are essential.

Matrix management depends on shared responsibilities and leadership, and it is often ruefully noted in matrix organizations that, 'Shared leadership equals no leadership.' When responsibilities are shared there is a greater cost in terms of the time needed for discussion and coordination.

Relationships and goodwill are key to resolving 'shared leadership problems', and good communication is as fundamental to making a matrix work as electricity is to a lightbulb.

To stop erosion of goodwill a wider view of the whole is necessary. Staff are at different locations, often feeling isolated and uncertain about future work. They work in teams that are physically separate, serving a range of different clients, providing pieces of a jigsaw whose whole picture they cannot see. Large projects can become a loose federation of mini-businesses, in which individual employees are constantly monitoring their own job security, and where self-interest can never be far from their minds.

Regular communication is the antidote to many of these problems, but communication is the first thing to be discarded when time is tight. The strong focus on cost, time and resource budgets often means that there is little time or budget to spend on communicating. As a consequence, it can be viewed as an overhead to be minimized or to be hidden away on client project work. People focus on day-to-day pressures, and lose sight of the bigger picture. At junior levels, they keep their heads down, intent more upon their professional development than on the organization's direction. This makes retaining good people all the more difficult.

Individuals are likely to have a reasonable degree of clarity on their day-to-day objectives, and on what they personally are supposed to be doing. They may also have a fairly clear view on what their immediate team is doing. Beyond that everything is much less clear. If your nose is close to the grindstone, your horizons tend to be low. This leads individuals to identify with their immediate teams, and to be much less familiar with other parts of the organization, and their priorities and problems. The result may be an 'archipelago' organization where a scattering of insular teams have little contact with each other.

The most important lesson that professional service firms teach us is that a matrix organization must consciously create the glue of goodwill by investing in regular communication between its people.

Where organizational structures become both complex and ambiguous, it is people's relationships that make the system work. People who get along with each other help each other out. They do not stand on their dignity or insist on keeping only to their own precisely worded job description. Goodwill and cooperativeness form a safety net for the inevitable imperfections of any structure. Where good relationships do not exist, or are allowed to erode, that safety net quickly unravels.

Project workers have to feel connected with the wider organization and the leadership. Giving them an understanding of the business gives them a greater sense of control and reassurance. However, where leaders are largely invisible, and there is no opportunity for contact, trust is undermined. Employees then fill the vacuum by building a picture of the leaders' motivation and agenda from isolated incidents.

Where leaders are largely invisible, employees tend to be unclear about their roles and responsibilities – what exactly do they do up there on the management floor? Employee attitude surveys and communication reviews consistently reveal that greater contact between individuals creates greater familiarity, greater familiarity creates greater trust and greater trust creates greater cooperation. The reverse is also true. Lack of contact and familiarity leads to distrust, and lack of familiarity leads to a lack of respect. Where one team does not know or understand what another team does, they rate them poor at doing it – the 'unknown incompetent' syndrome, mentioned earlier.

Organizations which use multidisciplinary teams to address customers' problems have to encourage collaboration, and to share knowledge gained in different parts of the organization. To achieve the benefits of cooperation, they will have to increase their employees' willingness to collaborate, reduce interpersonal friction and reduce the cost of coordination. For such organizations internal communication is both a corporate glue and a corporate lubricant.

They will also have to avoid overengineering, and added cost, by better project management. This, in turn, will entail educating their employees to understand the best business balance of customer satisfaction and commercial management and the trade-offs involved between them.

Internal communication is needed to make an organization's people able and willing to do all this. It has to give employees the information they need to do the job, while motivating them to want to do the job well both for the customer and for their company. It has to help decrease self-interest and increase mutual interest.

Improving the bonding of project teams, with a shared sense of direction and common understanding and values, requires using communication to link three agendas:

1. The company's agenda – the strategy and direction of the business.

2. The customers' agenda – what they need and how they want to receive it.

3. The employee's agenda – a clear career path and what experience and skills they want to gain.

This is a clear remit for communication. But to fulfil it, professional communicators need to understand how the shifting sands of organizational structure can swallow their well meant messages and bury their traditional communication channels.

WHAT'S THE PROBLEM?

There are two problems that often undermine global communication. First, the way communication is managed does not fit the organization's structure. The second is that communication does not match the way corporate reputation and brands are managed.

One of the reasons employees do not deliver consistently on the strategy is that in different parts of the organization they have different views of what they are supposed to be doing. They identify with different sets of values and different priorities. Different organizational barons compete for their employees' loyalty, time and attention. Managing competing claims on employees' loyalties is important.

There are a series of 'Russian dolls' of identification. While people do understand that they are part of a wider organization, they also identify strongly with their own division. In fact, they identify with a number of different claims to their allegiance:

- the corporate brand;
- the division brand;
- the product or service brand;
- the location where they work;
- the team they belong to;
- the customers they serve and have in common.

The organization has to decide with whom or what it wants its employees to identify and what behaviour is needed to support its strategy. In short, it must decide where the 'centre of gravity' of its identification should be. Is it, for example, more strategically important for an employee to identify more with the product division than with the corporate brand? Having answered the question based on what is best for the business rather than on what suits corporate or baronial egos, it can then organize communication around that centre of gravity.

RESTRUCTURING MEANS REWIRING

When organizations restructure they put themselves in danger. New organization charts may show the new formal structure, but the old informal structure of the past can linger to haunt management. Changing the structure does not change the informal network of allegiances and relationships which feed the grapevine.

When organizations restructure, they rarely pay enough attention to refitting the communication lines to a new structure. As employee survey after survey has shown, people prefer to hear from their immediate line manager and, in times of change, that is who they turn to. It does not matter, for example, that the reorganization says that they now report to a new manager of a new customer unit based in Houston. If, each day, they still go into the Glasgow office, they will still continue to talk to their old manager who is close at hand and with whom they have an established relationship.

The term 'phantom limb' syndrome is used to describe how amputees continue to feel sensations from their amputated limb long after it has gone. Without a conscious effort to realign the communication structure with the new organizational structure, organizations can suffer communication phantom limb syndrome. The old structure continues to make its presence felt long after the reorganization says that it should have gone, causing endless frustration to senior management.

CHANGING THE ROLE OF THE CENTRE

Corporate structure rethinks have extended to reviewing the role of the centre and putting under the microscope the value of both corporate parenting and head office functions. Numbers of staff in head offices have fallen sharply in recent years. Technology has made some former head office functions redundant and other functions have been decentralized to the operating companies or outsourced together. Some companies are outsourcing parts of finance, others are moving it into shared services. IT and human resources have been outsourced and decentralized with more reliance on SAP type systems to reduce the need for large numbers of information collators.

These changes reassure shareholders that greater value is being squeezed from all parts of the business. Reviewing the role of the centre goes beyond reducing numbers to identifying the most valuable role that the centre can fulfil. In the past, head offices either acted merely as banker to a portfolio of diversified businesses or, at the other extreme, involved themselves in operational detail. Both business models have now largely fallen out of fashion. Towers Perrin surveyed 50 large companies such as Glaxo Wellcome and Cadbury Schweppes. They showed that the majority of corporate centres described themselves as guiding and giving strategic guidance to the operating units, and shifting to a more networked approach in order to realize the advantages of leverage and size.

A corporate group may comprise a number of business units, each of which has its own chief executive operating within a clear strategic and financial framework. The primary role of the centre is to ensure that the business units benefit from being part of the group through its role as a 'parent'.

DUAL CITIZENSHIP

Gaining the advantages of leverage and size in an organization which is evolving from working in separate national markets to applying common approaches across all markets puts a high demand on communication. One of the key demands is the need to create 'dual citizenship' among employees so that they identify with their own business locally, but feel part of a wider family and are willing to swap information, share success and adopt ideas from elsewhere. In this way employees can balance short-term parochial interests with the longer-term interests of the organization as a whole.

The task of internal communications is to help enrol employees in the business strategy so that they reduce costs and improve efficiency. This means engaging managers so that they feel sufficiently part of the business as a whole to understand investment decisions being made elsewhere. Communication is also important for balancing a strong country focus with a greater focus on processes running across different countries, especially where there is an increasing use of cross-country teams.

Managing the transition from, say, a divisional organization with a strong national focus, to a matrixed, networked organization requires careful management of lines of communication.

When organizations shift their structure, internal communicators have to identify new answers to four questions:

- **Purpose and direction** – what level of understanding of corporate direction is needed at different levels within the business units?

- **Information** – who needs what information (for example, for strategy and direction, performance information), and how they can best receive it, how often, in what style and via which distribution process?

- **Identification** – what is the right balance of identification between corporate, and business unit, and how corporate communication should best support that; to what extent people should feel part of the wider whole, and how should communication best act as a 'corporate glue'?

- **Collaboration** – how should communication encourage the exchange of best practice, and foster sharing, learning and networking?

The pay-off for good communication is a unified group of people who know where the business is going, with less speculation, misunderstanding and fear.

COMMUNICATION ADDS VALUE OR DESTROYS IT

Normally, the change in an organization's structure is an attempt to find a solution to a problem. For the organization to succeed, communication has to match how it manages its brands and corporate reputation, and fit how it has chosen to structure and run the business. If the management of communication does not match and fit these, it will destroy value rather than create it. Communication that does not fit does not help; it hinders.

Organizations which are trying to get the benefits of global scale need to ask what they need their employees to think, feel and do? Answering this question is slightly trickier for such organizations because it depends on answering two other questions – how are we structured, and how do we manage our corporate reputation and our brands?

These two factors have a big impact – how an organization is structured usually determines what activities are done where, and therefore what behaviours are needed from employees.

If, for example, an organization decides to run its IT function on a global basis, this will change what it needs from employees in the IT function. They will need to feel a greater affinity with a global function, understand and adhere to global best practice, and be more disciplined in how they respond to the requests of their colleagues.

If an organization shifts its corporate identity, and creates a single global brand from a portfolio of national brands, this again will change what employees need to think, feel and do. Employees need to feel part of a larger global organization, need to understand the rationale for the change and need to behave in line with the brand values.

Unfortunately, agreement around these issues can be difficult. Local barons may still want to hang on to their local brands, and focus their people's loyalty on the country rather than the global organization.

Arguments then flare between corporate centre and business units about what is and is not legitimate to ask, and what the rules of engagement are.

One starting point for resolving, or at least clarifying, some of the arguments is to base the approach to an internal communication strategy on what business value it is supposed to add rather than arguing about the rights of different barons to access or protect their own people.

How communication is managed depends on an organization's degree of centralization. In more centralized organizations the corporate centre had a claim on the employees' brain space; in more decentralized organizations, the local barons run their own communication show.

When organizations want to turn their employees into brand ambassadors and ensure that they deliver on the brand promise, the question should be asked, 'For which brand?' – corporate, business unit or product? Where does the business strategy require the focus of employee loyalty to be? Employees who are expected to deliver on a brand promise should identify with the right brand.

In a business like Marks and Spencer, consistency and reliability are the core of what customers are offered at whatever shop they happen to use. It is therefore important that employees at any one of the network of stores identifies with the values of the brand proposition. Similarly, the essence of McDonalds' offer is consistent standards, wherever you go. There is therefore an obvious advantage in employees feeling part of the whole of McDonalds, its approach and values, and not trying to reinvent any of its wheels.

However, a customer looking for a pub may be more interested in one with quaint individuality, rather than looking for one that is part of a uniform chain. Should the bar staff feel part of the King's Head, or part of the pubs division of a diversified leisure group? While pub managers may feel happier as part of a larger group, seeing its range of career opportunities, do the part-time bar staff need to feel the same corporate connection?

When an organization's strategy is to present a local brand to the consumer, communication should be focused on encouraging employees to identify strongly with their local unit.

Having decided where the employee's identification should be, managers have to abide by the discipline which that decision entails. This discipline depends on both business structure and brand structure. For example, what freedom do decentralized, autonomous country managers have when they are marketing a global brand? Can they do what they like or must they follow guidelines from the centre?

WHAT IS THE CORPORATE IDENTITY AND BRANDING OF THE ORGANIZATION?

Any shift to operating as more of a global network will highlight the issue of corporate names and brands, and with whom employees identify. Brands and logos are the tribal flags and totems around which employees form their loyalty and identity. When organizations become more global, people become more tribal.

In every organization identity and structure go hand-in-hand. Organizations have to reconcile how they want to manage their brands with how they want to structure and run their business.

When it comes to brands, organizations fall into three groups: monoliths, portfolios and federations.

The *monolith* has a strong single business identity which is shared by its divisions: examples are 3M, BP and Virgin. The fundamental strength of the monolithic identity is that, because each product and service launched by the organization has the same name, style and character as all the others, then relations with staff, suppliers and the outside world are clear, consistent and easier to control and manage. Employees in each of its divisions will have a strong loyalty to the name and will be constantly seeing it in advertising and on the High Street.

The *portfolio* is an organization with individually branded businesses, owned by a group which is itself branded, such as Kingfisher, WPP and Whitbread. The companies forming a group are perceived, either by visual or written endorsements, to be part of that group, such as Nestle. Consumer goods companies traditionally have portfolio identities while banks traditionally have monolithic identities.

The *federation* comprises a collection of businesses, each with its own identity, owned by organizations such as Hanson or Tompkins. The owners' identity may be visible only to the City, and is irrelevant to the consumer.

Such federations have grown largely by acquiring competitors, suppliers and customers who have their own individual name, culture and reputation. They are concerned to retain the goodwill associated with the brands and companies which they have acquired. At the same time, however, they want to overlay their own management style, financial practices and rewards on to their subsidiaries. They have certain audiences, such as the financial world, opinion formers and corporate customers, who they want to impress with their total size and strength. Communication to these audiences aims to emphasize uniformity and consistency as opposed to diversity.

Of these three types of organization, portfolios have the most difficult job. Some portfolio organizations have acquired competitive ranges of products in different countries with varying reputations. They therefore have problems of competition and confusion among suppliers, customers and often their own employees.

Companies seeking to create an identity covering a wide range of activities, with subsidiaries that often compete, face a complicated task. At the corporate level and for corporate audiences, they want to project a single but multifaceted organization that has a shared sense of purpose. However, at a local level they also want to allow the identities of the companies and brands that they have acquired to flourish in order to retain goodwill, both in the marketplace and among employees. Different portfolio organizations take different approaches to this balancing act.

There are two types of portfolio organization – the high-profile portfolio, such as WPP, and the low-profile, such as Procter and Gamble, the giant American company behind names such as Duracell, Pampers, Ariel and Head & Shoulders.

The high-profile portfolio owner's name will be known to its customers and to its employees, whereas the low-profile portfolio owner operates through a series of brands or companies which are apparently unrelated, both to one another and to the corporation – especially in pharmaceuticals, food, drink and other fast moving consumer goods. Such organizations separate their identities as a corporation from those of the brands which they make and sell. A good example is Britain's Reckitt Benckiser, with brands including Dettol, Finish, Disprin and Lemsip. In such set ups, so far as the final customer is concerned, the corporation does not exist. What the customer perceives is only the brand. This allows the brand to have a life cycle of its own, distinct from that of the company. It also allows brands from the same company to compete with each other. That perceived competition might be reduced in the eyes of the consumer if they were known to all belong to the same owner.

A company has to identify the right 'centre of gravity' for its employees by matching the brand they need to understand and deliver with the structure and way of managing the business. The way of communicating should differ according to how centralized, centrally coordinated or decentralized it is.

BALANCING BUSINESS STRUCTURE AND BRAND STRUCTURE TO CREATE BEST VALUE

Internal communication should match the organizations' structure and fit the brand. Matching the management of corporate identity and brand against how the business is managed yields a chart which helps identify the best fit. Figure 3.1 shows how different organizations combine their approaches to management and brand.

The vertical axis looks at how you manage your brands – are you a monolithic brand, are you a high-profile portfolio or are you a low-profile portfolio?

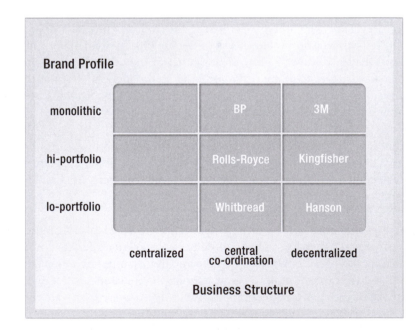

Figure 3.1 **The balance between brand structure and business structure in different companies**

The horizontal axis simply asks are you centralized, decentralized or centrally coordinated?

Rolls-Royce, for example, combines strong stewardship of its brand with a desire to allow business units to get on with their job, while retaining the advantages of any synergies. It has a monolithic brand, and manages its business units by central coordination.

WHAT BOX ARE YOU IN?

The diagram in Figure 3.1 gives communicators a quick way of engaging senior managers by asking them the following questions:

- What box do you think the organization has been in until recently?

- Which box do you think the organization is trying to move to?

- How fast do you have to make the shift?

One organization that has been moving between boxes is Unilever. It is a good example of the shifts being made by many global organizations to greater central coordination.

For years Unilever has been home to some of the world's best-known brands: Flora, Hellman's, Ben & Jerry's, Persil, Knorr, Dove, Pond's. By breaking down the barriers between its national businesses, Unilever is trying to exploit its global strength rather than simply its local presence.

Historically, Unilever was run as a federation of national businesses. This encouraged an entrepreneurial spirit among the heads of the national businesses. The chairman of a single country operation was in charge of everything – development, for brands and for going to market – effectively running their own mini-business.

However it inhibited the exploitation of innovations which could have been applied across a number of markets. The chairmen wanted to be self-sufficient and this led to fragmentation and complexity. Unilever's old federal structure led to some extraordinary examples of complexity in their product ranges. At one point Unilever was selling 64 variants of tomato soup in Europe alone.

A shift to greater central coordination took responsibility for many of the functions from individual country chairmen and gave it to specialist global teams. This left the country chairmen the sales job at national level, dealing with retailers and making sure that the job of selling and distribution was done efficiently.

Central coordination of marketing means taking a more cohesive, global approach which can save huge sums. For Lynx deodorant – known as Axe in most overseas markets, Unilever now make two or three adverts a year, compared to the 30 or 40 it would traditionally have done in local markets. Similarly with their Pond's range, they went from 64 pieces of advertising for Pond's in Asia to four in 3 years.

Unilever's shift to greater central coordination, with a greater focus on the global game, has brought significant changes. More than two-thirds of the chairmen of individual country businesses in Europe have been changed since 2005.

This shift to greater central coordination can increasingly be seen in organizations seeking greater value through greater unity. Figure 3.2 provides examples of different organizations making the same shift.

IMPLICATIONS FOR COMMUNICATION

Communication in a centralized organization

A centralized organization is characterized by close, central control of decisions. Typically, a small number of people at the centre have the authority to take decisions which affect the whole organization. In a centralized organization with a monolithic brand, for example, communication is run on the 'Roman empire' model. Strategy and planning happen at the centre, and prepackaged messages are distributed with minimal local change.

There may only be a few organizations which are actually completely centralized, but there are certainly a number of organizations who run their communication as if they were.

Communication in a decentralized organization

Decentralization allows greater closeness to the customer and faster responsiveness to the market. Senior managers in business units are allowed to get on with the job, within clearly established frameworks.

In the decentralized organization, communication should create greater closeness to the customer and faster responsiveness to the market. Employees should feel that they are working for the local business unit, so that greater identification and loyalty encourage greater motivation and productivity. Employees should be focused on local issues and priorities, with low exposure to the wider corporate picture.

Senior managers in business units can be allowed to get on with the local communication job, reporting regularly to the centre on their progress against agreed responsibilities. Managers at the centre should maintain a hands-off

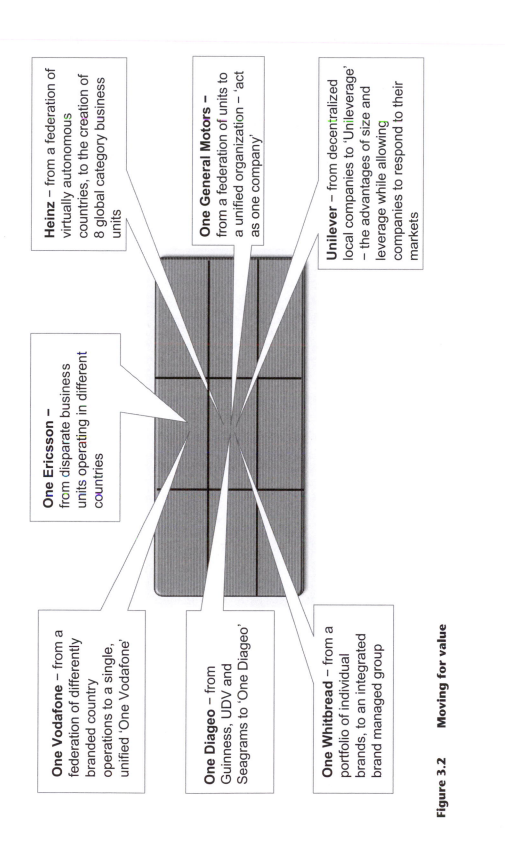

Heinz – from a federation of virtually autonomous countries, to the creation of 8 global category business units

One General Motors – from a federation of units to a unified organization – 'act as one company'

Unilever – from decentralized local companies to 'Unileverage' – the advantages of size and leverage while allowing companies to respond to their markets

One Ericsson – from disparate business units operating in different countries

One Vodafone – from a federation of differently branded country operations to a single, unified 'One Vodafone'

One Diageo – from Guinness, UDV and Seagrams to 'One Diageo'

One Whitbread – from a portfolio of individual brands, to an integrated brand managed group

Figure 3.2   Moving for value

approach and concentrate on identifying opportunities which can be rolled out across the divisions.

Communication at the business unit level should aim specifically to foster strong identification with the unit. The centre will communicate only occasionally to all employees and have only the top management tier as its regular constituency.

Communication in a centrally coordinated organization

Typically, in a centrally coordinated structure, technical functions, such as IT support, are centralized at headquarters, while daily operating decisions remain decentralized. Centralized purchasing takes advantage of group negotiating muscle and common Human Resources policies are often adopted across the business.

When organizations become more centrally coordinated, communication should prompt managers to look beyond the needs of their local units and to feel part of a greater whole. Employees can still identify primarily with their local units, but occasional communication from the centre can create an additional sense of being part of the wider organization.

In internal communication, common planning frameworks are needed to ensure consistency and coherence. Communication needs to be coordinated more strongly by the centre, and common standards, planning frameworks and measurement should be adopted across the business units.

Chapter 8 looks at how internal communication should best be managed for each of these types of organization with some rules of engagement for internal communicators, both at the centre and in business units.

SHIFTING THE CORPORATE COMMUNICATION REMIT

Communication is the glue that allows structures to thrive. Change in structure from decentralization to central coordination demands shifts in identification, information and relationships. The bad news is that it also increases the number of communicators active in the network, and the need to manage and coordinate them.

The traditional remit of the corporate communication centre is ownership of the corporate communication channels – the corporate video, the corporate newspaper – and drafting, crafting and distributing senior management thinking and messages. However, restructuring is likely to change its remit.

Redefining that remit depends on addressing five issues:

1.   management of communication responsibilities;

2.   managing the lines of information;

3.   redefining the role of the corporate communication function;

4.   redefining the role of the communicators' network;

5.   managing corporate and brand identity.

1. Management of communication responsibilities

A renegotiation of the relationships between the centre and the individual businesses should include redefining the communication responsibilities of the individual businesses. Managers tend to revert to past behaviour, and existing communication channels are often outdated and not designed to carry the business into the future. Clear expectations and targets for communication should be set, and managers tracked on their communication performance.

2. Managing the lines of information

Managers of corporate communication at corporate headquarters compete with operational managers in the divisions for employees' attention and loyalty. What share of voice each should have, and the degree to which business units filter information from the centre, will depend on clear agreement between communicators on both sides. Without agreeing explicit 'rules of engagement', the traditional tensions between the centre and the businesses will continue to damage communication.

3. Redefining the role of the corporate communication function

Becoming a unified business, and taking advantage of all possible synergies, means taking key strategic decisions centrally and coordinating key activities across the group. Communication to support this must itself be centrally coordinated with the communication function, proving that it can take a more value-added role. The role of the corporate internal communication department should change to match the new role of the centre, and the following questions should be answered:

- What are the current expectations of corporate internal communication, and how well does it perform against them?

- What should the new role of internal communication be in supporting the new role of the centre?

- What are the new communication criteria and standards for success?

- How should communication best support other changes (for example, sharing knowledge and creating common values)?

4. Redefining the role of the communicators' network

Creating networks of professional communicators who collaborate closely translates into greater familiarity, improved relationships and trust, so that change happens more easily. Any alteration to structure changes the responsibilities of communicators. Communicators need to work together in a network to ensure that the organization enjoys 'joined up' communication.

Redefining the role of the corporate communication function and the communicators' network is discussed in Chapter 9.

5. Managing corporate and brand identity

Business units will have distinct targets and measures. Those targets may encourage units to focus on their own market and customers, and may encourage self-interest. Therefore some force for cohesion is needed to counter possible separatism. When an organization restructures, it cuts across existing identities and loyalties and creates new ones. The corporate identity and employees' identification with it is a force for cohesion.

Rebalancing the 'Russian dolls' of identification depends on managing the balance between corporate and local identity and agreeing how far into each business corporate communication should reach. This means balancing the group-wide 'big picture' with local information and agreeing a share of corporate airtime in local communication.

Organizations need to ask themselves what is the role of the centre, what is the size, location and branding of the business units, and how important is having a common culture across the group? If some employees need to feel part of the wider business, how far down the organization should identification with the corporate name extend? In a decentralized business does the employee on the shop floor really need to know who the ultimate owner is and is there any value, beyond corporate vanity, in them having this knowledge? The following section provides a basis for agreeing this balance.

Operating across the world, organizations have to balance how they communicate at global and local levels, manage the increasing volume of communication and reflect structural and cultural differences.

The demands on employees are more complex, and the job for internal communicators more challenging. The same forces for change are multiplying the number of communicators – whether at global centre, global division, region, product line, function and global initiative.

As communicators multiply, they come under the spotlight applied to other functions – how many communicators are there, what value are they adding, what can be outsourced or offshored, are we duplicating activity and cost?

Internal communicators have to raise their game to meet the wide range of challenges global organizations face:

- They operate across different time zones which makes it difficult to manage information and keep employees up to date at the same time.

- Different countries will have different ideas about what is confidential and what is appropriate to share with their people.

- Thanks to the Internet and the introduction of multiple reporting lines, communication in one part of the world can rapidly migrate to another, which means organizations have less chance of compartmentalizing their communication.

- Organizations have varying quality of communication channels – some parts of the organization may be effectively wired up for e-mail and webcasts, other countries may be more geographically dispersed and have far less access to IT. The logistics and timing involved in translating information, and the cultural differences between different employees, add further complications.

Internal communicators in multinational organizations need to consider national and regional cultural differences.

There are very few truly global organizations; most international companies tend to have a dominant style which reflects the location of their headquarters. The danger is that the corporate centre takes on all the traits of the country of origin, so although a company happens to have global spread, its culture remains, for example, British, American, Dutch or French. Truly global organizations manage to combine unity and diversity into a cultural mosaic whereby regional differences contribute to the character and style of the whole organization.

Different nationalities within a single organization can apply different interpretations of corporate values and principles to the way they do business. Americans, for example, may interpret the corporate value of 'integrity' as sticking to your word on a deal, while their Japanese colleagues believe in being flexible and changing a deal if new information becomes available.

National differences also shape the internal workings of an organization and its underlying corporate culture. One organization believed that its American colleagues were more focused on individualism and promoting individual achievement – reflected in their belief that anyone can become President – while UK colleagues believed they tended to focus on teamwork. Conflicting cultures and attitudes can play out in the systems and infrastructure of an organization.

One company introduced acknowledgement awards for performance. They tried to adapt their reward and recognition system to local cultures and values, but they came unstuck when they attempted to include international teams. When presented with an award at the awards ceremony, the Japanese team member would say nothing; the British team member would say that it had been a team effort and the American would say that it had all been largely down to his own leadership.

In one international organization, global teams working on product innovations needed to collaborate closely together. American members of the team tended to be upbeat, positive and look for positive outcomes in the conversation.

The British, by contrast, saw themselves as more realistic and pragmatic, while they saw the Americans as 'cheerleaders' accepting every idea with unqualified enthusiasm. Meanwhile the British were perceived by the Americans as negative, obstructive and complaining.

CULTURAL CLASHES

Internal communicators in multinational organizations need to incorporate cultural differences in designing a global communication strategy that ensures that company-wide messages remain consistent and get through to their intended audience. Effective internal communication can help to build a corporate culture that glues together the different parts of a global organization. Conversely, inappropriate communication can lead to misunderstandings and compound cultural conflict.

In one organization, the global chief executive regularly e-mailed all employees worldwide each week on his activities.

The e-mail went out to non-English speaking employees, who printed it out and pinned it up on the notice board for everyone to read. It was full of baseball metaphors. A typical sentence read, 'We're at the bottom of the ninth innings, all the bases are loaded, and we have to swing at every ball.'

Confusion was widespread. Employees in Spain, for example, were unclear who this individual was, why he kept sending them e-mails, and why the business was apparently in the hands of a manically enthusiastic baseball player.

This example illustrates a number of points:

- Over reach – why is the global chief executive reaching employees who are located in manufacturing plants, reporting up to a country manager, through to a European regional head, through to a division chief executive – and only then to the rarefied heights of the global chief executive of all divisions?

- Selecting the wrong channel – why is e-mail being used to target mainly manufacturing employees who do not have access to computers, and therefore have to have print outs of e-mails pinned up on their notice boards in the factories?

- Language – why is this in English for an audience that is unlikely to be able to read it?

- Frequency – some contact from the global chief executive might be desirable for all employees – but weekly?

- Metaphors – why is it expressed so strongly in baseball metaphors which may mean a lot to the author, but may simply confuse the recipients?

TOOLS AND TACTICS FOR OVERCOMING CULTURAL BARRIERS

Translation and interpretation are critical to ensuring that cultural differences don't get in the way of effective internal communication. There are several factors that need to be taken into account.

Language

Although a company's business language may be English, people in different regions are likely to have different levels of understanding. For instance, English speaking ability tends to be more widespread in Northern Europe and less so in Southern Europe.

Some organizations, for example, follow up management presentations by providing chat rooms that provide easy-to-understand information for employees who speak English as a second language. This allows them to talk to each other to clarify what they have heard, and deepen understanding. This is particularly useful in Asian countries where people may feel less comfortable asking questions in public at the end of a presentation. It enables them to explain corporate messages to each other and reassure each other that they have clearly understood them without having to ask their boss. Oracle, for example, uses webcasts and webconferences to get the message across to its people, and then involves them in debate by using chat rooms. This allows those who are less voluble or who are not communicating in their native language to reflect and respond without feeling slow or stupid.

One approach is to punctuate management presentations with frequent opportunities for the audience to talk among themselves. This allows for interaction between the presenter and the audience, and between individuals and teams in the audience.

Interpretation

It is important to allow managers and local communicators to add value to global messages by explaining what they mean for each local business unit and team. If announcements are sent from the centre without warning, they wrong-foot local managers and communicators.

One of the basic issues of managing international communication is to allow time in announcements for different time zones; translating English language material into local languages and distribution.

Coordination

While there are a wide range of cultural factors that affect communicating, cultural nuances are often less important than coordinating messages and their delivery. It's not a matter of cultural misinterpretation, for example, when three different executives from headquarters show up at the same time to do in-country road shows.

Cultural sensitivity

Global executives and communicators need to align their messages and behaviours to local cultures and customs. For example, Western managers should avoid talking about challenging the past in Japan, where people have a deep-seated respect for history. Incoming leaders particularly have to respect cultural boundaries.

A chief executive went to the operations around the world in a series of road shows to update employees on the group strategy, to hear their issues and answer their questions. Wherever chief executives come from, they bring with them their own individual style, and their own cultural baggage. What works for Europe, may not work as well for Japan. In Asia, employees tend to be less forthcoming when asked to respond in open forum.

An executive opened a presentation to Japanese employees by tearing up the rule books as a sign of his intention to make dramatic change. Unfortunately, rather than dramatizing an end to bureaucracy, he instead shocked his audience, who saw the gesture as disrespectful to the policies that had been carefully developed and scrupulously followed. This apparent disrespect for the past silenced the employees since he was seen to have violated many of their cultural rules.

SHIFTING HOW COMMUNICATORS WORK TOGETHER

As companies operate globally, their internal communication needs to shift. A business strategy of greater unity and collaboration requires communicators to make the connections between strategy and the individual's daily life, connecting 'what it means for the business as a whole' with 'what it means for me in my part of the business'. It may also mean creating 'dual citizenship', where employees feel both part of their immediate business unit, and also of the wider enterprise.

Matrix organizations increase the volume of communication geometrically as managers increasingly belong to several teams – for example, geographical, functional, product and client. Leaders of each line of the matrix can hire their own communicators, which breeds competition between the volume, the profile and the timing of communication coming from different parts of the organization. With information overload such an issue, how, for example, does the Asian region cope with unannounced communication arriving from global headquarters?

Operating in a matrix creates a number of communication problems:

- Different communication strategies and different plans can create different messages and signal inconsistencies to colleagues at the same location but in different business units.

- Functions – like finance – in the business units, can be asked for information both along their functional line – finance – and within the operations line leading to duplication, competition, and confused priorities.

- Communicators adopting different approaches and different timescales can make difficulty for each other as formal communication in one business unit is leaked on the grapevine in its neighbouring business unit.

- Employees are able to compare and contrast the messages, and tend to select the one that confirms their preconceptions and suspicions.

- People's loyalty is often stronger to the location rather than the business unit which means they sift information not from a business unit perspective but in terms of what it means for their site, plant or location.

- Employees receive multiple copies of the same presentation from different leaders.

For a global business, creating coherence depends on establishing an integrated chain of communicators working in partnership. Otherwise, competing communication will create cost and clutter, and uncoordinated communication will destroy credibility.

AGREEING GLOBAL AND LOCAL RULES OF THE GAME

The relationship between corporate centres and their operating units can have a huge effect on managing communication. Managing a cascade so that it actually works is a challenge in any environment, but across a global business it can be a nightmare. Operations that regard the centre as a costly and unnecessary hindrance often fall into the habit of filtering out any information coming from the corporate centre as irrelevant or distracting.

Managing communication in international organizations entails building a partnership between the centre and local communicators in the business units. It is also important to establish clear rules of engagement to create a chain of communication incorporating each level of management.

This avoids competition between leaders and ensures that communication is consistent. For example, if a charismatic global chief executive decides to e-mail everyone directly, this can undermine the role of country leaders, who also need to have a voice. If local leaders are bypassed, they'll either duplicate the message or they'll disagree with it and create a communication disconnect between their business unit and the centre.

It's critical, therefore, to identify which leader is going to talk about what subjects to which audience. Global leaders often want to talk about the good news and leave bad news to the local management. Each level of leadership needs to have a role in helping global messages to penetrate every part of the organization.

Building a partnership between the centre and local communicators in business units means agreeing clear rules of engagement about who is communicating what to whom and how. A vital first step is agreeing common communication standards and principles:

Purpose   How are we trying to shift employees' views, attitudes and behaviour in light of the business strategy and structure? How much should people feel part of the wider whole, their business unit, location and team? What level of understanding of corporate direction is needed at different levels within the business units? How should communication encourage the exchange of best practice, and foster sharing learning and networking?

Reach and regularity   How far into the organization can the centre reach directly? Who, for example, should communicate the quarterly results – the global chief executive, the local business head or the global line of business leader? How frequently do local and central communicators have contact with employees? How often does the strategy need reinforcing? Should there be regular updates on how the diversity initiative is progressing?

Channels   What channels should be used – should the centre limit itself to e-mails rather than road shows? Do business units have to ensure they have a full range of fit for purpose channels, and ensure they are doing regular face-to-face communication sessions?

Content   What types of content should go down what channels? Who needs what information (for example, for strategy and direction, performance information), and how can they best get it, with what frequency, in what style and via which distribution process? Is strategy best explained by voicemail? Should restructures be communicated via the Intranet?

Priorities   How important are different types of information – financial results, strategic direction, global initiatives, sustainability, diversity, compliance – to different audiences at different levels in the organization? How does our view of what employees need compare to what employees actually want? How important do business unit communicators think it is for their people to know about the initiatives being promoted by communicators at the global centre?

Planning and coordination   How do we adopt common approaches to planning? How do we alert each other early to possible communication collisions and interdependencies? How do we renegotiate priorities with each other if we reach communication overload?

Freedom to adapt   It's important to allow local communicators to add value to global messages by explaining what they mean for each local business unit and team. However, it's not always clear what can be tailored and what should be passed on with no change. Chief executive's messages, for example, in some organizations, have been edited by local business heads to put their own spin on news. Without clear direction local communicators can claim this is mere localization. What's needed is clear guidelines on where communicators should tailor and where they shouldn't tinker – where messages should be passed on intact, and where they can be tailored and amended to reflect local differences.

In global organizations, engaging employees in business strategy means finding ways to make the same message resonate with a variety of different audiences. Sony Europe found this meant empowering local operations to bring the strategy to life. The key, says Jane Sparrow, Sony Europe's Head of Employee Communication & Change, is developing tools that allow local managers and communicators to adapt messages.

Communicating global strategy consistently across a large international organization requires guidance from the centre. Communicating some strategy locally, however, requires flexibility to account for local differences in corporate culture, values and business practices.

The global or European communications team worked with business heads to articulate key messages. Developing a broad core message and providing customized toolkits for delivering it in each country is an effective way to allow for some localization without losing sight of the global strategy.

The most successful programmes have been the ones where the implementation of those tools, and the message, have been tailored to local needs.

The European team works with communication teams in each country to tailor global strategy specifically to the local employee audience. The core message will be the same, but the delivery mechanism is different in each region.

The amount of support and guidance for regional communicators in adapting core strategy messages differs according to local needs. In some countries the directors work with the communications team to interpret enterprise-wide messages and integrate them into existing communication initiatives. In others, they work closely with the local communication team to devise a detailed campaign to engage employees in the company's objectives.

Although this takes more time than a 'one-size-fits-all' approach, there are two key benefits.

First, the overall message remains consistent because the core stays the same, but the interpretation of what this means for the audience is much clearer. This means the understanding gained and action taken as a result is much more effective. Second, the communication models devised in partnership with one regional team can often be replicated in another region, so local teams can benefit from each other's ideas and save time.

This serves to strengthen core strategy messages as they are delivered across the globe. It also develops a close connection between regional communication staff and those at the centre. This partnership approach works particularly well where regions or countries have fewer people in communication. They find it all the more valuable to take on some of the initiatives that have been devised in collaboration with other countries and regions.

Connecting the strategic big picture to the local day-to-day activities can also be helped by collaboration between communicators at global and local levels.

The company's global business plan is captured in a series of key messages. Different levels of strategy are set out like chapters of a book. These show employees the global corporate goal and what it means for the European business. Employees are provided with the big picture strategy for the whole organization, and are then asked to create the detail of what it means for their country or function, department and finally for them and their teams.

Providing toolkits helps employees align their day-to-day work, as well as their objectives and priorities, with the company's overall strategy. One toolkit, for example, included a strategy map, facilitation guides and exercises to create discussion and action planning. Every team could use these to align the strategic direction with their day-to-day activity.

CASE STUDY: ABN AMRO

ABN AMRO is an international bank which has been acquired by a consortium of Royal Bank of Scotland, Santander and Fortis. With European roots, the bank has been present in over 60 countries with the Netherlands, Brazil, the USA and Asia being its key markets. The bank aims to combine strengths from different markets, product and client business units, services and corporate functions, to serve a wide range of clients who required a combination of global and local capabilities. It serves as a good example of an organization aiming to cope with a complex global structure in times of rapid change.

At the beginning of 2006, ABN AMRO shifted its structure to support the group's strategic goals, adopting a matrixed structure to enable idea sharing and removing boundaries between units. This was a shift from an earlier Strategic Business Unit (SBU) structure that created independent pockets across the organization. Bringing the group together to develop more integrated solutions for clients therefore presented significant change for the communication function.

The implications of operating as one group for communication

In the former structure, communication teams across ABN AMRO operated in devolved SBUs. However, the new group structure demanded increasing interdependence of all areas. This interdependence demanded joint planning of communication activities since these would be visible to many internal and external audiences simultaneously. It also gave the opportunity to rewire channels and allocate resources in a more efficient way. It required a revised view of how decisions on priorities, issue resolution and running the function were made. The professional challenge became a lot more complex in a matrixed organization, requiring building relationships in a new way.

Defining a new structure for the function

A first step in making this shift was to redraw the structure of the communication function. This had to reflect the group's structure of five regions, global products and services business units. It also had to enable communication professionals to develop a more integrated brand and more consistent messaging. Previously, communication activities were staffed and resourced in each SBU, with group communications taking responsibility for the group's brand, reputation and shared messaging.

In the new matrixed structure, regional communication teams and group communications were responsible for execution of marketing and communication activities. The primary goal was achieving a consistent application of the brand to all initiatives and aligning activities both globally and in specific geographies. For example, a global campaign for a specific product would need to be consistent internationally for global clients, but also align with other campaigns and activities taking place in a specific country.

Small, dedicated teams remained in place for global units and services. These were primarily responsible for partnering with their business to shape requirements, internal communication to their specific audiences and the development of specialized information.

The communication function operated as a matrix rather than a fully centralized organization because the proximity to markets was also key. The challenge was to find the right balance between global alignment, and local responsiveness.

Working in a matrix

To move to greater integration, a 'Communications Board' was formed to bring together the heads of communication from across the bank. This Communications Board shifted from an idea-sharing forum to a strategic decision-making team. It led the function as a whole, and was collectively accountable through shared KPIs for strategic items, alignment of activities and coordination.

At departmental level (for example, press, internal communications, branding and marketing, issue management), alignment was achieved through coordinated networks. The heads of each department in group communications were responsible for bringing together a network of professionals in each field. The network's role was to focus on sharing best practice, tools and channels; planning future activities; and feedback on how global initiatives were being implemented at local level.

For internal communications, this network defined operating principles to clarify how audiences were managed and agreed how to handle the multiple interfaces that exist in a matrix, for example, between region and global product, between group and region and between global project and region. Since all the units depended on each other for execution and delivery, these networks also helped all parties involved to gain a better understanding of requirements from other units, whether that was understanding cultural issues or simply managing supply and demand.

The links between communication professionals across the group were also strengthened by a newsletter highlighting key initiatives and an annual conference focusing on shared strategic topics.

Two other factors are important to the successful operation of a matrixed, global communication function, such as that at ABN AMRO. Firstly, as the professional requirements shift, it is essential to get the right people in the right roles. This means moving staff across teams, developing competencies and at times funding external hires. Secondly, efficiencies need to be realized. Working in a matrix with strong interdependencies, there is an increased need for internal consultation and there is a cost of coordination in terms of more discussion, planning and offsite meetings. Balancing this extra cost requires rationalizing activities, channels and resources.

As Communication Director at ABN AMRO, Sabine Jaccaud provided strategic advice to the communication function. The lessons she draws from ABN AMRO's experience are:

- in a matrixed, global communication function, you need a strategic shared agenda to guide priorities across all business units;

- planning of messages and communication activities becomes a collective exercise: all units are interdependent and need to be able to appreciate knock-on effects and implications outside a given market;

- coordination is key: a mechanism for advance warnings, joint planning and resource allocation needs to be in place;

- structure is not the only solution: operating effectively as a more integrated function needs agreed principles and professional respect;

- significant efficiencies and removing duplication can be achieved through shared tools and practices. This involves an initial investment in new processes and channels.

Achieving a more consistent face to market, stronger shared internal messaging and better use of resources, activities and channels required clear shared goals across the function.

Defining common goals could be complex, involving extensive dialogue between 12 units, but once in place they provided clear direction. From these dialogues and the day-to-day work of coordinating activities, they found that professionals shifted rapidly from thinking within the boundaries of their unit to a willingness to participate in the broader agenda of the group as a whole. Making this shift meant being able to understand a number of key things – the knock-on effects of an activity or message in different environments; an ability to get up to speed quickly on the requirements of all units in the group; and the trust to let other people take responsibility for the delivery of services to audiences that were jointly owned by many different areas.

The ABN Amro case study illustrates the internal communication issues that are likely to be encountered by other organizations. Organizations will have to rewire lines of information to sustain new structures, reposition loyalties so that employees within individual companies also feel part of the wider family, and create a global network so that communicators in different business units work together effectively.

The communication function has to mirror the business as a whole by shifting from its traditional core of channel ownership and message provision to a more value-added role. This helps create greater business value through networking knowledge, fostering links between different parts of the business, encouraging a sense of global identification and creating a greater understanding of the new roles and behaviours that will be needed. These issues are taken up again in Chapter 8, 'Planning and managing communication', and Chapter 9, 'Repositioning the role of the internal communication function'.

REFERENCES AND FURTHER READING

Benbow, N. (1996), *Survival of the Fittest: A Survey of Managers, Experience of and Attitudes to Work in the Post-Recession Economy* (Institute of Management).

Frost and Sullivan (2006) *"Meetings Around the World: The Impact of Collaboration on Business Performance"*

KPMG (2006), *Post Merger Integration.*

Ollins, W. (1995), *The New Guide to Identity – How to Create and Sustain Change Through Managing Identity* (Aldershot: The Design Council and Gower Publishing).

Sirower, Mark (1997), *The Synergy Trap: How Companies Lose the Acquisition Game* (Free Press).

The Observer, (2007), Business and Media, 21 January.

Towers Perrin (1999), *The Role of Effectiveness of the Corporate Centre* (London: Towers Perrin).

II Leading Change

4 Leading Engagement

INTRODUCTION

In a world of turbulence and uncertainty, the job of leaders in setting direction and taking people with them is all the harder. With tough markets, uncertain demand and increasing competition, leaders need to build stronger relationships with their people and establish firm foundations of trust. Organizations need their leaders to lead, and good communication is vital to doing that job well.

Change for most organizations now means being in a state of almost constant flux. The stakes are high, both for the business and for its leaders. CEO departures doubled in 2005. The winners will be those organizations which are most fluid, anticipate change and adapt quickly.

Organizations now need more from their employees than simple compliance. They need to engage their creativity, energy and commitment. A business can only achieve its best when everyone's energies are pointed in the same direction and are not at cross purposes.

This chapter focuses on the importance of engaging employees and the key role of leaders in doing so.

UNDERSTANDING IS NOT ENOUGH

If companies want to engage their people, they must ensure everyone understands the key business issues – the 'whys' as well as the 'whats'. They must also 'make the connection' to show how individual success contributes to company success.

But understanding on its own is not enough. Commitment comes from a sense of engagement – the winning of hearts as well as minds.

Engagement involves employees feeling a strong emotional bond to their employer, recommending it to others and committing time and effort to help the organization succeed.

The importance of employee engagement was the centerpiece of the paper 'Putting the Service-Profit Chain to Work' by James Heskett of the Harvard business School (Heskett, 1994). Engaged employees create loyal customers who in turn create greater profit. Four years later in 1998 the Harvard Business Review carried a case study on the retail chain Sears' which had made employee engagement a fundamental plank of their strategy. Sears leaders estimated that a five-point unit increase in employee attitude led to a 0.5 per cent increase in revenue growth.

Sirota Consulting studied 28 multinational companies during 2004 and found that the share prices of organizations with highly engaged employees rose by an average of 16 per cent compared with an industry average of 6 per cent.

In 1999, The Gallup Organization published research that showed that engaged employees are more productive, more profitable, more customer-focused, safer and less likely to leave their employer. Watson Wyatt found that high-commitment organizations outperformed those with low commitment by 47 per cent. They also found that organizations where employees understand organizational goals deliver 24 per cent higher shareholder returns.

In a study of professional service firms, the Hay Group found that offices with engaged employees were up to 43 per cent more productive in terms of generating revenue.

'Driving Performance and Retention Through Employee Engagement', a 2004 Corporate Leadership Council survey of 50 000 employees in 59 global organizations, found that highly committed employees were 87 per cent less likely to leave their organizations and performed 20 per cent better than fellow disengaged employees.

The key to creating engagement lies with a company's leaders. It is their job to make the connection for their people and to communicate in ways that win commitment. This chapter describes how to do just that, and outlines critical lessons for success that every leader – at all levels of the business – needs to apply.

It is no longer enough simply to communicate and hope for compliance. Now the job has changed to one where leaders at all levels need to understand how to engage and motivate their people and lead their people through change, both good and bad.

A 3-year study of 40 major global companies (ISR, 2003) confirmed that a key driver of business profitability was the level of commitment shown by a firm's employees. The key factors behind this were the leadership skills of managers, the opportunities given to staff for personal development and the extent to which employees were empowered to discharge their responsibilities effectively.

Organizations are typically keen to engage their people for a variety of reasons. They want to unleash the talent and energy of their people, to give them strong personal ownership for delivering their goals, give them the sense that they are all working for the same business and to harness their drive to achieve extraordinary things. They also want to create a buzz around the workplace so that people enjoy coming to work, feel it's a great place to be and create a virtuous upward spiral of engagement and energy.

With all that to play for, it's no surprise that leaders are trying to raise the standard of leadership throughout their organizations.

They know that channelling their people's energy in the same direction will get the best from their people both for themselves and for the organization as a whole.

The leaders' role in achieving this can at times seem fairly daunting. The list of qualities expected of leaders is seemingly endless. They have to be brave themselves and motivate and energize others, drive performance, support the organization's vision and create positive working relationships across different parts of their organization.

Organizations with these kinds of aspirations for their leaders tend to benchmark themselves against high performing organizations, and therefore the standards they set for their leaders are continually rising. Whereas employee surveys in the past would typically ask employees to rate their managers on giving them the information they need to do their job, now employees are more likely to be asked to rate their managers on their ability to inspire them to do their best.

Research shows that executives often suffer from an 'inspiration gap', the difference between how they rate themselves and how their staff rate them. A DTI report, 'Inspirational Leadership' found that the chief executives they surveyed expected workers to show trust and respect for the people they work with and their customers. But, when 700 white collar staff were questioned, only 40 per cent thought their MD or chief executive had the same characteristics. 60 per cent said they were out of touch, and only 10 per cent said they inspired them. Four in ten executives 'talk more than they listen', staff felt, and just 50 per cent of staff felt there was a 'good buzz' at work.

So, at a time when leaders want more engagement from their employees, leaders are inadvertently disengaging their people through poor communication.

WHAT IS IT THAT PEOPLE WANT FROM A JOB?

Employees have a range of needs from their jobs. They want clear direction on where the organization is going and how it is doing. They want to know how they fit in, what they are supposed to do, how they contribute and how they will be judged. Once they are clear what their job is, they want to know where they can get the information they need to do it.

They also want meaning, excitement and a sense of purpose – what are we about, what are we interested in, are we playing a bigger game than making and selling widgets?

They want feedback on their progress and performance, and the opportunity to develop. They also want to know how they should behave, what is important to the organization, and who should they emulate. Finally, they want to feel part of a community, to enjoy working with colleagues who they can talk to for information, trust and rely on.

The Corporate Leadership Council emphasizes the importance of gaining employees' commitment because it has an impact on two things (Corporate Leadership Council, 2004):

- Their discretionary effort, which is the extra work they put in which therefore has an impact on improved performance.

- Their intention to stay or to leave, which has an impact on retention.

They identified two aspects of commitment:

- Rational commitment – the extent to which employees believe that following managers, teams or organizations is in their self interest – whether that's financially, professionally or in terms of their development.

- Emotional commitment – the extent to which employees value, enjoy and believe in their jobs, their managers, the teams they're part of and their organizations.

These two sides of the coin of engagement – rational and emotional – are reflected in global survey company ISR's useful description of three components of employee engagement:

- How employees feel – employees' sense of belonging to, and pride in the company.

- What employees understand – the evaluation of the company's goals and values.

- How employees act – the willingness to go the extra mile for the company and a preparedness to commit to the future.

These three components add to the rational and emotional the vital component of action. However, poor internal communication often undermines employee engagement, by failing to help employees feel, think and do:

- Employees may not feel that they truly belong to the organization, are valued by it, or feel pride in the company they work for.

- Employees may not understand what the company is trying to do, or why it is trying to do it. Kaplan and Norton (creators of the 'Balanced Scorecard') discovered from their research that on average, 95 per cent of employees are unaware of, or do not understand, the organization's strategy (*Harvard Business Review*, 2005).

- Employees may not know how the overall strategy relates to their daily job, what precisely they're supposed to do to contribute, and how, concretely, they can help.

There is a clear link between poor leadership communication and low employee engagement. Engagement is damaged by leaders' shortcomings in communicating, when:

- they lack clarity about strategy, and a clear focus about direction;

- they do not translate corporate rhetoric into concrete specifics, so their communication sounds like 'motherhood and apple pie';

- inconsistent messages from different leaders signal a lack of alignment, and a lack of certainty which only encourages employees to wait a little longer for a clearer picture to emerge;

- leaders tend to communicate in a way that is rational rather than emotional, and fail to paint the bigger picture. They use management speak and an impersonal style, and cannot bring a vision to life or generate enthusiasm in themselves or others;

- leaders are reluctant to give employees the freedom to ask tough questions or to answer those questions without dodging the issues. This signals a lack of respect for employees and undermines the credibility of leaders. Employees take from this that they are not valued or listened to, which undermines their identification with, and pride in, the organization;

- leaders do not walk the talk – there is an obvious disconnect between the espoused values of the organization and the behaviour of its leaders. Employees then listen less to what leaders say, and instead watch how they behave.

WHY LEADERSHIP COMMUNICATION IS IMPORTANT

Leadership guru Warren Bennis identifies the central role of communication for leaders:

> *'Communication creates meaning for people. Or should. It's the only way any group, small or large, can become aligned behind the overarching goals of an organization.'*

Survey after survey reports that employees feel the most important and preferred channel for communication is their line manager. This shifts depending on the kind of information which is being communicated. For example, where significant structural changes that have an impact on people's jobs are concerned, employees often want to hear it from the most senior manager available, on the principle of getting it straight from the horse's mouth.

Line managers and leaders have a clear influence on employee attitudes and behaviours.

Towers Perrin's and Tom Lee's useful piece of research highlights the primary sources of communication which have the greatest impact on employees. They report that while formal media such as newsletters, Intranets, and publications have a 7 per cent impact on employee behaviour, the impact of leaders on their employees is far greater at 61 per cent.

Ironically, many of leaders' communication shortcomings described above are inadvertent. The disengagement of employees can be the result of leaders playing to what they see as their own communication strengths, and using the winning ways which have helped them succeed so far. Unfortunately, many of these ways were developed in organizations that did not require high levels of employee engagement, and in times which were less complex and demanding. What has helped the leaders succeed so far may not be what will help them succeed in the future.

Part of the problem is that there is no one ideal model of a leader. There are different types of leaders who are good in different situations. They each have different communication styles, communication strengths and, inevitably, communication weaknesses.

Different people react differently to different leaders. The charismatic chief executive, who passionately paints the company vision that inspires the sales and marketing teams, can seem a little short on substance and specifics to the engineers in the manufacturing division.

A good first step for leaders is to understand what kind of leader they are, and what kind of leader they need to be in future.

In any leader's role there are two aspects: the task dimension of the role – setting a clear direction and helping employees understand their role and what their efforts mean to the organization; and the relationship side of the role – communicating with people in the way that builds constructive relationships and makes them feel valued and respected.

Authors of 'Primal Leadership', Goleman, Boyatzis and McKee, identify six styles of leadership based on research data from 3871 executives. These six distinct styles are very helpful in identifying leaders' communication preferences and styles.

- Visionary – describes leadership that inspires people by focusing on long-term goals. An effective visionary leader understands the values held by the individuals within the organization, and can explain their overall goals for the organization in a way that wins support.

- Coaching – describes leadership that delegates responsibility for elements of the organization's strategy. An effective coaching leader listens one-on-one to employees, establishes rapport and trust, and helps employees identify how their performance contributes and where to find the resources they need.

- Affiliative – describes leadership that creates a warm, people-focused working atmosphere. An affiliative leader listens to discover employees' emotional needs, and how to accommodate those needs in the workplace.

- Democratic – describes leadership that involves everyone in the group, listening to everyone's opinions before proceeding.

- Pacesetting – describes leaders that lead from the front, set ambitious goals and continually drive progress.

- Commanding – describes leadership that issues instructions without asking for input, and says 'do it because I say so'.

Each of these leadership styles lends itself to one element of the leadership communication job. Some lean more toward the task side, and the rational; others were toward the relationship side, and the emotional.

The problem is that leaders tend towards one dominant style, and either find it hard to adopt other communication styles, or do not realize that they are supposed to do so.

Visionary, Pacesetting and Commanding leadership styles tend to be used by leaders who are task focused, high energy and 'make it happen'. Their tendency can be to shoot from the hip, and get messages out rather than think them through. The temptation among such leaders is to communicate at, rather than with, their people. Such leaders have usually succeeded in the past by being directive and task focused. The communication skills they have developed are usually more suited to telling than to asking and engaging.

The skills needed to engage and create conversation are different from those required to make a strong PowerPoint presentation. Leaders who believe they can simply apply their existing communication skills to a different communication job usually do not get the results they hope for. A typical pitfall is to focus only on what messages they want to tell employees, rather than an understanding of how employees may interpret and decode their communication. Without a good understanding of their different audiences, and without a good feedback channel, such leaders are not communicating, just broadcasting.

If you are trying to engage your people, adopting a campaigning approach will seem like a superficial 'flavour of the month', which will hurt rather than help your credibility as a leader. People need to feel that their views are understood, and that they are reflected back in any communication. It is important for the leadership team to understand their people's concerns and likely reactions, before they start communicating.

More people-focused leadership styles such as Coaching and Affiliative, create a warm, people-focused working atmosphere. An affiliative leader listens to employees closely, with the danger of focusing more on the emotional climate and ignoring the work itself.

Democratic leaders listen to everyone's opinions and gather information. The danger for them is being seen as 'dithering', such as when meetings drag on for weeks without making progress.

There is no one best style of leadership. The directive approach, for instance, is useful in crises or when a leader must manage a poor performer, but overuse stifles initiative and innovation. The affiliative approach is appropriate in certain high-stress situations or when employees are beset by personal crises. Pacesetting can get results in the short term, but it's demoralizing to employees and exhausting for everyone over the long haul.

The most effective leaders are adept at all six leadership styles and use each when appropriate. Typically, however, leaders default to the styles they are most comfortable using. Leaders who are motivated mainly by achievement, for example, tend to favour pacesetting in low-pressure situations but to become directive when the pressure mounts.

In 'Leadership Run Amok, The Destructive Potential of Achievers', authors Scott W Spreier, Mary H Fontaine and Ruth L Malby warn of the impact of overachievers, who, they say:

> *'Tend to command and coerce, rather than coach and collaborate... take frequent shortcuts and forget to communicate crucial information, and may be oblivious to the concerns of others. Too intense a focus on achievement can demolish trust and undermine morale, measurably reducing workplace productivity and eroding confidence in management both inside and outside the corporation.'*

Leadership teams usually comprise different functional specialists who have developed different leadership styles. So it is no surprise that they focus on different elements of communication with different priorities.

These differences in style can reinforce the danger of leaders not being seen to sing from the same song sheet.

Pacesetting leaders, for example, may not spend enough time agreeing precisely what they are saying and how they are going to say it, or thinking through the possible negative perceptions of what's proposed, and agreeing their responses. Lack of preparation and discussion drives inconsistency, and inconsistency drives conspiracy theories. 'Kremlin watchers' in the organization look for differences in tone, interpretation and emphasis between the leaders that they then take to be signals of discord. A communication about change, for example, is then undermined when the top team is not seen to be united behind the proposals.

BUILDING TRUST IN LEADERSHIP

At a time when trust is declining in leadership, leaders are casting around to find out why. Trust is declining in a number of institutions – religion, government, the media – and sceptical employees are equally sceptical about their leadership.

Only 51 per cent of employees have trust and confidence in the senior management of their companies (Watson Wyatt) and only 44 per cent of employees believe senior leaders are trying to 'do their best' for their employees (Melcrum Research, 2007).

There may be a number of different reasons why employees do not trust their leadership:

- they don't see them, and so don't have a sense of what they're like;
- they suspect their competence – they seem like good people but not capable people;

- they're not approachable or human;

- they're not credible – they've got a strategy which doesn't seem to hold water, and no clear rationale for having arrived at it.

Employees seem to look for five things if they are to trust their leaders. To be trusted, leaders must be seen to be:

- Competent – judged to know what needs to be done for the company to succeed, and felt to be capable of leading the organization effectively in the right direction.

- Open and honest – telling the truth and feeding back the 'whole story' not just good news.

- Concerned for employees – showing they understand why staff feel as they do, and demonstrating empathy.

- Reliable – making sure that commitments they make are followed through and that 'words and figures' match.

- 'In the same boat' – perceived to share a common identity, experience and commitment with staff.

However, there are a number of things leaders do unwittingly which do not help them build trust:

- Leaders leak – what they are like inside leaks out of them, usually at unguarded moments. Any difference between what they espouse and what they actually believe quickly becomes apparent.

- Leaders emerge from meetings at which they've agreed a collective line and then communicate a different version, often more favourable to themselves.

- Leaders react under stress and say something which is completely uncharacteristic – which is then taken to reveal their personality. Employees have an 'aha' moment – they see the mask of their leaders slip, and feel they have detected the true person beneath.

There are other brakes which leaders unwittingly put on their own efforts. While one foot is pumping the accelerator of engagement, the other is firmly planted on the brake of poor communication.

Where employees perceive there is a lack of urgency, and where they cannot quickly perceive how they can help, they tend to disregard increasingly strident urgings from the boardroom to change and change quickly. Where they do not understand how the strategy was arrived at, where the strategy would take them and how they can contribute to it, employees are slow to put their hand to the plough. Where the strategy is simply not credible, where it is an apparent repeat of something already tried some years ago and where the leaders themselves are not seen as credible enough to achieve it, employees slow down again.

Finally, where the destination is unclear, it is unlikely to be motivating, and so employees feel neither willing nor able to head in the recommended direction.

WHAT MAKES A LEADER A GOOD COMMUNICATOR?

It is useful to be able to give leaders an understanding of the different components of the job they have to do as communicators. Each leader usually has in their head a leadership role model – someone admirable, who is effective and is a great communicator. However, each of these leadership role models can be quite different.

While leaders talk to each other around the boardroom table about the need to communicate, they usually mean quite different things depending on their personality, their character and their values.

A useful exercise is to ask leaders to identify another leader who they feel is an effective communicator. The leader they choose can be from any walk of life – political, sports, military, religious – living or dead, known by all or simply someone they've worked with during their career.

People will pick leaders such as Winston Churchill, Bill Clinton, Jesus Christ, Nelson Mandela, Colin Powell, Akio Morita, Lee Kwan Yew or even Mother Teresa.

When asked why their chosen leader is effective as a communicator they come up with another wide range of answers. Winston Churchill, because of his ability to articulate the feelings and determination of a nation and express them compellingly. Nelson Mandela, because of his strong sense of values, being a model of compassion and understanding, and embodying reconciliation within South Africa. Bill Clinton because of his charm and his ability to make people feel like they're the only one in the room he's talking to.

What's useful about this exercise is it shows that leaders incline towards a favourite way of communicating, and tend to neglect or downplay other styles.

Each of the leaders they choose tends to reflect the chooser's own priorities and values. Someone with a strong task focus and a desire to set strong direction may choose Margaret Thatcher. Someone believing in the importance of articulating the mission of the organization in an emotional and compelling way may pick Martin Luther King. A person who believes in the importance of 'walking the talk' and the importance of demonstrating values may pick Nelson Mandela. Someone who believes it is important to get on the same wavelength as people, to relate to them empathetically, and to 'feel their pain' may choose Bill Clinton.

These are four very different types of leaders, with different characteristic strengths.

Research done by Synopsis showed that effective leaders – in business or otherwise – excel in four key areas of communication. This enables them to engage their people in both good times and bad, throughout stable times and turbulent times.

These four areas are Focus, Articulate, Model and Engage – summarized as FAME.

For successful communication, leaders need to understand that all four aspects of communication are important, at different stages and times. They also need to be able to build on their existing strengths and to adopt new styles so they can adapt their communication to different audiences at different times.

Senior managers' selection of leaders who they believe are effective communicators are usually clues to whether their own leadership style leans towards the task side or the relationship side. Task and relationship in leadership are like the two pedals of a bicycle, you need to be able to push on both. However, senior managers tend to lean more heavily on one or the other.

Task focused leaders tend to be good at providing focus, setting direction, giving a clear sense of mission and direction and setting a challenge for the organization to fulfil.

They may be less good at articulating their vision in emotional and compelling ways that bring their people with them. They may not be able to see things from their employees' point of view, or be able to engage with them.

Conversely, some senior managers have a strong sense of values and are deeply empathetic with their employees – but they don't put enough time and effort into clarifying what the direction is, what the specific and concrete examples of what employees could do are, and they do not feed back on progress and how well targets are being achieved.

Effective leadership means balancing the 'hard task' and 'soft relationship' aspects of communication. The task side includes helping employees understand their role and what their efforts mean to the organization and its stakeholders. The relationship side involves communicating with people in ways that build constructive relationships, and make them feel valued and respected.

Making leaders more effective communicators means acknowledging that they have been successful by using the skills they have developed to date – it requires building on those skills, and understanding those areas where they are not yet as strong as they need to be.

Senior managers in organizations have often been promoted for their 'task' side – they have high drive, clear vision of where they want to go and can deliver results. However, in the past they may not have had to exercise their 'relationship' side – the ability to empathize, engage and articulate.

This is reflected in the drive with which organizations pursue employee engagement. Task-focused organizations often find themselves aspiring to relationship-based engagement – but pursuing it in a task -ocused way, adopting detailed step by step processes optimistically intended to create engagement with their people. A clear case of stamping on the brake and wondering why we're not going any faster.

However, research by management consultancy Marakon in 2005 suggested that most company strategies deliver only 60 per cent of their promised value. Under half the executives surveyed by consultancy McKinsey in 2007 said they were satisfied with their company's approach to making strategic decisions.

Part of the problem may be taking a purely rational approach to developing strategy. Research by strategy consultants Cognosis suggests that managers are crying out for strategies that engage both heart and head.

Only a quarter of the 1600 managers surveyed said that they found their organization's strategy exciting. Half didn't feel sufficiently involved, and did not believe that their opinions were listened to.

According to the research, there is a strong correlation between emotional and rational 'buy-in' – and both are needed to succeed. Stronger engagement and commitment can only be achieved where employees are persuaded, emotionally as well as rationally, that a planned strategy makes sense and is credible and doable. The Cognosis survey also revealed that 10 per cent of managers were 'super-engaged'. Intellectually they liked the rational rigour of their company's thinking, and were committed to achieving clearly understandable goals, but emotionally, they also felt their organization had a common purpose and that leaders were united round it.

The Corporate Leadership Council survey mentioned above found that emotional engagement was four times more valuable than rational factors in driving employees' effort.

The vital combination of rational and emotional is reflected in the words of Professor Henry Mintzberg of McGill University in his co-authored work 'Strategy Bites Back':

'Strategy doesn't only have to position, it has to inspire. So an uninspiring strategy is really no strategy at all.'

Thus, many high performing organizations are impatient to drive up engagement by having leaders who are inspiring. However, few are helping their leaders connect with their people in any way which is inspirational.

The section below expands on each of the four areas of leadership communication:

1. Focus

The chief aim of the leaders' communications is to ensure that everyone understands both the external and internal issues facing the organization and what each must do to contribute to the organization's success. Mercer Human Resource Consulting discovered in a study in 2000 that when senior managers do not communicate a clear vision for the future, employees are more likely to consider leaving the organization (Melcrum Research, 2005).

Employees often complain about the lack of connection between initiatives and the inconsistency of leaders' messages. Leaders therefore have to communicate a clear focus on business issues, set a few clear priorities, which they repeat and reinforce consistently, and identify clearly what they want employees to do.

The 2004 Corporate Leadership Council survey identified the top levers for driving employee effort as the employee's understanding of the connection between their work and the organization's strategy and the importance of the employee's job to the organization's success.

Employee research consistently shows that less than 50 per cent of employees know where their companies are going or what they are trying to achieve. This indicates that organizations are not telling their people the thing that would most increase employees' efforts. The same research also shows that employees are convinced that they themselves are doing a great job. They do not know where the business is going but they are all too confident that they are helping it get there.

This break in the 'line of sight' between a company's strategy and what individuals at the sharp end are expected to do is a common failure of leadership focus. Giving people clarity about what is expected of them, and how their efforts relate to organizational goals, has been shown to have the strongest link to productivity (Spreier, Fontaine and Malby, 2006).

2. Articulate

Great leaders can turn a vision into words succinctly. They paint a picture of what they want to achieve, turning 'management-speak' into plain language. They make messages memorable and ensure that everything they say fits together into an overall picture.

Leaders may want to engage employees' emotional commitment but they tend to appeal for it in dry, intellectual language. Leaders have to be able to turn the vision into an elevator speech, and paint a picture in a more emotional language. Effective leaders invest time in planning how they will convey their message. Leaders such as Martin Luther King and Winston Churchill painted their 'bigger picture' messages in emotional, engaging language, which they took the time to prepare and craft.

3. Model

In a Melcrum survey of over 1000 communications and HR professionals, 'actions of senior leadership' was rated as the most important driver of employee engagement. Effective leaders are champions of the values they stand for. They lead by example, and model the right behaviour for others.

If leaders want to inspire and motivate their people then how they behave and what they signal are often the most powerful parts of their communication. Commitment goes beyond simply agreeing and repeating messages, or going out on the road to meet people. Senior management need to walk the talk, and be committed, because lack of commitment is transparent and readily detected.

Nelson Mandela is not famous for his words, but for his actions. When South Africa hosted the Rugby World Cup in 1995, he walked out on the field wearing the South African rugby shirt. This was a symbolic action, signalling reconciliation across racial divides, in what Mandela saw as the creation of 'the rainbow nation'.

Modeling also involves understanding your own communication style, and adapting it to meet the preferences of a particular audience. Leaders such as Bill Clinton and Richard Branson use this skill to great effect.

Since 70 per cent of communication in organizations is informal, and employees consistently report that they get 70 per cent of their information via the grapevine, it's important to understand the impact of leaders' informal communication.

Leaders are influential, and have greater impact on their people when they are communicating informally – whether around the water cooler, in the bar or in a car on the way to a meeting.

Employees pay far more attention to leaders when they are apparently 'off duty' than when they are standing on stage in a formal setting.

It is important for leaders to understand that 'leaders leak'. What leaders truly believe, and how they really think 'leaks out' of them, unbeknownst to them, as they talk informally in off duty moments.

So it is that employees become experienced 'Kremlin watchers', looking at the behaviour of their leaders rather than just what they say. Informal communication is the most powerful, but it is also the most likely to lead to misunderstanding.

Even where leaders believe that it is formal communication events that have the greatest impact, they typically do not prepare for them. Leaders fly to vital management conferences only finalizing their slides on the plane. They do not allow rehearsal time with each other, and do not ensure that each individual leader is singing from the same song sheet, and harmonizing with their colleagues.

Such a lack of alignment and consistency may be survivable in a formal setting, but is deeply damaging when it comes to informal communication.

Inconsistencies in messages between leaders are almost inevitable. Leaders tend to agree on generalities, but disagree on specifics, since they do not take the time to dig further down into the issues on which they disagree. So their informal chats inevitably signal differing views. Employees perceive there is a gap between different leaders and then watch more carefully to see how these disagreements will be resolved.

This costs an organization time. Where strategy has to be translated into actions as quickly as possible, and there's urgent need for action, unprepared communication and lack of alignment between leaders act as brakes. Employees slow down rather than speeding up, because they get mixed signals, and so await a clearer signal of direction before proceeding.

4. Engage

Bill Clinton described leadership as, 'The art of getting others to do something you want done because they want to do it.' Effective leaders engage people by providing context and making the connections between their agenda and the individual's agenda. They are good at listening, facilitation, asking effective questions and handling difficulty.

Increasing employee engagement means understanding what engages people.

Employees want to work for an organization that is succeeding and is going somewhere. They feel it is fun to work with interesting people in an organization fulfilling a bigger purpose. However, how leaders engage with them is a vital part of whether they feel valued, involved and heard.

Employees report that what engages them is the chance to talk and the feeling they are listened to. They want to feel safe to speak, to have their say and to be able to exchange ideas with their leaders.

Leaders who are thought to be engaging are described as being approachable, enthusiastic and interested. They ask questions and listen carefully to the answers. They can get on the same wavelength as the people they're talking to, they can ask thoughtful questions to explore issues and they understand the concerns that their people express.

AREAS FOR LEADERS TO FOCUS ON

Work with leaders to improve how they engage their people has provided some useful lessons. One key lesson is where leaders focus. Typically, task focused leaders have a very clear idea of what they want to achieve but they tend to be less good at understanding what their various stakeholders want.

In one organization, for example, leaders had the clear aim of improving the margins of their business. Their intended message to their employees was clear – we have to compete more effectively, reduce our cost base and get our margins up to provide greater shareholder return.

Asked to identify what was the focus of their communication, leaders looked at a few simple questions:

- What's the outcome I want in this situation?

- Where are my people now and how do they regard the current situation?

These are deceptively simple questions, and it is surprising how often leaders find them difficult.

Take the first one. Leaders tend to be very clear about what they want to say to their people, for example 'reduce cost, improve margins and increase shareholder value'. They tend to be less good at identifying what communication is supposed to achieve. What should be the change in attitudes and behaviour as a result of successful communication, and how would they recognize success if they saw it? What this often reveals is that leaders focus on the message they want to give, rather than the change they're trying to make.

Leaders should focus on the outcome by asking themselves the question, 'What do I want my people to do differently, how do I want them to behave and what is my picture of success?'

Grappling with these questions, leaders often come up with abstract terms with few specifics, such as, 'I want people to buy-in to the change', or, 'I want people to feel energized and empowered.' The point is not that these answers are wrong, but they're not specific. How would you know whether your people bought in? Would it be enough for them to nod and smile pleasantly in agreement or do you want them to behave differently with customers?

Where are your people now?

It is extraordinary how often the leaders of initiatives are convinced that employees are waiting with baited breath to hear more about their programme. Because something is so important to its owners, it's easy for them to overestimate the enthusiasm of employees elsewhere.

Enthusiastic project owners tend to project their enthusiasm onto others. A typical response to the question, 'How do your employees regard this initiative?' is 'fantastic, very positive, very keen, very enthusiastic' and so on.

In one organization, the global IT function was about to launch a major change programme across the organization. Asked about how employees might regard this new initiative, they were initially positive and enthusiastic. Questioned a little further, they began to become less certain and less enthusiastic.

Why were employees so positive? How did they regard the last IT initiative, what was their perception of the global IT function as a whole and how did they regard the level of service that the function provided? Rapidly, the assessment of employees' views shifted. The last IT programme was widely perceived as being a disaster. Why was that? – 'Because it was a disaster,' said the IT team.

Senior managers need to take a slightly more sceptical view of their own initiatives, and to identify employee attitudes as they are rather than as they wish them to be. This is because if you're trying to get on the same wavelength as people, and trying to connect your agenda to theirs, it helps if you have a realistic picture of their views.

However, leaders can often view this as 'being negative' and can be unwilling to acknowledge and confront employee attitudes that they regard as negative, ill-informed and uncooperative.

This may explain why so much communication adopts a relentlessly cheerleading tone, and focuses on the positive – an approach that is reflected in employee attitude surveys which say that management too often tell employees the good news, but does not tell them the bad. This in turn undermines the credibility of the leadership, the trust of employees in them and the levels of engagement in the organization.

Articulating

Senior managers or project owners can find it difficult to articulate their message. This is often because:

- they do not put themselves in the audiences' shoes and see things from their viewpoint;
- they express things in 'management-speak', using jargon which is meaningful only to management;
- they favour complexity over simplicity and make things complicated not simple;
- they create communication to be read not said.

Articulating is about the leader's ability to put things into clear pictures, memorable phrases, compelling words. Articulate means being able to drive home your point by using language expressively. Leaders who are seen as great communicators such as Winston Churchill and Martin Luther King are often praised for the masterly way in which they use language. People remember Churchill's rousing call to action, 'We shall fight on the beaches', and they remember Martin Luther King sharing, 'I have a dream.'

Both of these leaders were trained in oratory, and had studied how to write their speeches and how to use their powers of speech to create a powerful impact upon their audience. That they could connect so closely with their audience testifies to their ability to express so precisely the thoughts, feelings and aspirations of their people.

Their expressiveness, their spontaneity and their impact was helped, not hindered, by the preparation and forethought they put into their words.

Margaret Thatcher, facing a rebellion among her own political followers who wanted to perform a u-turn on policy, memorably said, 'You turn if you want to, the lady's not for turning.'

Ronald Reagan was famously called 'the great communicator' because of his ability to reflect the thoughts and feelings of his constituents, through his simple and sometimes folksy use of language. Often criticized by the press for his short working hours, for example, he turned this to advantage in one press conference. Referring to a policy he had been working on, he said that he had 'really been burning the midday oil on this one'.

These are all phrases that live on, and are remembered and repeated when people think of those leaders. It is noticeable that the quotes of political and religious leaders can be recalled and repeated. It is much harder to recall the sayings of business leaders.

Politicians are trained in the skills of oratory. They understand the impact of the right words on their audience. They understand the impact of the cadences of their words, the construction of their sentences and the style of their delivery.

They take advantage of the fact that, for most of us, the rules of communication are based on an oral tradition – on words said rather than read. Literacy in the west is a relatively new phenomenon whereas the oral tradition of story telling is thousands of years old. Formal communication depends on the rules of written language, whereas informal communication is based on conversations using the rules of an oral tradition – the rules of storytelling, joke telling and anecdote swapping.

This may explain why so few employees can remember and repeat their business's strategy, but they can repeat a joke they have heard. This may also explain why the grapevine is such as powerful means of communication; because it relies on rules of communication we're all so familiar and comfortable with – the rules for telling and repeating stories. Seventy per cent of the communication within organizations is informal, whether that is networking or gossiping. Formal management-speak communicated occasionally via formal communication channels cannot match the power and influence of day-to-day informal storytelling.

What is remembered gets repeated. For example, the story of Goldilocks and the three bears is familiar and repeatable for a number of reasons. There are three bears, which is easy to remember. Each time Goldilocks tries something – a chair, a bed, food – the first is too this, the second is too that and the third is always just right. Imagine the confusion had there been six bears, and not just three bowls of porridge, but a buffet of food, each kind of which had to be remembered and repeated.

In the stories I told our three daughters, there were 'Three Billy Goats Gruff'. In fairy stories, magic rings provided three wishes, there were three sons who competed for the hand of the fair princess, and three wise men.

Three is a magic number. It features strongly in oral tradition, perhaps because people can remember three to five things before they start losing detail. This may be the reason why although Snow White met seven dwarfs it is so hard to remember all their names.

Three is the magic number in speaking. There are often three words – 'liberté, égalité and fraternité'. There's Tony Blair saying the most important issue is 'education, education, education'. The most important issue in buying property is 'location, location, location'.

There's the good, the bad and the ugly; lock, stock and barrel; hook, line and sinker. Politicians always seem to answer questions in three ways. Listen to any bulletin and you'll hear spokespeople giving their lists of three, 'We will protect American lives, restore law and order and prevent chaos,'

There's an important lesson here for leaders. Use rules of communication which are already established, rather than trying to overlay less successful rules. Your employees will not remember your PowerPoint slides, but they will remember your jokes. They will remember your strategy if it is structured in a way that helps it to be more memorable.

Seventy per cent of internal communication is informal conversation in the corridor or around the water cooler, using the rules of oral communication. If you can craft your communication to follow the same rules, your messages will be remembered. What gets remembered gets repeated, and what gets repeated gets reinforced.

The more formal the communication, the less likely it is to be repeated. Managers often feel uncomfortable 'communicating' with their people because the language they're asked to use is so unnatural and artificial. Leadership communication that is written in 'management-speak', as bullet points on a PowerPoint slide, stands less chance of being translated into day-to-day action.

The secret to effective leadership communication is to make it simple, memorable and repeatable.

As a first step this means avoiding complex words, and exploiting words that already work.

Before the advent of widespread literacy, techniques were used by people passing information to each other to ensure its memorability and repeatability. One of these techniques, for example, was the use of alliteration – using words that begin with the same letter, or the same sound. We have phrases in our language such as short and sweet, heaven and hell, chalk and cheese, cheap and cheerful, which owe their use to their alliteration.

News media are often very good at simplifying a story, and expressing it with alliteration so that it is remembered and repeated.

Affluent ladies who were opting to pay for caesarean delivery of their babies, rather than waiting for natural labour, were labelled as 'too posh to push'.

Alliteration is an aid to memory developed by oral tradition. Another is adapting phrases that already exist. For example, in one news story recently, controversy had arisen about four-wheel drive vehicles being used by affluent drivers who claim they are for off-road use, but only use it to go to the supermarket. The press started referring to these as 'toff roaders'.

Another aid is metaphor. People think in pictures, and a picture is worth a thousand words. If a chief executive exhorts his people to, 'Increase operational efficiency, raise the quality of product development, and focus on higher quality products and services,' his message is more likely to be remembered and repeated if he summarizes it by saying we want to be a 'Ferrari, not a Ford'.

We use metaphors in everyday conversation. We say things like 'we won't even get to first base', we will 'leave no stone unturned', we complain 'the baby has been thrown out with the bathwater'. One director talking about the future of his industry said, 'The traditional business model is sinking like the Titanic, and it's the small boats that will survive in the future.' Such pictures have high impact and are memorable.

A manager of a risk management department was frustrated at trying to engage other departments in the vital but apparently boring process of risk identification and logging. Each time they contacted colleagues for meetings to discuss the 'risk evaluation process' (REP) they couldn't get the time of day, as colleagues remembered they had to be elsewhere to do something much more important.

In a burst of frustration, the risk manager said that the way they were currently operating was, 'Like a fleet sailing into troubled waters without a minesweeper – at some point they were going to hit the mine field.' Most of his colleagues didn't understand what the REP process was, but they did understand what a minefield was. Communicating in this more vivid way got them greater engagement and greater cooperation.

Unions' very effective communication is often due to their very good use of metaphors. Whereas management talk about 'optimizing processes and rightsizing resources' in an apparently abstract and bloodless language that may conceal more suspect motives, unions fight back with vivid metaphors in protest. Plans are, they say, 'the thin end of the wedge', this is simply 'death by a thousand cuts'. One union recommended its members reject management's proposals by saying that 'this deal has more strings than the London Philharmonic'. Few of their members understood the details of the deal, but they repeated the sound bite knowingly. In the race for employees' hearts and minds, the metaphor beat the management-speak.

Metaphors are, of course, a two-edged sword. They can work for you or against you. One chief executive described to his senior managers the journey they had embarked upon. He was keen to get them engaged, and reluctant to be side-tracked by long debates about detailed issues of implementation, which could only become clearer once they got started, and at a later date.

Unfortunately, he described the journey in terms of being on a boat sailing troubled waters. What he wanted to say was that some details would only become clear as we got closer to them. He could have said that we were sailing towards the horizon and details would emerge as we got closer. Instead he described the uncertainty as 'sailing in fog', which, his senior managers muttered was like him – thick and wet. When he declared 'We're all in the same boat,' the rejoinder came, 'Yes, and it's the Titanic.'

Elevator speech

A number of these oral techniques come together in having leaders summarize their strategy in an 'elevator speech.'

The elevator speech is a brief encapsulation of an idea, concept or argument. It is named after the challenge of stepping into the elevator, and being asked by a colleague about something you are working on and being able to give them the short version in the 30 seconds it takes for the elevator to travel between floors.

The more conversational you can make the summary, the more likely it is to be remembered and repeated. However, to encapsulate everything in 30 seconds, requires some clear structure.

Stories and jokes have a clear structure. They have to, if the storyteller is to remember them, and the listener is to be able to repeat them.

For example, many jokes begin, 'An Englishman, Irishman and a Scotsman walk into a bar.' The Englishman goes first and does something, the Scotsman follows with his version, and then the Irishman does something different and brilliantly clever. In telling the joke, the teller knows that there are 3 cycles he has to remember. He knows there is a set up, three cycles and a punch-line. That gives the teller a clear structure and a roadmap of the story. It helps organize the ideas, not omit anything and put the emphasis on the punch-line.

Similarly, for the listener there are clear signals about what to expect. There's a clear structure, there's a simple sequence and there's a clear takeaway – the punch-line.

Importantly, structure helps both the teller remember what to tell and the listener what to expect and what to repeat in turn.

So, when leaders are asked to write an elevator speech, and then follow a clear structure, it must be written to be said, not read. It must be short, clear and simple. It must use conversational language, not management-speak and jargon.

The structure for the elevator speech is taken from storytelling and joke telling, and follows the 'rule of three'.

- A one sentence summary of what the strategy is trying to do – for example, 'We are changing the way we serve our customers, so that we focus on what's most important to them and more profitable for us.'

- Three reasons why we're doing this – for example, because customers are demanding higher levels of service, need greater levels of resources and are becoming more demanding about price.

- Three things we're going to be doing – for example, we're going to focus on those customers who spend most with us, we're going to retrain our sales people to act more as account managers and we're going to provide a smaller number of customers with higher level of service.

- Three benefits of this approach – for example, this way we will make happier customers, have more demanding but more interesting jobs, and securer and more interesting careers.

Typically, leaders are bought together in groups to translate their strategies into elevator speeches. They're then challenged to stand up and deliver these in 30 seconds against the clock. What's interesting about this exercise is that leaders often protest that their strategies are too sophisticated to be boiled down into such a short amount of time. In the BBC, for example, one broadcaster said he couldn't possible encapsulate his pet project in under 40 minutes if people were to understand the full richness of the subject. However, he acknowledged that BBC radio news programmes covered complex geopolitical issues in 30 seconds.

The challenge of condensing your story into 30 seconds is a useful discipline. It forces you to focus, prioritize and emphasize what is important. What becomes clear from the delivery is that the strategy is clearer, sharper and more memorable. This is not to say that all strategies must be restricted to 30 seconds – merely that the exercise helps crystallize what's important, valuable and necessary.

Why are elevator speeches useful?

Employees frequently complain that the communication they receive lacks clarity, simplicity and impact. This is often because it is coming from senior managers who take great pride in messages they have developed. They may be so proud of their initiative, and so wrapped up in its complexities, that they can't see the wood for the trees. Explaining to these managers that they can make greater impact in a short amount of time by crystallizing their message motivates them to think again.

Writing an elevator speech forces would-be communicators to get their message down to its bare bones. The rule for doing so is greater clarity, greater memorability, and greater repeatability.

Some organizations have also used elevator speeches to get greater consistency among their leaders. For example, at the end of a leadership conference at which the strategy has been discussed, a final session prepares leaders to communicate the strategy to their people.

As part of this, leaders work together in small groups to develop elevator speeches. This has been useful in a number of ways:

- it forces managers to remember what they've actually been told;

- it helps them begin preparing for onward communication – so they don't simply neglect to do so;

- it checks for consistency of message across different managers before they go out and communicate.

Once they have had time to prepare, one individual from each group stands up and delivers the elevator speech within the time limit of 30 seconds. They initially feel that this is too short a time to get the message across. However, on hearing each other they tend to be impressed for a number of reasons:

- short communication conveys greater punch and energy;

- it sounds conversational;

- it sounds clear and complete.

Sounding conversational is important to managers. Forcing them to think about an informal conversational setting – like an elevator – shows how ludicrous some of their strategy communication is – filled with management speak and dependent on a long PowerPoint presentation to back it up.

Managers are reassured when they hear their strategy encapsulated, sounding like normal conversation rather than some outburst of management speak.

CASE STUDY: DIAGEO – DEVELOPING LEADERS' COMMUNICATION SKILLS

Sixty-five per cent of CEOs are actively involved in developing leadership talent in their organizations (Hewitt Associates, 2005). Diageo is a good example of a company making precisely this investment.

Diageo, the world's largest producer of alcohol beverages including Guinness, Smirnoff vodka, Captain Morgan and Crown Royal, was formed in 1997 as a result of the merger between Guinness and Grand Metropolitan. Two years later, the company acquired the Seagram's drinks business.

After 5 years of continuous change, the company decided it needed to rally its leadership in an effort to unite and engage employees. Because of the mergers and acquisitions, and the loyalty people felt towards the company they had come from, it was difficult to unite employees around the new company that had formed. While Diageo was performing well, its leaders were confident they could boost performance to higher levels. The key was getting their senior leaders to connect with and inspire their employees.

They worked on the principle that, if you want to motivate and engage employees, you have to start by getting senior leaders to role-model positive communication behaviour. The communication team tackled this challenge head on through the development and implementation of a leadership communication workshop.

Diageo began implementing leadership communication workshops for its senior leaders. Finding innovative ways to address leaders' communication styles, behaviours and skills is a difficult task. However, the communication team were able to get leaders to evaluate themselves critically, by using real-life leadership examples, a number of hands-on exercises and a variety of practical application techniques.

During the company's leadership conference, the theme 'inspirational leadership' was unveiled and promoted as a key objective for Diageo's senior leaders. Diageo was serious about wanting leaders to develop the capacity to truly engage their teams. A fundamental part of that was helping them understand how their communication styles and behaviours impact the engagement of their people.

Diageo developed a programme of intensive, 1-day workshops designed to improve the communication skills and styles of Diageo's senior leaders.

The workshop curriculum was based around the FAME leadership model and designed to focus on Diageo's leadership and business objectives using specific practical examples of the situations leaders faced. The workshop was designed to be very hands-on, focusing on the practical application of skills and techniques.

As preparation for the workshop, leaders completed a personal style assessment to get them thinking about their own communication style. They were also asked to think of a current project or particular issue to use as a practical example throughout the day (for example, the launch of a new programme, a change initiative or an issue they had to communicate to their teams).

To kickoff the day, the facilitators helped workshop participants to brainstorm a variety of exemplary leaders from all walks of life – politics, business, sports, military and personal. The group then went through the list and pinpointed key attributes that have made these leaders successful and inspirational. Then, drawing from the list of leadership attributes, participants were asked to conduct a self-evaluation of their own leadership strengths and weaknesses. They then applied those attributes practically to a specific challenge they were facing, and had chosen to use during the workshop.

Participants were presented with the four essential leadership communication behaviours outlined in Synopsis' FAME model to help guide them during the workshop's discussions and exercises.

Leaders took part in a variety of practical activities, including analyzing case studies, role-playing and engaging in exercises around listening skills, using language with more impact and engaging people through the use of stories and metaphors.

According to Diageo, the workshops were less about training leaders on tactical communication skills, and more about increasing leaders' awareness of their communication styles and behaviours. Diageo does not claim that any one style is ideal. Instead, they highlight the positive and negative aspects of a variety of different styles and discuss which are most appropriate in different situations.

The overall objectives of the workshops were to help senior leaders to understand what Diageo expects from its leaders; identify personal communication strengths and weaknesses and use these to engage employees more effectively.

Diageo provides a good example of a world-class company that takes the impact of its leaders seriously. For Diageo, leadership is not limited to the top echelons of the organization, but is a responsibility for those leading people, initiatives and brands at all levels of the company. While they would pride themselves on having strong leaders at the top, they want to build an organization in which people are clearly led, leading in their own areas and strongly connected from top to bottom.

In other organizations, the danger can be that a single charismatic leader does not provide a good role model for others in the organization, but overshadows them. The danger with charismatic leaders is that they can be tempted to go direct to employees, bypassing the line management and undermining their role. Such leaders often feel frustrated that their messages are being stifled by the middle manager 'permafrost'. However, the first disconnect in the line management chain is usually between the board level and the next level down. This is the area of greatest schizophrenia where people have strong views, but are political enough not to voice them.

The relationship between these two tiers is often a problem, and tends to have a knock-on impact on the rest of the organization.

The role of the leadership group can be unclear. Are they there to discuss simply how to implement strategy, or to challenge, test and contribute to strategy? There is usually confusion about how directive the board should be, and how empowered and engaged the leadership group beneath should be.

The composition of the group can be unclear. Are people there because of the grade they inhabit, or because of their role as leaders of people? Grades may not spread consistently across different parts of the organization, and those outside the chosen grades but who are influential may be included.

The role of their forums can be unclear. Is the purpose of their meetings to transfer information, or to discuss emerging strategic tends and encourage a broader view outside functional silos? Meetings are often stilted and unproductive because of the confusion of the leaders' roles, and their caution about speaking up.

The net result of this is that there is often a disconnect between the board and next tier down, and because of that confusion there is usually a further disconnect between the leadership group and their direct reports.

A study by HR research organization, Hay Group, revealed deep division between senior and middle management caused by a widespread failure to communicate. The report showed that more than a third of senior managers – 38 per cent – believe their organizations are being 'paralyzed' by middle managers who can't understand and don't feel committed to their strategic goals. Based on the report's findings, Hay Group estimates the middle management problem is costing the UK service sector alone £220 billion annually (The Hay Group, 2007).

However, this 'paralysis' is being caused by middle managers struggling to come to grips with the challenge of engaging their people. While leadership includes making the motivational speeches, it also requires managers to have challenging conversations with their people. They often have tough questions about communicating that they need to get answered:

- How can I support the 'party line' of this message? Managers are uncomfortable about having to sell a party line that they do not fully understand and do not agree with. They feel it undermines their relationship with their people, their personal credibility and their sense of integrity.

- How should I lead the team through this change programme? How do I explain the interrelationship between the multiple initiatives which seem to be running inside the organization, explain the apparent contradictions between them, and feel able to shepherd my people through the various stages of the change cycle?

- How do I bring our strategy to life for my team? Confronted with a ream of management-speak and PowerPoint slides, which threatens to kill off any remaining spark of interest, how do I make sense of it all, speak plainly and paint a picture which is engaging, clear and motivating for my people?

- How do I get the company's message across meaningfully? How can I make a connection between the concerns, preoccupations and agendas of my people and those of the organization?

- How do I tell my people bad news? How do I explain the apparent contradictions between our desire to make this a wonderful place to work and our continuous lay-off programmes which undermine any sense of security employees might have?

These, and more, are key communication issues for leaders. These are the kind of questions they ask when they are encouraged to act as leaders and engage their people.

Leaders should be helping their people to see a clear line of sight between company goals and their daily work, by providing direction, describing the larger business context, building understanding and commitment to the organization's strategy, and establishing priorities. Organizations whose employees understand their goals deliver 24 per cent higher shareholder returns (Watson Wyatt), and highly committed employees are 87 per cent less likely to leave their organizations, and perform 20 per cent better than disengaged employees (Corporate Leadership Council, 2004).

Leaders can have a huge impact simply by being visible and by being approachable. By walking around, running 'meet and eat' breakfast or lunch meetings, and town hall meetings, leaders can have a disproportionate impact by showing what kind of person they are and acknowledging their people. 'Leadership visibility' programmes run by some organizations are simply a structured way of making this happen.

Communicators have to step up to the challenge of engaging their leaders in being effective communicators. Communicators are vital in helping leaders understand their impact, clarify their goals, crystallize their messages and meet their responsibilities.

Communicators should be providing communications counsel to leaders, identifying where they can most have impact, and challenging their thinking, their messages and their behaviour. Communicators can help their leaders provide clearer direction by helping them articulate their messages, increase consistency of messages, and by helping them remain 'on message'. They can also help leaders make the connection between the big picture and employees' contribution by helping leaders identify the 'so what?' of their messages for different audiences.

In terms of leaders' ability to model the right behaviour and 'walk the talk', communicators can help leaders identify where they should spend their time being visible and available. They can prepare leaders for these face to face sessions, and provide feedback about leaders' communication styles. They can coach them to align their style with their audiences' and identify the impact leaders will have through formal and informal communication. They can provide feedback on how well leaders have performed, and how employees have interpreted their messages.

Communicators have to be the eyes and ears of the organization, keeping their finger on the pulse of employee sentiment. They can help upward communication by raising issues which need to be resolved, and provide leaders with a barometer of employees' mood and level of engagement.

CASE STUDY: ASTRAZENECA R&D LEADERSHIP

The AstraZeneca R&D internal communication team took up the challenge of engaging leaders in being effective communicators. Faced with major and sustained change, the R&D organization of pharmaceutical giant, AstraZeneca, decided to coach, equip and support its leadership teams to engage people in what was happening.

Communicators worked with leadership groups to align them, help them understand their roles and responsibilities and play to their combined strengths, and showed leaders how communication could help achieve real solutions to key business problems.

The whole pharmaceutical industry is facing change – cost pressures, new markets, outsourcing and changing regulations are just of few of the factors they face. Like its competitors, AstraZeneca is responding to these broader changes in the industry and R&D is a key area for its focus. Pharmaceutical R&D requires a huge amount of investment, and efforts there to bring about greater innovation, greater productivity and new discovery will result in real and worthwhile savings.

Engaging employees in this change, particularly after earlier waves of productivity improvement, constant process improvement and change was a key task for R&D's Head of Global Internal Communication, Alex Kalombaris. Working with communication consultants, Synopsis, he and his team adopted an approach which focused on coaching leadership teams and equipping communicators to support them.

AstraZeneca R&D based their approach on the Synopsis FAME model of effective leadership communication. Each leadership team in R&D participated in a one-day workshop. A total of 200 senior managers took part.

The workshops were practical and focused each team on what they needed to do to bring about the necessary changes in their area. The entire day looked at how each group of leaders should articulate the direction for their teams, align behind the messages to their people, and prepare to engage their people in the changes ahead. Many participants were delighted that not only did they acquire new skills and techniques but they were also coming away with practical approaches to real communication situations that they were due to face.

A key aspect of the workshop was helping leaders understand their preferred communication style. A major distinction was whether the leaders were extroverts – lively, persuasive, and entertaining, or introverts – accurate, logical and factual. AstraZeneca used a detailed analytical tool to help leaders understand their natural styles and what this meant for the way they communicated.

Looking at communication styles helped the leaders in three ways. Firstly, they could plan to make the most of the strengths of their preferred style and minimise the impact of its downsides. Secondly, they could spot other people's preferred styles and shift their approach to match and therefore increase their chances of getting onto the other person's wavelength quicker. Thirdly, looking at communication styles helped them understand that different people were likely to react differently to the messages they were putting across, and that more than one approach was needed to reach everyone.

Early in the programme, a workshop for the R&D network of communicators who would be working alongside the leadership teams was run. In this workshop, communicators learned the key leadership communication skills, and practised ways to support their leaders long after the workshops were over.

AstraZeneca's investment in coaching their leaders highlighted the importance of the relationship between leaders and communicators. Their experience also provides useful lessons in how leaders should communicate in times of change.

10 LESSONS LEARNED

1. Communicators and their clients often have different styles which can cause misunderstanding. At AstraZeneca, communicators tend to have a different set of values and priorities from their internal clients. Whereas the communicators tended to be upbeat, spirited and considerate, their clients, most of whom were trained scientists, were by nature more likely to be lower profile, systematic and considerate.

    Understanding more about communication styles helped the communicators change their approach to get onto their clients' wavelength and achieve common ground from which they could agree a way forward. Without this understanding, it was easy for the scientists to dismiss the communicators as 'all show' and for the communicators to see the scientists as too fact-focused, with both parties coming away from meetings frustrated.

2. Members of leadership teams have different styles which can result in mixed messages. In one team in particular, different styles were reflected in different strategies for communication. A spirited and direct, energetic and charismatic member of the team was keen to talk to people in an unscripted and interactive way. More introverted members of the team were, however, uncomfortable with what they saw as an unstructured and undisciplined approach. The risk here was that different members of the team might take different approaches. The inconsistency that was likely to result could undermine alignment, and send mixed and confusing signals.

    This was addressed by working with the team to agree the key messages and the 'story' and also reinforcing that the leaders needed to consider the preferred communication styles of their audiences and flex their approach to cater for them. They should be energetic and upbeat for those in their audiences who were extrovert, but also make sure they clearly link what's happening with business objectives and have detail and evidence for the more fact-hungry introverted types.

3. Communicators have different styles which can result in mixed messages. At AstraZeneca communicators came from a variety of backgrounds and disciplines and had different styles themselves. Several communicators had been scientists themselves, and moved over to specialise in communication. Others came from journalism, and some through PR.

    Communicators were helped to understand their preferred style and think through how to get the most out of it. They also had chance to assess the preferred styles of the leaders they supported and how they could use this information to provide them with an even more effective service.

4. R&D leadership teams focused on collaboration. Many of the teams were successful because their leaders were skilled in building strong teams, bringing together functional and technical experts, and fostering co-operation. Their natural style was to be considerate and collaborative.

    In many ways, this style is useful during times of change – people expect greater empathy from their leaders, and to be reassured that they understand the pressures they're under and the pain they're feeling. On the other hand, the collaborative approach can also bring problems during change - leaders have to provide a strong sense of direction, and to be able to engage and motivate their people around the context for change, the compelling reasons for it, and the need to summon up another burst of energy for the new challenges ahead. Doing this means a shift to being more direct and upbeat.

5. Scientists like fact and process. Many appeared to be uncomfortable with emotion and story. The more introverted audiences such as many of the scientists do not like "arguing from analogy" – they don't want images and metaphors of how one thing is like another. They believe that a thing should rest on its own merits and be tested for itself. Scientists may also want time to reflect on information, to process through its implications, and to have a later opportunity for challenge and discussion. They are used to informed argument, to establishing hypotheses and then gathering data to test them.

6. Leaders can be too close to the information and too far ahead in their thinking. Many of the leaders were so close to the information that they forgot what their people did and did not know. This can cause difficulties when communicating change as an unwise word or unhappy choice of phrase could trigger concerns that had not existed before. Leaders can also become impatient with teams that are grappling with facts and detail they themselves digested some time ago and misinterpret their slow take up as resistance.

7. Leaders can project their concerns and uncertainties onto their people. For many leaders, the toughest objections to answer were those with which they privately agreed. Sometimes leaders would raise issues and concerns which their people may not have considered because the leaders did not want to be seen as corporate propagandists, or because they had their own concerns about how change has been rolled out, and the degree of detail which was available to them. Often, the end result can be extra confusion and concern.

8. Leaders need to develop their own questions and answers. Rather than having the communication team develop question and answer documents, leaders responded better when they challenged each other with tough questions, developed their answers, and tested out how real, credible and reliable these responses were.

It was also very helpful to challenge leaders to raise the questions they feared they'd be asked. In part this helped them prepare to deal with their fears, and it also helped them investigate what they were concerned about, get to the underlying issue and try and address and resolve it.

9. Meeting format matters. The leaders were especially interested in how best to put across their messages. The traditional way of communicating is to run large site events in which 200 – 300 people get the message at the same time. This minimises the grapevine, as everyone hears the same message from the same person in the same way.

However, these leaders also needed to ensure high degrees of engagement in order to maintain productivity and keep people focussed. Therefore they believed it was important to have discussion with their people, flush out their issues, and increase their sense of confidence about the change.

This meant they could not rely simply on the one off large scale events, since interaction at these would be low, and there would be little time or room for discussion. Indeed, it was more likely at any Q&A session the vocal minority would dominate, even if their views did not represent those of the majority.

Many leaders therefore decided to follow up larger scale events with smaller group discussions in which people could discover what the changes meant for their particular area of the business, raise their concerns and ask questions. They would also be able to challenge how well their leaders had created the vision for change, defended their interests, and developed a feasible plan for successful implementation.

10. Consistency is possible even when people see things differently. One of the group heads was especially worried about consistency of message. He knew this would be difficult to achieve because his department was spread across three sites, each of which had a distinctive identity and its own strong local leader.

Also, the sites were likely to be affected differently, and therefore would need not only different messages, but a different approach. For example, a site that was being severely affected by changes would not welcome an upbeat recounting of the benefits of the change to the organization.

Each of the team clearly had different styles and different mixes of how much telling and discussing they were likely to follow. Therefore, even when the messages and slides handed out to the team were identical and consistent, they would inevitably be used and delivered in different ways, to audiences who were themselves different and distinctive – and who would start selecting different elements of messages that they might remember and pass on to others.

Faced with what looked like an almost inevitable guarantee of inconsistency, lack of control of what people might take out of the sessions, selective memory and decaying recall, the leader was naturally concerned. He was able to reduce his concerns by:

- Preparation – spending time together working through what the members of the leadership group actually thought, believed and felt confident saying.

- Agreeing as a group an elevator speech, key messages, and answers to tough questions.

- Rehearsal – in which they could challenge each other, simulate tough situations they were likely to face and develop responses together, rather than coming up with something on their feet when delivering 'live'.

- Summaries – rather than leaving their answers in the Q&A sessions dangling, giving summaries of what they believed to be good about the changes and why they personally felt confident about them.

SUMMARY

Leadership is a subject which is constantly debated in organizations looking for inspiration and engagement. There are some simple, practical ways communicators can focus the debate on how important good communication is to good leadership.

Leaders are the most effective way of influencing employees' attitudes and behaviour, and are at their most influential when they are communicating informally, in water cooler conversations and corridor exchanges. Communicators need to move away from concentrating their time, effort and money on their formal channels, which are less effective, and need to get better at engaging their leaders in engaging their people. In all this, it's worth remembering that leadership is less about technique and more about attitude.

People all have their own favourite definitions of leadership, and one of mine is Peter F. Drucker's :

Leadership is not magnetic personality – that can just as well be a glib tongue. It is not "making friends and influencing people" – that is flattery. Leadership is lifting a person's vision to higher sights, the raising of a person's performance to a higher standard, the building of a personality beyond its normal limitations.

(The Peter F. Drucker Foundation for Nonprofit Management, (c) 1996)

In helping their leaders show this level of leadership, internal communicators have the responsibility to show their own leadership, and the opportunity to be leaders of their leaders.

The following chapters discuss how leaders can address some of their communication challenges – communicating change, communicating bad news and engaging their people more effectively.

REFERENCES AND FURTHER READING

Accenture (2006), *High-Performance Workforce Study*.

Bennis, W. G. (1989), Managing the dream: leadership in the 21st century, *Journal of Organizational Change Management*, 2(1).

Corporate Leadership Council (2004), *Driving Performance and Retention Through Employee Engagement*.

Department of Trade and Industry (2004) *Inspired Leadership: Insights into People Who Inspire Exceptional Performance*.

Drucker, P. F (1996), *Foundation for Nonprofit Management, The Leader of the Future*.

Farkas, C. and Wetlaufer, S. (1996), The way CEOs lead, *Harvard Business Review*, May.

Gallup (2005), Employee engagement index survey, *Gallup Management Journal*.

Goleman, D., Boyatzis, R. and McKee, A. (2002), *Primal Leadership* (Harvard Business School Press).

The Hay Group (2001), *Engage Employees and Boost Performance*.

The Hay Group (2007), *Corporate Soufflé – Is The Middle Giving Way?*

Heskett , J. (1994) *Putting the Service-Profit Chain to Work* (Harvard Business School Press).

Hewitt Associates (2005), *US Top Companies for Leaders Study*.

ISR (2003), *People Management Magazine*, 29 May.

Kaplan and Norton (2005), *Harvard Business Review*, October

Melcrum Research (2005), *Communicating Business Strategy to Employees*.

Melcrum Research (2007), *Effective Communication from the Top*.

Mintzberg, H., Ahlstrand, B. and Lampel, J. (2005), *Strategy Bites Back* (Pearson Education Limited).

Philpott, J. (2005), *People Management Magazine*, CIPD.

Sirota, D. et al, (2005) *The Enthusiastic Employee: How Companies Profit by Giving Workers What They Want* (Wharton Business School Publishing).

Spreier, S. W., Fontaine, M. H. and Malby, R. L. (2006), Leadership run amok, the destructive potential of achievers, *Harvard Business Review*, June.

Stern, S. (2007), *Financial Times*, 19 February.

Watson Wyatt (2006/2007), *Debunking the Myths of Employee Engagement Survey*, WorkUSA.

Watson Wyatt (2007), *Secrets of Top Performers: How Companies With Highly Effective Employee Communication Differentiate Themselves*.

5 Making Change Happen

Chief executives are generally preoccupied with becoming more competitive and more innovative, improving processes and reducing cost. All of these are likely to require some kind of change in their employees' attitudes and behaviours. Chapter 3 looked at the changes involved in globalization and restructuring, and the implications for organizations and their employees. This chapter continues the theme of change, focusing on how to bring employees along, rather than leaving them behind.

Managing change has become an important issue among senior management, yet studies consistently show that most change initiatives fail to deliver their planned benefits. At the heart of this failure is poor communication, despite the recognition that well managed communication is central to managing change.

When change shoots communication to the top of the management agenda, it exposes the weakness of existing communication practices. Like agreeing suddenly to run a marathon when you have not routinely kept fit, you realize, too late, that day-to-day fitness is vital. If you want to be able to use communication to achieve change successfully, you have to get your internal communication up to daily fitness. Effective communication minimizes the pain of change, prevents problems and helps the organization arrive at its desired goal more quickly.

This chapter describes the case for change, why change can fail and how communication can be used to bring about change more effectively. It identifies specific approaches to communicating different types of change, and addresses the problem of selecting the right communication media. Finally, it provides a case study of how one company used communication to support change, and concludes with some advice on how to communicate change more effectively.

There is no doubt that businesses are in the midst of a period of turbulence and uncertainty. New technology has plunged us into a 24/7 global society where we can shop at midnight, bank at dawn and pull off a multi-million pound business deal from a yacht in the middle of the Pacific.

In a bid to keep pace, organizations are specializing, generalizing, merging, acquiring, downsizing, expanding and restructuring at an alarming rate. Nothing is certain any more. The new chief executive that arrives in a blaze of publicity, promising a clean sweep, could be gone within a year. Today's competitor is tomorrow's ally. The next development in technology could potentially wipe out a whole market overnight – or give birth to a whole new breed of business. Organizations will be under intense pressure to reinvent themselves and deliver the goods fast for some time to come.

If businesses are to survive and thrive in these challenging times, they need to become more agile and responsive.

Businesses need to know how to take their people with them as they navigate the waves of change and uncertainty. This chapter sets out how communication can be used to drive change and cope with uncertainty.

WHAT LIES AHEAD?

If there is one thing we can be sure of in turbulent times, it is that if the only constant is change, the only certainty will be uncertainty.

The average tenure of chief executives is down to 4 years. The average time between organizational restructures is 18 months. The rate of change within sectors is astonishing. Who would have predicted that a stalwart such as British Airways could come under intense competition from a relative newcomer like Ryanair? Who would have thought that a reliable giant like Marconi could fall, or that a venerable firm like Arthur Andersen would disappear in the wake of Enron.

No one can accurately forecast the changes that lie ahead – and they certainly cannot predict the impact, implications and knock-on effects of them. But if organizations cannot deliver stability, certainty and predictability, they need people who are not shocked by events.

They need leaders who can translate shifts in strategy to specific action, and who can be specific with their people about the actions they need to take. They need employees who are clear about the direction of the organization and the part they need to play in it.

How can this be achieved? First of all, organizations need to build a sound bank balance of trust, so that when the board tells employees to move quickly – but cannot discuss specifics or predict the outcome – they are willing to do so. Trust needs to be built before you need to call on it. In uncertainty, doubts arise about the capability, credibility and preparedness of those in charge – so leaders need to establish their credentials up front. This means being open and honest with employees, sharing the thinking, showing empathy and making sure that when commitments are made, they are followed through.

Leaders also need to help employees overcome the feelings of powerlessness and loss of control that are typical at times of major change. If employees are to embrace rather than resist change, they need to understand what freedom and influence they still have – and which are the non-negotiable areas. Organizations are often afraid of giving people this room to manoeuvre. They want to publish their plans and have the workforce comply. But giving people this 'decision space' helps create focus and commitment and helps drive change through more effectively.

Those organizations brave enough to bring communication to the fore will be rewarded by the loyalty and engagement they need from their people to operate successfully in an uncertain future.

Change cannot be conveniently lumped together under one heading. It comes in many guises – all of which pose different communication challenges for the organization. Most organizations now face continuous waves of change, whether created by regulatory changes, competitive pressures or technological advances. Launching initiative after initiative means they face almost continual uncertainty.

There was a time when employees could rightly suspect that their leadership had a hidden agenda and an already worked out plan. Today it is more likely that leaders themselves are unclear how it will all work out. The uncertainty organizations are typically faced with today fall under four broad headings:

Driving in the fog

Organizations at the start of a restructure, the announcement of a merger or who are about to enter a new market, find themselves in this position. There is often a lack of clarity about exactly where it is all going to lead, what will happen and who it will affect and how.

Encountering turbulence

This situation arises when an organization suddenly finds itself under pressure in its marketplace (witness the unexpected troubles of Marks & Spencer or Vodafone). In this scenario, it is not clear whether the organization will survive and, if so, in what form. There are often rapid changes in top management, followed by a raft of new initiatives, and employees find themselves living from day-to-day.

Storm warning

The organization is motoring along quite happily, but the signs are warning of disruption ahead – a threatened private-equity bid for Sainsbury's for example, or Barclays' merger talks with ABN AMRO. Rumour and speculation are rife – but it is unclear if anything will happen, or if it does, how employees will be affected. In this scenario, people need regular 'views from the bridge' and updates on progress.

Meteor strike

The organization is doing fine when a sudden shock shatters the peace (Arthur Andersen and Enron, Societe Generales 'rogue trader' or AIB's 'brogue trader'). It is unclear how, or even if, the organization will come out the other side.

THE CASE FOR CHANGE

Change is a given in today's business environment, and the ability to make change happen is now a core competence. Organizations face a stark choice; manage change or become its victim.

Change is difficult to carry out. Hammer and Champney, in their book 'Re-engineering the Corporation' (1995), found that between 50 and 70 per cent of organizations failed to achieve the results they wanted by changing processes and procedures. A survey by Larkin and Larkin (1994) in the US showed that 66 per cent of companies which underwent change did not achieve the cost savings they sought. Although, for example, a large mineral extraction corporation achieved 50 per cent of their training goals and 50 per cent of their participation goals, they only achieved 5 per cent of their results targets. Similarly, one of the largest US financial institutions implemented a Total Quality programme. After 2 years they had experienced no bottom-line performance improvements.

Managing change well minimizes the risk of failure. Change itself usually involves a large investment in people and resources, and it takes time to bear fruit. Minimizing the time it takes to make change happen is at the top of the management agenda, because allocating business resources to implementing changes diverts them from their day jobs. If momentum flags, people become demotivated and sceptical and eventually the process runs out of steam.

WHY DOES CHANGE FAIL?

Most of the factors which undermine change relate to people.

Lack of motivation

John P. Kotter (1996) found, from his research, that over 50 per cent of companies failed in the first phase of change because they did not establish a great enough sense of urgency. Other researchers have found that only 9 per cent of companies implementing a change programme had any success in actually converting people to the new values involved.

Not understanding the full picture

Failing to understand the context for change is a barrier. If people do not understand the 'why' of change, they are less able and willing to implement the 'what'. For example, the implementation of a new computer system for a subsidiary of a large manufacturing organization failed because neither the system developers nor senior management understood the wider context. They did not realize that the project would involve so extensive a redesign of their business processes or their management structure.

Loss of stability

While chief executives reassure their people that the only constant is change, people want to be in control of their environment and to preserve stability. People try to regain their equilibrium if it is disturbed. People welcome change to the extent that they have control over their environment.

Failure to answer 'What's in it for me?' and 'What do we want employees to do?'

Employees' resistance to change can stem from their lack of understanding. Poor communication is often cited as the single most substantial barrier to achieving necessary change within organizations. This is because it is too focused on announcing the 'what' of change rather than the 'why', and then fails to spell out the implications and the 'what now?'

Unfortunately for those trying to make change, the force of an organization's existing culture is designed to maintain the status quo and builds in inertia to protect it. Culture is the means by which we bring stability to the threat of change, by rationalizing our way out of it or by going into denial of it. The mental starting position for most people is, 'We do not need to change – we're already doing a good job. But if we do, it's them, not me that needs to change.' We are brilliantly equipped to rationalize our way out of changing.

Communicating company vision is fine, but people want to know how they will be affected, and why they should change. Employees are likely to be bemused by the failure of managers to specify what precisely they are now supposed to do.

In order to address these failings, organizations have invested in change management processes and teams, to help coordinate and make change happen. Change management has three main roles: the delivery of benefits; helping to arrive at the desired destination more quickly and with minimal pain; and accommodating the needs of the business and of the workforce. Good internal communication is central to each of these roles.

HOW MUCH CHANGE IS MANAGEABLE?

Rather than try to manage separate waves of change, organizations need to become flexible and continuously responsive. This involves becoming more knowledgeable about how their people respond to change, and how they can foster the responsiveness their employees need to compete. Organizations need to shift from managing incidents of change towards developing the capacity to respond fluidly to events as they arise. This is rapidly becoming a critical factor – the ability to change continuously in a continuously changing world.

Traditionally, leaders will drive change, alerting the organization to the need to respond to changed competitive conditions. They will spotlight an external crisis, or the 'burning platform' for change – something that threatens survival and demands urgent action. The aim is to push the responsibility for driving change further down the organization by creating greater understanding of business issues and allowing employees to make changes where they see they are needed. Change can then be driven from the bottom of the organization, and top management need not constantly rearticulate direction to employees.

However, before they can reach that happy state, organizations have to deal with the issue of employee 'change-lag' – a situation where employees, threatened with yet another "burning platform" and warned again of the dire consequences of not changing, cannot take any more. Suffering from corporate 'combat fatigue' they bunker down in their foxholes and take each day as it comes. Without good communication, employees are liable to become sluggish and resistant, with the consequence that each successive change introduced will become more problematic. Involving people early translates into greater understanding of change and smoother implementation. For this reason, a number of organizations include a communication team in their change management department.

WHAT IS THE ROOM FOR MANOEUVRE?

People are not keen on change which destabilizes them and reduces their ability to control their environment. Thus, communication about change has to highlight for people the freedom they still have and be clear about the non-negotiables. This strategy serves both parties well – it allays the nervousness of senior management who fear that allowing employee debate will undo all their good work. It also fulfils the desire of employees to identify their remaining areas of discretion.

Psychologists describe people's perception of the degree of power they have over how things are managed as their 'locus of control'. There are two kinds of locus – internal and external. Those who have an internal locus of control fundamentally believe that they call the shots and that they are omnipotent in their world. Typically, newborn babies feel that they are the centre of the universe, see no distinction between themselves and the outside world, and do not see themselves as victims of bigger forces. After babyhood, we all swing from an internal to an external locus – from a sense of omnipotence to a greater sense of helplessness in the face of outside forces we cannot control.

When change happens, people ask themselves what they can affect and what they are likely to be affected by. They tend to see themselves as more powerless than before and to worry about those things they feel they cannot affect.

Employees' apparent resistance to change can be a consequence of not clearly understanding the space for control that they will have in the future. People are more stressed by uncertainty than by bad news. With bad news, they can identify their 'decision space' and get on with regaining as much control as possible and making what decisions they still can. Where this space is not clear, people create ways of increasing their comfort and denying the control of others over their lives.

Communicating change therefore has to tackle the danger of a clash between the management agenda and the individual's agenda. Senior management typically wants to limit employees' locus of control – they want to publish their plans and have the workforce comply. They fear involving people in discussion in case employees come up with the wrong answer and that, like children, they will have to be brought back to the correct answer after a diversionary bout of discussion.

Employees on the other hand, try to maintain their locus of control and, if possible, extend it. Practically, this means that it is not enough to simply make people aware of the plan, or describe their part in it. It is also important to remind them of the areas that they still control, and the decisions that remain within their remit. This encourages employees to look beyond their area of immediate control, to areas which they can also influence.

In times of change, when people are nervous about what they can control, leaving that 'decision space' unclear can cause employees to become overcautious and resistant while they try and fathom their room for manoeuvre.

Sensible organizations plan ahead for different phases of change, rather than focusing on the immediate change that is in front of them. They look not to win the war, but to win the peace. For example, during the restructuring of their organization, and the reduction of their workforce, they plan ahead for a post-restructuring world. They want to ensure that once the difficulties of the restructuring are past they can re-engage the energy of their people and focus on the future.

There are a number of issues they therefore look at:

- What is happening during the change period? How are employees reacting, what lessons are they learning about their leadership and how are employees thinking through their own options for the future?

- How are managers coping? They often feel torn between their loyalties to their people, and their responsibility to be a good corporate citizen.

- How credible is the leadership going to be in the future when they ask everyone to draw a line under the past and look only to the future?

The best kind of communication during a restructuring is fast communication which is well thought through.

It is important to give people the context and the rationale for change, the need for restructuring and the likely scale of it. This is for two reasons. First, rumours start very quickly, and it's easy to lose the initiative. Second, as soon as restructuring becomes an issue, employees very quickly want specifics about how it will affect them. However, organizations rarely have that level of detail, but are pressed for specifics by employees who are increasingly unwilling to listen to communication about the bigger picture.

One of the key areas of good communication is preparing managers to communicate during periods of uncertainty.

There are three areas in which managers need to be prepared:

- Identifying how to keep their people engaged when the future is unclear and outside the control of the organization.

- Understanding their people's emotional reactions and how they should speak to them in an appropriate way.

- Communicating bad news – how to feed their people difficult information.

Unless managers are prepared to be able to tell the whole story, however tough, they will make up information themselves. It is important to make sure that managers are prepared both for communicating with teams, and for having difficult one to one conversations with people who may be exiting the organization.

Managers usually do a poor job of this if they are unsupported. This is because it is hardest for them to deal with objections from their own people with which they secretly agree.

One way to help managers is to educate them about the change curve, to equip them to identify where their people are on that curve, and to give them some guidance on what communication is appropriate at each stage. For example, in the first phase of change – denial – employees tend to be fairly shocked and angry and are less receptive to logic and rationale. The job of the manager at that point therefore is to listen rather than tell, to give people the chance to vent, and not to overload them with information which is purely rational.

There are three main types of information which emerge during periods of change:

- issues which are unchangeable, not negotiable and must be accepted;

- issues which are negotiable and can be addressed and resolved;

- myths – which are due to misunderstanding, lack of information or disagreement. These can be surfaced and dispelled.

Outlined below are the key emotional phases that people are likely to experience following the announcement of a major change. The Phases of Change are based on a model by Perlman and Takacs. Listed for each emotional phase is a checklist of what to look out for, together with some suggested communication responses for line managers.

Denial

Managers have to realize that this is the first likely response of their people to a significant change affecting them. People may be angry and resentful and others sullen or argumentative. They may be unwilling or unable to grasp the logic of any argument. They may simply object to the proposed changes, or, more likely, attack the rationale or thinking that led to it.

The manager's communication role is to listen, and empathize rather than arguing the point. During this phase of change people have to feel able to say what they think and feel. Managers have to both listen, and keep supplying whatever information they get, making clear, where they can, what the implications are for their people.

Anger

Once greater acceptance of the fact of the change happening sets in, people tend to become angry and frustrated. Proposals may seem unrealistic, poorly thought through and unfair. Reactions to the change may become personal attacks on managers and leaders. Resentment at the proposed changes may become active resistance and refusal, or attempts to bargain and compromise to reduce the impact of the change.

The communication job of the manager is to make it OK for their people to be angry rather than fighting it. Listening is all the more important because it helps surface real issues and concerns.

Managers need to be clear which aspects of the change are fixed and non-negotiable. They need to know what is the room for manoeuvre, so they can accommodate individuals' issues and concerns, and focus on problem solving that is feasible.

It is also important to separate out fact from myths. As change continues, stories often circulate which are due to misunderstanding, lack of information or disagreement, which result in distorted stories about what is happening. The managers job is to surface and dispel these myths.

Depression

In this phase, people go through a strong sense of disorientation at the loss of what they are used to, and strong nostalgia for the past. With a feeling of insecurity can come a greater sense of self pity, a loss of energy, insecurity and emptiness.

The communication job for the manager is to acknowledge people's feelings, to accept that it is natural for people to feel that way and to explain to people what is happening to them and others in terms of their emotional reactions.

Listening, and asking questions about how people are responding, helps employees reflect on where they are, and increase their feeling of acceptance, which may speed the process to the next phase.

Resigned acceptance

In this phase, people move on to a grudging acceptance to change, but still have a lack of enthusiasm for the change proposed.

The communication job for the manager is to listen to and accept where people are, and to keep repeating the key messages of the change – why it's needed, why it's important and what the benefits will be. This is because as people become more accepting they start listening more for detail which they might have had no patience for earlier.

This phase may be particularly difficult for those who have seen their colleagues leave the organization. In addition to the normal responses to change, they also suffer 'survivor syndrome' – the guilt that they have kept their jobs while others have lost theirs.

Readiness

It is at this stage that people feel themselves returning to their normal levels of energy and enthusiasm. People are more willing to focus on the task ahead, keener to make things work and more willing to make long term plans.

For the manager, this is the springtime after the winter of change. It is important for managers to avoid making comments such as 'it's about time', and important that they repeat key messages, provide clear direction and give specific tasks. At this stage a manager should make a clear connection between the big picture of the change, and the specific implications for individuals and the team. This is because at this stage employees are keen to get back to work, and want clear direction on what specifically they should be doing.

Renewal

At this phase employees are back to their usual levels of energy, and are growing in commitment and enthusiasm for the change ahead. At this point they are keen to ensure that the change has been worthwhile, and that the promised benefits are actually achieved.

The communication job for the manager is to help people to redefine their goals, to help them understand where their contribution fits in to the strategy as a whole, and identify how they can contribute.

It is particularly useful for senior managers to prepare, thinking through how their people will move through each phase of change.

Communication coming from the leaders tends to be out of sync with where their employees are, uses compelling business rationale when greater empathy is required, and is based on a set of values and a managerial ethos their employees may not share. Explaining how the industry has changed, underlining the urgency of competing more effectively and protecting margins and giving greater shareholder value may all be perfectly sensible to the senior management, but may be less compelling and more insulting to their people.

This is because leaders usually have more control of their destiny, have greater ownership of the changes and are usually further along the change curve than their employees.

Senior managers coming out of the change curve, re-energized and ready to make the change work, are usually in a very different emotional place from their employees, who are much further back.

Getting senior managers to compare where they are to where their people are, and looking at how best to communicate with them, sensitizes managers to different viewpoints.

COMMUNICATING FOR CHANGE

Managers who want to communicate change typically ask, 'How do I convince employees of the need for change?' 'How do I motivate people to change?' and 'How will I know when staff have bought into change?'

In times of change, companies have to communicate far more just to stand still. Change increases employee suspicion and reduces management credibility.

MORI's norm for employees' rating of the credibility of management is 66 per cent under stable conditions. For organizations going through change, it drops to 49 per cent. Similarly, the norm for employees understanding the organization's objectives is 48 per cent under stable conditions, but in periods of change it drops to 34 per cent. This is exacerbated by the communicators' desire to push change at people, as if it were a desirable product, with self-evident benefits. Organizations typically set themselves to 'sell' any change to their people and become frustrated when their people decline to buy. Managers pushing their views tend to create resistance as this appears to dismiss the views of others.

Too many managers see discussion as a sign of weakness, or fear that discussion will unravel what's already been achieved. Yet, by trying to limit discussion, managers signal that communication is a one-way process. To persuade means both listening to others and reflecting their perspectives along with our own.

Senior managers tend to focus on what they believe employees need in order to fulfil their task, rather than what they need to understand. This mismatch hurts most when those at the bottom of the organization receive only narrow communication on the specifics of implementing change. The lower down the organization you are, the less you are aware of the wider context. The less rationale you understand, the less sense the specifics make. This kind of approach makes it difficult to know when staff have bought into change, because it focuses on trying to convince them of management's case rather than allowing them to raise their concerns. For example, is the lack of questions at the end of a manager's presentation to staff a sign of acceptance or rejection?

The difficulty communicators encounter in assessing the impact of their communication is that they often have no clear idea of the impact that they are trying to create. Communication can focus on the distribution of mission statements and visions which are too abstract to point employees to what, specifically, they are supposed to do. If there are no clearly identified outcomes that communication is intended to produce, it will be impossible to measure whether they have been achieved.

At the outset of change a company's leaders can usually identify specific examples of what they need. The people in the finance department, for example, should be answering the telephone more quickly when the customer service representatives try to contact them about a customer's billing query. However, in communication, these specifics are lost, because they are turned into the more abstract 'need for greater interdepartmental customer focused responsiveness'. This translation of concrete examples into abstract exhortation makes it harder to achieve the desired result. It also makes it difficult to measure whether the communication is being effective. Ideally, what should be measured is whether, in this instance, the telephones in the finance department are being answered more promptly. Instead, what the communicators end up measuring is whether people attended the change road show and whether they can recall the key messages.

Hoping for culture change while carpet-bombing employees with management-speak is a recipe for disappointment. The first challenge is to be clear about the outcomes you are trying to produce. Once you have established these it is easier to identify whether you have achieved them.

A FRAMEWORK FOR COMMUNICATING CHANGE

This following section offers some principles for communicating change. These apply specifically to the issues of culture change and structure change – two of the four types of change discussed later in this chapter.

Create a sense of urgency

Senior managers are often grateful for a 'burning platform' – a crisis that provokes an undeniable pressure for change. In the absence of a crisis, organizations are often tempted to set fire to their own platform by creating a crisis that gives them a mandate to drive change through. This is a tactic that can backfire if employees see little sign of the threatened crisis materializing. It damages management's credibility and portrays them as doom-mongering Cassandras.

In the absence of a crisis, and where employees are mistakenly feeling 'fat and happy', it is best to try the re-education route, taking employees to the top of the strategic mountain and showing them the oncoming threat to continued survival. Urgency is best created by taking employees through the same learning process senior management have undergone. A shared sense of urgency comes from a shared understanding of the business threats, on the principle that, 'If you can keep your head while all about you are losing theirs, you do not know what's going on.'

Later in this chapter, BMW provides a good example of both approaches.

Communicate the context and the full picture

In their study of more than 200 big business managers, for their book 'Corporate Culture and Performance' John P. Kotter and James L. Heskett (1995) show that there is a positive relationship between the strength of a business's culture and its performance. They also conclude that a business's performance depends more on how well its culture is adapted to the business environment than on how strong it is. That means having employees who understand the business environment and knowing clearly how they need to respond to it.

A recent significant trend has been towards organizations' creating greater business literacy among their employees, educating them about the wider context of their industry, consumer trends, changes in competition and highlighting the likely implications for them and their job.

Pepsi, for example, places great emphasis on building business literacy. After its research revealed that employees were not sufficiently aligned with the organization's goals, they developed a programme for employees, centred around communicating an understanding of the business and its direction. This had the aim of closing the gap between individuals' and business goals. Similarly, the Royal Mail runs business education sessions on the changing mix of personal and business mail and the increase in competition. First Direct runs annual conferences on business direction, strategy changes in technology and updates all its employees on these twice a year. Intel runs business update meetings for all employees each quarter.

Rolls-Royce staged 'One Small Step', 1-day workshops for their employees. The intention behind these was to expose employees to the need for change as well as to give them the context and the rationale for change, and a unified picture of change initiatives. In addition to sharing the thinking, the emphasis was on how each individual could take one small step to make change in their own area.

Communicate the 'why' as well as the 'what'

When employees object to what they should be implementing, it can be a symptom of a lack of buy-in to the 'why'. Unless you draw the bigger picture, and prepare the way with the 'why', it is difficult to get change properly understood, let alone implemented. For people to accept and cooperate, they have to share the thinking and understand the context.

Those in the organization who have worked on change projects often already possess the rationales, detail, messages and benefits. That information has simply to be channelled into internal communication.

Nevertheless, crafting clear and well presented messages has much less impact than management style and visibility, and the leadership's willingness to be challenged and tested on their case for change.

The Body Shop keeps employees in touch with the big picture and uses local communicators to marry local detail to the wider context by means of two different processes. First, sessions are held to ensure that people understand what the business is trying to achieve so that they can help deliver it. Second, line managers run a monthly cascade meeting which includes corporate information. In addition they make use of the work of departmental communication coordinators to give information to, and get feedback from, employees on their understanding of issues.

First Direct takes a similar approach to educating their people about what is going on in the marketplace, changes in technology and what their customers need and value. Each year, each employee participates in series of sessions given by the managing director. These engage employees in debate about changes and their implications for the business. These are then followed by half-yearly updates by heads of businesses, who relate some of the broader business changes to their own individual areas. First Direct also has a series of cross-functional and cross-sectional communication groups which are used both to gather views and to disseminate information. They are also used to give people better understanding of what is going on in other parts of the business.

Maximize the sense of continuity and stability

To create a sense of urgency, change is often sold as a 'revolution'. Such an approach risks being perceived as too extreme and sudden a departure from traditional values. Employees who see change as violating their values will resist and cling to existing work patterns. On the other hand, employees who perceive change as evolutionary, not revolutionary, see a greater continuity with the past, which reassures them.

During the 1990s banks went through a financial services revolution which called for managers to shift from focusing on whether to grant loans to customers to beginning to sell them products and services. The resistance of some managers to this was based on their perception that this was a complete break from their previous jobs. Only when communication began to emphasize that selling was a natural extension of the good service they had traditionally provided did resistance decrease.

Do not wait

When faced with a situation in which you are uncertain of the outcome it is very tempting to decide to say nothing until you are certain. Failure to communicate is based on the assumption that communication is under the control of management and can be turned on and off like a tap. This is a mistake. The grapevine will communicate if management does not. Therefore, be proactive and manage communication rather than having to respond to the latest rumour. There will always be something that can be communicated, even in the most uncertain situation.

Communicate probabilities and scenarios

As part of its restructuring, Cable and Wireless sold off its pager business, Mercury. Its management team decided to communicate with staff from the outset of what was a long process. They took the view that, while you cannot predict the future, you can talk about what might happen. They did not know who might acquire them, so they talked to employees about the sorts of different businesses which *might* buy them. People would have speculated anyway. By being proactive, the management team were better able to manage uncertainty, to respond to outlandish rumours and maintain morale.

Run low-key open forums or management briefings to discuss what might happen and the different scenarios you envisage. By conducting them in a low-key way, you will be better able to communicate that you are speculating, rather than announcing, what is going to happen.

Give the timescale

As you will almost always know the timescale to which you are operating, you can tell people when you will be able to communicate specifics. Communicating a timescale allows you to say something while you are still analysing and debating the way forward. However, it must be a timetable that you can keep to. You will seriously damage your credibility if you fail to keep to your own deadlines.

Communicating a timetable brings two benefits. It allows managers to separate specific implementation questions from big picture strategy questions and respond to them separately. It also lets employees know precisely when they can ask specific types of question and receive answers.

Make face-to-face the main communication channel

Research shows that people prefer to receive information about change from their immediate manager, face-to-face. This is because people want to get news from a trusted source, in such a way as to allow them to ask questions and assess the truth of what they are being told. However, when it comes to significant change, employees also want to hear from the most senior manager they can get.

It's important therefore to have announcements of change by senior managers quickly followed up by communication from line managers who have been prepared in advance.

By communicating in this way you will be better able to assess what people's concerns are, correct misperceptions, gather feedback to inform further communication and minimize the chances of sensitive details leaking.

Communicating face-to-face also enables you to communicate nuances better, especially when specific details are still uncertain.

Explain the implications for the individual

Employees may understand intellectually the business's objectives, and recall its key messages, but to care they have to see the link between their personal agendas and those of the organization.

Often, employees' first questions concern how any change will affect them personally. This means that communication has to spell out the 'what's in it for me?' and specify what employees are expected to do. In addition to understanding the role they will play in the future, employees also need to understand how they can succeed and how they will be measured.

If details are not yet available at the outset, tell people when they will be.

Use involvement to get commitment

Commitment comes from a sense of ownership, and ownership comes from participation. People need to be actively involved in discussing how the change can be implemented in their area. The less they are involved, the less committed they'll be.

People dislike being presented with a fait accompli. Even where they may have agreed with the conclusion, being excluded from the debate can be perceived as a slap in the face.

Train managers in new skills

Managers often believe that the secret of communicating change lies in presenting great arguments. This is because managers are usually good at presenting information, rebutting challenges and winning the argument. In situations where they are challenged, they can be masters of the put down.

However, in communicating change, other abilities are more important. Success depends more on the manager's credibility, ability to listen, connect on the right emotional level with an audience and use vivid language that makes arguments come alive.

Invest enough time

Communication is affected by the quality of relationships, and relationships take time to build. Communication is a process, not an event. It is unlikely that a shared conclusion will be reached on the first attempt. Communicating change involves listening to people, allowing them to test your position, allowing them to share the thinking and process information, and then talking again.

Senior management must 'walk the talk' if they expect those they manage to do the same. This is true in terms of their following new procedures, letting go of the status quo and not holding personal agendas too tightly. In any organization going through a transition from one definition of successful behaviour to another, there is bound to be apparent hypocrisy. If this is not recognized, there are always going to be instances of an apparent mismatch between managers' behaviour and their words.

A FRAMEWORK FOR DEVELOPING CHANGE COMMUNICATION

If the above are some of the principles that underly communicating change, what are some of the practicalities? The following section offers a framework for developing appropriate communication. It outlines four types of change so that communicators can select the most appropriate communication approach. The section identifies what is most important to each type of change, and then advises on the selection of the most appropriate communication media.

As a first step to communicating change it is important to define what the change is. Change may be significant but limited to one part of the business, such as the reorganization of a function, or of a factory. It may be limited to a change in procedures or the redesign of a process. The introduction of IT or the restructuring of IT legacy systems may bring root and branch change intended to have a more long-term impact on people's behaviour.

The following are four types of change, each of which requires a different communication approach:

Culture change

'Culture change' can mean a wholesale shift in attitudes and behaviour, and a move to a completely different way of operating. However, the use of the term is itself often confusing because those yearning for it often cannot define in what ways they want to see things changed. If culture can be defined as 'the way we do things around here', culture change is changing the way we do things. This begs the questions, which things need to be changed, in what ways and why? Asking these questions is vital to turning 'culture change' from rhetoric to specific and observable outcomes.

Structural change

These are changes which affect the organizational structure of a business – for example, restructuring, divesting non-core businesses, making an acquisition or merging with another organization.

Initiative

A change initiative has more long-term impact and is intended to have a greater effect on people's behaviour. Introducing anything with a three-letter acronym – business process re-engineering (BPR), value-based management (VBM), enterprise resource planning (ERP) – usually qualifies as a specific programme of change, intertwining different strands of change projects under an overall umbrella theme.

Campaign

Often what is characterized as a change can be defined as a campaign. This is communication with a finite life and a clear end goal, which aims to raise awareness and influence perception. This may translate for some groups of people into action or changed behaviour. Communicating, for example, the changeover to a common IT operating environment would fall into this category. 'The Handbook of Internal Communication' (Scholes, 1997) defines the aim of campaigns as:

> '... to gain commitment from the targeted audience to a specific business objective. Typical examples might be a customer care or service quality programme, a cost reduction exercise, or an attempt to persuade people to join a voluntary scheme such as an Employee Share Ownership Programme.'

A campaign to raise awareness in the run-up to a workforce ballot can be one aspect of a wider cultural change, as part of a product improvement initiative, prompted by a restructuring. Raising awareness about the shift to a common IT operating environment may be a campaign that is part of a wider change in how the organization uses its IT.

It is important to distinguish between these different types of change to avoid over-communicating and under-communicating. Over-communicating is done by those managers who are tasked simply with getting employees to save electricity by turning off unnecessary lights. However, they launch a series of energy management road shows in the last quarter of the financial year when employees are most busy, because they see themselves as on a mission to create a more eco-conscious culture change.

Under-communicating can be more of a problem. This is the failing of the manager who, faced with communicating a fundamental restructuring of the organization, uses only a complex PowerPoint presentation and an attractively laminated mission statement.

Do not confuse one kind of change with another. Initiatives which are communicated as if they were campaigns, for example, create awareness but do not create long-term shifts in attitude and behaviour.

WHAT IS IMPORTANT TO EACH TYPE OF CHANGE?

Communication principles relating to culture change and structural change are set out earlier in this chapter, while campaign communication is dealt with in a case study later. Initiative communication is discussed in Chapter 7.

155

One of the key issues in communicating change is identifying the degree of change involved and its impact on the employee's sense of power and control. How much will it disturb employees' equilibrium and how easy will it be for them to restore it? The deeper the change, and the greater the disturbance, then the longer the learning journey you have to take employees through.

There are two strands intertwined in communication – information and interaction. Interaction involves managers' personal style and credibility and how they interact with employees. The degree of change determines which of the two strands will be more important to employees.

Some changes demand more information; others depend on more interaction. Changes to car parking arrangements might generate some temporary heat, but they would be less worrying than the announcement of a takeover. The communication need in car parking changes would largely be for information. However, the announcement of an acquisition would provoke a very high requirement for both information and interaction. People would need a great deal of information, and their reassurance would depend on the credibility of the managers delivering it.

In a campaign, for example, information issues will be more important than those of relationship. Clarity of presentation, the use of plain language with clearly labelled points will be what's needed. Reliable distribution, timely alerts to change and the relevance of information to individuals will also be key factors in raising audience awareness.

Where structural change shakes the bedrock of employees' working lives creating uncertainty and insecurity, relationship issues come straight to the fore. In addition to clear and reliable information, employees will look for managers to be open and acknowledge their concerns. They will be affected by how managers listen to them, and whether they have the opportunity to voice concerns. Employees will also want the time to feed back their concerns, to raise challenges and to have some input into the final outcome. The size of the groups in which they gather should be small enough to help staff feel comfortable and safe to speak up. This is because the degree of interaction between people in face-to-face sessions affects their relationship, their feeling of being respected and their willingness to respect others and their views.

This is why people's interpersonal skills are critical to creating a responsive organization. The main hindrance to becoming agile and flexible is too narrow a repertoire of skills held not just by managers but by any employees who have to work together to pool ideas and create solutions. The importance of interaction is examined further in Chapter 6.

Selecting the best balance of information and interaction depends on the degree of change involved and the nature of the change – whether culture, structural, initiative or campaign.

Typically, the formation of a communication strategy begins by asking what are the target audiences, what are the key messages and what are the best media and communication channels for delivering them? This traditional approach is based on a view that communication is distribution of information to readily identifiable audiences.

This is a good strategy for a campaign, because campaigns have a high need for information and a low need for relationship. However, this approach does not work well for the three other types of change.

To become committed to a course of action, individuals typically undertake a journey. They consider whether the broad concept of doing something suits them before moving on to examining its feasibility. Only when they are satisfied it could fit in with the rest of their lives do they become interested in how the 'nuts and bolts' details will work out. This is a journey from awareness to commitment. The full journey means becoming aware of the change, understanding its implications, supporting it, becoming involved, deciding how it might be implemented and finally being fully committed to making it work.

Different groups of employees need to go on journeys of a different length. Some may need, for the moment, only to be aware; others to be wholly committed.

Equally, there are groups of employees which the organization needs to move to different stages of the journey, and at a faster rate. For organizations trying to use communication for change, the focus has to be on the outcome – what the organization needs from employees in terms of attitudes and behaviours. Investing time and resources in communicating to employees should be based on their importance to achieving the strategy, rather than on their status in the hierarchy. The organization will need to prioritize from whom it needs what objective over what time period. The first step to this is identifying what is required *from* different groups of employees, not just what is needed *by* employees. This process is discussed in greater detail in Chapter 7.

Having identified what is needed from employees in terms of awareness, understanding, support, involvement and commitment, the next question is how to begin to achieve it.

WHICH MEDIUM?

Few of us have a clear sense of which channel is most appropriate for a given communication. However, communicators should be aware that wrong choices create information overload and confusion, and waste time.

Anyone who wants to communicate can use first-class mail, express mail, voicemail, e-mail, SMS text, fax, electronic bulletin board, video-conferencing,

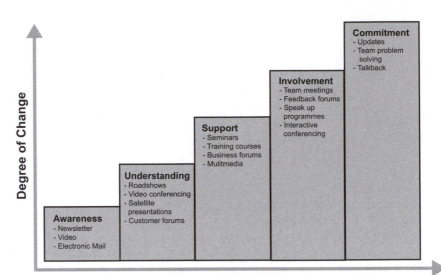

Figure 5.1   Communication Escalator

Intranet, newsletter, poster, business television, webcasts, or the telephone – not to mention a face-to-face meetings. The proliferation of technology has increased the options for communication but has created a new problem – how to choose from all the alternatives? One way of choosing is to understand the principle of 'richness' in information and media – that is, the capacity of different media to carry information and emotions. Whether a medium is 'rich' or 'lean' depends on how much it allows of the following:

- interactivity

- multiple cues

- language variety

- social and emotional cues.

Interactivity

Does the medium allow quick response, conversation and involvement? Examples of media which are richly interactive are those that allow conversation in real time such as face-to-face meetings and telephones. Media such as e-mail or voicemail are leaner on interactivity because they do not allow people to interact at the same time, but take place with a time delay.

Multiple cues

Does the medium provide a variety of signals which help convey both literal meanings and underlying subtleties of message? Face-to-face communication is richer since it provides all the non-verbal cues which aid further understanding. Written text is leaner because there is so little beyond the literal message to go on.

Language variety

To what extent does the medium allow a mix of types of language – for example, visual, musical and numerical? Different people respond to different types of language. The presentation of numbers on a spreadsheet aids precision but is not as engaging as the presentation of the same information in pictures and words which give a wider variety of cues and help spell out interpretation.

A spreadsheet or numeric database is lean on language variety, while video-conferencing is richer.

Social and emotional cues

To what extent does the medium allow personal feelings and emotions to infuse the communication? A high proportion of what is communicated is non-verbal, and we take our cues from each other's tone and gestures. Communication is not just the information transmitted, it is also the impact we have on each other. Emotion, emphasis and pace all have an effect. A rich medium such as face-to-face allows all of these to add to the communication. A channel such as e-mail is lean in these and would not, for example, be a good choice for communicating the chief executive's inspirational vision.

Telephones are a surprisingly rich medium, despite the lack of visual cues. Perhaps that is why Alexander Graham Bell initially thought that the primary use of the telephone would be for broadcasting opera.

DECIDING ON THE RICHNESS OF THE MEDIUM

There is a trade-off to be made between the desire to be clear and the need to use communication media efficiently. Choosing too lean a medium means the risk of too little information, which might result in different interpretations, misunderstanding and ambiguity. Choosing a richer medium than the issue warrants risks information overkill that results in 'noise', distracting from the key message.

Richer media are important for creating shared understanding where the risk of misunderstanding is high and there is a real need for minimizing ambiguity. If this need is low, leaner media are both more effective and efficient. This means, in practice, that you do not need face-to-face seminars to alert people to changes in the day's menu in the staff restaurant and that you should not try to enrol your employees in a major organizational change by sending them an SMS message. The first option would result in communication inefficiency; the second in communication ineffectiveness.

A general rule is: the less the chance of misunderstanding or misinterpretation, the leaner the media you can use.

WORKING TOGETHER

Every day we process information to assess the world around us and to coordinate the tasks that we are doing. These tasks usually involve an element of uncertainty either because information is missing or because it can be interpreted in different ways. To communicate successfully then, we try to do two things:

- reduce uncertainty by gathering more information;

- develop shared understanding with colleagues with whom we are working.

This means that we have to find the best way of using communication media as efficiently as possible so that we transfer the information we need without tipping into information overload. We also want to be as effective as possible in creating a shared understanding, without creating misunderstanding or conveying only part of the whole meaning.

Achieving the right balance depends on recognizing the considerable potential for misunderstanding and the importance of guaranteeing clarity. Where is the danger of misunderstanding greatest? At the outset of change. Where is the need for clarity greatest? During change. This is because there is no pre-existing shared context and because, in the early stages, general approaches and ideas are still being sketched out, and specifics are hard to come by.

THE STAGES OF CHANGE

There are three main stages in the change process:

Stage 1

Those planning change go through a process of funnelling their thinking from 'blue sky' possibilities where any option can be considered, to developing a specific option which promises the greatest value.

Stage 2

The specifics of a preferred approach are worked through and investigated.

Stage 3

A detailed implementation plan is developed with milestones, key responsibilities and performance indicators.

The 'funnelling' process progresses from general aproaches to specific proposals and, finally, to concrete action plans. All those involved in the funnelling are familiar with the issues, have an input to the changes proposed and have had the time to work out the implications. In terms of their 'locus of control' they feel that they have a good handle on the change.

In the first phase of this process there are few specifics to share. However, the change planning team realizes that they must get the organization's leaders to understand the whole picture in order to prevent later disagreement. Since senior managers have the power to veto or derail change, they are courted and prepared for any developments long before they emerge. For this purpose, rich media, such as face-to-face meetings, are used and are recognized as important: no project leader would simply e-mail his conclusions to the chief executive and hope for the green light. Later, once a shared context has been established, less rich media, such as written progress reports, are fine for efficient project communication and effective collaboration.

However, the sound logic behind this process of communication and enrolment is often abandoned when the time comes to communicate with the rest of the organization.

The communication process with the rest of the organization should involve taking people through a line of logic – a thinking process. Those whose attitudes you want to change have to go through the process; they cannot just be given its end-product. The aim of internal communication should be to share the thinking, not to announce conclusions.

The communication task at this point is twofold: take people through a thinking process from 'blue sky' proposals to concrete plans; and use communication media of the right degree of richness to do so. However, there are some obstacles at this point. First, managers may have mastered the issues involved and may want to cut out the debate and jump to implementing the solution. However, employees will resist any attempt to push them to the specifics; they will not cooperate until they have assessed how much the change will disturb their equilibrium and how difficult it will be to restore it. Second, those managers who are driving change have been using lean media such as e-mails, graphs and project reports to manage the change project. Having all that material ready to hand makes it tempting simply to package it up and use it to communicate to everybody. Third, although the change team may have done a good job in enrolling powerful and influential senior managers in the change, they neglect to consider the power and influence of employees in making change happen.

The greater the degree of change, the more likelihood there is of misunderstanding and the greater the need for shared understanding. This means sharing the thinking using rich media at the outset.

If you do not take employees through the thinking, communicating to them can feel like trying to herd cats. Discussion of nuts and bolts issues can suddenly veer into debates about rationales and hidden agendas. Carefully prepared and pithy presentations can suddenly erupt into argument. This is not necessarily because employees are resistant. It is more likely that presenters are making the wrong assumptions about where employees are in the learning process, and are using an inappropriate channel to communicate.

Employees must be allowed to match their own agendas to that of the organization. If they do not have the time and information to do that, they will be forced to find some other way of increasing their decision space.

Specifics are often rejected by staff because the foundation of shared understanding of the general approaches has not been laid. Pushing too quickly for compliance can actually cost more time than taking things more slowly at the outset. Change communicators find themselves having to run more time-intensive sessions to flush out the real issues and repair the damage. Once suspicion has set in you have to use richer media, such as face-to-face meetings and seminars to explain even simple operational details which normally could have been communicated via the noticeboard.

Trying to move change along too swiftly only succeeds in putting you further back. However, if you take people with you from the top of the funnel, sharing the thinking, you can then use leaner media to clarify operational detail.

Taking your employees through the thinking can seem expensive in terms of time and resources. However, those who want to take their people with them cannot afford to push them down the road of change without a good look at the map. As in trying to beat road traffic jams between you and your destination, sometimes the longest way round is the quickest way there.

Avoiding the information overload and initiative indigestion that seem to clog the path of change requires four things:

- the right identification of the type of change involved;

- the right selection of communication approach;

- the appropriate selection of rich and lean media;

- the correct application of both to the stage of change.

Earlier in this chapter four types of change were outlined – culture change, structural change, campaign and initiative. The following case study is an example of a campaign, which was part of a wider structural change and culture change.

CASE STUDY: BMW

The importance of matching media and message is underlined in BMW Group's communication.

The organization needed the commitment and contribution of the entire workforce and its recognition of the pivotal role of internal communications was central to making that change happen.

The company had been faced with an environment in which both upward and downward communication had traditionally been done through the union shop steward. They had to re-establish the communications channels and infrastructure in the company to ensure that their people understood their job, the job of their team or department and the company's goals and strategies.

BMW paid £800 million for the Rover Group. While Rover had been working to improve quality and productivity, the competition globally had been doing it better and faster. The competitive threat came not just from the UK but from the Far East, Eastern Europe and the US. This required BMW to introduce a number of changes in including flexible working practices which were used by its competitors.

BMW invested £400 million in its Oxford plant to produce the Rover 75, the first vehicle to have been entirely developed under BMW's ownership. After the sale of Rover, BMW kept the Oxford plant and used it as the birthplace of the new MINI in 2001 when it brought the MINI One and MINI Cooper onto the European market.

Since the introduction of MINI production at the Oxford Plant, BMW Group has made further significant investment in the plant as a state-of-the-art manufacturing facility.

Today, some 4500 employees make around 600 MINI cars a day at one of the most modern BMW Group production sites. All production processes and cars must meet the high quality standards of production applied at all plants in the BMW Group network.

BMW and senior trade union representatives reached an agreement on shift arrangements and working practices at the Oxford plant. This culminated in a draft agreement which was put to the workforce by ballot. In the run-up to this, there was a need for clear communication of the issues and the options, so that employees could decide which way to vote. This task was divided between senior managers and union representatives. Senior managers communicated first with all the managers, and the union then communicated with its members.

Managers prepared themselves for the task by first understanding the issues themselves. In small groups, they worked through the complex and detailed proposals in order to understand what the agreement meant for their staff and for the business as a whole. The aim was to prepare them to brief their staff and feel comfortable dealing with questions and concerns. More importantly, they were given the time to ask questions and challenge assumptions behind the proposals.

Managers participated in a half-day workshop by way of preparation. The presentation of the proposals was followed by a break-out session in which managers identified their questions and issues.

Senior managers often find it hardest to communicate when they themselves have unresolved issues. In most organizations it is difficult to raise such issues without being perceived as negative or self-interested. At the time of this communication process, one of the unclear issues was what the new role of managers would be under the new system. This meant that managers were trying to answer their staff's specific questions without knowing the answer to one of their own fundamental questions.

However, by acknowledging the issues, it was easier to get managers involved, since it demonstrated a willingness to grapple with tough issues – be they managers' or employees'. Managers were then able to work together to resolve employees' questions and propose new roles and responsibilities for their own future.

What was good about the managers' approach to communicating the changes, and what helped them to succeed were the following underpinning principles:

- Communication was face-to-face. The only way to communicate changes which affect how people do their jobs is face-to face. Videos, publications and large meetings can be valuable, but should not be used alone.

- Facts, not exhortation. "How will this affect me?" Employees need hard facts about change first and, in the absence of facts, will resist exhortation, hectoring and threats. Briefing packs and information literature should present the facts of the change, without management 'spin'.

- Create advocates by adding context. Managers and supervisors must feel that they can support the proposals, in addition to delivering the facts. People are influenced by those they trust and whose opinion they value. Managers and front line supervisors need to be aware of the context, arguments and counter-arguments for the changes. That way they would be prepared for face-to-face conversations with their people and to act as advocates for change.

- Prepare the briefers/session leaders. In change, communication is often contaminated by the concerns of senior management rather than those at more junior levels. Senior managers find it most difficult to counter those objections with which they secretly agree.

  Enrolment of the management is essential – they are not necessarily already convinced. The context and facts should first be discussed between the senior managers associated with the change and their immediate subordinates. Only then will managers feel comfortable and able to lead discussions at the frontline.

- Use feedback to retune the messages. At each stage of communication, employees' questions and recommendations need to be captured to keep track of how facts are being interpreted, and to amend the content for the next round of communication.

- Provide more information than communicators need. Managers who are running sessions must be given more background information than they are likely to need. This gives them the confidence to lead a discussion rather than sticking rigidly to the line of a presentation. It also gives them credibility, in that they can be seen to be adding value to the information they are presenting, rather than simply reading from a script.

- Make questions and answers as straight as possible. Most question-and-answer documents are written to rebut queries and questions from the audience. They follow the format of question-and-answer sessions designed for handling the media and aimed at controlling the discussion. This has the effect of closing down any conversation. The aim here should be to open up conversation, and to encourage people to feel safe about speaking up about what some of their, or their friends', issues are. Questions and answers should therefore couch questions in the audience's language. Answers should be as straight as possible, with the promise of further detail where it is not yet available.

- Explain the benefits to employees, not just those to the company. Because the internal team first has to sell its proposals to senior management, the implications of change are usually spelled out as benefits to the company rather than to the employee. However, using the same slides for employees can be fatal.

  The benefits should be reworked to reflect employees' concerns, not management's. This means being able to see information from the recipients' viewpoint.

The success of BMW's approach was a result of the partnership between management and union in their communication roles. Once managers had prepared, and briefed the management population, the union presented to its members.

Traditionally, at BMW Oxford, the union would have gathered 2500 people in a mass meeting on the lorry park, and then addressed them through a megaphone. This time, the union appreciated that it was a complex issue and that the traditional approaches were not going to work. Instead they brought their members together in groups of 150 people at a time, for a presentation. Management cooperated by stopping production for 4 to 5 hours so that the union could walk their people through the rationale, issues and their recommendations.

The investment of time in the preparation and communication of a complex set of issues by both management and union teams paid off in producing a clearer understanding of what was needed for the future. It also helped that, for all the hours of discussion and the numbers of slide presentations, the issues were summed up in a series of simple key messages – it was the best deal on offer, any alternatives would be worse and the union were happy to back it.

As a result, 85 per cent of associates turned out to vote, 70 per cent of whom voted 'yes' to the proposals.

COMMUNICATING CAMPAIGNS EFFECTIVELY

The BMW case illustrates some of the issues of campaign communication – aiming to raise awareness and influence perception, with a clear end goal.

Give managers something to say – or they'll make it up

When it comes to dealing with uncertainty, middle managers are in the front line. They will be asked by their staff what they know. While this may actually be no more than their people, they are believed to be privy to the latest thinking. Middle managers may wish to create the impression that they do know more than their staff, or they may wish to protect their relationship with their people by joining in with the speculation. The solution is to give them something to communicate in order to fill the vacuum.

Set up a feedback loop

Do not rely on feedback just from management briefings. Set up hotlines, e-mail addresses, Intranet sites or electronic forums to allow staff to raise questions and give feedback. Doing so will help you keep your finger on the pulse and allow you to respond quickly to the changing currents of communication. Make sure the feedback loop is connected to senior management, since they may be the only ones who will be able to address many of the issues raised.

Assume there will be leaks

It is wise to assume that anything which is written down will leak at some stage – hence the emphasis on face-to-face communication. Plan in advance how you will respond to leaks; make sure your internal and external communication plans are linked.

Ensure that the words and actions match

Management credibility is determined by the extent to which managers do what they say they are going to do. Do not plan one thing and then try to communicate something else. People will either catch you out as you go along, or figure out afterwards that you lied to them. Either way, you will destroy your credibility and have to manage a workforce which resents you.

Use plain language, not management-speak

Plans are usually sketched out in management-speak, with the benefits of proposed actions being benefits for the company – rather than for employees. The same information is then used to sell the change to employees. Without the same strategic insights as board members, and access to the same market and company data, employees often find the plans difficult to follow.

Acknowledge employees' concerns

It is important for people to understand why change is needed, so you should communicate about such things as market and industry pressures and rising customer expectations.

However, it is equally important to acknowledge employees' needs and reuqirements – such as job security, job interest and pride in their employer. This does not mean that you must guarantee job security, but does mean that you should explain the options that you considered and why redundancies, for example, are the only feasible way forward.

Communicate change even-handedly

People are not stupid and will ask you difficult questions. If you are being 'economical with the truth' they will quickly sense it. Therefore you have to be straight and credible about what changes are involved; overweighting one side of the argument will be seen as either incompetence or deviousness. Make sure there is a summary that spells out both the good and bad implications for change – people usually forget the positive aspects and focus instead on the negative aspects and drawbacks, and only stumble on the advantages some time later.

Explain the options

Expand on the rationale and need for the change, and the likely scenarios if the organization does not change. Do not use this as an excuse for scare stories that will damage your credibility. Discuss the likelihood of new and different competitors entering the market, and project the consequences of not responding to competitive pressures. Finally, discuss other options that have been considered by the organization and why they have been rejected.

Crash test your change presentation

A good way to test senior management cohesiveness and understanding is to get them to make a presentation to each other. Getting them to role play being a union official or a cynical employee helps flush out misunderstandings, misinterpretations and lack of agreement among the management teams.

Put it in writing

Managers have different philosophies and value systems, as well as differing hopes and expectations for the change. Creating a brief summary document as a handout for employees is a good strategy for flushing out those implicit disagreements and ensuring that there is a robust, coherent story that all can agree. The process of drafting it and getting it approved will take much longer than you think, especially since you should assume that anything written will leak.

Many of these approaches will help engage employees in making change happen. The following chapter looks further at engaging employees, especially in face to face communication.

REFERENCES AND FURTHER READING

Hammer, M. and Champney, J. (1995), *Re-engineering the Corporation: A Manifesto for Business Revolution*, revised edition (London: Nicholas Brealey).

Kotter, J. P. and Heskett, J. L. (1995), *Corporate Culture and Performance*.

Kotter, J. P. (1996), *Leading Change: Why Transformation Efforts Fail* (Harvard Business School Press).

Larkin, T. J. and Larkin, S. (1994), *Communicating Change, Winning Employee Support for New Business Goals* (New York: McGraw-Hill).

Perlman, D., Takacs, G. J. (1990), The ten stages of change, *Nursing Management*, Vol. 21 No. 4.

Scholes, E. (1997), *The Handbook of Internal Communication* (Aldershot: Gower Publishing).

6 Engaging Employees Face-to-Face

In a rapidly changing world, employees' understanding of the commercial context is increasingly important. However, the first casualty of communication is often context. This chapter argues that if organizations want to create understanding, they need to help their people to explore, test and understand the implications of the information they receive. This happens best through conversation, which enables them to develop a shared understanding through discussion.

Conversation is important not simply because it creates understanding, but also because it creates value. As the proverb reminds us, 'As iron sharpens iron, so one man sharpens another.' People prompt each other to think, build on each other's ideas and, together, discover new ways of doing things which alone they would have missed.

The moment of truth for communication is in conversation, whether this is in formal meetings or around the coffee machine.

Formal communication is outgunned by the informal. The most influential communication happens day-to-day, informally and in passing. Its effectiveness is most affected by a manager's style in dealing with their team. Time is one of an organization's scarcest resources, and face-to-face meetings represent a significant investment of time – 50 per cent of working time is spent in meetings, many of which are badly managed. Improving face-to-face communication is critical to increasing the return on that investment. The impact and effectiveness of communication can most easily be improved by improving the communication skills of the manager. Therefore, this chapter concludes by looking at the skills managers will need in future.

THE CHANGING ROLE OF THE MANAGER

The role of the middle manager has changed for good. Where information used to be power, now power comes from the interpretation of information.

The manager adds value by putting information in context, painting a compelling 'big picture' and creating understanding. As people work more in teams, dealing in ideas and information, managers and team leaders will need to facilitate and explain. They will have to create greater understanding of different parts of the organization and how they fit together. Managing will be less about instructions and directing, and more about making interconnections clear, engaging colleagues to identify issues and working together to solve them.

MIDDLE MANAGERS: THE MISSING LINK

Managers under time pressure need to learn how to make better use of time spent in face-to-face communication. The middle manager has always acted as a distribution channel for information, for example through team briefings, and has also often been suspected of blocking and holding back information. Technology is now being used in some organizations to bypass middle managers, thereby removing from the communication chain the one person who is best placed to turn information into meaning for the employee.

However, Tesco, for example, has used managers to educate its people. Tesco's retail business involves frequent day-to-day communication on detail and logistics. Traditionally, employees have been told only the essentials needed for operating the store.

Now the company has shifted from communicating purely operational information to communicating the broader view, so that its people know the business plan, understand the local implications for them and are able to take specific local actions. Tesco has learnt that communicating down to the shop floor means talking in simple terms, with a focus on customers. Sessions are run in-store by managers using desktop presenters, which reflect the external advertising and sales promotion material. Tesco found it more effective to communicate simply, in plain language, face-to-face via the manager, to help staff understand the whole picture and to play their part better.

MAKING THE LINK

The role of the middle manager has changed for good. No longer needed simply as a conduit for the dissemination of information, managers should be adding value to communication, by providing the wider context and acting as coaches and advisers to their people. However, filling these roles requires training in the right skills. Management style and skills are keys to success, but communication skills are often seen as 'nice to have' rather than 'need to have'.

THE CHAIN OF MEANING

Increasingly, companies want their people to have a better understanding of the economic environment and how they are doing within it. They want them to understand the issues the organization is facing, and to focus on how best to tackle those issues. Finally, they want them to be clear on how they are expected to contribute.

In short, what organizations want from their communication is an unbroken chain of shared meaning. They also want to avoid having to keep spelling out the issues. They want their people educated enough to spot them for themselves, so that, to borrow a phrase, 'They won't need a weatherman to know which way the wind blows.'

CASE STUDY: BAA TERMINAL 5

These two objectives were very much at the forefront of Terminal 5's approach to equipping their leaders to communicate.

The construction of Heathrow Airport's fifth terminal (T5) by BAA began in 2001. Designed to accommodate 30 million passengers, the £3.7 billion project is reckoned to be the largest and most complex construction project in Europe.

The scale of work is breathtaking. On a site the size of 500 football pitches, T5 provided a wide range of construction challenges: extensions to the Heathrow Express and London Underground's Piccadilly Line, the building of a new junction on the M25, and the re-routing of a river and the boring of a 3.5km overflow tunnel. All this to allow the building of an 87 metre high state-of-the-art control tower and a terminal building with a 400m by 150m roof, one of the largest single-span structures in the country.

To deliver this demanding task, BAA assembled a virtual organization comprising engineers, contractors and partners. Having put together a team with some of the best names in the business, T5 faced the challenge of ensuring the effective leadership and coordination of an organization numbering some 6000 people.

Communication had to ensure a clear 'line of sight' between the strategic objectives and priorities of the project as a whole and people's understanding of what they needed to do in detail locally.

This task focus was balanced by a focus on relationships. The leadership team knew that they needed to create a 'one team' feel across the project.

According to T5's Managing Director, effective communication was vital to the project's success. The scale and complexity of the project meant that alignment with project objectives and clarity about ways of working were vital. To build a high performance organization, the communication role of leaders would be critical in ensuring two-way, open communication that built a culture of trust, commitment and enthusiasm.

They decided to put time into face-to-face communication in order to build relationships with their people. They aimed to create a strong sense among the various team members that their contribution was valued and they were all on the same team, pulling in the same direction. All line managers were therefore trained in the communication skills needed to make the connection for their people.

There are a number of lessons that come out of Terminal 5's work.

One of the key lessons is that line managers must have the skills to understand the likely emotional reactions of their people, to be able to bring rational information to life and to paint a more engaging picture of its meaning.

Another lesson was that people enjoy the meetings when they get something out of them, either by solving a problem, or having their views aired and heard. The corporate information is rarely enough to excite them. What makes the session worthwhile is the team leaders' style, their ability to keep energy up and to involve people, and the cross-conversations between team members.

Another lesson they learned is that effective communication is not a cascade, but a chain. Companies are increasingly frustrated by the break in the 'line of sight' between their strategy and what individuals at the sharp end are expected to do. Typically, employees do not see a strong connection between the strategy and what they are expected to do – 50 per cent of employees do not know the strategy but 100 per cent of employees think they are doing a good job.

What businesses want from their communication is an unbroken chain of shared meaning. While the classic cascade passes information from level to level, what organizations actually need are much stronger links between information and its implications which will differ from department to department and from tier to tier.

However, the information that companies produce and distribute does not always help create that understanding. Information makes sense in context. Without the same context, it doesn't make the same sense. Information and context fit together like a lock and key. Either without the other is useless.

For example, consider the dilemma of the finance director of a successful multinational company. He is passionate on the subject of internal communication and feels that there should be daily bulletins alerting all employees to the fact that the company's share price on the Nikkei – the Japanese share index – has shifted. For him, that information is crucially significant. It will have a major impact on the business – an impact that he can already foresee. It will have repercussions that will extend to the lowest level of the business – repercussions that he can already predict. For him, seeing the share price shift is like a valley dweller hearing the dam burst. His overwhelming urge is to be an organizational Paul Revere riding through the darkened corporate corridors, alerting the slumbering natives to the imminent danger – with the clarion call, 'The Nikkei has shifted, the Nikkei has shifted.'

Unfortunately, what is clear to him is not so clear for others. Most of the 'slumbering natives' he sees working in his organization would not understand what a Nikkei is, or the significance of it having shifted. They would resettle themselves at their desks, muttering about the excitability and typical lack of consideration of finance directors.

Paul Revere may have had the original communication road show, but no matter how often the finance director takes to the road, unless he finds another way of speaking to his employees, he is never going to get them to that 'Aha!' moment of discovery, where they share his urgency and understand his concerns.

The finance director therefore has to find another way of communicating that urgency to his people. The significance which the finance director attaches to the information needs to be translated into other people's contexts. As a first step he has to realize how likely it is that he will be misunderstood.

Misunderstanding costs all organizations time and money and is due to the basic nature of language. All words have multiple meanings, but these meanings are narrowed down by the context in which the words are used.

The meaning of words is not a simple equation; a word does not have a single meaning, it has a large number of possible, and very different, meanings. Unless the speaker tells us explicitly which definition is intended, we must work it out from the context of the talk.

Consider the unsuspecting tourist in the US looking for some place to park and joyfully finding a sign saying 'fine for parking'. Does this mean that the space is allocated to parking, or the opposite, that anyone parking there will be penalized?

Because words take their meaning from the context in which they are used, and because the context is created by each one of us making our own interpretation, there is always the possibility of misunderstanding.

People expect us to make sense of what they say even when they do not say it clearly or precisely. They assume we already have enough background knowledge to understand much more than they actually say. Nor do people expect to be asked what they mean, even if those who hear them do not precisely understand. When we ask people to be more precise about what they are saying, they can become annoyed and defensive, partly because the request implies that they are not expressing themselves clearly. Questions can be perceived as reflecting badly on the speaker.

However, we cannot use one-way communication to tell people what to do, or what we think and want, and expect them to understand. One-way communication does not allow us to discover whether there is a shared context for understanding. Unless there is opportunity for conversation, we have no way of checking.

Conversation and shared context make understanding each other possible. Conversation turns information into understanding. We give explicit information that the listener might not have, and we ask questions to make sure what we have said is understood. But the more complicated the communication, the more depends on extensive shared context. And when clear communication is important, we cannot afford to assume that we share a context.

ASKING QUESTIONS IN BUSINESS

So, questions are necessary to check understanding, and any situation in which we are discouraged from asking questions risks creating misunderstanding.

The bad news is that, in business, we are routinely discouraged from asking questions or limited by the organization's culture as to the questions we can comfortably ask. Coupled with that, there is a cultural reluctance to speak up. Typically, employee survey research shows that 69 per cent of employees do not feel they can speak up without being perceived as negative (Bloomfield, Lamb and Quirke, 1998).

However, more insidious is the fact that asking questions can be difficult simply because people think language is basically clear and unambiguous and expect us to understand them the first time. We also believe that asking questions exposes some failing in the speaker or the listener. Therefore, if we ask questions, it is our fault for not listening properly or, worse; we are implying that the speaker was not clear.

Across most organizations there are topics and areas of concern that people feel they could never talk about with their boss. Believing that words are normally clear and unambiguous, they are afraid that they are at fault for not clearly understanding. This belief hinders people in making sense of each other and leads to managers sitting in company conferences, determined not to admit that they have lost the plot.

Added to this comedy of errors is the negative effect that communication media can have. Whatever aspirations managers may have for two-way communication, most presentation media are one-way and are not designed to encourage conversation. Worse, room layouts are often unwittingly designed to signal to participants in meetings that they should passively accept presentations from the performer at the front and not engage in conversation. Organizing groups in sizes that expose the maximum number of eyeballs to corporate messages suppresses conversation. Furthermore, managers are routinely trained in presentation skills that relegate conversation to a question-and-answer session at the end. This led in one organization to the chief executive passionately appealing for feedback and tough questions at a management meeting whose slick professional staging and theatre-style seating guaranteed no such feedback would be forthcoming.

Finally, employee feedback is usually solicited to check whether there are any problems. Exploration of understanding is superficial. If employees seem happy, the communicator's job is done.

Misunderstanding between people is normal and highly likely because talk is routinely vague and ambiguous, and you cannot eliminate the inbuilt ambiguity of language. You reduce the problem of misunderstanding by creating a shared context for understanding through conversation and checking on feedback. Inconsistency is inevitable without feedback, and understanding is unlikely without conversation.

Most face-to-face cascade briefing processes are based on the belief that everyone is entitled to receive information on the company's direction and progress, and that each should receive a single consistent message. This pursuit of consistency can, however, become a production-line approach to communication. The desire for uniform standards means a single core brief has to be read out, with some local tailoring and some local addition.

While it is sensible to minimize mixed messages by agreeing core information, inconsistency is almost unavoidable. It makes more sense to encourage conversation in meetings to check interpretations and then to fine-tune the communication in response to feedback. Unfortunately, current approaches to communication in organizations do not always encourage conversation.

Approaches to writing information further undermine the imperfect face-to-face systems we have. Poor planning and coordination and poorly written communication increase the barriers to effective face-to-face interaction.

INFORMATION TO INTERACTION

As organizations have realized the need for employees to be more engaged, they have also realized how important the interaction is between managers and their teams. Therefore, communication has to be managed for the best chance of creating understanding during that interaction.

This means removing the barriers which currently exist to interaction, and reorganizing information to make it more comprehensible. This calls for restraint and coordination among information and message providers, and better use of time, better skills and greater accountability among managers.

In a classic team briefing, the manager adds value to the process by adding in local items of information. This is not enough for the future. Managers have to add value by turning information into meaning and highlighting the implications and significance of information for their people.

Managers have to be able to make the link between the organization's agenda and that of their people. This means seeing the significance of information from their viewpoint and then being able to make the connection between the information and employees' needs and concerns. What employees say engages them is a chance to talk, feeling safe to speak, feeling that you are being listened to and the exchange of ideas.

As first outlined in Chapter 1, effective communication is a four-step process of conversation:

1.   providing content

2.   creating context

3.   having conversations

4.   gathering feedback

All four steps are needed and each is a vital link in the chain of communication (see Figure 6.1).

WHAT BREAKS THE CONNECTION?

Although this may be the ideal, the internal communication process is often managed as a series of discrete and disconnected elements. Each has its own problems and is managed by different people with different ideas of what they are doing. For each of the four ideal stages of the communication process, there are characteristic barriers to success which undermine the intended outcome:

•   **Content.** Information is provided in non-user friendly fashion with unclear meaning and intent.

•   **Context.** People with different background contexts and mixed perceptions of each other's credibility are unable to relate to each others' contexts, and use information that is unclear.

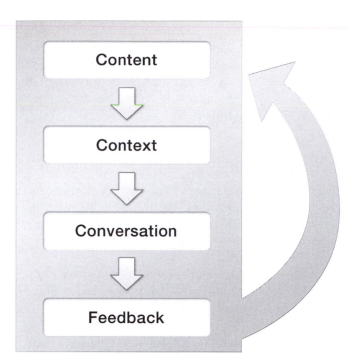

Figure 6.1   Four step process of conversation

- **Conversation.** The format of meetings prevents interaction, skills are lacking and the mode is one of presentation, not discussing. There is not enough time or opportunity for dialogue between people to digest and assimilate information, with the result that the more they are force-fed with it, the less they digest.

- **Feedback.** Organizations are unclear what feedback they actually want – acknowledgement of receipt of messages, satisfaction with the way the meeting was conducted or innovative ideas for improvements? Managers can filter out feedback or feed all the unresolved issues up the organization where they clog up senior managers' time.

The number of people in the room directly affects the degree of interaction in a meeting, as does room layout. The volume and clarity of corporate information has an impact, as does uncertainty about its intended purpose, what feedback is expected and what will be done with it. Much therefore depends on enough time being available and the manager's skills in making the best use of it.

WHAT IS NEEDED AT EACH STEP OF THE PROCESS?

The challenge is to manage communication as a process that gives managers the best chance of turning information into meaning for their people.

Content

In terms of infrastructure, organizations need distribution processes that can efficiently deliver information to identified audiences. In terms of information, they need to have clear messages, well articulated in plain language and presented in a familiar and recognizable format, with the intended meaning clearly highlighted.

Context

The value of the manager is in adding context, painting a clear picture and creating understanding. For managers to put information in context, they need to have the context themselves. This means giving them an opportunity to discuss information, unpack its significance and challenge its rationale before they are asked to go and do the same with their people.

Managers should be provided with key messages and user-friendly information, with clear meaning that gives them a reasonable chance of being able to translate it into local relevance.

Conversation

Managers and team leaders should be provided with the appropriate skills to prepare information, breathe life into it and engage in a conversation with their own people to create clear understanding. Given the low level of communication skills of managers, and their focus on presentation skills alone, communication coaching and skills training is vital.

Feedback

There should be upward channels for response, together with clear guidelines for managers in prioritizing areas for feedback, with timescales for reporting back on actions taken as a result.

As a minimum, feedback should be used to test understanding, not simply to report exceptional complaints. Managers should feed back to authors on how their information was interpreted, what employees made of the information and what action this has created. Feedback should be treated not as a check on employees' happiness with the message but as a means of continuing the conversation and providing input to the next round of communication.

GREATER FORWARD PLANNING

All this demands a more disciplined approach to forward planning. Managers want to be able to add value, so there should be no sudden shocks, surprises or inconsistencies which they would find difficult to explain. This means that the top management team has to agree a limited number of prioritized messages and be able to present them in a unified picture.

LOSING CONTEXT

The cascade process of communication is well designed as a means of distributing information in a stable organization, undergoing little change. However, when organizations move the goalposts, and redefine what their communication should deliver, the cascade process can be left behind.

In a cascade process, managers further down the chain become successively less able to add meaning to information. They lose more and more sight of what was the original impulse behind the information and have less and less shared understanding of the context which gave rise to it. The absence of any translation and context setting means that, when those messages do reach the bottom of the organization, they often have little meaning or relevance. This inevitably reduces people's ability to make any useful contribution to the team meeting and results in a lack of upward feedback.

Such a situation arose when Lyons Tetley, now the Tetley Group, conducted a root and branch review of its face-to-face communication. It was focusing on product innovation as a way of increasing its share of the beverage sector. After a restructuring of senior management responsibilities, an announcement that the two most senior jobs in the UK and in the US had been restructured was disseminated through the team briefing process.

This was duly briefed down through the workforce who received it either with apathy or with resentment. Why on earth should they be interested in the senior promotions? Wasn't this just fat cats dividing the cake up differently amongst themselves? Would they now be receiving higher salaries for their new responsibilities? What about the workers? Why was it that the senior people could get more money while the workers were still demanding air-conditioning in the factories?

This was a classic comedy of errors. There was actually very good news and great significance in the announcement. However, that meaning had been successively extracted from the communication as it was passed down the cascade process.

So, why had these two senior jobs been restructured, and why had responsibilities been changed? The focus for the business was on product innovation. Resources for the research and development of products had to be tightly allocated to make sure that the business was not diverted into fruitless areas. From being production-focused, Tetley changed the business culture to become much more customer-focused and market-led. The company was looking outside to the market, identifying different consumer trends, spotlighting those areas for product development and organizing their leadership in order to direct resources to areas with the best chances of pay off.

In the UK, tea drinking was in slow decline, while coffee drinking was on the increase. In mainland Europe, the opposite was true. Coffee drinking, long since traditional, was in slow decline, while tea drinking was becoming more fashionable. In Europe, tea is drunk hot. In the US, tea is drunk cold, as iced tea, and there are even tea-flavoured popsicles.

The reorganization of responsibilities between the UK and the US was therefore a reflection of consumer trends – a way of organizing around products which different consumers preferred hot or cold. It should have been a positive signal to the workforce about the future of the business, the extent of investment in new product development, and about where the opportunities for extra jobs, interesting work and exciting marketing activity were likely to be.

All this was initially included in a one-page brief, but briefers announced only the 'what' – the change in the roles and titles of the chief executives and dropped the 'why' – the context and the explanation.

It is easy to get the wrong end of the stick when that is the end being presented to you. This example is not at all unusual. Many organizations which have put basic team meetings in place are frustrated by the outcomes.

A telecoms company introduced a regular face-to-face communication meeting they called 'Face 2 Face'. This involved staff getting together for between half an hour and an hour on a regular basis – usually monthly. The leaders at each level talked to their team and updated them on how the company and their own area were doing. This meant that all employees were kept informed by their immediate boss on what was relevant to them. This should have been a winning formula because, in most communication surveys, employees rate their line manager as the most important channel of communication. People also say that they prefer face-to-face communication, and they like to get information in groups, so that everyone hears the same messages and gets to hear each other's comments and questions.

The instructions to managers for Face 2 Face stated that it was the manager's responsibility to create discussion. The aim behind Face 2 Face was to generate conversation, in the belief that conversation creates greater understanding, greater ownership and greater impact of information.

However, things started to slide when managers found it difficult to follow the instruction to create discussion. They agreed with the principle that creating discussion might be useful, but the teams were unclear why they should be discussing anything.

The number of people in the meetings tended to vary, and it was difficult to create any real discussion among groups of 20 people or more. Even if managers succeed in provoking discussion, some of their questions remained unanswered. What's the intended outcome and response? Who is interested in the outcome of the discussion and what sort of response or reaction will there be as a result?

The teams appreciated the time together but wanted to use the time to discuss their own issues and performance, and there was a limited amount of patience for other information.

Items that were included in the Face 2 Face briefing notes were far removed from the team's interest and its day-to-day focus. Issues which were too corporate with no apparent impact seemed irrelevant and a waste of time, so it was difficult to raise anything beyond a token discussion of them, that soon petered out. This was because the principle that underlay the process was being defeated by the practice.

This company had invested heavily in face-to-face communication in the belief that it was important, but they were not getting the results they wanted. While the initial aim of the process was to create understanding and conversation, Face 2 Face had come to be used as a catch-all for distributing all manner of information. Different senior managers could insist that they have their own items – however irrelevant – included in the session, whether it was operational information, the discussion of a large-scale change programme or a change to the stationery requisition form.

This reflected the different perceptions of the purpose and role of Face 2 Face. Some senior managers believed that it was intended to give employees a fuller understanding of business context so that they would be able to embrace change better. Other senior managers believed that it needed only to tell employees what was necessary to carry out their jobs.

This difference of outlook translated into practical difficulties, as both groups of managers simultaneously used the process for different purposes. Some senior managers happily provided information for disseminating via the Face 2 Face process which they saw as an efficient means to distribute instructions; others added information on changes to car policy, for example, because it was a convenient way of getting the information out.

This resulted in poor-quality briefing material, unfit for the intended purpose of creating engagement and designed with a very different purpose in mind. Information was provided, which might not be of interest to the team but which senior management believed staff should welcome. Consequently, managers found themselves asked to lead lively discussions on such subjects as changes to the car policy, which did little for their own credibility and produced little value for the team.

COMMON PROBLEMS AND HOW TO RESOLVE THEM

This organization is not alone – many organizations are finding that face-to-face communication in teams shares some common problems:

- **Lack of clarity at the top.** The 'management-speak' used to formulate the messages in the core brief can be misunderstood by those putting it together. If these people do not fully understand the brief, by the time the messages reach the end of the management chain they can be impenetrable.

- **Lack of translation.** The failure of local managers to set corporate messages in a local context often results in the core brief being seen as both remote and irrelevant to the local job.

- **Management style.** Various forms of heavy-handed 'management style' can inhibit the team and prevent them becoming engaged and involved.

- **Disowning the brief.** Managers can be guilty of distancing themselves from the information they are presenting. The 'do not blame me, this is what they have told me to tell you' approach immediately undermines the credibility of the messages. It also means that the manager will not bother to set the core brief in a local context or add any local information.

Getting value from face-to-face communication and improving the quality of interaction require the simple ground rules described below.

Be clear why you are doing it

There are often confused and different perceptions about the purpose of face-to-face communication. At board level, for example, the aim behind team meetings might be to create a flow of creative ideas for improvements within the business. At business unit level, senior managers may see its value in creating a greater focus on customers. Within a team, however, the purpose may be to swap updates on day-to-day activities.

A problem arises when at each level in the organization there is a different perception of the value and the purpose of communication. If the corporate centre sees the role of communication as the dissemination of corporate information, if the business units use it to create a sense of identification within the business unit and if local managers see it as a means of engaging employee enthusiasm and empowering them to solve problems, then there will be conflict and confusion. Communication from one level to another should form a chain of shared meaning, not a cascade of confusion.

Unless there is a common understanding all along the chain – between all parties – on the purpose and intended value of communication, the links will not be forged and time, effort and energy will be wasted.

In the past, face-to-face communication has been seen as a distribution channel for giving instructions, reminding people of procedures and regulations and alerting them to issues and complaints. Now it is likely to be used more valuably in stimulating discussion, creating greater understanding of issues affecting the business and fostering greater support for the business strategy. Engaging team members in problem solving and seeking their responses to particular issues uses managers' and employees' time better and produces more value both for them and for the business.

Nowadays, meetings are also more likely to be used to put previously distributed information into context, and for creating discussion and prompting feedback. This does, however, rely on people actually reading the information beforehand, which may not always happen.

Agree what information face-to-face meetings will contain

The aim of the process should not be to deliver efficiently a series of messages tailored to different audiences. There are more effective ways to distribute information, via more neutral media – electronically or in print. The aim should be to use team meetings to strengthen the relationship between team leaders and their teams. Making managers translate information helps connect managers' and their teams' agendas, and forces leaders to consider carefully what the messages they receive actually mean.

Avoid overload

Employees will tolerate some non-local messages, if the rest of the meeting is useful in addressing their local problems. The core brief rides on the back of local issues – too heavy a core brief and the horse dies beneath the jockey.

One of the general principles of team briefing, for example, is that 70–80 per cent of the information should be 'local' items, with the remaining 20–30 per cent being the information passed down from above. This emphasizes the importance of allowing time at each level to discuss and understand information. More importantly, it demands preparation time on the part of line managers as their ability to translate corporate information into local significance will be vital.

Prioritize a limited amount of information

When it comes to communication channels, clutter kills. Avoiding clutter requires prioritizing issues and only using face-to-face meetings for information which requires context and is worthy of discussion.

Linking employees' and the business agenda is easier if the core brief is not developed as a mere summary of discussions at board level. It is better to develop it as a combination of what the business needs to tell people, and the responses to concerns fed back by employees.

Senior management need to understand that their employees' have limited capacity for absorbing information, and that information coming from management will not have the highest credibility. They need to concentrate on a limited number of key issues and messages, and adjust these in response to feedback, which they should actively seek.

Do not overload the time

Creating conversation takes much more time than announcing an item of information. The capacity of meetings to carry corporate information is radically diminished by using the process to create understanding. That, in turn, means switching information that does not need putting in context, or discussion, into other channels.

Local team leaders have to understand that it is in the team's interest to include both local and business-wide issues. Equally, the board has to understand that only by creating interesting local meetings can they generate interest in wider issues. They cannot afford to overload them with non-local information, since this will kill interest, create boredom and ultimately ensure that no one attends.

Advertisers know that they attract attention by putting their advertisements alongside interesting editorial. They also understand the necessity of an advertising/editorial ratio to retain readers and prevent an off-putting advertising overload. The same principle applies to internal communication.

If the focus of the session is the team's issues, there is likely to be room for only two or three additional information items. This demands restraint from would-be communicators and a 'local to corporate' ratio that leaves most of the time for discussing issues.

Raise the energy

People enjoy meetings when they gain something from them – either solving a problem that annoys them or being able to air their views. Rarely does corporate information excite them – it is usually the team leaders' ability to maintain energy levels and involve people, and the cross-conversations between team members, that make the session worthwhile. This puts a premium on the team leader's style and skills.

If you want discussion, make the information discussable

In face-to-face meetings, teams are usually more comfortable talking about specific task-related items close to their experience. Thus there will be a greater interest in local items and their implications. People will be able to discuss them because they have experience and understand the issues.

If a mix of corporate and local issues is included, there is a danger of a breakdown. Any meeting takes time to warm up, and putting the corporate information first risks it being passed over without discussion or interest during the warm-up period. This is a particular danger when people have a relevant experience to draw on and few opinions to volunteer. Discussion cannot be jump-started with items that have low mileage for discussion. Such items should be reserved for later in the session.

Make it a cycle, not a cascade

Team briefings cascade communication monthly over a period of 48 hours. Although feedback channels usually exist, cascading information can be like dropping a stone down a well and hearing no splash. Spreading information around the business requires more frequent and more active contact to keep communication moving. Feedback from communication meetings should form the agenda for the next round so that people can see a cycle of continuing conversation, not a monthly offloading of corporate information.

Build in time for discussion

Time for discussion should be built in between tiers of managers. Briefers can only sell what they own, and ownership grows from discussion and understanding – which takes time at all levels. The chain of communication usually breaks because not enough effort has been put into forging the links at the top.

To get the most from the meeting, team leaders need to be able to create a sense of common purpose as a basis for addressing real areas of disagreement and resolving conflict. That means focusing on issues of common interest and finding a link between business issues and issues at the top of the employees' agenda. Finding that common ground, and speaking to the needs of the team, is a key skill that managers need.

For communicators, the biggest challenge in aligning the business's and the employees' agenda is to close the gap between the language spoken by senior management and the language that employees speak and understand. We use words to denote categories of similar things, and to help make the world manageable. We speak in generalities, emphasizing the common traits and ignoring the specific individual differences of things. However, while people may speak in generalities, they tend to think in specifics. This is what makes the use of 'management-speak' such a danger. It trades in generalities and abstractions so that the underlying specific point is not brought home. Language is a tool, and when employees do not get the point, it is often because management has blunted its edge.

Words have multiple meanings; all occupying what is called a word's 'semantic field' – its range of possible meanings. Generalized language raises the likelihood of two people conversing without ever making a meaningful connection. We all take refuge in abstract language, especially when it lends significance or helps us avoid discomfort. This may explain why, for one maintenance company, 'vegetation management' turns out to mean cutting the grass and, for another, 'multi modal logistics transfer' means taking a parcel off a truck and putting it in a van. Similarly, managers making employees redundant are often masters of the euphemism because the plain facts are so painful.

In the same way that Dr Johnson rewrote parts of Shakespeare because he thought his choice of words was too plain and basic, so managers take plain speaking and inflate it with management-speak until all edges and outline are lost. Give them generalized terms and business abstractions to discuss with their people, and the danger is that they will start from the abstract and work outward, making it all indistinct.

LANGUAGE AND TRADING LABELS

Engaging employees is often undermined by the terms we use, such as 'professionalism', which are so broad, and therefore easy to misinterpret.

Key to effective communication is turning abstractions into concrete examples. Without this translation into specifics, without getting feedback and exploring what meaning the other person has selected from the field of options, we are not communicating but simply trading labels.

Although successful communication relies on translating abstract nouns into concrete examples, leaders' impulses can be in the opposite direction. In one engineering organization, a project manager felt increasingly frustrated by the lack of enthusiasm that teams in other areas expressed about his initiative. He was closely involved in the project and enthusiastic about its potential. However, he was disappointed by his colleagues' failure to become similarly engaged in the subject, and infuriated when presentations to them fell victim to the 'MEGO' syndrome – 'my eyes glaze over'.

The project was called by the three letter acronym FMA. This name conveyed little meaning but signalled that it was vaguely technical and yet another initiative. Few people understood its purpose, and fewer still were interested in finding out more. Referring to the initiative by its three letter acronym extinguished any flicker of interest they might initially have had.

Pressed to explain the original idea behind the project, the manager explained why he was so enthusiastic. FMA stood for Failure Mode Analysis. So what was that? It was the term used to refer to the new practice, 'We're only going to service equipment when it's actually needed, not just because the service book tells us to do so. We've got some clever ways of monitoring the state of equipment so we can predict and anticipate when it really is going to require servicing. This way we put our efforts into where they are needed, avoid wasting money on equipment that doesn't need it and stop hampering our own people by taking their equipment away unnecessarily.'

Teams which had been deprived of equipment they needed when it was removed for totally unnecessary servicing could immediately identify the benefits of such an approach. Finally, someone had the good sense to tackle the issue in a practical way.

An original, vivid and compelling idea had been turned into a generalization, and then abbreviated to a three letter acronym. The original inspiration had been like a light bulb being switched on over someone's head but the communication of the idea had turned the dimmer switch down on it.

Talking about FMA was an immediately effective way of killing interest and hiding the project's light under a bushel. However, referring to his colleagues' frustration about being deprived of vital equipment, the manager quickly got their attention. That is because he followed the principle of 'lead with their need' – framing communication from the recipient's perspective, not from the communicator's viewpoint.

Hooking people's interests and relating information to their concerns can be done by 'leading with their need'. Without that, people do not see any reason for or urgency about taking the action that's being urged upon them. They do not see how the action – apparently part of management's agenda – relates to their personal agenda. One of the tenets of communication with employees is that it should always spell out 'What's in it for me?' – the implication or benefit for the individual.

Ironically, however, the chain of meaning is often broken not at the 'What's in it for me?' stage but at the 'What exactly is it?' stage. It is impossible to get commitment and compliance if there is not first clarity. One of the most common failings in communicating an initiative like the earlier example of FMA is not making clear what exactly is its point and what precisely it entails.

If companies want to use communication more effectively to create understanding, they will need to raise the clarity and relevance of their information and reduce the amount of gibberish inflicted on employees. Information needs to be written in plain English, from the recipient's viewpoint, explaining the purpose of the communication, whether for information, consultation or action.

For employees to be clear about what, specifically, the organization wants them to do, information must be integrated. Focusing on individual initiatives one after another, for example, gives employees a distorted view and, more importantly, confuses their priorities.

Organizations tend to ask employees to focus in turn on shareholder value, customer focus, productivity efficiencies and cost savings. However, if they keep sending them individual bits of the jigsaw, with no big picture, it is no surprise that people fail to fit the pieces together.

The art of a salesperson is being able to make the connection between the specific needs of a prospective customer and the capabilities of the product or service. Managers have to learn the same skill of making the connection between information and implication. They are well placed to make the important connection to the individual's agenda because, from their daily contact with their own people, they are best placed to know what their issues and concerns are likely to be. Managers have to understand the individual hooks and interests of their people; they are best placed to 'lead with the need' – to connect individuals' agendas to that of the organization.

To make the connection between the organization's agenda and that of their team members, managers must do two things with information:

- start with the hook of whatever is at the top of the employee's agenda, and in which they are most interested – in order to lead with their need;

- make the connection to the 'So what?', and translate the significance of a message into the implications for the employee.

To make these connections they have to understand their teams' preoccupations and the underlying point in any news or information they are expected to communicate.

To do this, managers have to be able to review the information they receive and tease out the connections – which items are capable of discussion, how information relates to their team and what implications need to be spelled out. They have to follow the first rule of face-to-face communication – start from where your people are, not where you would like them to be. In other words, they should start with the team's express needs, talk about the underlying issues and show the link to a proposed solution. This can only be accomplished by describing an unbroken chain of logic between context and action, with the links answering the question, 'So what?'. For example, an instruction to car manufacturing workers to cover up personal jewellery provoked suspicion and annoyance. Would management next insist on covering up tattoos? Then the line of logic was shared with supervisors:

- competition is increasingly fierce from low-cost economies such as Malaysia;

- consumers are more demanding, and able to demand higher levels of quality for lower cost;

- so we have to find ways of reducing cost, and raising our quality to meet their standards;

- so we have to be rigorous not just about quality of build, but absolute unblemished perfection of paint finish;

- therefore we are going to be all the more careful to avoid the smallest of blemishes;

- the most frequent form of blemishes is inadvertent scratching from personal jewellery;

- so we are going to ask you to tape up belt buckles, rings and watches at the beginning of each shift.

In this way, it was explained, they could make sure that inadvertent blemishes did not cost the company its reputation for quality. It would also reduce their workload in vehicle preparation, because they would not be putting time and effort into rectifying inadvertent mistakes.

The supervisors then took their own people through the rationale using a short form of making the connection – 'Why? What? So'.

- **Why?** The most frequent form of quality blemish is a scratch from personal jewellery;

- **What?** We're asking employees to tape up rings, watches and belt buckles to avoid inadvertent scratches;

- **So** – we'll reduce the workload in vehicle preparation, and free them up to do more of the work we currently pay dealers for.

CASE STUDY: REXAM

Rexam PLC is one of the world's largest packaging companies, with 20 000 employees and 110 production sites around the world. Built from a range of acquisitions in key markets around the world, Rexam rebranded itself to become a unified global company with common approaches and consistent processes. With customers like Coca Cola, Nescafe and Budweiser, Rexam was keen for customers to get the same world class standards of service everywhere. As importantly, Rexam was keen that the organization was linked by the corporate glue of common values and management style.

The introduction of 'the Rexam Way' was designed to create a common culture, and to focus managers from a traditional manufacturing background on the broader attitudes and skills they needed to attract, develop and engage employees.

An employee attitude survey designed to test the progress of the Rexam Way identified two key issues – employees wanted to see a change in the management style, and greater two-way communication.

Rexam's leadership was keen that all employees should have a clear sense of being part of the whole Rexam organization. They felt it was important that all their people, whether at the global centre or at production sites, should be able to make the connection between the overall global strategy, what their sector's priorities were and what they were expected to do at site level. It was even more important that employees realized that they were vital to turning strategy into action, and that they and their ideas were valued.

To make the connection from top to bottom, Rexam's human resources and corporate communications leaders developed a quarterly process of conversations at global, sector and site levels.

Every employee would get the chance to hear what was going on at their site, what impact it had on them, how the sector was doing, what was happening at global level and what impact it might have on them. Leaders from top to bottom of the organization were trained in the same skills, and communication coaches were trained for every site.

In classic team briefing, the manager adds local items of information. This usually means that there is so much information to present by the time it reaches those at the sharp end, that managers insist employees keep quiet to enable them to get through all the slides.

One of the lessons Rexam learned was that 'less is more' – put less volume of information in, but make sure employees take more out. The manager's job was to turn information into meaning, and spell out what the information meant for their people.

Employees often think the communication they receive is boring and irrelevant because the communicators do not answer three key questions:

- Why am I telling you this information?

- Why you should care?

- What does it mean to you?

As well as 'unpacking' the implications of information, leaders also need to be able to communicate issues from the viewpoint of their people, not from their own, occasionally skewed, perspectives. This helps show more clearly the overlap in agendas between the leaders and the led.
Part of Rexam's strategy, for example, was to reduce its factory capacity, so it could focus on high value work in its factories. One of its key strategies was also to focus on continual improvement in quality and standardizing its processes.

For plant managers this made life challenging – they had to engage with their people in improving processes, adopting standards and sharing best practice

– while also having to manage downsizing, and explain to employees why higher quality is needed at a time when capacity and jobs were being reduced.

Plant managers were asked to pull together groups of employees with the aim of explaining the need to reduce costs, and engage them in identifying where costs could be reduced.

Plant managers groaned. The prospect of having to talk to employees yet again about cost cutting was not appealing. It was not a popular subject with employees, and was not getting any more popular each time they revisited it.

From the employees' viewpoint, being asked to reduce costs at a time when the organization was also likely to be reducing jobs, added insult to injury. However, plant managers learned that both their own automatic concerns and those of their employees were misplaced.

Plant managers learned how to view subjects they wanted to discuss from the employees' point of view. Any agenda item that seemed to be purely for the benefit of the management was unlikely to be warmly embraced.

Plant managers learned to think through the implications of what they wanted to discuss and to look for the shared agenda. What impact would cost reduction have on employees? What were the key areas of cost, and how could they reduce costs through better processes rather than simply demanding cuts in budgets?

One of the key areas they identified was the cost of printing 4-colour images on cans. When things went wrong in this part of the process it could be costly. As customers increasingly wanted to use colourful on-can branding, 4-colour cans were becoming more common. This was an area likely to produce more headaches for the operators, and more costs for the plant manager.

What was it that contributed most to problems in colour registration? Poor performance in the printers, and errors in the printer cartridges, caused by lack of maintenance. What was it that most annoyed operators? Downtime of the printers while they were maintained and fixed.

This was a good example of a shared agenda – something that concerned both managers and their crews, although for apparently different reasons. The shared agenda for both operators and plant managers was getting better performance out of the printers which would reduce the irritation for operators, and reduce unnecessary cost for plant managers.

Plant managers therefore introduced this particular agenda item in their team meetings – not as cost reduction, but as 'How to improve the printing process and reduce the frustration of downtime for operators.'

One result of this approach was that employees could see a connection between what was bothering them, and what was bothering the company. Encouraged to participate, they then told the manager what they really thought. The more employees feel they can say what they really think, the more likely they are to understand what the organization is trying to do and the more likely they are to support it. Rexam's training encouraged leaders to smoke out underlying concerns and address them, having learned that employee advocacy comes more from lively argument than passive acceptance.

A key lesson was that there is a better chance of aligning the business agenda and the employees' agenda if employees do not think managers talk an alien language of 'shareholder value maximization and process excellence optimization'. Leaders learned to pull such points out of the PowerPoint slides, translate it into plain language and put it across in their own words.

Another lesson was that typical communication cascades leak meaning.

In a cascade process, managers further down the chain become successively less able to add meaning to information. They increasingly lose sight of what was the original impulse behind the information, and have less and less shared understanding of the context which gave rise to it.

The absence of any translation and context meant either those messages never reached the bottom of the organization, or if they did, had little meaning or relevance. This kills energy, involvement and feedback.

These are often the penalties for not asking the question, 'So what does this mean for our employees?'

An insurance company was briefing some of its middle managers on the launch of a new pension product. The leadership believed that this was a good news story, and were keen to use it to raise the spirits of employees, demonstrate their innovation and illustrate their commitment to investing in product development.

The product manager making the presentation emphasized that they expected this to be a high volume product, although with slightly lower margins. They believed the market was buoyant and they would get a large market share with this innovative new product.

Following the briefing, the product manager's slides would be made available to managers, who could use it to brief their own people on this good news story.

Those at this leadership forum were politely interested, and relaxed about the positive prospects of this new product. Only as an afterthought, one manager asked how this might affect employees further down the organization.

The product manager replied that with lower margins on this product, they would expect customers to do more of their own administration via the Internet. What implications would this have for employees in administration? Well, there would obviously be a need for fewer employees, since the administration volume would be lower.

What, then, would be the impact on back office staff? Well, the business would start looking at rationalizing headcount in back office services.

So what would this announcement mean for administrative staff? The possibility that they would not have jobs in the next 6 months.

Only because managers kept asking the question 'So what?' did the implications of this apparently good news story emerge. This allowed managers to start considering what might happen, and be more balanced in their communication of this apparent good news story to those that might be affected later.

Had the manager not asked the product manager 'So what?', it's likely that the good news story would have been announced to all employees, to be followed some months later by the surprising news that some of them no longer had jobs. It is important to ask the question at the outset, 'What does this information mean for different audiences in the organization?' so as not to be wrong footed.

It is also important to translate generalities into specifics. One pan-European porcelain manufacturer had invested considerable time and effort in communicating the organization's vision and strategy. By all accounts, they had done a good job and employees reported that they were clear about where the organization was headed.

One night, one of the plant managers was taking time to walk the floor talking to some of his people. One of the kiln operators, responsible for baking the porcelain, was reporting back how clear he was on where the organization was headed and how exciting it was.

As an afterthought, his boss asked him, 'How many units have you got in the kiln tonight?'. The proud answer came '17 units'. 'Unfortunately', replied his boss, 'you need to be putting 19 units in the kiln – we only make profit on the last 2'.

This story illustrates the point that however engaged people are in the vision, they need to be able to translate engagement into the right actions.

Internal communication often focuses on giving employees a sense of meaning in their jobs. The story is often told of the bathroom cleaner at NASA who, asked what he was doing, replied, 'Putting a man on the moon.'

A sense of vision and purpose is important, but the bathroom cleaner also has to know how thoroughly to mop the bathroom or stray bacteria might infect the astronauts and delay the space mission.

FACE-TO-FACE – ONE SIZE DOES NOT FIT ALL

In recent years there's been an explosion in different types of face-to-face communication. Although the classic team briefing/cascade process is most widespread for face-to-face communication, it is not the only approach.

Employees are facing a wide range of different workplace situations, and not all of them are working in offices with access to meeting rooms. For example, the Automobile Association patrolmen run their team meetings in the cab of a low loader lorry. Retail staff meet with their section head in a huddle beside the chiller cabinet in the store. Factory workers meet on 'hotspots' – a designated, branded part of the factory where they get together to brainstorm ways of improving processes.

Similarly, companies are looking at different ways of using the time they get face-to-face with their people. The drive is for greater flexibility, greater engagement and more innovative ways of doing things.

A recent pilot training programme in the health service is teaching managers how to tell jokes, so that they can use humour in their meetings to diffuse the tension of stressed out employees.

Appreciative inquiry is another innovative approach that uses structured dialogue to generate a collective image of a new and better future for an organization. Rather than asking people, 'What's wrong?' you ask people what's good about their organization and how it could be made even better. Asking people what's wrong tends to create problems rather than resolving them. 'Appreciative Inquiry' focuses people on what's possible, unlocks experience and knowledge and releases employees' creativity.

In mid-2002 the BBC used Appreciative Inquiry in an ambitious exercise for employees called 'Just Imagine'. Over 10 000 employees (approximately 40 per cent of the total number of BBC staff) took part in over 200 meetings across the UK and around the world. Attendance was voluntary and, in sessions that ranged in size from 25 employees to over 200, people shared their experiences of being at the BBC. They talked about successful moments and about what made them proud. Participants were asked to consider three key questions:

1. What has been the most creative/valued experience in your time at the BBC?

2. What were the conditions that made that experience possible?

3. If those experiences were to become the norm, how would the BBC have to change?

Over 98 000 ideas and suggestions were produced, leading to 35 concrete initiatives for change at the BBC, from new insights into the BBC's audiences to new flexible working and holiday arrangements.

'Open Space' is another way organizations are trying to get more out of their people's time together. The approach was created in the mid-1980s by organizational consultant Harrison Owen when he discovered that people attending conferences preferred the coffee breaks to the formal presentations and plenary sessions.

Open Space conferences have no keynote speakers, no pre-announced schedules of workshops, no panel discussions and no organizational booths. Instead, participants learn in the first hour how they are going to create their own conference. Anyone who wants to initiate a discussion or activity writes it down on a large sheet of paper in big letters and then stands up and announces it to the group. After selecting one of the many pre-established times and places, they post their proposed workshop on a wall. Participants mill around the wall, putting together their personal schedules for the remainder of the conference. The first meetings then begin.

Organizations trying to engage their people in the strategy and educate them about the pressures facing them have used learning maps. These present corporate strategy using an imaginative, interactive visual that looks like a board game. It puts all the strategic and marketplace issues that a company wants its staff to discuss into one big picture. Employees acting as facilitators walk their colleagues through the picture and lead group exercises and discussions. In this way, employees educate themselves, discover the issues and identify what it means for them and their jobs.

Storytelling is another approach that organizations have found useful. Storytelling uses a range of techniques to engage, involve and inspire people, using everyday language and a narrative form that people find interesting and fun.

Storytelling has existed for thousands of years as a means of exchanging information and creating understanding. It is alive and well in organizations – as 'the grapevine'. Typically, the grapevine tends to spread stories which are bad news. What gets lost, ignored or buried tends to be the stories of successes. This approach to the storytelling ensures that those stories are collected, collated and shared. This in turn increases people's sense of pride in the achievement of the organization.

Getting leaders together in management conferences or employees together in team meetings, organizations are encouraging storytelling as a way of tapping into their people's natural abilities as storytellers. Stories are memorable – their messages tend to 'stick' and they get passed on. They can also provide concrete examples of how to do something and why it works, which means people are more open to their lessons.

Organizations tend to become more ambitious in their approach to face-to-face communication when the stakes are high or the challenge is complex. One example is leaders' desire to engage their people in redefining the corporate culture or aligning themselves with corporate values.

An organization's corporate culture can be a business advantage as customers, investors and employees are increasingly drawn to organizations that share their principles and values. Leaders want their people to be empowered to make the right decisions, but they know they cannot create a rulebook to resolve every issue that might arise. A strong corporate culture, with clearly stated values that everyone understands, gives employees a sense of how they are expected to behave and what's appropriate in any situation. If organizational values are defined and communicated clearly and consistently, and embedded in people's everyday roles and functions, corporate culture becomes a flexible substitute for a rulebook.

While organizations cannot always design their culture precisely, their internal communication plays a key role in fostering corporate values and bringing them to life. Companies often display value statements in their offices and include them in their external and internal presentations, literature and websites. However, these need to be backed up by defining the behaviours needed from employees, and the systems and infrastructure to support them. Making value statements that aren't backed up is like posting Bibles through people's letterboxes and hoping they will convert themselves.

Internal communication has to help translate leadership's aspirational value statements into actual practices and behaviours that employees can apply day in, day out. That is what makes corporate values an integral part of an organization's culture.

Organizations have a greater chance to embed their values if they link them to how they serve customers and make money. Otherwise employees see values as an irrelevant paternalistic exercise that will soon be dumped when times get tough. People buy more into corporate values that are based on creating actual value.

As a first step it is helpful to define the problems that the values are designed to address. Why do we need values? As corporate glue, to give us a consistent approach and to make us attractive to potential employees.

Second, define what specific behaviour needs to be changed. Leaders rarely wake up one morning and decide that something's wrong with the corporate culture; they become increasingly frustrated by the gap between what the company needs for the future and the behaviours they observe. The first step in culture change is for the leadership to identify which behaviours among their employees they want to change and which they want to encourage.

Third, make the values concrete. Corporate values often refer to concepts like teamwork, respect and integrity, which mean different things to different people. Get groups of employees together to agree a shared definition of the corporate values and find examples of where they apply to their various roles and functions.

Fourth, having defined what the values mean, ask people to identify when they're *not* applied within the organization. This raises questions such as, 'Why do we give more attention to high-value customers and disregard low-value customers when we're supposed to be customer focused?' The answer may be, for example, 'Because we're also profit focused.' This demonstrates to employees that not all values are equal and sometimes people subordinate one value to another. These questions and answers expose the dilemmas employees face in trying to balance different organizational values.

To change the culture of an organization, you have to make sure people understand the words you use. Language is the raw material of culture and certain words and phrases carry basic assumptions. A significant barrier to culture change is the tendency among managers to translate concrete problems into abstract concepts. The internal communication function can address that difficulty by giving employees a clear explanation of what is required of them.

Employees need to know what the organizational values are, why they are important, what they are seeking to achieve and how they translate into their individual roles and functions.

Organizations use different ways to communicate values to employees and help them understand what they stand for and how they apply to their day-to-day work. These include team discussions, games, painting pictures and telling stories.

Team discussions are particularly useful. They help teams define together the specific behaviours and practices that would be in line with the organization's values. They also help the team work out ways of building them into the workplace.

People get together in their teams to talk about dilemmas and values. If you ask people whether they work with integrity, nobody will say that they don't. If you ask them what they would do if they found money on the street, there are a lot of possible options. People end up having a debate about what they would do, and how they define the behaviour that fits particular values.

Organizing cross-functional meetings is also useful as these discussions highlight actual and potential conflicts relating to corporate values. For example, service engineers might define the value of 'integrity' as telling customers exactly what they're getting, while salespeople may see it as recommending the best product, regardless of price. This approach identifies how people in various parts of an organization interpret the same values in different ways, which can sometimes lead to clashes between departments.

An extension of this is getting employees to play a game where members of departments, teams or cross-functional groups ask each other how they would apply corporate values to specific workplace scenarios. This is something similar to the moral dilemmas game, 'Scruples', where players have to second-guess each others' responses. As people laugh and chat about organizational values, this approach encourages people to connect their own personal values with the principles espoused by the organization. The purpose of fostering values is to influence behaviour, and this is a way of getting people to discuss what behaviours they apply to various situations.

Another way of making corporate values memorable is to interpret them visually. Employee groups talk about situations in which following values would be important, and then produce pictures illustrating each of the corporate values. A key value for one company was 'taking prudent risk'. Employees were presented with a picture of a naked man cutting a hedge. The illustration depicting 'ingenuity' as a value showed an Automobile Association patrolman fixing a fan belt with a pair of tights. These visuals bring the values to life as they show people what behaviours they are designed to encourage – or discourage.

Asking people to produce their own pictures of how the value of, say, 'determination' applies to their jobs will produce different pictures depending on people's roles and functions. For example, a salesman will see determination as getting the sale no matter what; an engineer may see determination as tuning an engine perfectly, no matter how long that takes.

Getting people together in teams and either having a cartoonist draw the values as they describe them, or simply providing pens and paper and asking them to draw what they mean by values, can be very revealing.

In one professional services company, for example, where one of the values was 'adventurous', one group of employees drew a twin-hulled catamaran. When asked why they had drawn a twin-hulled boat they said that it was to illustrate that the business was actually two separate businesses bolted together – and in danger of breaking in two. Pictures enable people to share quickly their perspectives on their organization's culture and values, and where they fall short.

Publishing stories that show where values have been applied effectively and have contributed to the organization's success gives all employees a chance to assess how they're doing. Corporate culture is a journey. On a good day we're doing brilliantly, but on a bad day we may fall behind. It's important to reflect and consider how we're doing, and look at what holds us back and what moves us on. Stories help people assess where they're doing things right and where they're not. They give people a chance to work out how they could apply the values better to their actual jobs.

GETTING FACE-TO-FACE COMMUNICATION RIGHT

Often, leaders are ambitious to engage their people, but they are undermined by the way that face-to-face communication is designed. For example, one Chief Executive gathered his senior and middle managers at a leadership conference to engage them. He wanted to give them a clear idea where the business was going, the options open to the business, the scenarios the leadership had investigated and the strategy they had developed. He wanted to enthuse them about the future, excite them about the options, engage them in the strategy and enrol them in translating that strategy into action in their areas. He wanted to present information, share the thinking of the board, clarify any questions then jump-start a debate. He wanted his people to challenge the thinking, stress test the strategy and buy-in to the way ahead so that they could take it on and own it.

How could he best do this? In a bid to be seen as professional, his communication department hired an event management company that created a beautifully slick stage set, found an attractive venue and created glossy versions of the slides presented by the strategy consultants and the chief executive.

Managers were ushered on arrival into the sizeable conference room, to the accompaniment of galvanizing music. The room, laid out in theatre style, focused attention on the beautifully lit stage set with the theme of the conference emblazoned above it.

The rows of chairs in the room quickly filled up – but from the back. All the cynics and sceptics quickly occupied the back rows, far from the watchful eye of the chief executive. As the lights went down they exchanged whispered jokes about both the chief executive and his strategy.

The event was not the success the chief executive had hoped for. The next section details what undermined his good intentions.

There are six key areas that communicators need to look at if they want to improve face-to-face communication:

1.   the purpose of the session;

2.   group size and its impact on interaction;

3.   format and layout of sessions;

4.   content and messaging;

5.   preparation and training of session leaders;

6.   feedback and measurement.

1. The purpose of the session

In face-to-face communication, leaders do not get what they want because they are not clear about what they are trying to do. They are often disappointed by the results, because they have not clearly defined the outcomes.

Why are you getting people together and what do you want out of the conversation? Are you planning a small informal 'get to know you' breakfast or brown bag lunch? Are you trying to make people familiar with the leader, create a greater sense of relationship and trust and make a human connection?

Are you, on the other hand, trying to stage a rally for hundreds of people to showcase a charismatic leader presenting a compelling vision?

Are you trying to present financial information in a crisp and clear way so as to ensure that employees are better informed about the business progress? Are you rather trying to get people together to create a sense of community, to encourage relationships between siloed departments, in the hope of fostering greater familiarity, trust and collaboration?

Is the purpose of the meeting to have an efficient presentation – exposing the greatest number of eyes to the greatest number of PowerPoint slides? Is it to jump start a debate and conversation, and involve employees in identifying ideas, implementation plans and practical next steps?

It is important to be clear what the purpose and objective of the session is. It is also important that expectations of those hosting and leading the session are pretty much the same as those attending. Confusion on both sides is often created when leaders think they are there to give a detailed exposition of the financial results, while employees attend thinking they are going to be asked their opinion, and given an opportunity to have their say.

Why is it so important to be clear on the purpose? Because the purpose dictates almost every element of the process – who will attend, how large the group size will be, what the mix of presentation and discussion is, what the layout of the room is, down to the positioning of any audio visual equipment.

2. Group size

The number of people in a room or at an event will have a direct impact on the degree of interaction there is:

- 6–8 people can chat over breakfast or an informal lunch;

- 8–12 people can get involved in a team meeting, feel they are part of the conversation and feel they can have their say and will be heard;

- 25–30 people can feel part of a training session or seminar, and expect both to listen and to be called on to contribute;

- 100 people at a conference can expect a more structured series of presentations followed by a period of questions and answers.

The larger the number, the lower the likely degree of interaction. This has an immediate bearing on the purpose of the meeting. If you, as the leader, want interaction, debate and discussion there is a point at which the group size will militate against it.

If you want people to feel safe to speak up, to ask questions and to engage in debate, it is less likely if you have relatively large numbers of people, especially if they are arranged theatre style.

3. Format and layout

The number of people in the session is not the only important factor. Trade fairs, for example, have large numbers of people going around to small stands, with the possibility for lively discussion at each. Open space meetings engage large numbers of people in a range of different discussions.

Therefore it is possible to create more interaction, even with large numbers, if you pay attention to the way the meeting is designed and the room is laid out.

The way a group is arranged in a room has an impact on how well its members connect with each other, and how well the discussion flows. Rooms have rules. The layout of a room creates roles and expectations within the group. So changing the physical layout of the room will change roles and expectations.

For example, when people enter a room that is laid out theatre style for a presentation, they automatically pick up the signals the room is sending them, and slip into the role it requires of them.

Laying a room out theatre style signals that the presenter has all the answers, and everyone else is required to be a relatively passive audience. In Shakespeare's play, 'Romeo and Juliet', when Juliet asks from her balcony,

'Romeo, Romeo, wherefore art thou Romeo,' no one in the audience feels moved or permitted to shout out a reply. In the same way, positioning a chief executive on a stage set behind a podium, on a brightly lit stage, presenting into a dimly lit theatre style conference room, will not help create interaction and engagement.

There are alternatives. If you simply have to communicate to relatively large numbers of people at the same time – as you might have to do with sensitive information which will otherwise rapidly spread via the grapevine – there are some ways of reducing the drawbacks:

- set the room up cabaret style, with mixed groups at round tables;
- move away from formal stage setting, allow speakers to roam using radio microphones;
- create clear divisions between presentation sessions – which should be kept short – and discussion and debate sessions at tables;
- give table leaders flip charts with which to catch the thinking of people at their table;
- use networked laptops to capture information and project it onto a screen for simultaneous sharing.

Diageo's global finance leadership were keen to 'think outside the box' and to shift their traditional way of communicating strategy. They deliberately took an unusual approach to communicating with a relatively larger number of key managers, while also creating greater interaction. They set up a series of workshops in which managers participated, one workshop after another.

A number of different workshops looking at different facets of the strategy ran simultaneously, and participants moved from one to another in sequence – like watching a series of different movies at a multiplex.

A final workshop was designed to help finance managers engage their people creatively in the global finance strategy – something which might otherwise be seen as relatively prosaic.

Leaders were only allowed to communicate the strategy to their teams using pictures – effectively a game of finance 'pictionary' in which key elements of the strategy were conveyed only in pictures.

This forced managers to use the right side of the brain more, tapping into their creativity. It also forced them to engage with the actual meaning of the words, rather than simply repeating received phrases of management speak.

Using pictures not words was far more compelling and appealing, because many of us tend to think in pictures and translate words into concrete images.

First Direct took a similarly innovative approach to engaging their people. They brought their employees together in groups of 100, but to create greater interaction, they turned the whole idea of 'rooms have rules' to their advantage.

They set spaces up to look like TV studios, as though employees were the audience watching the taping of television programmes. They used the format from existing TV programmes – 'Panorama' for an overview of strategy industry changes, 'Watchdog' for a more challenging and irreverent overview of consumers demands and 'Any Questions?' in which politicians are quizzed by an audience. Using each of these television programme formats signalled to employees the roles they were expected to fulfil.

4. Content and messaging

Boring content, irrelevant information and unclear messages are some of the main killers of face-to-face communication.

Anyone preparing content for a meeting has to ask themselves:

- What do I want to tell them and why?
- What impact am I trying to have, and what's the result I am trying to produce?
- What are they likely to be interested in, and what is their current perception of what I intend to talk about?

This is all the more important when the subject is contentious and emotional.

Employees may forgive being asked to go to monthly team meetings to be updated on production figures which have a relevance and impact on their day-to-day work. They may be less forgiving about being told at great length in impenetrable terms about HR's new performance management process. They will certainly be more attentive and more challenging if the subject is a significant change to their pension and healthcare benefits.

It is tough enough to get people in one place, cope with scheduling difficulties, and manage the logistics of accommodating people in the right rooms at the right time.

The real killer is when the well intentioned session leader presents impenetrable, irrelevant and turgid information to colleagues. It is all the more tragic when underlying the impenetrability is a vital issue that needs to be got across.

Leaders do tend to fall into the trap of using 'management-speak', trading management terms such as 'gaining traction, going for the low hanging fruit' or 'drilling down to granularity'. Simple phrases like 'tell customers when we can deliver' are translated to 'proactively inform the customer base of the optimum e.t.a'.

Management clichés are a particular problem – especially when the managers confuse them. One manager in an organization was famous for confusing his, becoming a management version of Mrs Malaprop. He would combine 'keep our eye on the ball' with 'let's keep things on the boil' to produce 'let's keep our eyes on the boil'. This left his listeners with a particular nasty image that was neither galvanizing nor motivating.

5. The preparation and training of session leaders

Managers are often guilty of two faults. They believe they are already naturally good communicators and they believe that they need little preparation, and can rapidly pick their slides off the e-mail and wing the presentation.

This may have worked when their only job was to read the slides from screen without falling asleep themselves. In a world where managers are expected to present meaning, not simply bullet points, and therefore need to prepare their messages, this can be disastrous.

Part of the manager's job is to think through the implications of information for their people. Failing to do this ensures that information will be irrelevant, unclear and lack impact.

Under increasing time pressure, managers may feel preparation is a luxury. Taking as their role models expert leaders who seem to speak effortlessly and fluently, they may believe that spontaneity is the key to charisma. What they may not realize is that some of the greatest speakers put a lot of time and effort into rehearsing their spontaneity.

Managers need to understand that they require different skills for different communication tasks. They also need to understand that they have a natural communication style which will suit them in one situation, and be a liability in another.

In small group settings, where the aim is to foster discussion, managers need to be good at listening and influencing.

Team meetings with a larger number of people require the leader to be able to create rapport, get on the same wavelength as the team, translate information into relevance for them, handle any difficulty amongst the team and agree necessary actions.

Presentations to large groups of people reduce the opportunity for interaction and discussion. This puts more onus on the manager's ability to bring information to life, to structure the presentation in a clear way, and to deliver it with a lively and energetic style.

Different managers have different communication styles, and are better suited to some of these than others.

While chief executives, for example, are often expected to be charismatic, many of them are actually introverts. They may be very good at listening, good at empathizing and understanding the people they speak to, and good at processing and structuring information to come up with a solution. Much of this goes on behind the eyes, and may be invisible to the people they're talking to.

They may be perfectly suited to small groups and informal conversations. They may be completely unsuited to rousing the sales force at a kick-off rally. Equally, senior managers who are brilliantly engaging when addressing a crowd may be less able to listen patiently to a group of back office workers in a cafeteria.

One of the jobs of the communicator is to identify the style and strengths of their managers, and match those to the kind of sessions they are expected to run. Often it is more effective to use an introverted chief executive in small group settings, with informal discussions, rather than forcing performance in the spotlight on stage in an amphitheatre.

When the purpose of the meeting is primarily to pass on information, managers will need to be able to write succinctly, to chart up information, present clearly and use audiovisual equipment. If the purpose is to involve team members in innovative problem solving, more advanced skills are needed, such as understanding group dynamics. To change from presentation to conversation requires the ability to present information from the recipients' viewpoint, to put information in context and to engage employees in discussion.

Launching out on face-to-face communication without preparation and training does not work. Deciding to use team meetings for creative idea generation or problem solving, and then only providing team leaders with a 3-hour module on the use of an overhead projector is not a formula for success.

In a survey of chief executives, carried out by the University of Sheffield, 94 per cent of them identified communication skills as a key management attribute for the year 2010. Communication skills for the twenty-first century will include listening, influencing and eliciting feedback. Facilitation skills are as fundamental today as presentation skills were yesterday, and there will be a greater need for coaching colleagues on their personal communication skills. Added to these basics, managers will need an understanding of the best use of media – for example, when to use e-mail versus face-to-face communication – a subject discussed in Chapter 7.

Managers and team leaders need training in assembling information, preparing and putting it into context, leading discussion, stimulating and handling questions and feeding back. Professional communicators – including HR managers and internal communicators, initiative and project leaders – will need training in planning and preparation, how to assemble the big picture information, creating key messages, assessing the communication needs of their internal customers and skills for influencing and negotiating.

Before managers learn new skills, they need to realize that they lack them. This calls for holding the mirror up in front of them by means of tools such as 360-degree appraisal.

6. Feedback and measurement

Managers can often get away with lack of preparation and poor performance because the purpose of the session and its desired outcome has not been specified.

If the definition of success favoured by managers is to avoid complete humiliation, to bluff their way through the slides they do not themselves understand and to get a few laughs for their more politically incorrect jokes, then they will probably feel they have done a good job.

If there are questions they could not answer, information they did not quite understand and messages they forgot to mention, little of that will show up on the manager's self evaluation.

One of the underlying assumptions in face-to-face communication is often that the team is there to witness a performance, and it is the leader's job to turn in a professional performance.

Any evaluations of events therefore tend to focus on the performance of the leader, and feedback from colleagues is often focused on the wrong things.

Evaluations of a leadership meeting, for example, may be focused on the participants' satisfaction with the venue, ranging from its location and choice of beverages, to a rating of each of the individual speakers' performances. What you may actually want to find out is, 'Did we achieve what we set out to?' If we are trying to create clarity about the strategy – how clear are people now? If we are trying to get across three key messages – can people remember and repeat them? If we're trying to engage people in debate and discussion, did they feel able to speak up and did they feel that they were heard? If they left with questions they want answered, how confident are they that we will get an answer back to them as promised?

If we are trying to make the connection between strategy and action, how clear are people about the strategy, their part in it, and about what, specifically, we want to do as a result?

Engaging employees involves identifying what you want them, specifically, to think, feel and do.

Tracking the outcome of communication, and using measurement to improve it is vital. This is taken up again in Chapter 10, which looks more closely at measuring impact, tracking engagement and improving the return on investment in face-to-face communication.

The next chapter looks more closely at engaging employees in changes, projects and initiatives.

REFERENCES AND FURTHER READING

Bloomfield, R., Lamb, A. and Quirke, B. (1998), *Talking Business – New Rules for Putting Communication to Work*, (London: Synopsis Communication Consulting).

Cooperrider, D. L. and Srivastva, S. (1987), Appreciative inquiry in organisational life, *Research in Organizational Change and Development*, Vol. 1, pp. 129–169.

Sheffield University (1998), *Survey by the Institute of Work Psychology.*

7 Communicating Initiatives and Projects

Change has forced organizations to look at how they communicate and improve. Today's world has very different rules for communication and, to succeed, organizations have had to learn them.

The following chapter continues the theme of communicating change but focuses on using communication to achieve the intended benefits of projects and initiatives. It looks at the specifics of communicating initiatives, campaigns and projects, with some rules, hints and tips for doing it better. It presents key steps for using communication to produce better results:

- dealing with the pitfalls of project communication;

- coordinating project team members, and linking them with other communicators;

- linking different communicators together to form an internal marketing approach to project communication;

- developing a communication plan.

Some of the issues in communicating initiatives are highlighted by the following case.

A business decides that, in order to secure its future, it has to reorganize its internal processes to get more for less. Part of this reorganization includes unifying IT into a single business-wide system. This is a major change programme in which the way people work together, and the processes which they operate, will all alter.

So important is this change to securing the organization's future that it is carefully planned and programmed. Recognizing the importance of good communication to successfully achieving the promised business benefits, a dedicated communication team is assigned to it.

209

Initially the team's job looks relatively easy. There is already high expectancy and a strong desire for information within the organization. Senior managers are keen to show their commitment and start the implementation. They appeal for information, videos, brochures and road shows with which they can begin to motivate and inspire their own people.

The communication team includes members who are very familiar with their organization's culture. They are personally enthusiastic about the project and believe that the right kind of communication is vital. They have seen so many previous initiatives run aground because of internal competitiveness and sudden surprises about detail, that they view this as their opportunity to strike a blow for clarity. Personally they feel that it is important that people like them are involved, since their colleagues on the project tend to be far more technically focused. Although excited by the technical developments, their colleagues are uninterested in, and naïve about, the likely human reactions of the rest of the workforce.

The team develops a painstakingly scheduled and carefully produced communication plan. It includes which audiences should receive which messages, via which communication media, and with a calendar of events. They then begin assembling some communication products – a dvd for communication to the workforce, scheduled road shows by the team and its leaders to begin education, a newsletter to keep everyone updated on developments and slide packs for use both by team members and by senior managers. An Intranet site is also developed, where updates on the team's work can be seen.

All seems highly satisfactory on the communication front, until a review of the initiative's progress at the end of the year. The actual implementation programme has gone well, meeting all its milestones, but the promised business benefits have not materialized. The problem is that, although the changes have been put in place, none of the behaviour changes, the shifts in attitude or the re-engineering of processes has been delivered. This is partly, they now realize, because the communication of the changes has neither been wide enough nor has addressed the wider change-management issues. Communication has focused on the announcement of changes, rather than enrolling those who need to change.

Communicators had identified constituencies and had given each of them different relevant messages. However, they failed to understand that each had to go through a different mental journey and that different degrees of engagement and commitment would be needed from each. Mass communication to all employees took place simultaneously with communication to managers, thereby treating managers as any other audience, rather than as a vital link in the chain of communication.

The project team's communication focused on announcing the changes that they needed to meet their timescales. It did not signal the implications or significance of those changes to the various constituencies throughout the organization. The adoption of a campaigning approach positioned the change as basically an IT project, run by 'techies', which would have few far-reaching implications. Those affected did not realize the implications of the change, and resisted making the changes once they did.

The adoption of an acronym, logos and newsletters signalled that this was only a 'flavour of the month' initiative and created the expectation that it would have a limited lifespan. Nor was there a signal to managers and employees about the relative importance and priority of the change initiative. Although the project was launched with the full commitment of the chief executive, the 'big bang' approach, with little follow-up, meant that it became simply one more initiative on the list of initiatives being reviewed regularly by the board. It dropped down the order of priorities to join the other acronyms, regardless of their relative impact on the future of the business.

This is not an unusual case and it highlights some of the problems encountered in achieving the benefits of crucial projects.

Beginning on a major project is like getting the builders in. There is an initial resistance to, and inertia about, starting the job, but the vision of how beautiful it will all look when the work is completed is seductive. Senior management stand on one side of a valley of change, gazing over to the far side, and to the sunlit uplands of the business benefits. Then the descent into the valley begins. As with building works, the day-to-day upheaval is underestimated. The sudden implications of making the change come forcibly home. Deep outrage is felt despite the project manager's claim that careful reading of the project plan would make it blindingly obvious, even to the uninitiated, that such steps were required. This is when the trouble begins. Senior management's optimistic support given at the outset is suddenly withdrawn. People claim that they did not understand the full implications and, had they known, they would not have committed.

This familiar descent into confusion, unrealized benefits and mutual frustration on all sides is often the result of poorly managed communication. Although good internal communication alone will not guarantee that a project delivers its anticipated benefits, poor internal communication alone can derail the initiative.

Any organization with a number of different change initiatives underway should question its people's capacity to assimilate change. The Jensen Group's (2000) research into complexity in the workplace found that part of what drove an 85 per cent increase in work complexity was an average of over 35 separate change initiatives juggled by everyone in the workforce – on top of their regular, daily tasks. The same research showed that up to 80 per cent of the workforce could not make sense of the information they received.

THE PITFALLS OF PROJECT AND INITIATIVE COMMUNICATION

Employee confusion and apparent management incoherence is not helped by a laissez-faire approach to internal communication, especially by those running initiatives and projects. Ironically, such projects are usually highly important, with a high potential for success or disaster, and have large amounts of money at stake. They can command communication budgets which are only a minor proportion of promised benefits, but are nevertheless usually bigger than communication budgets in corporate communication departments. Such budgets allow communicators to use their purchasing power to get things done their way. Where enthusiastic 'gifted amateurs' have large chequebooks, they can quickly become loose cannons.

The way in which communication is managed can actually prevent the anticipated business benefits materializing. Companies tend to confuse selling with marketing in internal change communication. They use push communication to persuade people that the change is good, focusing only on creating awareness rather than translating awareness into action.

During a study by the Jensen Group (2000), 38 companies shared detailed change management and change communication plans for driving new business strategies or major change efforts. All 38 plans concentrated on preparing messages and sending them out via a variety of media and events. Only one of the 38 plans provided an in-depth analysis of the audience's readiness for change, which identified what specific behaviours for each stakeholder group needed to change. Only two of the 38 plans detailed how the audience's behaviours would specifically change and be measured as a result of the planned communication.

THE MISSING LINK

In communicating an initiative, the first step is to help the company's leaders understand why change is needed, and identify what specifically should change. Communication of the initiative should not focus on the tools and means too quickly, but concentrate first on the goal of change.

Project leaders can themselves be a source of confusion. If they are left to carry the burden of communication, without any link to a corporate communication effort, they can unwittingly cause confusion. Under pressure to deliver, and focused on their milestones and deliverables, the risk is that team leaders run their projects as separate stand-alone efforts.

Project managers tend to be passionate about their project and can lose sight of what is most relevant to the people they are addressing. The risk is their feeling that, even if people may not be that interested in what they are doing, they damn well ought to be.

The typical approach to selecting project communicators does not reduce the risk. A programme is established, and each project within the overall programme has a communicator. They are selected for their enthusiasm and interest rather than any experience or skill and do the job part-time, along with their other responsibilities. Together they try to coordinate their efforts. They see communication as promoting their project and informing everyone about the changes to be made. The communicator's job is seen as relatively straightforward and requiring little specialist knowledge, but a great deal of willingness and enthusiasm.

Once recruited, such communicators fall prey to 'logo mania', developing new identities and slogans for their project. If they have been selected for their experience in desktop publishing, a project newsletter is certain to follow, whether or not it is appropriate. If they like blogging, the project leader will be persuaded to start a blog. When the only tool you have is a hammer, the solution is always a nail.

Initially, it is decided to coordinate communication and present a single face for the programme. But individual project teams begin to break ranks, producing their own communications in isolation. Although they know that this could cause confusion, project team leaders feel that they are being tasked to deliver on their own project and so work for their project's benefit, not for that of the programme as a whole.

Project teams can see themselves as independent entities with no obligation to work alongside their colleagues in other teams. Their focus is on achieving their own objectives, sometimes in isolation. There is often no reporting line to corporate communication, human resources or whoever is responsible for managing day-to-day communication. This means there is a greater danger of uncoordinated, and competing, communication leading to incoherence.

COMMUNICATION AS IMPLEMENTATION

Project leaders, selected for their project experience to drive change initiatives, concentrate on making things happen. They communicate only specific task-related information designed to help them achieve their timescale and milestones. This translates into a communication plan which is designed to announce implementation details. This can create misunderstanding and resistance, rather than creating widespread understanding of the need for, and the implications of, change.

FAILURE TO SEE THE RECIPIENT'S VIEWPOINT

Project leaders create their own identity and promote themselves and their teams among senior management to gain recognition and advance their careers. Even when they are convinced champions of change, they can be seen as pushing a solution for a problem which most employees either do not understand or do not recognize.

Initiative communicators can be caught in a double bind when they try to promote their own initiative and sell it to their internal customers like a product. Employees are given information about the project and asked what more they need to know about it. Employees do not know what they do not know and can't say what they need. So initiative communicators go back to pushing more information at them.

COMMUNICATION CONTAMINATION

Consultants can contribute to the problem of poor communication inside organizations. Their terminology becomes others' jargon, and, as a result, contamination by jargon swiftly spreads among managers who are keen to be seen to be 'in the know'. Those who work closely with consultants end up adopting their language, using their slides and imitating their presentation style. They become the carriers of the epidemic of half-understood and confusing language around the organization.

WHO SHALL COMMUNICATE WITH THE COMMUNICATORS?

Where there are many uncoordinated communicators, they may not themselves fully understand the relationship between initiatives and therefore cannot clarify it for anyone else.

It is not uncommon for project team members to be unclear about their project's key messages, or to disagree fundamentally about the anticipated benefits. Yet, who else is going to be able to provide clarity for employees? The first place to create clarity is among the project leaders and team members by getting them together at the outset to agree the central purpose and key messages of their project.

The success of any initiative depends on successful communication. One source of continual and credible communication is the project teams, in their daily contact with the organization. As research within companies continually shows, informal communication is more influential than formal. Project team members' informal daily contact with staff will have a greater influence than will formal communication.

Team members may be focused on getting the task done, but also affect the climate of acceptance for the project. They are in regular contact with the rest of the organization, working out the details of implementation and often thinking aloud about the feasibility of different options. Without realizing it, they can contaminate communication and create concerns. However, since they have regular contact, understand the issues and can spot problems early, they can be huge assets if they are managed properly. Their day-to-day contact with user groups and members of departments which will be affected by change is likely to be more influential than occasional formal communication. Issues can often be identified early at grassroots level before they swell into serious concerns.

COORDINATING PROJECT TEAM MEMBERS: BEING ON MESSAGE

Using these assets depends on managing members of project teams as a network of formal and informal communicators.

Project teams are both a key audience for communication and ambassadors for the project. As such, they need to be provided with clear messages to help them communicate consistently with their contacts in the rest of the organization. They also have to understand their roles and responsibilities, to commit time to identifying important issues and to ensuring feedback about those issues from their own teams.

Part of staying 'on message' could, for example, include a standard slide pack for presentations, rather than each project team creating its own and so increasing inconsistency. The team could also keep a record of who has presented and said what, to which audiences, and at what point in the project life cycle.

Agreed key messages should be circulated for reinforcement by all team members. Project team leaders should spend time communicating with their own team members, with whom they should hold regular briefing and debriefing sessions.

When problems occur in initiatives, it is surprising how often the underlying issue was known about long before it came to light. Project leaders are close to the issues but are not always aware of their possible implications for employees. Without understanding the issues that lie beneath the project milestones, those communicating the initiative can feel that they are flying blind. Developing the communication plan while so many project questions are still being explored can be like trying to assemble an airplane on the runway. Yet communication managers at least know what they do not know. Project leaders may not realize what they do know until an action taken as part of the project unexpectedly upsets the rest of the organization. Only then do the project leaders confess that they had a passing suspicion about such a reaction, but had neglected to mention it.

One way to avoid communication crises and to improve forward planning is to encourage project leaders to describe the path ahead and speculate about possible impacts and implications. Getting a project team to think through some of the implications of their work means having them report back regularly, not simply on their achievements, but on the benefits to the organization of those achievements. Telling employees that milestone number three has been successfully achieved means nothing unless it is spelled out why that is good news. Equally, project leaders need to include in their reports to communicators any alerts or possible reasons for concern they might have. Such concerns may not be for general communication, but sharing the project leader's thinking does help contingency planning.

AN INTERNAL MARKETING APPROACH TO PROJECT COMMUNICATION

'Internal marketing' of an initiative is often misinterpreted as applying glossy sales promotion techniques to internal communication.

Initiatives are often communicated in a way which is more akin to product promotion than change communication. Promotional communication is designed to let people know the initiative exists, but it does not communicate its relevance or benefit to its internal customers.

Project teams can feel frustrated because they are unable to make effective headway while communicating in this way. They are perceived as self-promoting and irrelevant to the business, and their communication effort is absorbed by having to explain what the project's acronym stands for.

Communication should aim to share the thinking from the broad concept down to the specifics. First, the whole organization has to be educated on the need for change and the rationale for the approach.

Without the right context, the initiative communicators find themselves at the sharp end trying to explain the specifics of their activity, but ensnared in debate about why change is needed in the first place – a symptom that the rationale for change was never established. Creating the right context depends on communicators at corporate and at business unit level consistently communicating supporting messages in their own areas.

In order to achieve the benefits of change, an organization has to ensure its various communication efforts are mutually reinforcing.

In external marketing, brand marketing and advertising create awareness of a product, preparing the ground for direct marketing and point of sale promotion. Then, the salesperson, the customer service representative and after sales support form the final links in the chain of marketing communication. Communication roles can be similarly shared in internal marketing:

- Corporate communication provides the overall direction and business priorities of the organization as a whole. On the principle that different types of leader have different levels of credibility, the broad picture of change can be communicated by the chief executive.

- Business unit communication talks specifically about challenges and day-to-day issues facing the business unit, the needs which the business has identified and the gaps it needs to close. This responsibility can be taken on by the business unit leader.

- The project positions itself as the means of closing those gaps, and as a tool for addressing the business issues. This can be communicated by the project champion or initiative leader.

The business units are best placed to communicate the relevance and application of the work being done in the initiative. They can best make the link between the general need for change and the specific implications for the business unit.

The initiative communicators should therefore stop trying to sell change directly to employees, and instead provide the necessary information to the business unit communicators. This approach shifts the traditional competition between communicators to one of collaboration. Each communicator plays to his strengths in terms of credibility, in a concerted internal marketing plan, to make the connection between the why, what and how of change.

MANAGING THE COMMUNICATORS

If a project or initiative team wants to make change happen and integrate it into the day-to-day working of the business, it must first integrate its communication with the existing communication structure.

In a complex organization results may have to be delivered quickly so existing networks should be used, such as HR professionals, internal communicators and marketing communicators.

It can make more sense for the initiative team to let the existing communicators use the existing infrastructure to speak to employees. This means that a project communicator can concentrate on enrolling the business's managers, and equipping existing communicators with the right information.

A better return on costs and more coherent communication can be achieved by limiting the number of communication channels. Project communicators often have the luxury of creating not just their project information and messages, but their own communication channels too. This creates a confusion of roles in which project communicators act both as PR people – seeking coverage of their initiative or message – and media or channel owners, providing or inventing the channels to carry the message. These roles are better clearly separated into two – content providers and channel owners.

Content providers are those with information that they want to communicate; these may be the initiative communicators or senior managers who want to raise awareness about issues. They act primarily as authors, creating messages and information and giving this to the channel owners for distribution using existing communication channels.

Channel owners are responsible for providing robust communication channels that reach employees, and are accountable to content providers for ensuring that they get airtime for their initiative and project messages.

This separation of roles puts a greater emphasis on forward communication planning. It also requires content providers to provide easily translatable, well thought-through and clearly labelled information for channel owners. The onus is on them to ensure that their channels are sufficiently robust to deliver the promised reach to employees. If they do not, initiative communicators will start creating their own.

MATRIX COMPLICATIONS

Collaboration between different communicators is particularly important in matrix organizations. Here, there is a danger of individual business unit communications having a knock-on impact on each other, especially where business units share locations, and employees from different business units can find themselves, for example, eating in the same restaurant. This leads to a situation where employees from different parts of the organization hear different things from outside. For example, there is a set of software applications called SAP, which enables users to access information about all aspects of their business. SAP is rapidly becoming the worldwide standard, and is used by over 15 000 companies across the world. In one organization implementing SAP, a manager in one business unit heard from an outside supplier which had done the same, that the letters SAP here had come to mean 'Stop All Production'. Another manager in a separate business unit in the same location learned from one of its suppliers that implementing SAP was the best thing they had ever done. Confusion set in between the two business units, as informal lunchtime chats undermined the formal communication.

These kinds of mixed message may well be inevitable, but they are exacerbated by different communication strategies and plans developed by different communicators who share the same location, but belong to different business units or departments. Communicators adopting different approaches and different timescales can make difficulties for each other as formal communication in one business unit is leaked as grapevine gossip in a neighbouring one. Employees are able to compare and contrast the messages, and tend to select the one that confirms their prejudice and suspicion. Because people's loyalty is often stronger to their location than to their business unit, they sift information not from a business unit perspective, but according to what it means for their location.

Communicators can make life easier for each other in these situations by integrating their efforts, agreeing common messages and timing, taking a united view on cross-business unit issues and keeping a calendar of upcoming events, likely developments and hot issues.

All of these highlight the need for a clear communication plan.

DEVELOPING A PROJECT COMMUNICATION PLAN

A communication plan allows you to smooth the path for change, allows people to put information into the right context and increases their comfort with your initiative. It keeps key people who can present your case in the loop, and minimizes disruption and confusion.

There are four sets of questions that communication needs to answer:

- What is the change? When will it happen? What will it entail?

- Why is it happening? What are its intended business benefits? How does it relate to other initiatives and the wider management agenda for change?

- What are the specific implications and likely impacts of the changes? What issues do these create as they are rolled out? What is the process for gathering feedback and responding to it?

- What lessons has the organization learned from other change efforts? How are these being incorporated in the latest proposal?

Developing a communication plan that will answer these questions involves six steps:

1. analyze your audiences;

2. set communication objectives;

3. select the communication approach;

4. develop key messages and themes;

5. match communication vehicles to your approach;

6. measure the outcome.

These are discussed below.

1. Analyze your audiences

Identify the different groups who need to know about your initiative because it affects them, who need to brief others about your initiative or who can influence its success. You should think through how they will be affected by your initiative and what concerns you think they will have. Remember to include the people who can influence the success of your initiative, even though they may not be directly affected by it. These are your potential champions and ambassadors.

This analysis of stakeholders should include what their key concerns are and what the desired behaviour needed from them is. Doing this well depends on two factors – the accuracy of your perception of the stakeholders' interests and whether you can retain some objectivity, and not define stakeholders' concerns only in terms of their acceptance or rejection of the proposed changes. The danger is that communicators will aim for stakeholders' compliance, not their commitment. Project communicators can confuse achieving buy-in with 'closing the sale'. Overcoming employees' objections and rebutting their concerns may silence employees but not convince them.

Team members may disagree about the desired end point. One may be concerned to surface employees' real concerns and deal with them, another may want to identify the reservations to the proposed solution and rebut or downplay them.

To avoid analysing stakeholders from the viewpoint of whether or not they will 'buy' the change, a different approach is proposed, as shown in Figure 7.1.

This approach looks at stakeholders in two ways – what impact the proposed change is likely to have on them and what their level of initial interest or concern is likely to be. It takes account, not just of those stakeholders who might be concerned about, and object to, the change, but also of those who are mistakenly feeling 'fat and happy' about the change. For each box in the grid here is a proposed focus to communication:

- providing a 'wake up' call for those who need to realize that they will be affected;

- educating and informing those who will not be directly affected, and therefore do not need to be concerned;

- reassuring those who are needlessly concerned;

- engaging those who are concerned, and who have cause to be.

This allows communicators to direct precious face-to-face communication on to the two priority boxes – 'wake up' and 'engage'.

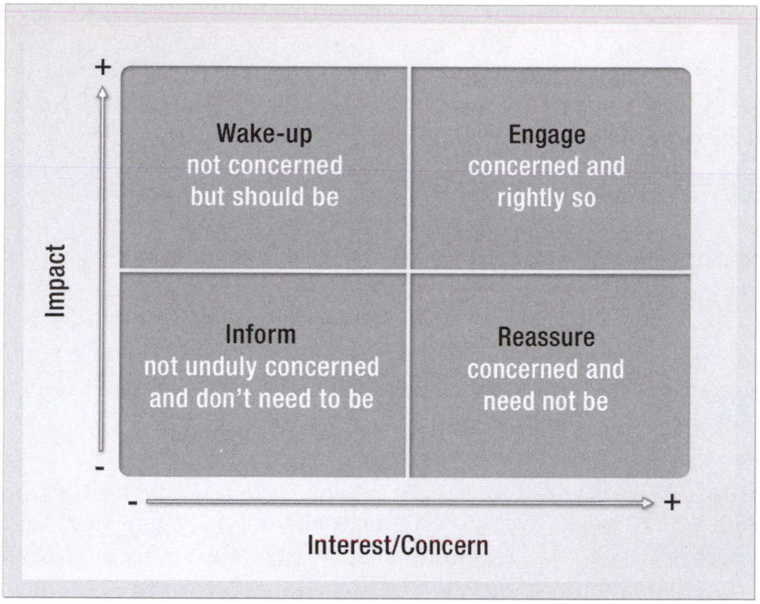

Figure 7.1   How different audiences will be affected by restructuring

By way of example, an organization which was globalizing restructured its corporate head office. A shop floor employee in the US might be little affected by, and little interested in, the change. This would put him in the bottom left-hand box. However, the story would be different for a first-line supervisor, who might be equally uninterested, but would be affected. This placed him in the top left-hand box, needing a wake-up call. Despite his initial lack of interest, the organization needs that supervisor to understand the implications of being part of a global organization. Future business would rely on changing some local procedures, at which point this need for cooperation would affect his job. He therefore needed to understand how to balance local self-interest with the interest of the global network as a whole.

The top right-hand box included those people who would be keenly interested and heavily affected – people at corporate headquarters and senior managers, all highly anxious about whether or not they still had a job. Areas of high anxiety demand more face-to-face communication, and more careful preparation on the part of those running communication sessions.

Walking a project leader through this grid makes it easier to identify the "hotspots" where the most concerned audiences are, highlights what different approaches should be taken with different audiences and stakeholders and prioritizes where time can best be invested.

These factors are illustrated in the following case study.

CASE STUDY: NYCOMED AND ALTANA PHARMA–COMMUNICATION AND ITS ROLE IN M&A INTEGRATION

Almost every industry has been through a period of consolidation and the pharmaceutical industry is no exception. Over 20 years the shape of the industry has changed tremendously, with the industry's major businesses combining to form several industry giants. It is now facing a new wave of mergers and acquisitions which will include the small and mid-sized companies.

It was against this background that Nycomed, a small Denmark-based pharmaceutical company purchased Altana Pharma AG, a mid-sized German pharmaceutical company. At the end of September 2006, after months of media speculation, it was officially announced that Nycomed would buy Altana Pharma from Altana AG for €4.2 billion.

The research-based pharmaceutical industry operates to a relatively simple business model. It discovers new drugs, establishes a patent on those discoveries, and then maximises the commercial return on those drugs before the patent life expires and other companies can sell cheaper copies. Recent years have seen increased pressure on this 'growth equation' and many of the large pharmaceutical companies are facing major patent expiries in the near future. These imminent patent expiries have coincided with a period of poor R&D productivity from the industry, meaning that companies are finding it ever tougher to replace lost revenues with sales from new products. As a direct result, a number of big pharmaceutical companies have decided to cut jobs, some by as much as 10 percent or more.

Altana had been very successful with Pantoprazole, a drug for the treatment of gastrointestinal disorders with sales of more than US$2 billion annually. However, in many of the world's largest pharmaceutical markets, Pantoprazole was due to lose its patent exclusivity within the next two to three years.

Altana Pharma had previously been part of a chemicals and pharmaceuticals conglomerate, Altana AG but Altana AG had been searching for a partner to safeguard the future of the pharmaceutical business. Throughout 2005 and 2006 a number of names were mentioned as potential partners and there was speculation in the media. This media discussion was not matched by internal communication within Altana, and the lack of any definitive message from senior management began to affect employee morale, especially at Altana Pharma's global headquarters in Konstanz, Germany.

In mid-2006, Nycomed's name was linked with Altana Pharma for the first time by the media. By now, the talk was less of partnership and more about an outright sale of Altana's pharmaceuticals business. This caused both surprise and concern among employees. Surprise because Nycomed was much smaller than Altana Pharma – something like 25-30% of the size of the German company. Concern because Nycomed was owned by private equity and the German media had been conducting a long campaign criticising the practices of private equity owners in Germany.

Immediately after the announcement of the acquisition an Integration Team was created with representatives from key functions from both companies. The formal completion of the deal was set for the end of 2006, which gave the Integration Team just 12 weeks to develop an integration plan. A 12-week window to launch a new company meant that speed was of the essence. The success of the communication effort depended therefore on understanding the different needs of different audiences, engaging stakeholders and employees, and using regular research to target communication and track progress.

Recognizing and addressing different audiences and their different information needs

The acquisition of Altana Pharma by Nycomed brought together two companies which had similarities and were complementary in many areas. Both companies were based in Europe, were small-to-mid-sized pharmaceutical companies, and they had both experienced a period of sustained growth. These similarities allowed both organizations to talk about the acquisition as a 'perfect fit', which was borne out by a comparison between the companies' product portfolios and their geographical strengths.

However, there were also some differences. Altana Pharma had had big ambitions and had created a large and complex organization to deliver them. They had begun to build up a large US organization, they had made a commitment to a specific long-term strategy and had created a framework of policies to deliver it. The core of the company was its Research and Development operations -- it prided itself on discovering new drugs 'in house'. By contrast, Nycomed was entrepreneurial and optimistic. The company had built a strong track record of in-licensing new products and had focused its sales efforts on niche markets – the hospital specialist market in particular -- and high growth markets such as Russia and CIS.

Finally, the company cultures were very different and communicators had to be aware that communication would be perceived quite differently by the two audiences. Some, but not all of this, was based on the fact that Nycomed was a Scandinavian company and Altana a German one. Most importantly, the *ways* of working in each company were different and the differences had bred very different working environments and cultural climates.

Employees across both legacy companies found themselves in very different situations. For Nycomed, this was a great story – 'little Nycomed takes over a company three to four times its own size.' In Altana, there was confusion, – 'if we are so successful and this makes so much sense, why didn't we buy them?' Additionally, the situation was different depending on *where* employees were based. Of the 50 countries where the combined company was present, only 14 had overlapping operations – all in Europe.

This meant that, for many, the integration process was a simple change of company name and logo and they could then move on. For those at the heart of the restructuring plans, it meant much more, as evidenced when it was announced that around 10 percent of jobs would be lost from the new company – mostly from the former Altana Pharma headquarters in Konstanz.

Aside from the obvious reaction to this news – disappointment, anger – something else happened. Communicators started to see feedback from the unaffected markets that they were growing bored by the integration story and eager to move on. By contrast, the affected markets would complain when any 'good news' was communicated from unaffected markets. They saw it as inappropriate and insensitive, given what they were going through.

Communicators' response to this was to create a communication project team which focused on the specific and unique situation in Germany and in Konstanz in particular. Comprising internal and external communicators, it focused on local media attention and employee communication, instigating weekly face-to-face forums for employees and large all-employee briefings whenever there were significant developments.

Developing a close relationship with the Integration Team

Closeness to the core integration team was essential. It was important firstly, to ensure understanding and support of the communications approach, secondly to ensure that the approach was tailored to deal with the business plan for integration. Some of the challenges of working with the integration team were the speed of the process, the requirement for every communication to be double-checked by the legal and human resources representatives, and the subjective input of other team members to the communication strategy. However, the greatest challenge of all was the management of enforced 'periods of silence' in various pockets of the business. This followed the announcement of restructuring plans and the start of 'behind closed doors' negotiations with works and employee councils according to local laws. Communicators overcame this by drawing up a map of the various activities and, viewing each function's communication schedule as a 'radio', ensured that not too many of the radios fell silent at the same time.

Developing a close relationship with the Senior Executive Team

The head of integration became the *de facto* representative of communication with the leadership team, which made the relationship between him and communicators all the more important.

The company's leadership team was new, drawing membership from both legacy companies. As a consequence, at the very time they were under pressure to be visible and vocal within the organization, they were also engaged in establishing themselves as a team behind closed doors and defining how they would work together in the future.

A real challenge was that the combined leadership team had differing experiences of integrating mergers and acquisitions. The legacy Nycomed team had strong multi-company experiences of mergers and acquisitions, although not all of it was necessarily positive. But the legacy Altana Pharma leaders had no experience at all. As a consequence, some leaders were operating from memory, while some were learning as they went. Different leaders therefore required different levels of support.

Finally, while the desire of the leadership team to take the time to discuss the future strategy of the combined company was understandable, this was at odds with the needs of employees to hear something 'right now'. As a result communicators found themselves 'filling the gap' with leadership profiles and statements about the positive future for the company without having specific and tangible plans of action to support their messages.

Using regular research to track progress

To ensure recommendations were based on facts and data rather than instinct, communicators instigated a company-wide employee survey, which was repeated twice more during the year of integration.

When Deutsche Bank acquired Bankers Trust in 1999, it conducted a study into employee perceptions of the acquisition in order to develop a targeted communications strategy. Similarly Nycomed and Altana's employee survey was intended to provide useful baseline data from which to shape a communication strategy. The earliest opportunity was taken to survey the organization in February 2007, with repeats in June 2007 and 2008.

The employee surveys showed that the messages were getting through. In the first wave alone (February 2007, one month after completion of the deal) 69 percent of employees said they understood the reasons for the deal (81 percent in legacy Nycomed, 67 percent in legacy Altana). In the ex-Altana organization, this level of understanding went down in the second wave of the survey (June 2007) largely as a negative reactive to the scale of restructuring announced in May 2007.

As a direct result of the first survey, the new company strategy and organizational charts were shared with employees soon after the deal. The surveys also revealed that line managers were very willing to fulfill their roles as communicators but were unsure of what to say. There were a lot of rumours and in the absence of line manager briefings, employees were turning to the external media for information. All of this input shaped and reshaped the communication approach and, among other things, led to Nycomed and Altana retiring the legacy company communication channels and replacing them with new ones. They also placed much greater emphasis on supplying line managers with what they needed to say. Cascade slide packs, supporting scripts and manager briefings were provided ahead of major announcements with key messages developed for different audiences facing different situations.

The Nycomed and Altana case illustrates the importance of understanding the different perspectives of different audiences and engaging the leadership team in articulating key messages explaining how different parts of the global organizations would be affected.

In one global organization, the global IT leadership team had decided what the key messages of their expensive and extensive IT transformation program ought to be:

- world class operating efficiency and project management;

- clear accountabilities between in-house IT business partners, and third party support partners;

- efficient IT at the lowest cost to the business;

- the phased introduction of a common operating environment.

They then identified a number of different audiences they were trying to address:

- The business leadership team of the organization – they wanted them to see the IT function as dynamic, keen to take action, taking a global approach and following best practice.

- Their own IT community – who they wanted to galvanize, and engage more directly in acting as business partners to the organization, and to work with third party suppliers to do the lower value support work.

- Third party suppliers – who they wanted to feel full partners, fairly treated and clearly instructed.

- IT users – the majority of employees in the company, who they wanted to feel were getting a reliable, quality service, at a lower cost to the business.

2. Set communication objectives

Having identified your audiences, you should describe what you need from them for your initiative to succeed. This involves describing the outcomes you need from each audience in terms of what you want people to think, feel and do as a result of communication. For each group you should add a 'by when' date, linked to the milestones in your project plan.

Looking at the employees who use IT's services, you might list what you want them to think, feel and do as:

- understand that we need to reduce the overall cost of IT to the business;

- be supportive of our outsourcing of IT to third parties;

- feel confident in the support they will get from offshored help desks;

- appreciate the decisive action being taken by IT leadership;

- balance their frustration at lower service with an understanding of low cost to the business;

- feel proud to work for an organization which is following global standards and leading edge practices.

3. Select the communication approach

Different initiatives need to be communicated in different ways. For example, the way in which a redundancy programme is communicated would be very different from letting people know about a change to the car policy.

The communication of change in initiatives is often not a mass communication issue. It is more important to enrol managers who have to make things happen. Although most people should be kept informed of the likely implications, the successful communication of change initiatives depends on the successive enrolment of tiers of management, so that communication ripples, rather than rolls, out. Some organizations that have communicated directly to the workforce have found enthused employees returning to their managers with questions the manager cannot answer.

Use both 'push' and 'pull' 'Push' is the favourable momentum created by senior managers, executives and key influencers. 'Pull' means the demand created by end-users who regard the change as something which can help them both professionally and personally. Key to achieving push is getting key players to buy-in, commit to and sponsor the initiative. Creating pull depends on marketing the process so that it emphasizes benefits to users.

Impact must be measured so that senior managers can track progress and 'push' where necessary, and also to allow the target audiences to see the benefit of the initiative, thus creating more demand and 'pull'. However, the initiative will only be 'pushed' by senior executives if they see it as a solution to one of the problems at the top of their business agenda. This means finding the key business issues concerning senior executives, and demonstrating a clear link between them and the initiative.

Avoid staging a big launch followed by a sustained silence and few updates on developments. Avoid also the communication of an apparently complex programme; it needs to be simple and memorable. If you create an umbrella brand for change or improvement programmes, ensure component initiatives are sub-branded as members of the same family. This will create consistency and continuity as new elements are introduced, and flag a clear link between individual initiatives.

As well as formal channels of communication, look to the informal. A communication plan outlines the target audiences, issues, messages and the best match of media to objective. There is another side, however, to the equation – identifying which people are best placed to present communication and be involved in the face-to-face sessions. Given the power of informal communication and networking, communicators need to know who are the influencers and credible communicators who could be likely ambassadors for change for each stage of the project.

At each stage of a project – from initial concept to implementation – different people have different levels of credibility and relevance. At the initial concept stage, the leader is respected and believed for creating the vision and setting the direction. At the scoping and planning stage, credibility is given to the more technical expert who understands some of the implications of the change, has some track record in making change happen, and combines both the will to push change through and the understanding to manage the implications. At implementation people are looking for their colleague, or a local authority, to be able to talk to them about the specifics of what they are likely to encounter at their desks or during their working shifts.

Avoid acronyms   What you call your initiative is important. Employees' complaints about initiative overload are as much a reflection of meaning underload. Employees report feeling deluged with an alphabet soup of three-letter acronyms. Selecting a three-word name for an initiative is a recipe for confusion. An initiative called, for example, 'Customer Improvement Initiative', is immediately collapsed into the shorthand of CII which goes into the alphabet soup with all the other three-letter acronyms.

Corporate identity experts always counsel companies when they change their name not to adopt three letters, such as ICI or IBM, because you either have to be very famous or spend a great deal of money explaining to people what those initials mean.

In one organization where employees reported confusion, some helpful soul compiled a glossary of three-letter acronyms which ran to 13 pages. This did not help; it merely highlighted the extent of the problem. However, the real problem is not the need for a glossary of three-letter acronyms; it's that acronyms convey little meaning. Managers trade three-letter acronyms, either pretending that they know what they mean, or genuinely knowing what they mean, but using them as terms which exclude the uninitiated. Then employees start guessing what the three letters actually stand for. One organization which had an initiative with the three-letter acronym 'ITP' ran an open competition about alternative meanings. While ITP actually stood for 'Innovation Through People', the favourite alternative meaning was 'Indiscriminate Termination of People'.

It is far better to choose a single word which is memorable and gives some sense of what the initiative is about. East of Scotland Water, for example, has a management development programme for their managers in the water industry. They call it 'Causeway', which gives some sense of a development path across water. Similarly Axa Sun Life's post-merger process for bringing together and uniting two disparate organizations was called 'Fusion'. This gives some sense of two things being bonded together, and gives you a clue as to what this initiative is about. While choosing a single word for an initiative reduces acronym confusion, you still have to choose carefully. One organization named its restructuring project with the biblically inspired 'Genesis', which brought the office wag's warning, 'After Genesis comes Exodus!'

In an attempt to increase clarity further, some organizations have turned to using the branding principles applied to their external communication for their internal communication. The perception of initiative overload can be a direct result of not thinking through the branding and sub-branding issues, or explaining the inter-relationship between different initiatives and their relative importance.

Brand guidelines and architecture are useful in external communication. They aim to explain the hierarchy and inter-relationships of different products, and between brands and the organizations which own them. Brand disciplines are increasingly applied to initiative communication, since they are some of the few available tools for creating context and clarity amid complexity. They do, however, require discipline, which is often lacking in managers who would never risk messing with their company's brand image in the marketplace, but who believe they are gifted enough to turn their hand to communication inside the organization.

4. Develop key messages and themes

Organizations can become too focused on their communication channels. Clearly it is important to have the right mix of appropriate channels, and to investigate new technologies for ways of reaching people more effectively.

However, a constant curse of internal communication is the low quality of the content that is communicated.

If communication channels are the armoury of the communicator, good messages are the ammunition. Unfortunately, people are bombarded by messages from all directions. Competition for their time and attention is increasing, so it is vital to be clear why you're communicating, and to make messages memorable so they stick.

Internal communicators get involved with messaging in a number of different ways:

- **Creation** – for example, working with the management team, or a project team, to help them crystallize their thinking and articulate their messages.

- **Localization** – where communicators in a division or business unit receive financial results and key messages from the corporate centre, which they have to localize and make relevant to their part of the business.

- **Unpacking** – where a site management team is developing messages to communicate to the site workforce, and the communicator helps them to identify the implications for, and impact on, different audiences who have different concerns.

- **Condensing** – where the long versions of messages for initiatives, campaign or projects need to be boiled down to simple, repeatable and memorable messages.

Internal communication tends to be 'sender driven'. Communication is created and sent to suit the convenience and the agenda of the sender, rather than the receiver. Senders are often so focused on their own agenda that they do not look at things from their audiences' viewpoint. They become obsessed with what it is they want to say, rather than trying to understand what the audience is likely to hear.

One of the key skills the internal communicator should bring to the table is being an expert on the audience, seeing things from their viewpoint and anticipating how they will interpret communication. Looking at things from the audiences' point of view should change how you articulate your message, and how you define the outcome you want.

To develop the key messages for your initiative you need to understand what behaviours and attitudes you need from people and their current perceptions of your initiative.

Identify where audiences currently are, where they need to be and by what date. This gives you the rate at which the gap between the current and desired states must be closed.

Even if people currently know nothing about your initiative, that does not mean they will listen to you neutrally. People will bring their own preconceptions to bear on whatever you have to say, so consider how they might react.

In addition to identifying what outcome you need from each key audience, identify the information each audience will need. This is likely to include the background to the initiative, its objectives and timescale, the rationale for the change and how it is likely to affect customers, suppliers and staff.

Messages should go beyond creating awareness to specifying what action employees need to take, as well as how they can get further information now, and what other information they can expect and by when. Motivating employees demands a realistic playback of their preoccupations. Messages must speak to their recipients' concerns and preoccupations, and present information from their viewpoint. Use 'hooks' – motivating, attention-getting statements which introduce the project in terms of the audience's need. Hooks are links between an individual's own agenda and the solution offered by the project or initiative. Different hooks need to be developed for each key audience.

Weed out the management-speak   When employees are on the lookout for a hidden agenda, they can view management-speak as a cover for some terrible surprise. Every additional example of management-speak in communication merely compounds that impression. Do not allow anyone to send anything out without having another pair of eyes review it, to guard against management-speak as well as misplaced assumptions about what employees already know or understand.

Research people's issues   Where there is a diverse range of audiences, the needs and concerns of each audience must be clearly understood, and addressed. Often communicators automatically assume that they already know what the issues and concerns are. It is often not information that managers lack, but perspective. They are willing to believe that employees will have substantial and serious worries, but are shocked to discover petty, but no less strongly held, concerns.

Initial research should be undertaken to identify the likely audiences' issues and reactions. This will allow planners to work out what the best outcomes for each audience group are, to identify what the key messages are and therefore to be able to track whether those outcomes have actually been achieved.

The Automobile Association wanted to introduce customer-driven rostering – basically a change to flexible working hours in order to be more available when customers needed help at the roadside. The organization declared that it would not introduce change before everyone affected had an opportunity to discuss the proposals and to fully understand the implications. The main benefit of its approach was that it communicated a proposal rather than announcing a fait accompli. There was still room for debate, and the purpose of communication meetings was to get reactions so that necessary amendments could be made to the proposal.

A further, and largely unforeseen, benefit was the extent to which, given the opportunity, employees discussed and fed back the detailed impact of the proposals on their day-to-day working and personal lives. What most concerned one individual was not the detail of the proposals but his realization that, with his friends on flexible rostering, getting them all together for their usual weekly football match could be impossible. For another, the concern was how would he be able to predict his regular finishing time so that his wife would know when to have his dinner ready? For yet another, the question was when would there be any quiet time, which could be used for cleaning their vans and organizing their tools?

This highlights the fact that, however well prepared the presenters of the proposal were, their audiences were preoccupied with very different issues, many of which were individual and personal, and often unpredictable. Early research before making presentations helps reduce unpredictability and allows communication to be more targeted and more specific about the 'What's in it for me?' for different audiences.

The global IT leadership team mentioned earlier began looking at the issues from their different audiences' viewpoints, which made them realize some of the dilemmas they were facing. The IT leadership team asked themselves the key question, 'What are the barriers to our various audiences thinking, feeling and doing what we'd like them to?'

The business's leadership team, for example, did, as hoped, see them as dynamic and leading edge – but that impression was being steadily undermined by persistent complaints about poor service from IT that were percolating up from employees. Changes to IT were being driven largely by the organization's need to reduce the unit cost of IT, which, like all the other functions in the organization, was being required to reduce costs substantially. The IT leadership team had enthusiastically shouldered their share of the organization's overall cost reduction target. While the IT leadership team understood the necessary balance between cost and service, they were being pressed to reduce cost by leaders who did not understand the likely impact on service. They were then not ready for the poor internal publicity that the reduction of IT service created.

Employees perceived that they were now getting a worse service than before. Their day-to-day technical support contact had been outsourced to regional support centres, so they missed the personal contact they had before. The help desk had been moved to India, and poor communication from the help desk was exacerbating users' frustration at the slow pace of getting their problems resolved.

The IT leadership team realized that their key messages were aimed upwards at their bosses. Any messages to employees would be filtered through deep scepticism and resentment about reduced quality of service.

The leadership team realized that they would have to start addressing their communication more directly to their users. Improving users' perceptions would result in better 'word of mouth' that would quickly feed back up to the business's leaders and reassure them. It would then, in turn get them to understand that cost reduction had to be balanced with maintaining a quality service.

Revisiting their key messages in the light of their new understanding of their audiences, the IT leadership team identified what messages they should be focusing on for their users:

- best balance between cost and service;

- the need to change processes to provide better service;

- users need to work differently with the help desk to prioritize the most important problems to fix.

Employees often do not see the connection between different messages about different initiatives, nor do they understand the implications of some of the things they have been told.

They receive one message about the organization intending to become truly global. Later, the IT department announces the launch of a 'unified computing environment'. Finally, the help desk e-mails them to say the server will be down for several days. These three messages are linked – but the links are invisible, to employees lost in the stream of separate, apparently random messages arriving.

Ironically, the organization's commitment to being truly global is demonstrated by its investment in IT developing a common operating environment. The consequence of this development is that the server will need to be taken down to make necessary upgrades.

Making these connections is not rocket science, but it does require a little bit of time and thought. A key part of messaging is being able to make the connection between information and its implication for different audiences. It's also vital to make the connection between assertions, and evidence of those assertions.

Sales people are paid to make these connections for their customers. They will have been trained in the simple process of FAB – Feature, Advantage, Benefit. This means that they will be able to present the characteristic of the product they are selling, explain the advantage that this brings and then underline the implications and the benefits for their particular customer.

Making the connecting between feature, advantage and benefits helps the customer take the right action. Presenting a customer with technical detail, which seems to have some significance only to the sales person, leaves the customer confused rather than motivated to buy.

The lack of these connections is one of the reasons why employees often say they are confused by unsupported assertions from their organizations. They either don't quite understand what they have been told, because the implications aren't clear, or they can see no evidence for the assertions being made.

Marketers and sales people know that they have to provide evidence for the assertions they are making, and be able to point out the implication for their customers. Internal communicators need to adopt the same discipline.

Volvo provides a good example of making the connections, when they emphasize their key brand attribute of safety.

They make the assertion, 'Safety is built in from the very start.' This, they explain, is shown by the fact that Volvo installs a unique side impact protection system (SIPS).

This system has the advantage that in a collision, SIPS dissipates a large part of the force that would otherwise penetrate through the body of the car. The benefit is that in 25 per cent of severe accidents, where the cars are hit from the side, Volvo gives you much greater protection.

Volvo provides an assertion, supporting evidence and the implications.

Adopting this simple approach to messaging for internal communication means that messages are more thought through. Message creators are forced to provide illustrations or evidence of their assertions and they have to explain the implications they think it will have for different audiences.

Table 7.1 shows how this works for an organization.

This framework allows communicators in divisions and units to take corporate messages, identify evidence to support them, and then make the connections to what it will mean for their part of the business.

Table 7.1   **Connecting assertions, evidence and implications**

Message	As shown by...	Which means that...
We'll be market leader in the next 3 years.	Our current rate of growth, the successful integration of our recent acquisition and the rate of new products being developed and launched.	For R&D, we will be investing more heavily, and will need to be better at identifying likely successes earlier in the process. For Marketing, we will be able to focus on our global brands, and will need to stop investing in peripheral products. For Operations, we will need to adopt common global processes and get good systems in place now before we are over-stretched.
We will take a more systematic approach across regions and reduce expensive inconsistency.	Our adopting a single approach to core processes rather than a country-by-country approach, the successful adoption of the new business planning process and the creation of cross regional process teams.	We have to be ready to adopt the processes that are 'not invented here', we have to be clearer about investing in areas which will give us good ROI, and we have to be willing to kill off those projects which are not vital.
We will work together more closely across the business to generate more revenue.	The successful cross-regional collaboration on key customer accounts, the successful introduction of the new Customer Relationship Management process, the creation of more profitable 'hybrid' products.	We will be working more often together in cross-functional teams, key account leaders will be asking for a greater share of managers' time, products will be examined for their individual profitability and we will adopt new ways of identifying where revenue is coming from, and ways to share the credit.

5. Match communication vehicles to your approach

Different communication processes achieve different objectives. If you are aiming to communicate with some audiences to create awareness and understanding, you may be able to use existing communication channels.

The most commonly used communication channels include e-mail, Intranet, newsletters, team briefings, notice boards and video. These are geared towards creating awareness and understanding. What the organization usually wants from its people is involvement and commitment, so extra time may need to be invested in creating additional communication channels that will deliver these objectives.

The more the organization needs an employee to move from awareness to commitment, the more face-to-face communication is needed and the more time is involved. If all the organization wants is awareness and understanding, the focus should be on the quality and the efficient distribution of information. If the requirement from employees is towards involvement and commitment, communication needs to concentrate on improving the quality of the relationships and interaction between people.

Figure 7.2 shows the 'communication escalator', showing how employees can be moved from awareness to commitment using different communication channels. The following are a range of different communication objectives with the communication channels which can best help achieve them.

Awareness   Means of creating awareness will range from the corporate identity, press coverage, announcements on the bulletin board, internal and external advertising campaigns to payslip inserts, memos, continuous strip displays, SMS text message, direct mail and employee annual reports. They may also include video, Blackberry bulletins, voicemail and e-mail. The focus of most channels like these is on the one-way distribution of information to a passive audience.

Understanding   The shift from awareness to understanding needs feedback and additional information, tailored to the needs of a more closely defined group of people. Communication is more interactive, and seeks feedback to check for understanding.

Communication vehicles could include management conferences, road shows, satellite broadcasting, web-casting, video-conferencing, teleconferencing and feedback forums. All of these allow more dialogue and more interaction.

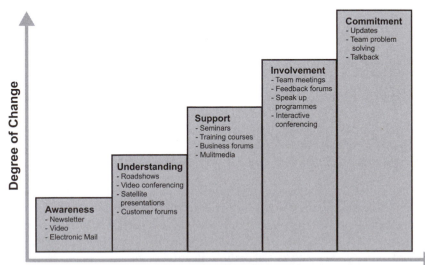

Figure 7.2   Communication Escalator

Support   Creating support involves a significant shift in interaction. The aim is to elicit acceptance, if not of the change itself, then of the need for, and the rationale behind it. Employees may not like what is happening but they can accept why it is happening and support the logic.

Support can be created through strategy forums, training events and seminars. Presentations will be less formal, with continual discussion rather than set question-and-answer periods.

Involvement   The aim here is as much to encourage employees to share their pre-existing reactions, concerns and objections, as it is to inform them about management thinking. There will be more of a dialogue – sharing thinking, assessing implications, exploring alternatives and reviewing the best means of implementation. Here, the focus is more on listening.

Commitment   Commitment comes from a sense of ownership, and ownership comes from having participated in the process.

Gaining commitment entails a high degree of talking through the pressures affecting the business and reviewing possible competitive scenarios and strategic options. The high levels of interaction and participation needed mean that this is a process that takes a good deal of time.

6. Measure the outcome

The final step in the communication plan is measurement. Impact can only be assessed if you know what to measure, so make sure that you identify observable outcomes and behaviours for each key audience.

Measure the changes in the level of your audiences' understanding and their recall and understanding of your key messages. Also, assess which channels were the most effective in getting the messages across.

Measuring impact and tracking results are discussed further in Chapter 10.

PLAN FOR THE UNEXPECTED

Finally, however good the communication plan, there are bound to be unexpected developments, unresolved issues and unexpected debate about how best to respond to employees' questions. Project communicators need to be in regular contact with each other and with colleagues responsible for communication across the business. They should be feeding back to each other on issues that are being raised and setting dates by which these issues need to have been resolved.

Sometimes a project or initiative can entail significant changes that mean bad news for some employees.

COMMUNICATING BAD NEWS

Andy Grove, one of the co-founders of Intel Corporation, gave sound advice when he said, 'The worse the news, the more effort should go into communicating it.'

This section looks at the issues surrounding communicating bad news, how people react to change and an approach to communicating bad news.

While bad news for an organization can mean the multimillion pound pay-off of a departing chief executive, bad news usually means bad news for employees. However, there's a wide range of different types of bad news:

- Closures – where particular locations, branches or plants are closed down.

- Head count reductions, right sizing and lay offs – where the number of people in the work force are reduced, redistributed, transferred or outsourced.

- Down turn – where there is a down turn in the market, an increase in competition or stagnation in the economy.

- Cancellation of orders or projects, a loss of clients or key accounts – usually with negative implications for people who have been working on them, or have expected to work on them.

- Resignations, particularly for senior management – or firings of senior management for poor performance, lack of cultural fit or unacceptable behaviour.

With all these different types of bad news come a wide range of issues:

- Uncertainty – not all the details are clear and it's not even clear when they will be. There's no agreed version of events, and issues which may affect the organization are outside its control.

- Confidentiality – there is material information which cannot be disclosed, either because of agreement with commercial third parties, or because there's a strict sequence of information and consultation as with unions, works councils, shareholders and regulators.

- Timing – there are interdependencies with other plans, a clash of timing with other changes, or there's a need to consult with different stakeholders in sequence, which means uncertainty is likely to continue for some time.

- Leaks – grapevines are not only very active, they can be very accurate. With the rise of industry chat sites, and the extension of the grapevine from the water cooler to e-mail and chat room, the likelihood of keeping something quiet for too long is low.

- Divisiveness – some employees are likely to be more affected than others, and as rumours spread, employees can rapidly divide into different camps, with different views and very different emotional reactions.

Dealing with such complex and emotionally charged situations cannot be done with a 'one size fits all' approach. However, the following section offers nine areas to consider when communicating bad news.

Build your radar

There are some changes which hit organizations which are unpredictable and unexpected. The majority, however, have usually been within the organization's control, and in the works for some time. Organizations often make it harder for themselves by waiting until they think they have something to communicate, before starting to think how they will communicate.

This is almost always a mistake.

The key first step is to build a radar of what changes are coming, and even if they're only possibilities, what's the probability that they will actually happen?

The 'radar' may simply be a list of possible initiatives, regulatory changes and possible restructurings. The point is to get out ahead of simply being the victim of circumstance and to develop scenarios about what might happen. This is something organizations tend to do with crisis preparedness, issue management and disaster recovery. They need only apply the same disciplines to the forward planning of internal communication.

It's useful to have a forward view of different initiative and likely impacts, and the inter-relationship between those initiatives – what happens for example if there's a regulatory change requiring more detailed work and more robust processes, at precisely the time we're thinking of downsizing?

The 'radar' should also give you some idea for each initiatives of who's going to be affected and how? How might those different parts of the organization react? As well as providing some sensible forward planning, this usually forces senior managers to put themselves in the shoes of audiences and see it from their point of view which is itself a useful discipline.

Planning

Organizations often wait until everything is clear before wanting to communicate. When there is a great deal of uncertainty about what is happening or what may happen, this is a luxury few organizations can afford. If you wait until everything is clear, you'll probably be too late. It is better to begin communicating as soon as you can, and to be proactive rather than find yourself reacting to rumour.

There is always something to communicate. Bad news doesn't spring out of nowhere. It is the consequence of a series of earlier decisions. Even when you don't know where things are going to end up, you can start communicating how they started, how the organization has started to respond to them and the likely criteria for decision making and options.

If you communicate early, you'll retain the initiative and build your credibility. Reactive communication is usually defensive and apologetic, and hands the initiative for communication to third parties.

Therefore, once you've built a full view of what is likely to affect your organization over the coming 18 months, it is important to have a sound internal communication plan that identifies issues, likely impact on audiences and communication plans for addressing it.

It doesn't matter that some of these may never be implemented. Organizations should be reviewing their communication plan at least quarterly to update likely factors affecting them and to revisit their scenario planning.

As part of the planning process, organizations also need to think through what communication process they will actually use to get to their people should they need to. If there's likely to be a sudden announcement about a merger, for example, does the organization have a 'flash' communication channel – by e-mail, voicemail cascade or SMS text message which can help them get to their people rapidly?

Conversely, if there is going to be a controversial and difficult ruling by a regulator, do we have the face-to-face forums to enable senior managers to explain the intricacies of the issues, to provide the bigger picture and to give their people the story behind the story?

Mapping your audiences

In any change, communicators need to think through their different audiences, both internal and external. External audiences affected by any particular change will include:

- customers
- suppliers
- prospects
- shareholders
- pensioners
- future employees
- stakeholders.

Internally, employees need to be segmented not just by grade and role or location, but by how the likely change will affect them.

Communicators have to think through how many employees will be affected and what proportion of the work force that represents. Often the scale of change gets lost in reaction to a change. What can look like a cataclysm to employees in a local plant, which represents a small proportion of the organization, may be of far less concern to the rest of the workforce.

It's also important to look at what options and alternatives employees have. For example, the shut down of a plant in a hot labour market where there's no problem getting another job is clearly less of an issue than closing a location on which the local community depends heavily.

Similarly, organizations which have had significant head count reduction may feel that after the initial pain they can continue with the survivors in a positive direction. However, in some cases, existing employees have former colleagues for neighbours, so while employees disappear off the organization's radar screen, they're all still present at the neighbourhood barbeques.

Employees who keep their jobs don't always feel the unqualified gratitude their bosses think they should. They're often affected by 'survivor syndrome', the guilt of having escaped while colleagues have lost their jobs.

It's important to identify which audiences have different likely reactions and needs in order to identify how best to communicate with them.

When organizations are under time pressure, it's best to put their time and attention in where it's going to have the greatest impact, and where there's the greatest need. This is usually with employees who are going to be most affected by changes, and are most concerned about the impact on them.

For employees who are less affected, who are virtually spectators on changes affecting other parts of the organization, there may be less immediate need to put a lot of time and effort into them – unless their very detachment is likely to be a problem in the future.

In one organization that was merging its global operations, mapping its various employees and locations on this grid highlighted three key employee audiences:

- Head office staff who were concerned – and rightly so – that they would lose their jobs when head office functions were merged. This was an audience group you could predict would be concerned. What might not have been predicted were the other two:

- Employees in locations that duplicated each other – where both of the parties merging had sites. They believed that their jobs were at risk when, in fact, part of the merger was actually to get more critical mass in some of these locations. They were therefore concerned unnecessarily, and wasted time worrying with each other when there was no need.

- Salespeople in regional offices, who saw themselves as the backbone of the new organization. In fact, theirs was a product area which the business was going to drop as part of their future strategy. They were not concerned, but were living in a fool's paradise, and were, from the organization's point of view, 'fat and happy'.

- A further group at a small production site saw the merger as a good thing. They felt unthreatened because they did not have new colleagues located in their neck of the woods competing for jobs. They felt that life would continue much as before, but with a brighter future. They were not unduly concerned, and didn't need to be.

Mapping employees out in this way gave the merged organization a clearer direction to take in communicating with its people.

The chief executive put his time into face-to-face sessions with head office staff. The emphasis here was on engagement – making the sessions relatively small for the greatest degree of interaction, encouraging people to ask questions and giving them as much information as possible to help them understand the change and the likely implications for their jobs.

Senior management put their time into these sessions because they wanted to signal their commitment to the merger, and their respect for those employees who are going to be most affected by it.

For this audience, the best communication channel was face-to-face. At the end of each session, a summary of the likely changes and the implications on areas such as pensions was produced. This was distributed so that people could go away and reflect on their future options and begin to plan for their own futures.

For those employees who had wrongly been concerned, line manager cascades were used to give them the right information and to reassure them that their future was secure.

Although face-to-face communication was used, had time and resources been more limited, reassurance could have been given by arms length channels such as e-mail, Intranet or even bulletin boards.

Similarly, for those audiences for whom there was little immediate direct impact, and who simply needed to get information about the changes, media such as newsletter, Intranet and e-mail were used effectively.

However, for the employees who were 'fat and happy' – unconcerned when they should be – face-to-face communication was used. It was important to be able to paint the broader picture of change in the organization, to unpack the implications of the strategic move to new products, with the likely impact on locations and jobs. It was important to use face-to-face communication, because as soon as people realized what the future might hold, their emotional shift from secure confidence to anxious resentment meant the sessions became more emotionally charged, and people wanted a broader range of questions answered.

In effect, running face-to-face sessions with the 'wake up' group shifted them into the 'engage' box – people who were now concerned and rightly so.

Method of communication

As the preceding section shows, it's vital to get the right kind of communication channels used to get to the right audience. When communicating bad news, there's likely to be a greater range of emotional reactions, and greater potential of damage to the trust between the leaders and their people, and credibility of the leadership team.

Therefore, there are some simple rules to use when choosing methods for communicating bad news.

Make face-to-face communication the main channel. While this puts managers under greater pressure to deal with emotional reactions, the very fact of leaders being brave enough to 'face the music' creates greater trust in them. Communicating live is higher risk, but it means the leaders can get rapid feedback to what they're saying, and allows them to correct any misconceptions.

Face-to-face communication isn't always possible. There are problems of geographically scattered employees, different time zones and having to synchronize internal communication with external communication – especially where information is share price sensitive.

Where face-to-face channels aren't possible, the next best is at least a 'live' channel. This means using the telephone, video-conference, teleconference, dial-in audio or radio – any channel that allows people to hear the message directly from the horse's mouth at the same time.

In communicating bad news, any organization has to assume that information will leak. While being open and honest with employees, and asking them to respect confidentiality often reduces leaks in organizations, they won't be eradicated.

It's a healthy assumption that written materials, whether in print or e-mail, will find their way to interested third parties.

Avoid, if possible, using e-mail, voicemail or fax to communicate sensitive information which will have an impact on people – not because that information might leak, but rather because of what it says about your respect for the people you're communicating with. The apparent insensitivity of an employer in making their people redundant can be compounded by the communication channel used. News stories are rarely about people being fired – but they're often about the means used to do it – such as firing employees by fax and texting them their termination.

Roles

Since stakeholder's sensitivities means communicating bad news is often high risk, it's important to have agreed clear roles – who is saying what to which audience, and when?

- What is it that leaders are going to say, and which audience will they address and when? Who will cover the different issues – financial, structural, HR, community impact?

- What is the role of managers? – can they follow on from the leader's communication by telling their own people what the likely impacts and implications are in their area?

- Employee association or union representatives – who will they talk to, how and when? How will their communication fit with the leadership's line? How will they provide independent information for their members?

- What's the role of supervisors – can they communicate successive waves of information and act both as a sounding board and as a feedback channel for their people's concerns?

Timing

The sooner organizations begin to plan at the first sign of trouble, the more room they'll have for manoeuvre. However, even the best plan may not survive contact with reality.

Timing is a key issue of planning. Who the organization tells first says a lot to employees. Will employees learn, for example, about the bad news in the newspapers or from their supervisors?

- Senior managers responsible for making change in delicate areas – such as site closures – can be tempted to hold on as long as possible before communicating. Instead it is better to identify the earliest point that people can be told.

- If you don't know what's going to happen specifically in the future, it is possible to communicate what may happen in terms of probabilities and scenarios. Employees appreciate it when their leaders communicate as much as they can, as soon as they can.

In one telecoms organization, for example, there was the likelihood that the business would be divested and sold off. Senior managers did not know who the eventual buyer would be. It rapidly became known to employees that their organization was in play and speculation was rife on the grapevine. Senior people in the organization who were likely to be affected began asking questions about their pension provisions, sales people started talking to competitors about possible jobs.

The leadership team was keen to start communicating, but had little concrete information to communicate.

Instead, they communicated what the process was likely to be for a sale. How bidders would be identified, what due diligence they would undertake, how they would tour and inspect the business and how the successful party might be selected.

Although they didn't know the names of actual bidders, they communicated who might interested, and for what reasons. A European competitor might acquire them in order to get economies of scale to share back office systems and to reduce the cost base. A US based telecoms company might acquire them in order to give them a launching pad into the European market. A private equity firm might be interested because they could see ways of increasing efficiencies, getting greater penetration of customer base and increasing margins.

The important thing about this approach is that it tackled the speculation rife on the grapevine. Senior managers channelled the corridor and water cooler conversations into face-to-face meetings where people could raise their questions and concerns. They got the fullest answers possible at the time – and the commitment to give more information as soon as it became available.

Employees appreciated particularly that their leaders gave the timescale for the sale and, where they could not yet be specific, there was a date given when they could be.

This put the leadership back into the discussions with their employees and allowed them to regain the initiative from the grapevine.

Be clear what the bad news is

In communicating bad news, managers often shy away from being clear. The straight facts of closure, downsizing and redundancy can be painful for managers, who then use abstract management-speak to soften the blow and conceal their blushes.

Employees cannot answer the question 'What does it mean for me?' if they are not clear what the 'it' actually is. Therefore, in communicating bad news, it's important to describe the news in a clear and straightforward manner.

Employees need first to understand the 'what', and then they need to understand the 'why'. Therefore, you have to explain why the action is being taken, what is the problem to which the action is a solution, and what is the urgency to take action.

Then, you have to explain the rationale for the decision, how the decision was made, who made it and what process was used to arrive at it.

You have to describe the effort that went into the decision, outlining some of the alternatives that were considered, the options that were reviewed and the means by which they were assessed and rejected.

Finally, you have to explain how the decision that has been reached is as fair to as many groups as possible, and then describe what happens next.

Getting that degree of clarity is not that easy when there are, often, a number of people involved in the process. It is often difficult to get a clear agreement on the rationale for decisions, often because they are taken by a team of leaders, each of whom has a different priority and a slightly different agenda. They can therefore believe that there is an 'official' reason for the decision, and a real reason for the decision.

This makes them cautious about how they phrase and communicate the 'official' reason, lest they inadvertently reveal the true reason. It's important therefore to have an approval process for messages, which involves the whole leadership team – ideally together in the same place at the same time. Otherwise, there is a round robin of draft correction, with each successive leader amending the changes of the leader before.

It's obviously important to integrate messages which are going internally with those that are going externally. If the messages are different, because they have come from different departments who want to put different spins on the message, employees will want to know which is correct and which isn't – otherwise they simply disbelieve both.

It's important to 'stress test' the messages. Get senior managers in a room, and get them to pull the messages apart, question them, challenge them and adopt the most negative counterview they can think of.

If senior managers are uncomfortable in this exercise, because they feel it's being unduly negative, they'd do well to remember the negative impact of the grapevine. It is often the case that the grapevine spreads as gospel truth the worst alternative that management has ever considered. Organizations often start with a 'worst case' scenario, simply to shock leaders into confronting difficult situations. However, it is often that shocker that has the most impact, taking on a life of its own as it is spread by the grapevine. One of the reasons that there are employees who are 'concerned and need not be' is that they're the ones who first believe what the grapevine is telling them.

Preparation

While getting the message clear is important, just as important is preparing those people who are going to communicate. The most overlooked audiences are managers involved in communicating and handling employees' responses.

The more senior the communicators, the more they will feel they are already good at communicating. However, it's important to get senior people in the same room hearing what each other is saying, particularly in response to questions. While senior people can read the same bullet points from the same PowerPoint slides, inconsistency starts when they start giving different responses to the same questions.

The key issue in communicating bad news isn't how well you can present, it's the leaders' ability to listen, connect with and engage with their people. What's most important is to get people to say what they think rather than harbouring what are often unfounded suspicions.

Making employees feel comfortable, valued and listened to encourages that kind of disclosure. Under pressure, senior managers can revert to using the power of their status to shut down awkward questions, or, worse, to use their media training techniques to dodge the underlying question.

Delivery

If you're going to use face-to-face communication as the main channel, it's important to plan a clear sequence of who is talking to whom and when. It's useful to assume that those who have been briefed first will call up all their friends in their personal network and spread the news. Therefore, it's worth planning for the fact that different audience groups will start the meeting at different stages – the first group may know nothing, the fourth group may know the basic outlines and the rationale for the changes, the twelfth group may want to get straight to questions about, for example, the impact on their pensions.

Involve senior managers in delivering the message. Using a cascade to communicate bad news is playing to the greatest weaknesses of the cascade – using managers who may themselves not yet know how the changes will affect them.

Who communicates the change says a lot about how much the organization cares for its employees. While local managers are useful for translating the big picture messages into local implications, employees usually want to see a senior person explain the rationale for the change and be willing to take reactions on the chin.

The lack of senior management involvement, on the other hand, tends to raise questions about control, responsibility and leadership amongst employees. Do more junior managers really know what's going on? Can they really speak with the authority of the organization, or are they themselves next to go?

A useful sequence is to tell managers and supervisors first so they have some time to prepare themselves to talk to their own people. The most affected employees are then told next.

In one organization, there was some bad news to be communicated. One product line had not been very successful, and although it had been on site for a long time, the factory was going to be closed down. The factory was co-located with a number of other factories producing other products for the same organization.

Mapping the different audiences showed that, unsurprisingly, one factory was deeply concerned and should be, and that's where communication efforts should be focused for the future.

Their neighbouring factories would be concerned, because the closure of their neighbour might signal a problem with the organization as a whole. They therefore duly got their reassurance, and a picture painted of the bright future of the organization and their factory in particular.

However, one issue on the radar had not been spotted. While one factory was being closed down, another new factory was to be opened with state-of-the-art equipment which would focus on those international markets promising the greatest growth for the future.

In the event, the senior management decided not to put too much effort into communicating with and engaging with workers in the factory they were closing. After all, the redundant employees would be gone, so it did not seem worthwhile to invest leadership time.

However, shortly before the communication – or lack of it – began, there was a review of the initiative radar. Looking at the future opening of the brand new factory, the question was raised, 'Where would they hire new operators?'

HR said the best place to hire people from was the factory they were closing down. The most disillusioned and annoyed people were about to be transferred to the new factory as the guardians of the organization's new future hope.

This led to a quick recalculation of where time could be best invested – and a greater communication effort in the closure of the old factory.

In summary, managers being asked to communicate bad news need to be:

- Clear about the message they are being asked to communicate – do they know what it is, and can they describe the key messages clearly, succinctly and memorably?

- Comfortable with the rationale – do they understand why we have been driven to take this action, what other options we've considered, how we reviewed those options and why we've identified this course of action as the right one?

- Prepared for the meeting – they've put time into understanding the overall communication, they can explain how it relates to their people, they can anticipate the questions they are likely to get and they're happy that the answers they give are in line with the rest of the organization's communication.

- They've 'stress tested' the message – they've looked at it from the most negative viewpoint of the most cynical employee and they feel that where there are objections they're able to address them.

- They feel able to talk to a group – they've identified the size of group they feel comfortable with, and they feel they can manage both themselves and their own reactions and manage the group and its reactions.

Communicating bad news can often be so traumatic that having once successfully completed it, communicators don't particularly want to do it again.

However, communicating bad news is usually only the first step. The next step is to keep people up to date on developments, so it's important to keep a constant pulse of communication. If you have promised to go back to people with information as it arises by a specific date, you've got to go back on that date – if you don't your credibility will be damaged and employees won't accept your reassurances in the future.

It's important to keep a finger on the pulse, and to provide a number of feedback channels so people can give responses, raise questions and get answers.

As part of that, it's important, when using face-to-face communication, to debrief communicators. Senior managers who have run sessions will tend to judge them in terms of whether their performance has been successful. What communicators want to know is how did it go, how did employees react, what questions did employees have, what questions could the senior manager not answer and what did they think their people did not say?

Communicating in uncertainty is inherently unstable – things change quickly, assumptions shift and options open and close. Therefore, it's vital to keep a constant update on what's developing.

Different communicators will have different views, and may recommend different approaches. Communicators at the corporate centre may have an interest in local bad news because of its possible impact on the organization's reputation. The site communicators may have different priorities from those in HR, or from communicators attached to the project.

When the news is bad, communicators need to be at their best, and pulling together. The following chapter looks further at the need to manage and orchestrate communication.

REFERENCE AND FURTHER READING

The Jensen Group (2000), *Changing the Way We Work: The Search for a Simpler Way* (London: The Jensen Group).

III Pulling It Together

8 Planning and Managing Communication

The preceding chapters have looked at how to achieve business ends via better internal communication. First, organizations have to do the right thing by focussing their internal communication on achieving their business strategy and, second, do things right – have efficient and effective processes. This chapter and those that follow are about doing things right.

So far, this book has listed a number of formidable tasks. Organizations need both to keep their people informed and create understanding. They must be able to tap into creative thinking and innovation. They need to align personal values and brand values to deliver value to customers. They need employees to feel part of a global network and collaborate in a matrix of teams while living and working in local communities. They need to do all this and cope with change and ambiguity too.

Achieving all this with existing communication practices is a tall order.

This chapter describes how to manage communication to meet these challenges. It makes the connection between two of the key elements of good practice outlined in Chapter 1 – Communication Planning, which helps reduce the quantity of information, and channel management, which helps increase the productive capacity of communication channels.

It argues that communication management has lessons to learn from supply chain management, whose principles can be readily applied in order to create greater value from internal communication.

It also proposes three main ways in which to bring greater coherence and improved quality to communication:

1. Better management of communication quantity through coordination, planning and communication 'air traffic control'.

2. Better quality of messages and information throughout communication supply chain management.

3. Better design and presentation of information.

COMMUNICATION AS OVERLOAD

The limit to effective communication is not the number of trees left standing from which to produce newsletters or the number of e-mails that can be distributed in a single day. The limit is the extent to which people have the inclination, time and goodwill to engage with the communicator. Employees' mental capacity to absorb and process information is limited and this capacity has to be treated as a strategic resource.

Employees' willingness to consume all the messages aimed at them is shrinking, as is the time they are willing to give those competing for their attention. Uncoordinated and inconsistent communication, and poorly thought-through and badly presented information makes matters worse. Employees get half-baked information which they do not have the time to 'bake' any further. No time is given for employees to assimilate information, discuss key issues and their implications, and few channels exist for feedback from employees so information can be improved.

PULLING COMMUNICATION TOGETHER

Making communication coherent is a tough job in an increasingly complex environment. The problems that organizations are encountering highlight two issues – the limited capacity of organizations to organize and distribute information, and the limited capacity of individuals to process and turn information into something relevant and valuable.

Businesses must therefore more carefully manage access to communication channels, prioritize messages and manage the threat of information overload. There are three ways of improving communication management:

1. Better management of the capacity of the communication channels through more selective use.

2. Reduction of the quantity of messages through better planning and clearer prioritization.

3. Better quality of messages and information by ensuring that suppliers of information provide higher-quality raw material.

All of these call for better planning by senior management, clear prioritization and the agreement of a limited number of key messages.

WHY PLANNING IS IMPORTANT

Planning is high on the agenda for effective communicators for a number of good reasons. Communication directors are tired of having to keep a wary eye out for unexpected, unpredicted and unwelcome communication from within their own organizations. It is hard enough trying to cope with a volatile external environment without fearing you may fall victim to the 'friendly fire' of unplanned internal communication.

Global heads of communication want to ensure that they've got a coordinated picture of what's going on in individual countries, divisions and functions. For their part, individual countries don't want to have unexpected, time consuming and inappropriate communication initiatives dropped on them out of the blue from the global centre.

In matrix organizations, the number of communicators seems to increase geometrically. As soon as one baron within the business hires a personal communicator, the air quickly becomes thick with newsletters, mousemats and road shows. Large change programmes with large budgets enable gifted amateurs or outside consultants to engage in 'cheque book communication', in which they can buy share of voice by outspending their more constrained colleagues in the corporate communication departments.

COMMUNICATION OVERLOAD

Organizations are waking up to the fact that while internal communication is a good thing, you can have too much of it. They are shifting from an informal competition between various communicators to creating greater collaboration, which allows the company to present a more coherent face.

Employees continually complain of initiative overload, while functions at the centre, change initiatives in the change programme office and global chief executive's office all pursue 'flat pack communication'. This is where the employee receives communication from all corners of the globe, without any coherent picture about how it is all supposed to fit together.

They are forced to bolt bits of communication together in the hope of building a coherent picture. No wonder the final result often looks skewed.

Organizations are now waking up to the need for far greater coherence so that each piece of communication reinforces rather than contradicts others, and so that all stakeholders get a consistent picture. Getting that degree of coherence and consistency in complex organizations demands careful planning and collaboration between communicators.

INCONSISTENCY UNDERMINES CREDIBILITY

In external communication, inconsistent messages undermine brand and reputation. Internally, different and inconsistent communication can unnerve employees and reinforce their suspicions. In times of change, employees look for the signals to indicate what could be the real agendas of their leaders.

Employees become 'Kremlin watchers', watching every nuance of communication from each of the leadership team to find out where the splits are, who's in and who's out, and what's really happening. Inconsistent messages from the top team can signal splits and fuel conspiracies that are often based on simple misunderstanding.

Unless the organization is clear on its priorities and focused in what it says, people will tune out. More and more organizations are finding that far from generating greater illumination, increasing communication actually creates inconsistency, confusion and clutter.

Good planning can reduce unpredicted and unwelcome communication from random people within the organization, and unexpected, time-consuming initiatives from the corporate centre that have not been planned or prepared for locally. It can also reduce the overload of messages that have little strategic relevance, that drown out more important communication and that leave employees with an inconsistent or incoherent picture of the organization's business priorities.

GETTING PLANNING RIGHT

There is an old saying that, 'To fail to plan is to plan to fail.' This is a salutary reminder that as communicators we cannot rely on last minute inspiration to pull our chestnuts from the fire. But too much planning can also bring its problems – as John Lennon reminded us when he commented, 'Life is what happens when you're busy making plans.'

The secret to successful communication planning is getting the balance right. The communicator who focuses on reams of beautiful communication plans will fall victim to analysis paralysis, hypnotized by all the interdependencies. On the other hand, those who plan on the proverbial back of an envelope will eventually trip themselves up and fall flat on their face.

DEVELOPING A COMMON LANGUAGE

In today's fast changing business environment, communicators cannot afford to fly blind. They need planning processes and disciplines to help them avoid overloading the organization and to make sure that communication activities are focused on the right business priorities.

Without some kind of common planning framework and process in place, it's difficult to manage the different agendas and communication priorities of individuals. Having a common planning process helps ensure a common language, greater consistency and easier coordination of plans.

COMMUNICATOR OVERLOAD

The lack of coordination of communication in many organizations is a result of the number of communicators working within them. There has always been a traditional rivalry between corporate centres and business units, between global headquarters and country operations, and between one country and another. Communicators have had to negotiate and cooperate to work across those tensions. Now life is becoming even trickier as organizations add to the mix the complexities of matrix structures, the decision to either centralize or decentralize and the need to manage a common brand consistently. All this calls into play a new layer of communicators who operate along different lines of the matrix, whether in functional networks, product divisions, market sectors or key customer teams.

A matrix structure geometrically increases the amount of communication and multiplies the number of competing tribal loyalties. The more complex the matrix, the greater the number of communicators, the higher the level of competition for the employee's attention and the more jigsaw pieces the recipient has to assemble to produce a coherent picture.

Then, after the matrix has created warring tribes of communicators, an additional group of communicators emerges working on organizational initiatives, programmes and projects, which are important to the success of the business and usually have a high profile.

All these communicators effectively compete for the time, attention and brain space of employees. Each has a different preoccupation and a different offer. At the centre, they want to achieve a cohesive unity behind the brand name and have common standards and processes, where it makes sense, across the business units. They also want a reasonable share of employee brain space for corporate issues and to build employees' loyalty to the organization as a whole.

Within the business units, communicators want to serve the management agenda of their immediate boss. That may be promoting the success of the business unit and focusing employees on specific objectives, even if that means blinkering them to the wider picture.

Initiative communicators see their job as promoting their initiative, and compete for as much time and attention as possible. They are very aware of the importance of visibility, not just to employees, but to the initiative owners, bosses and colleagues. Their communication runs laterally across the business units, cutting across others' communication, using independent communication channels that they develop themselves, such as videos, Intranets, newsletters or road shows.

As well as having different agendas, corporate, business unit and initiative communicators may actually have a different definition of how their communication is supposed to be adding value. In a number of organizations, those at the corporate centre see themselves as consultants, the business unit communicators see themselves as the efficient distributors of management messages, and initiative communicators see themselves as internal PR campaigners. This brings further dimensions of complexity, confusion and possible trouble.

It is an old adage that too many cooks spoil the broth, especially when they each use a different recipe. Organizations pay for all the cooks, provide them all with the tools for the job, pay for all the ingredients and can still end up with no broth.

This is not all the fault of the communicators. They have a difficult job intertwining a number of different strands of communication. They have to provide relevant information, create a common sense of identity across the business and build teamwork along different lines of the matrix.

Communication channels are limited but everyone's got a key message they want everyone else to remember. In today's organizations this is a complex task and can seem at times like playing three-dimensional chess. However, organizational communication is a team sport, in which coordinating all the players is the only way to score the goal. The rules of the game have to be set by the leaders, and there are six steps to helping them plan communication better and manage channels more effectively:

1. Plan communication with senior management.

2. Agree a communication policy with the board.

3. Involve senior management in forward planning.

4. Ensure that change initiatives have communication plans.

5. Create greater coordination between internal communicators.

6. Practise 'air traffic control'.

1. Plan communication with senior management

There is a clear need for a more systematic and disciplined approach to communication planning. Research by Synopsis shows that only a third of boards actually approve the communication strategy and plan (Bloomfield, Lamb and Quirke, 1998). But 69 per cent of Fortune 1000 companies do not have a communication policy at all.

2. Agree a communication policy with the board

Too few businesses involve their top team in approving the internal communication strategy and plan. Businesses may say that they want their people to sing from the same song sheet, but they fail to ensure that the top team agrees the words. It is small wonder then, that the result is mixed messages.

In one organization, the failure of the top team to develop a prioritized communication plan left individual areas to do their own thing. Enthusiastic individuals unleashed their creativity on communication activities, competing to be louder, bigger and better than communicators elsewhere. Finally, like rival salesmen sabotaging each other's product displays, communicators ended up covertly tearing each other's posters down under cover of darkness.

Unresolved board-level disagreements translate into communication competition further down the organization. Although everyone can easily understand that coordination is needed for coherence, it does not mean that they will practise what they hear preached. For senior managers, charged with driving forward an initiative, for whom success is a career issue, altruism is likely to give way to self-interest, as they drive their communication ahead anyway. Prima donnas are generally reluctant to join a formation dancing team.

The only way of reducing the pressure is for senior managers at board level to commit to a more prudent management of that strategic asset, employee brain space. That means having all the initiative owners, the business unit leaders and the chief executive, in one room, committing as a group to the common interest. Trying to tackle the issue leader by leader is likely simply to perpetuate the problem.

Different views on the role, value and purpose of internal communication need to be agreed by members of the board, including the best balance of openness, and the sensitivity of information. Consensus should be reached on the key messages and the amount of airtime they should receive, which messages need only go to specific managers or locations, and which initiatives should have greater emphasis and prominence. With an agreed overall picture for the jigsaw puzzle, employees will be better able to assemble their own picture from the pieces they receive.

3. Involve senior management in forward planning

Senior management should be involved in communication planning well in advance and should focus on business, rather than communication, objectives. They should develop an annual calendar of communication events and milestones, explicitly linked to the business plan, and then review the communication plan quarterly. The emphasis should be on educating people about the rationale for change, rather than simply announcing conclusions. This will require involving communicators earlier in the planning process, rather than – as is frequently and unfortunately the case – when the implementation of a change begins and they are asked simply to make the announcements.

4. Ensure that change initiatives have communication plans

Without a common format it is that much harder to be clear on how and when different change initiatives will affect people in the organization. This results in change managers competing for communication time and resources, with the risk that change fails through initiative overload – too many changes hitting people too quickly. This may explain why employees keep experiencing sudden, apparently unexpected and uncoordinated change. This only serves to increase their anxiety, their frustration and their perception that the management team does not have its collective act together.

Organizations need to think ahead, show clear linkages between different initiatives and give people the bigger picture of change. Initiatives should have individual communication plans that are linked to the business's umbrella strategy.

5. Create greater coordination between internal communicators

The number of communicators within organizations is increasing. Reasons for this include managers taking their communication responsibilities seriously, initiative leaders wanting to create support for their programmes and new divisions and departments and business units hiring their own communication specialists. If these communicators are not coordinated, they inevitably compete for time and attention, contribute to communication clutter and create inconsistency and mixed messages.

Different functions – human resources, corporate communications, IT, marketing and operations – own different pieces of the communication jigsaw which must all be assembled correctly for success. It is not enough for communicators to coordinate their diaries of events; they have to share their plans, priorities and thinking. Cooperation is not enough unless all plans are integrated.

Members of the communicators' network – whoever they are in the matrix – should work together to devise ground rules for sending messages down the communication channels, to map out who owns which communication channels and to decide what the requirements are for each.

Organizations should differentiate between the roles of channel owners and content providers. Corporate communication, for example, can be responsible for managing communication channels such as the corporate newsletter or the briefing process. It can also be responsible for providing corporate messages to other communication channels owned and managed by other parts of the business. One rule of engagement, for example, could be that the corporate centre provides the content to business units, leaving them responsible for disseminating it via their existing communication channels. Confining some would-be communicators to providing only content can reduce the problem of their inventing new channels and get more value from the investment in existing channels.

6. Practise 'air traffic control'

Communication will continue to be viewed as a soft area until leaders take a harder line. Unless business leaders insist that early planning, coordinated communication, and clear and consistent messages with identified actions are agreed at the top of the organization, communication will continue to fail to deliver changed attitudes and behaviour.

Companies face the choice between self-regulation and confusing clutter. To reduce information overload, organizations must adopt a more sophisticated approach to managing information and interaction via greater communication 'air traffic control'. They will have to shift from the current 'factory' model of communication, in which more and more messages are pumped down communication pipelines, to regulating the amount of information being circulated.

This raises the dilemma of being perceived as a communication 'policeman', filtering out and depriving employees of information. Of course, some degree of editing is required, to reduce overload. Saul Thurman identified the 'information anxiety' syndrome – the fear that somewhere there is vital information you need but are lacking. What he did not identify is that employees within organizations also suffer 'information paranoia' – the persistent suspicion that the truth is out there, and that vital information is being kept from you by a communication conspiracy.

The Intranet allows people to access information for themselves. Perhaps in the future, using intelligent agents to alert individuals to relevant information might be a way of replacing filtering and editing, since a filter excludes and an adviser alerts. However, for the present, there is a need to reduce the complexity at source. It is not the job of communication managers to keep making rescue attempts on poorly thought-through planning and decisions, like throwing lifebelts to drowning men. They need to walk upstream and see who is throwing them off the bridge in the first place.

Communication has to be orchestrated carefully via an 'air traffic control' which has an overview of communication activities. This prevents mid-air collisions caused by would-be communicators taking to the air as and when they like.

The linkage between business strategy and communication planning at the centre and at business unit level should be closely coordinated. Early planning and prioritization of messages is vital, even though this may cause some inconvenience to the senior management team, who may see their room for manoeuvre being restricted.

Some organizations set up an 'air traffic control' coordination group comprising representatives from corporate communication, HR, marketing and change management, to prioritize and coordinate business-wide communication. Such groups typically assemble all proposed communication activity on a single calendar or project plan to serve as a communication 'radar screen'.

An integrated communication plan should be prepared annually and reviewed quarterly. This should cover objectives, key messages and the use of communication channels, and outline how initiatives will be timetabled and coordinated. It should also identify the measures to be used in evaluating performance. The document should explicitly explain how action, messages and so on would be segmented by key audience. This should be approved, at least in summarized form, by the board, in order to ensure ownership by senior management and confirm that strategic objectives are being supported and sufficient resources and budgets are allocated.

Business units should have a similar local planning and coordination process, and their more detailed operational plans should connect to the integrated central plan.

USING ONLINE PLANNING TO IMPROVE AIR-TRAFFIC CONTROL

Organizations are well aware that employees can receive communication from their local unit, their function, from regional headquarters, divisional headquarters and from the corporate centre. Increasingly, communication is not simply up and down, but side to side, as global initiatives contact people directly, or one country swaps best practice with another. Communicators at the centre may want a more joined-up picture of communication across the organization, to make it more integrated and to engage senior management in better communication decision making and prioritization.

BP is a good example of a global organization managing complex communication. BP has a number of divisions or 'segments' with a global network of communicators. In a multinational, multicultural organization such as BP, communication initiatives occur at different levels within each specific business unit and country. At the same time, more information is coming in from above, from segment and group levels.

BP has adopted an online "air traffic control" tool that guides communicators in developing a plan and gives it a communication 'radar'. This means it can prioritize and schedule communication activity in order to reduce information overload and ensure that key messages get the right amount of airtime.

An interactive coordination calendar shows all planned communication, allowing overloads and clashes to be spotted easily. This 'radar screen' shows who owns each plan, and allows 'drilling down' into each plan and activity. Because the calendar can be filtered by date, target audience, location, grade and priority of the communication, users can see what communication is planned and which audiences particular messages are intended for. This increases the chance that important messages get the air time they need while less important pieces of communication get moved aside.

Communicators can use the calendar to avoid the 'friendly fire' of competing communication, spot opportunities to piggyback their message on existing communications and choose the best time to communicate their message.

While the tool enables specific events to be scheduled and planned, it also allows communicators to guide internal clients through questions about audiences, messages and desired outcomes. This enables the communicators to have a helpful, but challenging, conversation with their internal clients, positioning themselves as a solution provider, not merely an order taker.

The online planning tool allows internal communication managers in individual countries to see an overview of their communication activity, and see what incoming communication is planned by the centre. The online tool can be accessed by members of the same local team in a single business, or by colleagues spread around the world from different countries and divisions.

COMMUNICATOR NETWORKS

As more organizations wake up to the importance of communication, and invest in more internal communication professionals, more organizations are having to look at how best to connect those communicators in a professional network.

The communication audit has been a familiar tool for years. A more recent development is the audit of internal communicators – where the search is launched for all those involved in internal communication, with the aim of mapping just who is doing it, for whom and to what standard.

Organizations discover that they have got global communicators, divisional communicators, national communicators, site communicators, functional communicators and initiative communicators. Left to their own devices, internal communicators can duplicate effort, create unnecessary cost and end up competing with each other for employees' time and attention.

Other functions are under the microscope to see whether they are adding value to the business, justifying their costs and demonstrating professionalism. Internal communicators are no exception.

Establishing networks is a sensible way of ensuring that internal communication is being run as a team sport rather than a solo pursuit; with the same roles, same rules and the same goals. At a time when internal communicators are educating senior management about the true value of internal communication, it makes sense for networks of communicators to work more closely together to acquire skills, press for change and raise standards.

Naturally there are different kinds of networks, created for different reasons, and at different stages of development. What they usually have in common is a belief that together they can improve internal communication in their organization.

Vodafone, for example, operates a global internal communication network, connecting members from each of its country operating companies.

As Vodafone has evolved from a portfolio of acquired mobile phone companies, each often with its own individual brand, to a global, integrated organization under one brand, so the nature of the network has shifted. Internal communicators meet for planning and developing best practice. Rather than simply swapping good ideas, network members identify the key areas of internal communication they need to focus on, such as face-to-face communication, communication skills for managers or measurement. They agree which operating company will develop a solution, which will then be piloted in one market before being transferred to the others. This means that the global centre's role is to foster collaboration, not be the source of all wisdom.

Roche is another organization that invests in its network of communication. It regularly pulls together both its internal and external communication communities, underlining a commitment to an integrated approach to communicating with all their stakeholders.

Diageo's internal communicators see their network as more than a body for information exchange and coordination. They see part of their job as spreading good communication practice beyond their own function, to leaders of the business and to the leaders of change initiatives. Working closely together, members of the network have developed a 'Diageo way of communicating', which includes innovative leadership communication training, manager guides to improving their communication and training in communication planning.

A network is a useful way of spreading the greater experience in one part of an organization rapidly to another. BP's global Exploration and Production division operates in far flung corners of the world, and needs good internal communication to connect its operations. Its communicators network is specifically designed to help integrate communication, adopt common processes and allow experience in one market to be rapidly transferred to another.

NETWORKS GO THROUGH DIFFERENT STAGES

Networks are established for different reasons. Some get together to share information and trade best practice, others are created to reduce internal competition and confusion. Once created, they tend to go through different, but clear, stages:

Information exchange

They tell each other what they're doing, without any commitment to change what they're doing in the face of any objection. At this stage, network members tend to be wary of each other and are committing simply to exchanging information rather than renegotiating their communication plans.

This stage is typical of a decentralized organization in which business units have done things in their own distinctive way and see little value in anyone else getting involved. The nature of a network, and the relationships between its members, inevitably reflects the relationship between the centre and the businesses, or between the global headquarters and the countries.

Coordination

As relationships are established, and the fear of power grabs recede, members of the network start to coordinate their efforts, synchronize their communication plans and give each other early warning of upcoming initiatives. They look for synergies between their activities and for opportunities to piggyback on conferences, training courses and publications.

This stage is particularly important when the network of communicators is being used as a distribution chain – where the centre relies on divisions to localize, translate and pass on central communication.

Collaboration

Members of the network start swapping examples of good practice; sharing ideas with each other, trading communication materials, co-funding the development of training and contacting each other for coaching, help and advice. They explore new developments, report back on conferences and workshops and contribute to colleagues' professional development.

Integration

The network sees itself not simply as a federation of internal communicators, each with their own patch of turf, but as a team with different skills who consult with each other and coach each other. Individual members are recognized as subject matter experts, and take the lead on particular specialisms such as face-to-face communication or measurement.

Trying to pull together a network of communicators is not always easy. Added to the simple logistical difficulties of getting everyone in one place, and investing the time it takes to build relationships, there are other issues:

- Different reporting lines – often internal communicators can be reporting to different functions – corporate communications, marketing, human resources or strategy. These will have different bosses, with different priorities, and there will be some degree of internal politics to deal with.

- Different focuses – some see the roles as an extension of marketing communications, others may believe that they are there to effect culture change. Different interpretations of the job will cause frustration.

- Different levels of skill – networks tend to be of variable quality. People have often found themselves in the internal communicator's role as an accident of history. They may have very different levels of skills, little opportunity for professional development and very different expectations from their line bosses and internal clients.

- Different amounts of time – whereas centrally based communicators may spend 100 per cent of their time on internal communication, they may be working with a local internal communicator who is only part-time, and expected to cover external and marketing communication as well.

WHAT MAKES NETWORKS WORK?

Although establishing networks faces problems, lots of companies have learned what can make their networks work.

Clear rules of engagement

Networks are an important way of creating coordination, consistency and accountability. It helps for networks to recognize the balance between the centre and the business units. If an organization is trying to unify its different businesses into a coherent whole, internal communicators should help, not hinder, the move. Internal communicators in the businesses should not insist on independent approaches, or rebranding communication for their people.

Equally, where an organization is decentralizing, and allowing its individual brands more independence, the centre has to relax its role to support rather than direct. Often networks are established when the structure of an organization changes. Previously independent and autonomous units find themselves having to work more closely with communicators at the global centre, or at regional level.

Internal communicators who previously have only had to focus on their own business unit, often with its own brand and its own heritage and culture, suddenly discover that they have to collaborate as members of a family of businesses.

This is often the case where organizations are built up by serial mergers and acquisitions, and where independent brands suddenly find themselves as part of a broader portfolio.

Here, communication networks are a useful means of creating coordination, agreeing common approaches and striking a positive balance between the needs of the corporate centre with its corporate brand, and those of the individually branded business units.

Whitbread is a prime example of this kind of network. Internal communicators from such brands as Costa, Premier Travel Inn and David Lloyd have worked to ensure that there is a common 'one Whitbread' approach to internal communication, while ensuring that each brand pursues its own internal communication in a way that fits its distinctive style and culture.

A common communication planning process

Most communication networks discover that they can make life easier for each other by developing communication plans and sharing them. That way, the number of unexpected surprises is reduced, the chance for coordination and synchronization increases and those out in the operations get a better chance for early consultation and input which will improve the final result. Where networks adopt the same planning process, they get plans in a common format which can be combined to give a unified view of what's going on at global and local levels.

Meetings are not the only tool

Getting everyone together in one location is a good way of building relationships but can be expensive in terms of time and travel cost. If the network does not move on to doing useful work together, the take-up of invitations tends to decline, unless the locations become more exotic.

Networks that work together between meetings tend to hang on to the good intentions they had when they parted at the last meeting and keep the agreements they made. Networks can use collaborative software, team rooms and project video-conferences to make progress.

Acknowledging best practice

Members of networks often fear that they're going to have a 'one size fits all' approach to internal communication imposed on them. Often, individual members of the network have pioneered new and innovative approaches in their own areas, which are often superior to those at the centre. These have to be recognized as good practice, which can then be agreed as common practice for the network as a whole.

Rolls-Royce provides a good example of a network which has been built up by the functional leader at the centre providing regular forums to showcase good work in its business units, and providing collegiate support rather than imposing central solutions.

Professional development

Internal communicators are often lonely beings, trying to work with colleagues and internal clients who don't quite get it, and whom they feel they have to educate. Communication networks' members can offer each other sympathy and advice, but, more importantly, they can provide a forum for professional development and acquiring skills which will build their careers, raise their status and get them greater recognition.

Ericsson is a good example of a network looking ahead to the future, and projecting what business value internal communication should be adding, and what skills internal communicators will need. Ericsson has involved internal communicators from the global centre, its R&D units, its business units and its market units, in a systematic programme of development. As a network, they have worked to establish a common view of the value internal communication should provide, identify the priorities on which they should focus, map the skills they currently have and develop the skills they'll need to fulfil future roles.

What organizations like this have realized is that they need to marshal their communication forces if they are to have the impact their business needs from them. For a profession that preaches the importance of employee focus, alignment and engagement, it is good that we start with ourselves.

Planning is one key element of good practice because it helps reduce the quantity of communication. The other element is better quality of communication, and the following section looks at improving what actually flows through the communication channels.

Surveys consistently reveal confusion between the volume of information and its value. Organizations need to focus more on the refinement of raw information into meaning and relevance.

We all think that we are good communicators. Anyone who has either the seniority to insist on being heard or access to the right communication channels, can broadcast to the world. Unfortunately where there is no quality requirement for communication and where authors feel they are naturally good with the written or spoken word, the result is high volumes of low-quality material.

Organizations need a better understanding of their different audiences so that they can clearly link key messages from the centre with individuals' concerns and preoccupations. Where messages are mass produced and distributed, there is little tailoring of information to the recipients' needs. Making a stronger link between business direction and individuals' agendas requires more research to test employees assumptions, and better feedback channels to improve understanding of how employees 'decode' the communication they receive.

Businesses need to get more out of their communication, in terms of cost, clarity and credibility. Some are beginning to realize that information overkill is consuming precious time, creating clutter and creating mixed messages.

In an effort to reduce communication fatigue, IBM aims to reduce information and communication channels to the minimum. It has created an enforceable code of practice to reduce information to manageable levels. Its internal communication department acts as internal consultants and audits not only the amount of communication, but the effectiveness of channels. It also gauges the clarity of information as perceived by employees and whether or not communication has actually been effective in achieving the planned outcome.

IBM takes consistency and coherence even more seriously. To keep executives in harmony with corporate approaches, it provides a toolkit on the Intranet, specifically for managers. This toolkit contains the five top-priority business issues for communication, together with the context and background information for each issue. Managers are therefore supplied with the means of communicating plus the means of adding value and context as they pass information on. The toolkit also contains guidelines for preparing material, and is intended to help managers think through the communication issues before putting pen to paper. From the communication department's point of view, it is a framework for ensuring the managers who want to communicate provide them with a thought-through plan. It also reduces the risk that managers will appear unexpectedly in the department asking for a video to be made.

COMMUNICATION SUPPLY CHAIN MANAGEMENT

With more communication being forced onto people who are filtering the information they receive, we need to squeeze more performance from our communication channels and more meaning from information.

Communication management has lessons to learn from supply chain management. The traditional debate between communicators, whether between corporate and business unit, or between initiative and project, has been based on two things: the communicator's right to address the internal audience and the communicator's assumptions about what audiences want and need. This is a production-led approach and is reminiscent of factories forcing products into their distribution channels and insisting that their sales force offload them onto their customers.

The distribution of a message is too often mistaken for a communication. It is frequently assumed that if information has been sent out, it has been received and assimilated. Fighter aircraft have 'fire and forget' missiles. Pilots can fire their missiles at a target, and then peel off, confident that the target will be hit. Managers have a similar, but misplaced, confidence about 'fire and forget' communication – information sent out without highlighting its significance, why it has been sent or what response is expected as a result.

There can be a number of disconnects between different links in the communication chain. Messages are mistaken for communication, and success is defined only as the media's ability to deliver messages, with no regard for the final outcome. Competing communicators jealously guard the part of the communication chain they own, and managers are accused of filtering and blocking information, and disagreeing with its value. These disconnects are similar to those of another chain – that of supplier and customer.

For example, managers are currently used as a distribution channel to deliver information to an end-user. The distribution process is unreliable, not least because the information has not been designed for the use of either the manager or the end recipient. Both have to add the vital ingredients of meaning and relevance to make the information they receive valuable.

These are problems which organizations are already tackling and solving in their approaches to supply chain management. The problem faced by internal communication today is the problem confronting businesses with traditional supplier management – supply is divorced from the creation of customer value.

SQUEEZING MORE FROM THE SUPPLY CHAIN

The traditional communication cascade is a distribution channel that links a supplier to a final customer. The intention is that, as messages are passed down the chain, they will be localized, or sweetened with local information. The product being distributed is information and there is a great deal of waste, confusion, discarding and frustration along the supply chain.

This problem is now greater because organizations have redefined the purpose of internal communication. In the past they wanted it to be a means of efficiently distributing information, but now they need it to be a process for creating understanding.

In the traditional cascade communication model, information is handed from link to link in the chain, without an understanding of how the whole chain works, or what the different needs of each part of the chain are. Frequently, the information supplier creates problems for the customer by providing inferior material – written in obscure language, poorly presented and with no obvious point.

As the volume of information increases, the quality does not. Therefore, we have to make two changes simultaneously – identify what is the intended business value in communicating, and design a better process to deliver that value. We need to see internal communication as a process of conversion rather than a process of distribution. Just as assembly line workers convert or add value to a component that they receive from up the line, so we have to convert information into meaning for ourselves so that we can make the right decisions.

If assembly line workers receive poor-quality components, they can stop the line and reject the components. There is no such facility for employees who are continually receiving poor-quality information which they find difficult or troublesome to translate. The worse the quality of the material, the longer the employee takes to arrive at the desired conclusion. Better-quality information would make the process easier, would waste less time and create less exasperation. To achieve this, quality must be built into the creation of information and those who author information must adopt a more thoughtful discipline.

Communication consultant and author Roger D'Aprix (1997) captures the point well:

> '...the analogy in our old manufacturing economy would be to have assembly line workers digging through piles of parts and raw materials to find the components for their products. No manufacturing plant manager would tolerate that situation for a minute. If we are going to use information as the raw material to build other products and services we need to treat it as carefully and as deliberately as a Toyota, a Motorola or a Sony treats its raw materials and its production processes.'

As communicators, we have to make the same shift that companies such as Unipart have undertaken – from running a basic supply chain to running a supply partnership in which partners work together to increase the total benefit in the chain. The shift is from seeing the supply chain as merely a series of interconnected distribution channels to seeing it as interconnected partners who each have a responsibility to add value to what they receive and what they hand onwards – a value chain. A company's value chain is the whole string of activities – from procurement to after-sales service – which it combines to create and deliver value to a customer.

The aim of communicators in the chain should be to remove the steps that benefit nobody and eliminate procedures that add only difficulties and no value. They should have a clear view of what value the final customer is intended to receive, and understand the needs, constraints and capabilities of other partners along the chain. Furthermore, instead of accusing partners when the chain breaks down, they should work to identify how things can be improved for the future.

WHERE IS VALUE ADDED?

Some internal communicators have reached the same conclusion as supply chain managers – quality along the chain is only as good as the weakest link. Car manufacturers, for example, realize that final car quality cannot exceed the quality levels achieved by suppliers, so they share their quality know-how and training with their suppliers.

Working in a supply chain means identifying what internal customers want and need. What are the customer's constraints and idiosyncrasies and how should communication processes and content be designed best to suit these?

Managing the supply chain is about how best to meet the requirements of the end customer, while also meeting the requirements and the agenda of intermediaries along the chain.

Seeing internal communication as a process of converting information into meaning demands different rules. Partnership along the chain is vital, as is eliminating one party dumping a problem on the next party in the chain. For that to happen, the whole process not only has to be transparent to all, but also has to be managed by a process owner, from end to end.

Everything should be produced with the end customer in mind, with a common agreement about what value the final communication should produce. Finally, feedback from each point of the chain should be used to improve the process, and feedback from those at the end of the process should test whether the intended outcome was achieved.

CLARIFY THE POSITIONING OF THE COMMUNICATION DEPARTMENT

Much of the pressure to pump messages into the organization is caused by senior managers insisting that communication specialists give them access to communication channels. Those specialists are often seen by their senior clients as simply part of the distribution process. This issue, and ways of dealing with it, is expanded in Chapter 9.

One of the difficulties encountered by the communication department is the way in which its different customers perceive it as providing very different kinds of value. Senior managers, for example, want access to communication channels, while employees may pray for less information and more relevance. Communicators have to provide a valuable service to both sets of customers. This means that the communication team has to provide value for employees by reducing volume of information and increasing its relevance, while also providing value helping senior managers achieve their objectives via effective communication. This can all be accomplished by taking some of the following approches:

1. Focus on processes, not products.

2. Reduce the number of messages and make them more memorable.

3. Design information with the recipient in mind.

4. Budget time not paper.

5. Measure the outcome.

1. Focus on processes, not products

Managers have to be educated away from an automatic demand for a communication product, especially when that product is yet another newsletter, or their own blog. Their real goal is usually to create awareness and understanding, or create support and involvement for change. Communicators should help them to identify what precisely they do want to achieve. Equally, communications specialists should help them identify the best process rather than the best product. For example, combining an article in an existing newsletter, discussion in a team meeting, a reliable feedback process and a 'frequently asked questions' section on the company Intranet could provide the desired outcome without inventing new channels.

Reducing the volume of competing voices within the business means providing tools as well as rules. It is more acceptable to impose an 'air traffic control' structure if you also provide communicators with tools and processes that will still help them succeed.

Like IBM, Hewlett Packard and Microsoft give managers a planning tool to help them think through the communication needs of their project and to provide guidance on the effective use of communication channels. This allows them to clarify their thinking, consider options and refine their messages.

2. Reduce the number of messages and make them more memorable

Improving the communication chain means reducing the volume of information and using clearer and more accessible language.

There is only a certain amount of information that people will take in and remember. The more key points that are crammed in, the less chance there is to make information memorable. A survey among Church of England vicars spot-checked how many of the Ten Commandments they could recall unprompted. The average was two. If professionals can only retain a limited number of essential facts, what hope do the rest of us have of retaining the long list of key principles underlying the mission statement?

The less that managers put in, the more employees take out.

3. Design information with the recipient in mind

Communication is supposed to create meaning and relevance for employees. However, companies often push the burden of translating information into relevance on to the employee. Pushing out generic messages from the centre, with little concern for the needs of different audiences, may save time for the message senders, but takes up far more time elsewhere in the organization as recipients struggle to make sense of what they have received.

Just as mass marketing was replaced by segmentation marketing, so marketing to individuals will become the norm. The same holds true for internal communication.

By creating information with the end-user in mind and presenting it from the recipient's perspective, companies can improve their employees' quality of life. Relevance spells the difference between a welcome letter and junk mail. Messages that fail to register with employees merely add to the clutter.

In 'information overload' the volume of information is often less of a problem than 'meaning underload'. With time being so short in the working day, managers need to send out information that makes its point simply and clearly. Recipients need to know why they have received information and what, if anything, they are supposed to do as a result.

4. Budget time not paper

Written material should be easy to absorb and, if it is for use in face-to-face meetings, should provide a springboard for discussion. Information provided for face-to-face communication is often written as though it were going to be read, rather than spoken. This can make it turgid and time consuming. Instead, the material should be written and timed to be spoken, like a script for the radio, not a letter to the tax man. Information items should be allocated a time budget – how much of a meeting they will take up. This also helps identify whether an item should be included and whether it is worth the time it takes up.

Better prepared and written information is one way to improve the return on time invested in face-to-face communication.

5. Measure the outcome

The acid test for the effectiveness of communication is how people rate, prioritize and consume it. Regular measurement is needed to test effectiveness. Without this feedback we could end up with a more efficient distribution system for messages, without actually producing the desired outcome.

Researching recipients' reactions to communication should be more than simply checking whether they have received it. It should also focus on how user-friendly they found it and what they concluded from it. Research by the Jensen Group (2000) showed that only 14 per cent of companies consistently ask the recipient how they would prefer to receive information. The measurement of communication's impact is the subject of Chapter 10.

In external marketing, the effectiveness of rival media in delivering messages to target audiences is measured, as is the likelihood of the audiences taking action. The same principle should apply to internal communication: the cost of getting information to employees and the medium's effectiveness in achieving the desired outcome.

In surveys, employees invariably choose face-to-face communication as their preferred means of receiving communication, and their immediate boss is usually the preferred communicator. Why, then, do initiative communicators, for example, usually prefer the newsletter, the video and the Intranet? Possibly because they are convenient for the sender rather than the receiver, and aim to expose the greatest number of eyes to the greatest number of messages.

These kinds of channels have their place in the mix, but that place has to be earned. A decision as to whether a senior manager should produce a corporate video should only be made after comparing the cost of different methods delivering the message, its impact on the employee, the employee ability to recall key messages and the impact of the communication on the likelihood they will take the desired action. This can help persuade would-be communicators that low-tech means can have more impact, and reduce the pressure on communication departments to create numerous communication products.

EMPLOYEES' TIME AND ATTENTION IS A VALUABLE COMMODITY

Part of the internal communicator's job is to make the connection between the intent of the communicator and the impact on the recipient. Internal communicators need to shift from providing and distributing content to being experts in their audiences and understanding what those audiences need. Since employee time and attention costs the company money, it should be treated respectfully.

Internal communication, however, is still the playground of gifted amateurs. This is because it's predominantly seen as a pumping station for messages, using channels and processes that seem relatively undemanding to senior managers.

Senior management tend not to realize the risks they run in communicating to their employees. They can often have a naïve belief that, 'If we communicate it they will do it.'

What they do not realize until too late are the rampant misinterpretations, the mockery of management-speak and the increasing distrust of management's agenda caused by poor communication. Where trust is low and communication is imprecise, the danger of misunderstanding and over-reaction is all the greater.

Internal communication is often left to the enthusiastic but inexperienced. This is very much not the case in other areas of communication. In media relations, for example, there are very few organizations that will happily let any employee talk to the press. This is because misunderstanding, either of the journalist's needs or of the random comments of an employee, poses such a reputational risk that it's not worth countenancing.

In investor relations there are very few "gifted amateurs" being allowed by the chief executive to chat to analysts, because the risk to the share price would be so high.

In crisis communication, when an organization hits trouble, the senior management assembles the professionals and reaches for the crisis preparedness manual, the disaster recovery plan and the process manual for responding to the media.

Few of these disciplines are applied to internal communication, mainly because senior management perceives the risk of failure to be so low. This, in turn, is because there is often a lack of feedback from the communication that goes to employees, and its consequences. Make a mistake in talking to the press, to the analysts or to a parliamentary sub-committee and the feedback is immediate and painful – the chief executive's face on the 6 o'clock news.

Sending a few paragraphs of management-speak that further alienates employees may not bring immediate consequences. However, it can provoke a further degree of resignation from employees, further erosion in management credibility and employee trust, and misunderstandings about strategy and misdirection of effort. All these can happen without an immediate warning bell or shrieks of alarm. Since the risk of damage is so high, communicators need routinely to be tracking feedback on the impact of their communication.

SEEING THINGS LIKE EMPLOYEES

One of the key issues is to understand what is suitable for employees.

One automobile manufacturer revamped the magazine they sent to service engineers from portrait format to landscape. Unexpectedly, the magazine's readership declined, and engineers' understanding of their vital role in the overall strategy declined with it.

While the new publication had been beautifully designed and glossily produced, research to find out why it wasn't working discovered an important fact. Service engineers typically read the newsletter sitting in the lavatory. This is the one chance they had to clean up after working on a car, strip off their overalls and sit back and take in information. One of the unforeseen consequences of the redesign into landscape shape was that it was too wide for the lavatory cubicles.

No-one could have foreseen this in the design brief – but it is an extreme example of a good principle – find out how your communication is being consumed.

In a pharmaceutical company's sales and marketing department, product teams would compete for the time and attention of the sales force by sending them ever more glossy newsletters. Fatally, they started trying to create greater loyalty from sales people by using pretty, graphic PowerPoint templates.

They would send out information in a beautiful PowerPoint template, often including the photos of the team that was appealing to sales people to sell their product. Unbeknownst to them, their attempts to get sales people onside actually served to alienate them.

If product teams had looked at the sale people's experience they would have found a few problems. Sales people would get home at the end of a busy working week on a Friday evening and try and download their e-mails. The slow connection speed would mean that downloads of relatively simple messages took a long time. What exasperated them was the download of large files, including PowerPoint slides with complex graphics.

Once they had finally downloaded the slides, they would discover the beautiful PowerPoint template with inappropriate messages within it. The product teams would simply copy and paste what could have been a memo into the centre of their template. This confirmed sales people's worst suspicions about the self aggrandisement and vanity of sales and marketing people – and showed that those at the centre didn't understand what it was like in the field, and were wasting their time.

It was a perfect example of good intentions being frustrated by the wrong combination of information and channel. Worse, a sales and marketing in-tray analysis showed that 30 per cent of their e-mails were mistargeted, creating further frustration and unnecessary wasted time and cost.

INFORMATION OVERLOAD

Over the last 10 years, a number of studies have shown a growing problem with information overload.

In 2000, a survey by The Institute of Management linked e-mail to workplace stress in general. 'Keeping up with e-mails' was ranked number ten in a list of 18 prime factors causing stress in the workplace, and significantly contributed to the number one pressure, 'constant interruptions', reported by nearly one-quarter of the respondents.

In 2006, four-fifths of senior executives and managers said they received too many regular communications from both internal and external sources, based on a global survey by NFI Research. The survey was conducted across more than 1000 companies in 47 countries, with 237 senior executives and managers responding.

While a third of business leaders said they received 'significantly too much' communication, only 3 per cent said they sent significantly too much. Clearly when it came to information overload, business leaders felt 'more sinned against than sinning'. While e-mail, voicemail, messages and memos were all cited as part of the communication onslaught, e-mail was named the biggest problem.

Research conducted by Loughborough University has found that e-mail communication within the workplace costs UK businesses millions of pounds in lost productivity. The project, conducted to reduce the amount of time that staff waste on e-mails, found that the cost per year in Britain was more than £9.8m.

A report issued in 2006 by ntl: Telewest Business, the telecom firm, showed that on average, office workers spend 42 minutes a day chasing responses to urgent e-mails and 27 minutes responding to voicemails or managing telephone calls (*The Sunday Times*, 4 February 2007).

While the quality of the content was a frequent target of criticism, it was the method of communication which was often identified as the main issue (*The Business Communicator*, 2006).

A 1997 study undertaken by The Institute For The Future with the Gallup Organization for Pitney Bowes Inc., titled 'Managing Corporate Communications In The Information Age', showed office workers deluged by communications and technology. Pitney Bowes' annual survey confirmed that in the years since the original was written, overload has got worse.

The study of Fortune 1000 workers found that corporate staff are inundated with so many communications tools – e-mail, teleconferencing, video-conferencing, postal mail and voicemail – that they don't know which to use for which tasks.

The study found that the average manager in these companies was sending and receiving 178 documents a day through a variety of media. It reported that, '69 per cent of Fortune 1000 companies do not have a communications policy to guide and support their employees' ability to make decisions about communications tools.

However, a number of companies have provided a simple tool for giving both employees, and senior managers, guidance on which communication channels are best used for which purpose. After all, neither employees nor managers can be blamed for not knowing what channels their organization provides, or for what purpose they are specifically intended, if no one tells them.

Some companies provide a simple guide to channels, others provide toolkits which provide greater detail on when to use which channel, its strengths and weaknesses, and who to contact for advice.

It is important therefore for internal communication departments to be sure that they have a broad enough range of channels and the right mix to fit the number of jobs they need to do and objectives they need to meet. A guide to which kinds of channels meet which communication objectives was given in Chapter 7.

Each channel should have a clear purpose, a clear objective, a definition of the audiences it is aimed at and an assessment of its strengths and weaknesses.

Communicators should check that there is a good match between the channel being used and the information it is being used for. For example, if people want to understand changes to their pension entitlements, and to calculate how changes in their contributions might affect their final benefits, the Intranet will provide employees with an interactive means of doing so.

Internal communicators will be able to assemble information about the channels they operate, their intended purpose and the information they are best suited to carry. However, they will need regular feedback from their different audiences on their perceptions of channels' appropriateness, strengths, weaknesses and usefulness.

While internal communicators may maintain, for example, that the corporate newsletter is the source of information on strategy, research among audiences may well show that employees go elsewhere to get that kind of information.

An example of one organization's channel guide is shown in Table 8.1.

CASE STUDY: STARBUCKS

Companies have a limited capacity to organize and distribute information, and individuals have a limited capacity and willingness to assimilate it. Where resources are scarce, companies have to be more intelligent in the way they use them. Facing a communication equivalent of global warming, we have to learn to reduce our emissions.

Direct marketing companies have already learned this lesson. Customers grew weary of the deluge of junk mail, especially when much of it arrived simultaneously from the same company. Companies have now become better coordinated, more disciplined and more tightly targeted in their direct marketing. Some of these strategies are increasingly being applied to internal communication.

Starbucks provides a good example of communicators shifting from pumping messages to being the guardian of meaning, being the expert on the audience, and understanding issues from the audience's viewpoint. In particular, they have looked at communication as an end to end process: how do employees receive, prioritize and respond to the communication they get?

Table 8.1 **Channel Guide**

Channel	Description	Objectives	Audience	Frequency	Type of info	Strengths	Weaknesses
One World.	Company-wide internal magazine.	'To inform and entertain'. To make people feel part of the corporate family.	All staff.	Bi-monthly.	Business strategies and direction, product and performance news.	Well liked by audience, doesn't have a 'head office publication' feel to it.	Can't guarantee it will be read. Very little interaction from audience.
Info Cards.	Briefing sheets, principally for stores, displayed in staffroom in plastic holders.	To create awareness of issues and initiatives affecting day-to-day work.	All stores (main audience). Also displayed in HQ and regional offices.	Fortnightly.	Minimum text and focus on graphics. Message must have a clear relevance to all store staff.	Popular channel. Good way to grab attention of audience and cross refer to more detailed communication elsewhere.	Not good for detail. Must be punchy or won't catch attention. Can't guarantee will be read.
Management Update.	Management newsletter.	To help managers understand the broader business context.	All managers.	Monthly.	A management overview combining progress/news about vision, strategy and the 5 year plan and how things fit in.	Opportunity to communicate to a more focused audience on management issues.	Content doesn't always link clearly to strategy/vision. No guarantee will be read.
Management Forum.	Strategy conference.	To communicate the strategy to management, and allow them to challenge and gain ownership of it.	All management from store manager and above.	Quarterly.	Strategy and plans. May discuss results if the timing is right. Also recognizing achievements.	Face-to-face delivery. Chance to reinforce strategy and key challenges for year	Large group of people and can be very one way – must work to keep it interactive.
Team Briefs.	Store team meetings.	To brief local teams about priorities for the week/day and to stimulate discussion and create involvement in better customer service.	Local store teams.	Varies – up to three times a week.	Currently at manager's discretion.	Face-to-face channel. Easy to check understanding and raise issues.	No central feed into the process. No feedback process. Reliant on line manager for success.

Avoiding communications overload

As a Director of Internal Communications at Starbucks, James Greathouse has been responsible for defining and directing the communications strategy for corporate offices and remote locations. Part of the Starbucks internal communication mission is to manage the flow of information through defined communication vehicles to ensure the effective execution of company initiatives.

The vision for internal communication at Starbucks is to create a communication process that is more predictable and accessible, as well as easier to administer. Achieving this means streamlining communication efforts for both the reader and the sender. In practice this has meant reducing the number of communication vehicles, adding consistency and clarity, and reducing repetition.

Taking the gatekeeper role

Part of the Starbucks internal communicators' role is to fight for employees, and to keep them free of distracting and confusing communication. By doing so they are protecting business's interests, reducing wasted time and keeping employee frustration down. They also demonstrate to employees that the business is interested in what they need, when they need it and how to provide it in a form they find useful. It shows employees they are being considered as internal customers, and it shows that the organization is 'on their side'.

Starbucks found that the sheer volume of communication hitting employees was driven by a number of misplaced management attitudes. They felt for example they needed more vehicles to communicate, and that if communicating once was good, four times was great.

Similarly, managers believed that spinning a topic many different ways lead to greater understanding, and that employees just need to know what to do – not why they are doing it. Underlying a number of managers' approaches to communication were the strong beliefs that the employees would be dedicated only to working on the sender's pet project, with managers seeing their communication as important without asking 'important to whom?'

Cost of poor communication

Greathouse provides a 'rule of thumb' calculation of the cost of poor communications. A single, poorly written headline on an Intranet homepage in an organization of say 15 000 people costs US$1000. This calculation is based on:

- 5 seconds to ponder the headline;

- 10 per cent click onwards even though they found the first headline useless;

- employees typically spend 30 seconds reading before deciding to skip;

- 15 000 employees spending 30 seconds at an average wage of US$30 per hour equals US$1000.

It doesn't take many poorly written headlines to start costing significant amounts of money. More importantly, in a retail organization, where time is money, any time spent uselessly costs money and distracts people from doing the real job. To reduce the risk of wastage and distraction, Starbucks set out to focus their internal communication.

Asking employees what they think of communication

Starbucks brought together a working group representing both the functions that wanted to communicate with the workforce, and members of the workforce to act as judge and jury on their communication. Employees from the field were able to provide the acid test for the importance of communication from the centre – what they wanted more of, what they wanted less of, what they had never heard of and what they wanted in a different format.

This information allowed the internal communication department to contrast what communication head office departments wanted to send with what communication employees wanted to receive. The internal communication team then set out to create a system which would work both for those who wanted to communicate and those who were on the receiving end.

The first step was to identify the different types of communicating, which they divided into:

- procedural/operational

- reference/informational

- product information

- business strategy

- feedback

- recognition

- benefits

- executive/management

- legal.

The next stage was to identify the communication vehicles they had within the company:

- print – such as the newspaper, manuals and posters;

- electronic – such as the Intranet and e-mail;

- audio – conference calls and voicemails;

- video – training and company overview videos;

- face-to-face – management staff and marketing meetings.

Using the most appropriate channel for the type of information is vital, but the choice of channel is often for the convenience of the sender rather than the convenience of the receiver.

As a third step, Starbucks looked at what actually happened to communication once it hit the audience. One example was the updating of operational information. In almost every organization an operational manual sits on the shelf. Updates are sent regularly with instruction to insert them at the relevant page. What actually happens, they found, is that those updates are stuck at the front of the manual, not inserted carefully at the appropriate page.

A perfect example of mismatching the type of information with the communication channel was using voicemail to send out operational instructions. It is hard enough trying to catch the telephone number of someone on their voicemail, much harder is trying to listen to and remember operational information.

In the same way that employees don't want the burden of having to insert separate pieces of information into a binder, they don't want to have to memorize information for later reference when it comes through on e-mail. They also don't want to have to listen to operational information on a voicemail and race to write down what they're hearing. What they want is an archive of operational information they can search, as and when they need it.

Developing a communication matrix

The internal communication team had identified what channels existed and what types of information were being sent out. They also knew how employees rated the information and how they actually used the communication channels. Putting all this together allowed Starbucks to develop a communication matrix that identified what types of communication should go down what channel:

- reference information would be posted on the Intranet, so that it could be referred to;

- product information would go on the Intranet or electronically;

- business strategy would go in the newsletter or in print;

- feedback would go via the Intranet;

- recognition would be via a mail package of print material and graphics;

- benefits information would be communicated via video and print;

- executive and management communication would go via voicemail and at face-to-face meetings;

- legal information would go via hard copy.

In the same way that they assigned different types of information to specific channels, they also gave each channel a specific purpose:

- Newspaper and print – to provide business strategies as a background to explain daily tasks and events, and information relating to overall business direction that helps employees better understand the initiatives and sales drives.

- Video – as an effective way to communicate critical, over arching business concepts with the most impact, because it provides a great sense of emotion and allows people to see the style of their leaders.

- Mail packages – used for things like signage and display items, information that stores regularly need and which have to be presented in a visual form with graphics, to avoid the trap of trying to send large graphic files down small bandwidth.

- Voicemail – used for executive management messages, which are either motivational or urgent.

- Meetings – used by management to ensure delivery of one consistent message to all employees, to create interaction and to get immediate feedback.

Taking the audience perspective, they looked at what worked. For example, on their Intranet, they discovered that beautiful graphics were no substitute for extremely simple navigation in a simple language.

Now, keeping the use of graphics to a minimum, Starbucks uses the Intranet as a core business tool. Using the Intranet predominantly as a business tool, not a communication channel, has been vital. Its real value, they feel, is in streamlining business practices and providing a means of business management. It also provides a one-stop shop for the most current reference information on HR and procedures. On the back of that it provides daily messaging to help drive the business effectively and provides a two-way communication channel, allowing for quick surveys and rapid feedback from the field.

Starbucks has also walked away from e-mail as a corporate communications channel. They prefer to keep it as a business tool for people to interact with each other.

Providing the communication matrix to show which type of information went with the most appropriate channel was vital to creating shared responsibility for communicating. This was because it gives guidance both to employees, and to managers who want to communicate with them, about the rules of the game and what constitutes a foul. Clearly defining which channels should be used for which type of information, and their relative strengths and weaknesses, also highlighted which kind of communication would be inappropriate for specific channels. This helps keep everyone accountable to each other, so it is clear when either employees fail in their responsibility, or a manager is putting the wrong information down the wrong channel. 'When we gave the communication matrix to employees we created 1000 cops that could blow the whistle on the wrong use of channels', says James Greathouse.

Starbucks is a great example of an internal communication department that's making the connection between how employees want to be communicated with, with those who want to communicate with them. However, they emphasize that since communication is a two-way street, good communication is the responsibility of all employees. To equip employees to fulfil their communication role responsibly Starbucks provided them with training in good communication, tips on how to use e-mail and voicemail more effectively and examples of what good practice to follow.

CONCLUSION

Business success depends on employees being able to make sense of information and turn it into appropriate decisions. Organizations can increase their chances of success through better management of their internal communication. This requires reducing complexity, simplifying and integrating messages and using the most appropriate communication channel.

As the Starbucks case study shows, the role of the internal communication function is central to the better management of communication. The following chapter discusses how managing internal communication can be improved by repositioning the role of the internal communication department within the organization.

REFERENCES AND FURTHER READING

Bloomfield, R., Lamb, A. and Quirke, B. (1998), *Talking Business – New Rules for Putting Communication to Work* (London: Synopsis Communication Consulting).

D'Aprix, R. (1997), Partner or perish, *Strategic Communication Management*, (3), April–May.

Institute of Management (2000), *Taking the Strain*.

Jackson, Dr. T. (2005), *Email Use Within a Large UK Company* (Department of Computer Science, Loughborough University).

NFI Research (2006), *Communication Survey.*

Pitney Bowes Inc (2000) *Managing Corporate Communication in the Information Age,* Study undertaken by The Institute For The Future with the Gallup Organization.

The Business Communicator (2006), Vol. 7, Issue. 5, October.

The Jensen Group (2000), *Changing the Way We Work: The Search for a Simpler Way,* (London: The Jensen Group).

The Sunday Times (2007), 4 February.

9 Repositioning the Role of the Internal Communication Function

Leaders know that communication is vital to change and want to use it as a strategic tool. How exactly they should use it to best advantage is less clear to them. How they should use their internal communicators may also be unclear. They want support from communication strategists but feel they get message crafters and drafters instead. Communicators, on the other hand, may want to fill the crucial role of communication strategists, but feel that they are being used too often as writers and editors.

Chief executives want to get the best value from the business's tangible and intangible assets, especially the brands it owns. To do that they have to decide how the organization should be best structured, what the role of the centre is and what the best balance of corporate identity and branding is.

Once the corporate body is designed, communicators have to provide the communication nervous system to make it live and breathe. How do they tailor communication structures to the type of organization and the strategy the business is pursuing, as well as ensure some flexibility for the next inevitable restructure? How do they resolve the tribal warfare between communicators worldwide and how do they create clear rules of engagement between communicators?

There are four reasons why organizations need to improve their communication to add value for their businesses:

1. *The re-examination of the value of the corporate centre.* The increased emphasis on improving shareholder value has led organizations to focus more on the corporate centre's costs, and on the value it adds. This inevitably sparks a debate about the value of internal communication, and how the function should be structured, located and resourced to deliver what the organization needs.

2. *Restructuring and globalization.* There are many reasons for globalizing. Customers may demand global services, global consistency and a single point of contact for global purchasing. Companies may wish

to take advantage of their experience and their expertise by creating global functional networks to standardize what they do. The spread of global brands demands common worldwide approaches and consistency in marketing and manufacturing. These factors all put pressure on internal communication to help deliver these objectives consistently, across the globe.

3. *Brand discipline and the desire to protect the corporate reputation.* Companies whose value far exceeds their tangible assets are now commonplace, with a large part of this extra value coming from the value of brands and corporate reputation. To protect these assets, organizations are placing greater emphasis on ensuring that their employees' behaviour is consistent with their brand – yet another job for internal communication.

4. *The need to reduce information overload.* Making communication coherent and managing information overload is a tough job in an increasingly complex environment. Within an organization there may well be a host of different communicators, at the corporate centre, in the business units, at regional offices and supporting change initiatives. All these effectively compete for the time, attention and brain space of employees. In a world which is searching for value, this competition destroys it. To add value, communicators need to manage this complexity.

This chapter makes two important connections. First, it connects business leaders' need for strategic communication advice with communicators' aspirations to fill a strategic role. It looks at how communicators can place internal communication at the heart of the business and deliver greater value to senior management. Second, it describes how internal communication can be used as corporate glue to provide greater agility in shifting from one organizational structure to another. It provides a framework for ensuring that communication architecture is matched to the business structure, its corporate identity and brands. This can then be used for negotiating responsibilities between corporate and other communicators.

Finally, this chapter highlights the importance of professional leadership and the development of skills in managing communication networks.

VALUING COMMUNICATION

Internal communicators are continually trying to convince senior management about the importance of communication to the business.

In organizations seeking to change their people's attitudes and behaviours to deliver on a strategy, people with experience in change management or strategy and planning are increasingly taking responsibility for communication. Where the need for change is high on the agenda, the internal communication function is usually close to those trying to make change happen. This acknowledges the importance of internal communication.

However, just as communication finally finds a home, internal communicators may find themselves evicted, unless they can define their value to the organization and demonstrate a clearer return on investment. 'Nature abhors a vacuum' and, if internal communicators do not clarify their value proposition, the value vacuum will be filled by another department, or outsourced.

There are areas of businesses which are quietly getting on with harnessing communication to change cultures, re-engineer processes and build their brands. However, the internal communication departments are often busy elsewhere, either missing the action or being kept out of it.

Leaders are wasting communicators' expertise and experience by not making best use of them. Internal communicators are typically overloaded and frustrated as they try to focus on the strategic while having to deal with the tactics of drafting and crafting, managing logistics and producing events. The danger is that, despite good intentions, internal communication will be dragged down by leadership's outdated perception that communication is about newsletters and e-mails. In trying to fulfil a range of different expectations, communication departments may end up having to deliver to the lowest common denominator – acting only as a post office that distributes other people's messages.

BEFORE TRYING TO ADD VALUE, DEFINE IT

Businesses are learning a simple lesson – the solution they provided yesterday is taken for granted today. If you stand still you go backwards as your product or service becomes a commodity. The problem you evolved to solve may no longer be such an issue – and your solutions no longer seen as valuable.

Internal communicators need to do internally what their own organizations do externally – define a clear value proposition which their internal customers will value. They have to communicate that proposition clearly to manage expectations, and then organize themselves and acquire the skills to deliver it.

POSITIONING THE COMMUNICATORS

Organizations need to shape their communication departments to suit their strategy and their structure. Communication professionals need to be networked, coordinated, of a high standard and highly skilled.

Internal communication departments are often prevented from adding value by lack of access to decision makers and by their internal customers' perception of them as messengers. This is often exacerbated by their own narrow focus on internal communication activities, rather than on business objectives. Communicators do themselves no favours by measuring how efficiently messages are distributed but neglecting to measure how well they produce the intended business outcome.

Part of the pressure on communicators comes from internal clients' expectations, spoken or unspoken, of what kind of service they will receive. Internal clients tend to think through their problem, decide on a solution and then look for someone to implement the solution. However, they often ask for what they believe the internal communication department can provide, not what is actually needed. What they ask for depends on their perception of the department, and the skills and abilities of the people within it.

If, for example, a senior manager, who is responsible for a major initiative, wants to raise awareness of it, they might well feel entitled to some internal PR support. Faced with the demands of a powerful senior manager, it would not be surprising for communicators to jump to it and provide that support – whether or not it is appropriate.

In order to connect communicators with their internal clients, and avoid disappointed expectations, the role communicators play and the service they provide must be clearly defined. A lack of clarity in these is why internal communicators are often not involved closely enough with the functions which typically plan and drive change – strategy and planning, marketing and IT.

BY ANY OTHER NAME

Internal communication exists under a variety of different names in different organizations, such as employee relations, internal marketing and organizational communication. Although some organizations see these as interchangeable terms for the same thing, they reflect different expectations of internal communication and an unclear positioning of the department's role.

The position of internal communication depends on a number of factors: the structure of the organization; whether it is centralized or decentralized; what industry it is in; and whether branding and marketing are important to its competitive strategy. It also depends on where the department is located – unit, country, corporate, global – and the split between corporate and operational communication.

Where the internal communication function is located is largely driven by history. In some organizations it will have been seen as a hygiene factor and parked somewhere – such as with the company secretary. In other cases it has been put in a department where it was seen to be providing some value. In organizations whose focus is on manufacturing for example, and for which unions and industrial relations are vital, internal communications may be positioned within employee relations, industrial relations and personnel. On the other hand, in highly regulated industries, such as the pharmaceutical business, internal communications can be the responsibility of the financial and legal department.

Over time, however, an organization's competitive strategy changes, and the role of internal communication needs to change with it. If it does not, the internal communicators can be left high and dry, working in a no longer valued role. To be an ace industrial relations negotiator in, for example, an organization which is no longer unionized, is to fall from grace. The responsibility for internal communication does not have to move from department to department since, whatever the location, internal communicators merely need to form links with other departments. However, that does not stop organizations moving it around. The ideal role is as the communication champion, bridging human resources and the external marketing and public relations functions. For this, internal communication needs to be coordinated as part of a bigger communication picture.

In some organizations the internal communication function has developed along an evolutionary path. The value of internal communication to the business changes as what is needed from employees changes. Over the years, this may shift from employees' happy compliance with instructions to empowering them to innovate.

If it started life as part of personnel or industrial relations, the communication function may move to Corporate Affairs. This happens when the organization promises employees that they will hear news from the management before they hear it from the media. One of the reasons why internal communication becomes part of Corporate Affairs is the importance of consistently integrating internal and external messages, and getting a better return on marketing investment by using external marketing and advertising for internal audiences.

Corporate communications is often the natural home for internal communication, particularly for organizations which have learned the importance of good communication with their external stakeholders, via investor relations or coping with a crisis.

Once internal and external messages are coordinated, internal communication may be moved into Human Resources. This happens when the organization discovers that the managers' skills, and the way employees behave, is critical to delivering on the brand promise. Training, management competencies, appraisal, measurement and reward are all part of Human Resources' remit and exert a powerful influence on communication behaviour.

For those organizations in which delivering on the brand promise and increasing customer focus is vital to success, internal communication may become part of Marketing. Marketing may see the role of internal communication as focusing on the brand, driving customer service and achieving sales.

HOME IS WHERE THE HEART IS

For internal communication to bring value to the business, it has to have a home close to the heart of the business. It has to be positioned where it can support the way in which value is created for customers, and where the money is made – sales in a sales organization, innovation and quality in a product organization and knowledge sharing in a professional services business.

It is useful to be housed within a function that the business values and respects. Marketing is only a safe haven if the business understands and values Marketing. If Marketing is seen as glorified sales promotion, internal communication's role will be writing the wording to put on the T-shirts. If Human Resources is seen as a euphemism for collating sick notes, internal communication will be seen as policing the health and safety notice boards.

When an organization redefines its strategy, the heart of the business moves. Redefining its offer to the customer, or changing its target market, also redefines what attitudes and behaviours are needed from employees. This in turn redefines what information they will now need to do the job, and redefines the role of the internal communication function.

Putting the internal communication department within employee relations may make sense in a manufacturing company which depends on smooth industrial relations. When such a business redefines itself from being a manufacturing business to being a brand-owning, market-led business, the internal communication department needs to redefine what value it will now bring to the party.

The single most important factor in the success of the communication department is the personality of whoever leads and champions it. The most successful communicators operate at board level with a director, of whatever function, who is close to the heart of the business. This person has street credibility, is seen to add value and understands communication and its importance. Moving the responsibility for internal communication around departments is often a disguised quest for such a personality.

BUILDING PARTNERSHIP BETWEEN HUMAN RESOURCES AND CORPORATE COMMUNICATIONS

While some organizations keep moving responsibility for internal communication from function to function in the hope it will work, others have focused more successfully on creating partnerships between the different functions that own different parts of the internal communication job. This is particularly true of greater collaboration between Human Resources (HR) and Corporate Communications.

There are several reasons why HR is involved with internal communication activity more than ever before. First, organizations have redefined what they want internal communication to do. They used to want it to distribute information efficiently, now they need it to create understanding. They don't want simply to pump out messages; they want to create meaning and to translate communication into action. Second, companies are beginning to realize that where you put internal communication depends on what value you expect from it.

HR has a crowded agenda – and one that often includes change management: helping the organization restructure or downsize, introducing new ways of working, recruiting and retaining employees, improving performance management and ensuring clear career paths and succession planning. This, in turn, means HR has a challenging internal communication agenda as each of these strands needs to be communicated effectively. In addition, the introduction of new legislation, such as the EU Directive on Information and Consultation, means that HR professionals need to be heavily involved in ensuring organizations follow best practice when communicating with employees.

REDEFINING WHAT COMMUNICATION MEANS FOR HR

As a function, HR is rarely seen as being good at communication. This may be due to the fact that they have an impact on sensitive and sceptical employees. It may also be because many HR professionals view communication as simply passing on information, and pumping messages – mainly about the HR issues they want to communicate. While individual projects and initiatives are good at telling people what they're doing, what's often missing is the overall HR story and the bigger picture.

In addition, HR can also be seen as a tool of management, simply delivering the managing director's agenda and carrying out initiatives such as restructuring and headcount reduction. This can hamper HR's overall effectiveness when it is no longer assumed to be on the side of the employees or acting as an advocate for employees' interests and concerns.

Finally, HR may not fully understand the external brand and issues around reputation. When HR takes up internal communication it can end up focusing only on employees – leaving investor relations, stakeholder communications, community affairs and corporate affairs to the PR people. This separation of internal from external communication has a number of impacts. Alignment with the external messages can be broken, and the balance between employees, customers and shareholders lost. Listening to the voice of the customer can be forgotten, and employees can lose the external context which is often a pressure for change.

TREATED AS A TEAM, NOT A STAR PLAYER

Ideally, communication should not exist as a single department – it should be a process for which a number of functions are responsible. These functions – HR, corporate communications, IT, marketing, customer service and operations – should each own different pieces of the communication jigsaw.

Brand values, for example, are normally the province of the marketing department, corporate values are often developed by the corporate communication department, and the employer brand, employee values and managerial behaviours are often developed by the HR department. Rather than giving each function a time at bat, organizations should field a unified team that plays to its members' strengths. Instead of playing musical chairs with internal communication, they need to orchestrate the functions so that each have an influence on it. For example, Marketing comes up with brand values which are connected to corporate values, then HR develops a competency and reward framework that encourages people to act in line with the values. Corporate communication comes up with the communication plan and the key messages for key initiatives, then HR trains line managers in the skills of bringing messages to life for their people.

There are a number of ways the HR and Corporate Communication functions can partner.

Air traffic control

HR and Corporate Communication can help to plan and prioritize communication to greater effect, with early planning, coordinated communication, and clear and consistent messages agreed at the top of the organization.

Because HR has such a busy change agenda, it needs good communication planning. Some companies – like Diageo and Rolls-Royce – provide communication planning tools and training to equip HR initiative leaders with the process and skills needed to engage employees.

Developing tomorrow's leaders

More organizations are investing in the long-term development of leaders. Because communication – with employees and other stakeholders – is a vital part of leadership, HR and Corporate Communication can collaborate to develop leaders' ability to communicate. Managers' personal style and skills are often the most powerful communication. Training, management competencies, appraisal, measurement and reward are all part of HR's remit and exert a powerful influence on communication behaviour.

Building engagement and advocacy

Organizations want their employees to speak up for them with customers, with suppliers and with their friends. HR departments have spent time demonstrating the link between satisfied customers and satisfied employees. There is a strong link between good internal communication and greater profitability. Greater customer loyalty has been shown to produce greater profit. Such customer loyalty depends on greater employee loyalty and satisfaction. Employee attitude research over the last 15 years shows that better communication creates better employee satisfaction, and improves employee perception of their line managers. Higher satisfaction reduces staff turnover, and higher retention of staff creates higher customer satisfaction and greater customer retention.

Organizations want their employees to stand up for them as good employers, to say they are being managed well, and to provide customers with good products and services. HR departments can focus on the factors that build employee satisfaction, and make employees willing to be advocates. Corporate communication professionals can ensure that employees are not only willing, but able, to be effective advocates. This means providing employees with the information and knowledge they need in order to speak in an informed way about what is going on in the organization, why their products and services are good, and why their leaders are taking well informed and judicious positions on key issues.

Defining the employer brand

HR is increasingly involved with developing an employer brand as a way of attracting and retaining people. This means that HR has to be able to link its work to the corporate brand. To reduce labour turnover and improve employee retention, companies want to give employees a greater sense of belonging, so they have a deeper connection with the organization. Employees are more likely to deliver on the brand promise effectively if they feel a sense of ownership and pride in what the company stands for.

This means that HR, Corporate Communication and Marketing need to work closely together. In survey after survey, employees report that their loyalty is undermined because they feel that their benefits do not match the market rate. On closer inspection it often becomes apparent they do not know or understand their overall benefits package, or how it relates to what competitors say. This is often a simple communication problem.

Measuring outcome, not attitude

Working together, HR and corporate communication are using surveys as a more precise measurement tool. In the past, HR surveys have tested employee engagement and satisfaction, while communication surveys tested employee understanding and satisfaction with communication channels. HR often owns the employee attitude survey – which is shifting from checking employee satisfaction to a wider assessment of employee engagement.

Now, an integrated measurement between the two functions can look at how clarity about messages and satisfaction with channels translates into greater employee engagement and satisfaction, and whether that, in turn, converts into changed attitudes and behaviour that take the strategy forward.

WHAT EACH SIDE BRINGS TO THE PARTY

Good internal communication is usually the result of a robust partnership. If either HR or Corporate Communication is solely in charge, poor communication inevitably ensues. Turf wars between the functions undermine good communication. For every HR director who complains that corporate communicators are all form and no substance, packaging empty phrases in glossy brochures, there is a corporate communicator pointing the finger at HR functions for being all model and no message. So it's good news that both functions can bring complementary strengths to the communication table.

HR's involvement can broaden internal communication from messages and media to include managers' style and skills. It shifts internal communication from megaphone management to a process of creating shared understanding and meaning. A partnership means, while corporate communication provides the relevant content, HR creates the necessary capability.

HR typically brings a number of strengths to the partnership. HR professionals understand the impact of change on employees and how they go through the various emotional reactions on the change curve. They also know that senior management tend to have a rosier view of change than do employees, because they go through the changes first and feel more in control of their destiny. HR knows the practicalities of employment law, industrial relations and consultation as well as the constraints of confidentiality. In employee forums, HR professionals are often the first port of call for problems and grievances. They have a keen sense of the organization's culture, and understand how employees are likely to react to particular issues.

One shortcoming of internal communication can be a concentration on messages and channels to the neglect of how these are used by managers with their people. HR usually has the job of educating and developing managers to be good communicators, so it knows that good communication does not automatically come from distributing good PowerPoint slides. HR puts communication skills in the broader context. Good face-to-face communication practice has to be embedded in the organization through the right competencies, reward, recognition, appraisal and measurement programmes. HR owns succession planning, for example, and can highlight the importance of being a good communicator to getting on in the business, so that role models champion the cause of good communication.

On its side, Corporate Communications brings its own strengths to the partnership. Because some of their core skills include planning external campaigns, matching the right message to the most appropriate channel and looking to get the best return on media spending, corporate communicators generally have excellent planning skills.

Because of their experience in stakeholder analysis and crisis preparedness, corporate communicators tend to be good at issues identification and scenario planning.

Corporate communication departments know that they are dealing with a range of stakeholders to whom they cannot dictate, but whom they seek to influence. They are sensitive therefore to a range of different audiences and their needs. Bringing this attitude to internal communication is useful. It treats the employee as someone whose commitment and conviction has to be sought, not demanded. Good communication demands the simple skill of effective writing. Great strategies are often undermined by their expression in incomprehensible management-speak. Corporate communicators often have journalism training and are able to make dense language accessible. They can help ensure that strategy is translated into a few memorable phases that strike home.

RELEVANCE AND VALUE

Whoever is managing the communication function needs to understand the business strategy, the obstacles to achieving it and what frustrates senior management. They have to be able to develop communication solutions to the business's problems. To do this, they must have access to the chief executive and become involved early in planning and prioritization. Ultimately, they must be able to use internal communication to help the business deliver on its strategy. If they do not address these issues, internal communicators risk being without a home in their own organization.

The job of a communication specialist is to diagnose business problems and propose a communication solution. While this includes providing solutions requested by internal customers, internal communicators have to be the doctor, not just the pharmacist – educating senior management about different approaches to communication may be necessary. However, rather than trying to push communication up the management agenda, it is more effective to link communication with what is already at the top of it, diagnosing problems as well as filling prescriptions.

As communication is a means to an end, it is better to start at the end – what is the business trying to achieve and what obstacles are causing it pain? Depending on the strategy, points of pain for senior managers can include:

- low retention of customers;
- high cost of customer acquisition;
- high cost base;
- lack of internal cooperation;
- falling market share;
- increased cost of administration;
- low retention of staff.

Finding the points of pain for senior management and using communication to reduce the pain is central to creating value. Getting the opportunity and permission to explore those points of pain is the first step.

VALUE IS IN THE EYE OF THE CLIENT

Internal communicators can help solve business problems, but they have to find problems which concern the internal client. Value, like beauty, is in the eye of the beholder. If the internal client does not recognize the problem, nothing that is done for them will look like a solution.

Whether, for example, internal communication can valuably increase staff retention depends on whether staff turnover is a problem for the business. High employee turnover may be a key concern for IT departments and management consultancies because of skill shortages, but be a matter of some indifference to a retailer who accepts the seasonal migration of young shop assistants.

If the business has any aspirations, there will inevitably be barriers to achieving them. If it is happy where it is, there will be opportunities for improving what it currently does. Either way, some element of communication will be involved. The internal client may be unaware of the problem, or unaware of the link between their problem and a communication solution. Or they may be aware of both but not see the internal communication department as the place to go for help.

To be recognized as a source of help and value, communicators have to develop a problem-seeking mentality.

PERMISSION DEPENDS ON PERCEPTION, PERCEPTION DEPENDS ON POSITIONING

Internal communicators need to market their role internally and communicate how they add value. Mismatched expectations between departments and their internal customers inevitably create frustrations unless the service being offered is clear to both sides.

Communicators may want to reposition themselves in the eyes of their organization, to take a more strategic role and to provide advice and support. However, communication department staff may be viewed as skilled wordsmiths who can turn out beautifully crafted messages and then distribute them efficiently. While communicators often perceive themselves as facilitators and consultants, their time is frequently consumed in producing. It is easy to become preoccupied with tasks that you believe are valuable but which your internal customers do not – for example, developing strategy when they are desperate for a video, or publishing newsletters when what's needed is a major change in employees' attitudes.

More often, communicators complain about being deluged with requests for immediate tactical help that divert them from taking a longer term strategic view. The job that communicators feel they should be doing may not be the one that the rest of the organization expects of them.

THE POSITIONING OF INTERNAL COMMUNICATION

The department has to be clear about what it offers to the business. It may combine a number of roles, such as:

- **Post office** – providing an efficient message delivery service for management, getting the right messages to the right people at the right time, using the right channels.

- **Travel agent** – keeping track of communication traffic in the organization, helping internal clients identify good times to communicate, booking slots in communication channels and developing new channels for communication.

- **Consulting** – diagnosing problems and providing solutions, making the connection between communication strategy and business results, understanding the internal culture and adapting communication to match it.

Each of these roles is a different value proposition – ways in which internal communication can add value to the business. Each one of these demands a different set of skills, and the department needs to be organized differently to deliver on each.

THE ACTIVITY GRID

Internal communication teams need to identify where they should invest their resources, time and effort.

Figure 9.1 looks at the typical activity of an internal communication department in two ways:

- What is the balance of strategic work they do versus the amount of tactical work they do?

- What areas of communication do they effectively own and operate, and in which others are they providing advice and support?

The majority of the internal communications team's time and effort will usually be focused in the bottom left hand corner, operating those internal communication channels which they own. This is the core area for the team. The organization expects them to provide a range of effective communication channels, and there's not a lot of competition from other areas of the business to take these over.

While activities in this box may take the greatest amount of time, they do not provide the greatest amount of value. Those internal communication teams trying to add extra value tend also to cover the top left hand box. This is an area of greater added value, acting as a strategic partner to the business rather than as a tactical provider of communication products. This includes getting alongside senior management to link communication to business strategy, acting as experts in their audiences and offering insights into how employees will think and behave. They will provide coaching support to senior managers, 'air traffic control' of internal communication and partnering with other functions such as Marketing and HR to support them in their initiatives.

The left hand side of this chart shows those areas that internal communication departments can expect to own and move into. The right hand side of the chart shows areas which are more problematic, less clear and more contested. Those internal communication departments that have account managers or business partners tend to operate in the upper right

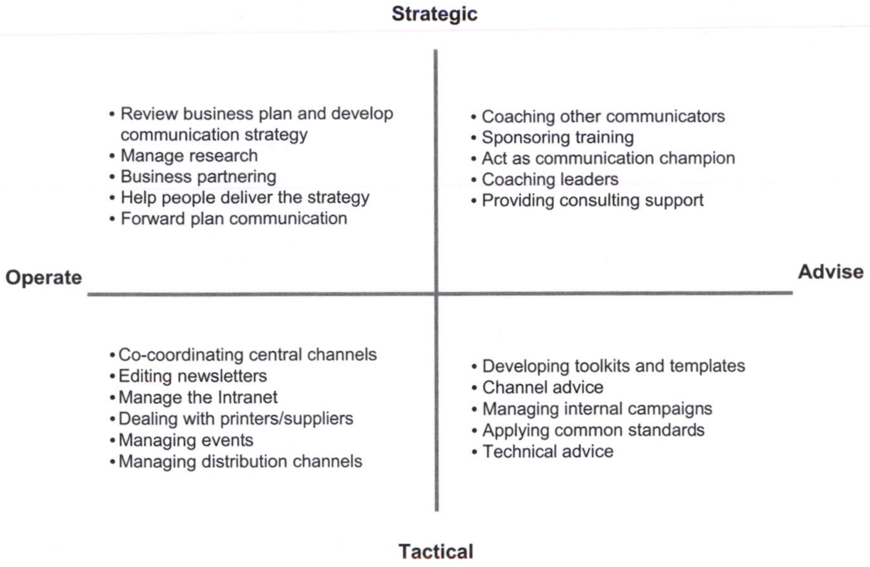

Strategic

• Review business plan and develop communication strategy • Manage research • Business partnering • Help people deliver the strategy • Forward plan communication	• Coaching other communicators • Sponsoring training • Act as communication champion • Coaching leaders • Providing consulting support

Operate   **Advise**

• Co-coordinating central channels • Editing newsletters • Manage the Intranet • Dealing with printers/suppliers • Managing events • Managing distribution channels	• Developing toolkits and templates • Channel advice • Managing internal campaigns • Applying common standards • Technical advice

Tactical

Figure 9.1   The Activity Grid

hand box – they provide strategic support and advice to business leaders, and may not necessarily get involved with providing tactical support and implementation.

This is perhaps the most important box for internal communication heads to focus on. This is because this box reflects a key area of need for the business – strategic advice from knowledgeable people who understand how communication can affect a business.

This kind of advice is sought by senior project leaders who want to make their name in the business, who understand the importance of communication to success and want to take innovative approaches to increase their chance of success.

The danger is that if internal communication heads don't look at this box, others will. This is the box where you find an influx of consultants, contractors and enthusiasts offering their services. Perhaps more importantly, it's where project leaders and senior managers enthusiastically buy support and where turf battles and initiative overload occur.

The fourth box in the lower right hand side is the area in which implementation is provided to those projects initiatives and functions that fall outside the core area of the internal communication team.

This is where initiative leaders go when they are looking for high impact events, innovative communication channels and novel media. It is also the area where the strangest communication support tends to happen. One IT department had its key messages printed on packets of condoms which were dropped on people's desks. The hope was that employees would associate the key word 'protection' with the IT department's campaign against viruses.

In another organization, one department's novel idea of providing a desk piece bearing the corporate strategy was hijacked by another department who tried to beat them to the punch. Unlucky employees ended up with two almost identical desk pieces showing them competing departmental mission statements.

WHAT'S THE POINT OF THIS CHART?

This should help the internal communication team identify where it is operating, and where it should be operating if it wants to add greater value. It should also help internal communication teams identify what other activities are going on outside their department that have an impact on the business. Finally, it will enable internal communication teams to identify what their individual members are doing.

In one organization, the internal communication team was providing a team member to support one of the most important strategic initiatives of the organization. This was the roll out of a Customer Relationship Management system which was fundamental to the future success of the business. What the business needed was strategic communication advice on how to create the attitude and behaviour change needed to make the system a success.

What it got instead was an enthusiastic former journalist who provided all the activities in the lower right hand box – lots of campaign material, merchandise such as key rings and mugs, a logo and posters for any meetings you might want to run.

At a time when the business was crying out for exactly the kind of strategic support internal communicators dream of, there was a vacuum in the top right hand box. Since nature abhors a vacuum, if you don't provide value, someone else will – and inevitably senior management started looking for outside consultants to fill the gap.

Working in internal communication demands the ability to work with internal clients at three levels:

1. **Strategy** – involved in the development of strategies, policies and frameworks; involved with the high-level alignment of communication strategies with business objectives and plans.

2. **Management** – planning and managing the implementation of communication strategies; managing communication resources.

3. **Execution** – designing events and newsletters, distributing materials and coordinating activities.

With luck, a communicator will be able to operate at all three levels. However, sometimes communicators are expected by the business to operate at one level while being restricted to another – expected to deliver change while only being allowed to deliver messages.

As shown by Figure 9.2, the internal communication manager may have to fulfil a number of roles:

- Coach

- Consultant

- Technical advisor

- Craftsman

- Distributor.

Alongside each of the roles is a range of skills that an internal communicator has to fulfil.

From the bottom up:

- **Distributor** – you have to have the channels to reach people, and this is the basic 'post office' service internal communication departments have to offer – the ability to guarantee getting messages from point A to point B via reliable channels.

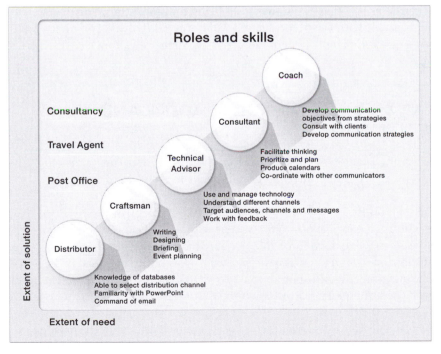

Figure 9.2   The variety of roles to be mastered by professional communicators

- **Crafter and drafter** – this is about being able to craft messages clearly, simply and memorably. This needs good writing skills which are usually desperately needed but not always in evidence.

- **Technical advisor** – this is about being the knowledgeable advisor on which channels to use, what the technical developments are, what emerging options are and what the strengths, weaknesses and best use of different channels are.

- **Consultant** – this is about being able to work with business leaders to understand what their business problem is, to identify the communication elements within that and to propose different communication approaches which will help solve the problem.

- **Coach** – this is about having a close enough relationship with managers, to be able to understand what the issues are, anticipate the problems they may find and alert them to issues proactively, even before they're aware of it themselves.

Typically, in an internal communication department, different members of the team will cover different roles. Even those who operate at the level of consultant and coach will still have to have the other skills. Whatever step on the roles 'ladder' you're on – you have to have all the skills of the steps beneath you.

The important thing is to have the range of skills in a team that allow you to deliver your value proposition to the organization. It is dangerous to have all consultants, when the business is looking for newsletters. Equally, senior management with bright ideas about what they need, often don't need an over-eager and complicit communicator, but someone who will challenge them to think again.

LINK BETWEEN THE ROLES LADDER AND POSITIONING

Earlier, the position of the internal communication department and the three options of post office, travel agency and consultancy were discussed.

The skills on this role ladder relate to those three roles. For example, to operate as an effective post office you have to have good distribution. To be an effective distributor you probably have to be good at collating information, finding new ways to bundle it so as not to overload recipients and synchronizing distribution to when people most want to receive it, rather than when the sender wants to send it.

To be an effective travel agent, you need to understand what the existing communication system is, what the range of channels that could be used is and what are the different routes open to would-be communicators to get their message across.

To be a good consultancy, you'll need the ability to see things from a business point of view, understand communication problems and propose communication solutions, and provide counsel, challenge and advice at a strategic level.

Therefore, it's important to be able to match the positioning you choose to the skills your team has. It's also important, as discussed earlier, to understand the expectations of your internal clients and their perception of you. You may be frustrated, for example, because you see yourself as a consultant, but you're forever being told at the last minute to send out e-mails advising every one of another culture change and restructure. If so, you're probably not seen by the business as the consultant you think you are.

If you decide that you need to raise your game, and on the activity grid occupy the top two strategic boxes of the chart, you'll need to invest in developing the skills of your team accordingly.

If, on the other hand, the business is expecting a good post office service and you don't have anyone who can find the employee database, or you don't have the employee e-mail list to get things to – the business is going to get very impatient with you very quickly.

STRUCTURING THE FUNCTION TO MIRROR THE ORGANIZATION STRUCTURE

The number of communicators in organizations is increasing as management recognizes the importance of communication. In matrix organizations in particular, each line of the matrix – geography, function, product line – often hires its own communicator. Faced with this growing band, more and more organizations are asking whether they need all these communicators and how they should be managed.

Chapter 3 included a discussion of the relationship between globalization, restructuring and internal communication.

Figure 9.3, first seen in Chapter 3, matches the management of corporate identity and brand against how centralized, decentralized or centrally coordinated a business is. How different organizations combine their approaches to management and brand should drive the rules of engagement for internal communicators, both at the centre and in business units.

In looking at how different businesses structure their internal communication functions, some clear principles emerge:

- there is a clear definition of the role of the internal communication department;

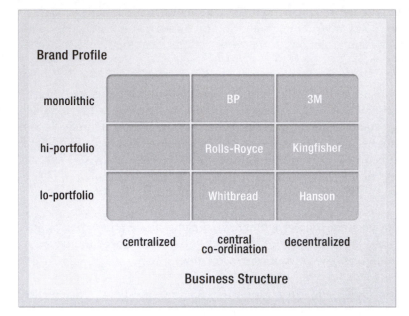

Figure 9.3   How companies balance structure and identity

- internal communicators form a professional network, which has professional leadership and development;

- there are clear roles and responsibilities between communicators;

- there are clear accountabilities, which are measured regularly.

ADDING VALUE BY GREATER CONSISTENCY, COORDINATION AND ACCOUNTABILITY

Most organizations are on a migratory path which may take them from decentralized low-profile portfolio to centralized monolith.

There are four areas which help the internal communication function to fit an organization's structure and identity:

1. Creating consistency;

2. Establishing coordination;

3. Agreeing accountability;

4. Clarifying roles and responsibilities.

Consistency

The more an organization raises its profile from low-profile portfolio owner to monolith, the more important consistency becomes. With businesses drawing on the assets of brand and reputation, and as the number of people using the brands increases, sticking to brand values and protecting the corporate reputation becomes more important.

The tools that help create consistency include communication templates, delivery guidelines, toolkits and agreed key messages.

Coordination

If an organization, other than a federal one, shifts from centralization to decentralization, the need for coordination increases. Individual businesses will still have some degree of corporate family membership to balance with local priorities, and coordination will help avoid duplication and get the most from resources.

Tools for helping create greater coordination include a communication 'air traffic control' discipline, a standard communication planning framework, planning and communication toolkits, and an internal communicators' network with professional leadership and skills development.

Accountability

As both the profile rises and the business decentralizes, the need for accountability increases. Businesses are able to take advantage of the brand but have greater freedom to do what they see fit. To balance freedom and responsibility, business units are required to work within strategic and financial frameworks, and are accountable for producing results. The same holds true for communication. Tools which allow freedom while ensuring accountability include shared communication standards and clear measures, regular tracking and measurement, and linking communication competencies to appraisal and reward.

Clarifying communication roles and responsibilities

This section identifies what the best mix of roles and skills is, and how consistency, coordination and accountability can best be used for organizations with different brands and structures.

If organizations are to win the game, they have to ensure that their internal communication is match fit – it has to match their structure and fit their brand. As the strategic goalposts shift, so too should the way communication is managed.

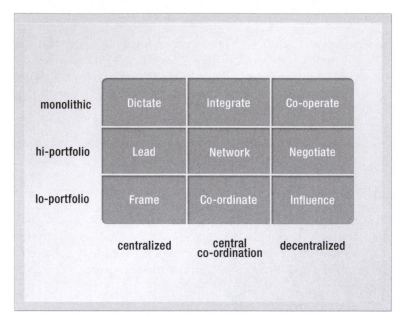

Figure 9.4   Different options for managing internal communication

Figure 9.4 labels different options for structuring and managing communication. Each of the options balances three aspects:

1.   The best location of the roles of strategy/management/execution.

2.   The mix of tools of consistency, coordination and accountability.

3.   The range of communicators' roles – distributor/craftsman/technical adviser/consultant – and where these should be located.

The individual options, indicated in the boxes, are discussed below.

1. Dictate

In a centralized organization with a monolithic brand, communication is likely to be run from the centre. There may be few organizations which are actually structured as centralized monoliths, but there are certainly a number of organizations who run their communication as if they were!

In this option, strategy and planning are carried out at the centre, with execution and delivery of pre-packaged messages done locally with minimal change. This is like being the McDonald's of communication – trying to ensure consistent delivery of a centrally developed communication product at all locations around the world.

The problem is ensuring that what is dictated is actually delivered locally, since there is a danger that local business units may feel the communication material they receive is so unresponsive to local differences that they substitute their own. This makes consistency more important, so the organization has to provide clear guidelines for what is mandatory for communication and what is discretionary.

This option demands that the consulting and planning roles have to be at the centre, together with the communication craft skills to develop messages and package them appropriately. At the local level all that is required is some degree of craft skills, to translate and tailor messages, and the skills for distributing them to people locally.

2. Integrate

In this option, local business unit freedom needs to be balanced with the consistency of the brand. With the complexity of matrices in the organization and a growing number of communicators, there is a need for a far stronger discipline than mere cooperation – integration.

While communication planning and execution will be devolved more to business units, strategy will be set at the centre. It will be important to have coordinated planning, communication 'air traffic control', a communicators' network with shared quality standards and strong professional leadership.

Strategic skills will be needed at the centre. In the business units, communication managers should be able to interpret the overall strategy in the light of their local needs, working alongside the local management team.

3. Cooperate

When monolithic branded organizations decentralize, the increased risk to the corporate reputation has to be managed.

While the risk to reputation may increase, the ability of the centre to command obedience, and the inclination of the business units to obey, is likely to decrease. In this situation, quality standards and frameworks are needed to create an 'eggshell of excellence' that reduces inconsistencies. Therefore, strong strategic and planning skills are needed at the centre to develop frameworks and toolkits which are suited to a wide range of different business units, and which reflect their different markets.

There will be a need for strong 'air traffic control', as well as strong local skills development.

Finally, the centre should actively quality assure local communicators, with clearly defined competencies and job descriptions, and regular professional development.

3M is a good example of a decentralized network of businesses, sharing a monolithic brand. It ensures cooperation between communicators through shared messages and tools across its different regions worldwide. The role of internal communication at the centre is to act as consultant and supporter, while the individual businesses focus on their own internal communication strategies and plans.

The role of the centre is to help create cross-business communication and to supply corporate messages to be tailored at local level. The individual businesses are responsible for local external and internal communication.

4. Lead

In a centralized, high-profile portfolio owner, where both the corporate owner and the businesses it owns are strongly branded, there is likely to be a network of marketing and communication professionals. They will have strong views on communication issues, as well as expertise in brand management.

Communicators at the centre may have the power to dictate, but they recognize that success depends on enrolling fellow communicators. This calls for leading the way, not dictating the rules. Developing new ideas, sharing approaches, importing leading practice from outside and providing professional leadership is a better way for them to build a functional network and ensure greater consistency.

5. Network

A business which is a high-profile portfolio owner and centrally coordinated wants the advantages of scale and synergies wherever possible. However, it also respects the individual brands' responsibility for issues that directly affect the customer, and the delivery of the product or service.

Communicators have to create 'dual citizenship' so that employees both identify with the group and are loyal to their own brand. This means that corporate communicators at the centre will have to work with the local business unit communicators to strike the best balance of corporate and local information, and the best emphasis on corporate and local brands.

There will be a strong overall corporate strategy set at the centre with a planning framework within which the individually branded businesses develop their own local communication plan. The centre is likely to provide a corporate newsletter, a corporate video and corporate information for the business-wide briefing process. It might also provide a corporate Intranet, with pages dedicated to the individual businesses.

The business units, meanwhile, will have their own communication channels, so there may be a danger of duplication. There will be a need for strong 'air traffic control' and an agreed channel strategy to avoid channels competing unnecessarily.

The relationship between the communicators at the centre and those in the business units will be a collegiate one of equals. Their roles will be similar, although their focuses may differ – one focusing on corporate brand, the other focusing on the business unit brand. The units will be given sufficient freedom to reflect their individual markets and to act in line with their individual brands.

This option is called 'network' because it entails shifting from occasional networking between communicators – meeting to exchange ideas – to a formal network of interconnected responsibilities.

In this network the relationship is as much between the business units as it is between the units and the centre, with resources and expertise shared from one to another. Business unit communicators with specialist expertise lead on particular areas such as face-to-face communication, Intranet, measurement and training. Measurement of communication takes place across the network, with common standards and measures.

6. Negotiate

Where a business is decentralized and has its own brand, its management team will feel very autonomous. They will want to focus communication only on their own local agenda. They will be sceptical about communicating group issues such as corporate values and corporate social responsibility, whether or not the group chief executive supports them.

Local brand loyalty will be strong, and employees will identify mainly with their location, product or service. Communicators at the centre and in the business units will continually argue and negotiate about business unit support for corporate initiatives and plans.

In this option, there need to be strong strategists at the centre who command the respect of local communicators. The corporate centre is likely to be staffed by the same kind of people as the business units – strong communication managers and able strategists, with good communication planning skills. Good craftspeople will be required both at the centre and in the business unit. Newsletters will need to complement each other rather than compete for the same employees' time and attention.

The balance of power lies with the business unit, and the central communicators are likely to seek, rather than demand, their help. They will negotiate for a share of voice and for support for corporate communication initiatives.

At this stage coordination is important. An internal communicators' network will allow communicators from business units to get together to share best practice. There they can identify how one business unit's solutions can be transferred to others, and discuss how corporate approaches need to be tailored to business unit needs.

The centre needs to develop a communication framework to ensure consistency, aid best practice exchange and avoid the reinvention of communication wheels in all the business units. These can include communication toolkits, a consistent planning process and communication skills development programmes. These enable communicators to come to the centre in order to learn consistent approaches which can be adapted locally, and also to spend time and network with each other.

7. Frame

A low-profile portfolio owner which is centralized, like Procter and Gamble, wants employees and customers to identify more with the individual brands and less with the corporate owner. Communicators at the centre provide strong frameworks, quality standards and clear processes for measurement. Those in the business units tailor the specifics to the requirements of their own brand and their business unit.

Such organizations allow local communicators the freedom within a clear framework to tailor and repackage communication appropriately. They provide a strong central framework without creating a straitjacket for communicators in the business units.

Once the strategic framework is set, the business unit's job is to interpret it in the light of their own brand values and market.

The relationship between the business unit and central communicators will be that of internal client to consultants. The business units will not be expected to set their strategy alone, but will be expected to draw on some of the expertise at the centre, and to get advice and guidance on how the corporate framework can best be adapted to their business's needs.

8. Coordinate

A low-profile portfolio owner which is centrally coordinating wants 'back office' synergies, while allowing the branded businesses to respond to their individual markets.

Whitbread Plc is a good example of this kind of organization and is also a good example of the coordination option.

Whitbread owns a range of branded businesses: Premier Inn hotels, Brewers Fayre and Beefeater restaurants and Costa premium coffee shops. Whitbread employs some 35 000 people and serves over 8 million customers a month.

The company combines high-quality 'front of house' customer service with the exploitation of 'back of house' economies of scale in purchasing, property and IT. The 'front of house' is managed by branded businesses in ways appropriate to their target markets.

Although Whitbread Plc sees its business as being brand-led, the Whitbread endorsement is not put on all brands. There are few benefits in being part of Whitbread – customers do not move from one brand to the other simply because they are part of the Whitbread portfolio.

The brands tend to have separate cultures, with employees identifying with those brands. The vivacious Italians staffing Costa coffee houses need to feel part of Costa – that is where their centre of gravity is. However, managers need to understand the whole Whitbread picture so that they can understand the reasons for some decisions being taken, and appreciate the trade-offs that need to be made. A sense of Whitbread among managers also helps to share resources, take advantage of size and to share best practice

While it aims to achieve the benefits of synergies where they exist, the centre allows the branded businesses to get on with the job. Each business has its own internal communication person who has similar leeway. In this decentralized approach to internal communication, the central internal communication function acts as a corporate message supplier, manages a professional network and acts as a consultant.

The central internal communication department communicates with the top managers, supporting them in communicating to their people, stimulating communication between the business units, and creating a feeling of 'dual citizenship' – of both their own business and of the wider Whitbread business. As a provider of content, it creates and sends out briefings to the top managers and provides a central news service into the brands' own newsletters. As an equipper and consultant it helps managers in the divisions translate corporate values and information into communication appropriate to their brand, and provides skills training.

Since it is a low-profile portfolio there is no common brand 'exo-skeleton' to keep the business hanging together. The relationship between business unit communicators is therefore an important corporate glue. Communication quality has to be maintained by close collaboration within the internal communication network. The head of communications therefore provides professional leadership to communicators in the business units.

In this kind of organization, not having a strong corporate brand puts the corporate centre in a weaker position to achieve its aims. It cannot create the goodwill to help cooperation that a shared identify fosters, and it cannot invoke the need for business-wide consistency that a monolithic brand provides. This can create a stand-off. On the one hand, the corporate strategy demands finding and exploiting those areas where cooperation makes sense for the business. On the other, each business unit has a strong and distinct brand and claims it has to do things differently and therefore cannot cooperate as much as it would like.

The danger here is of increasing frustration between the centre and the business units, as areas of cooperation, cost saving and best practice exchange are slowly and painfully wrung from internal negotiations. Internal communication will be expected to help accelerate cooperation, but the communicators themselves will first have to learn to coordinate.

This option places a great onus on the corporate communicators. They have to demonstrate their value if they are credibly to lead the network. This can entail providing opportunities for professional development, hosting events to enable best practice exchange and providing communication toolkits which save business units time, effort and money.

9. Influence

A low-profile group which is a portfolio of decentralized, individually-branded businesses is the exact opposite of a centralized monolith.

Being decentralized and with no shared brand, there are few other sources of corporate glue than communication. Here, the corporate centre has to be 'hands-off'. However, the group is likely to make investment decisions which can seem perplexing and frustrating for those in the business units without the wider context. So, there is a need to give the businesses a wider view of the issues.

It is important to maintain corporate glue and lines of communication. At some point in the future, there may be a need to shift to a more centralized structure. It is easier to make that change if the glue and the communication lines already exist.

Only the top management tiers of the business units will need to feel a broader loyalty and dual citizenship. The relationship between communicators at the corporate centre and those in the business units will be one of influence rather than command.

One of the cardinal dangers in decentralized, individually-branded businesses is the variable quality of the communicators they hire. In addition to lacking skills, they can also lack status with their local management team. Even where they have the same job title, they may be doing quite different jobs and may be expected to provide very different services.

A powerful source of corporate glue will be the internal communicators' network. Meetings are likely to concentrate on agreeing common standards and common approaches, and on ways to raise communicators' skills, status and influence.

The point of all the options described above is this: ask yourself which box you think your organization is in. Then ask yourself whether the way you currently run your internal communication fits that box. Ask your counterpart in another part of the business the same question. Chances are, where you should be, where you are now and how you manage, all need to be realigned. Communication either adds value or destroys it. If it is not aligned then it is destroying value.

MANAGING COMMUNICATION STRUCTURE TO ADD MOST VALUE

The preceding descriptions of options emphasize the importance of networks of communicators working closely together. The more important organizations consider communication, the greater the number of communication specialists, and the greater the need for close alignment between them.

In addition to full-time communication managers, there are two other kinds of communicators' network which organizations use effectively. The first is a network of part-time managers who work with local management and advise them on best practice and provide local support. The second comprises employees, with part-time communication roles, who are used as an information distribution channel and for gathering feedback. Body Shop, for example, used staff on the ground, trained to act as conduits for vertical and lateral communication. Such networks have common problems. Members tend to vary in terms of skills, motivation and status. Communication professionals at the centre cannot depend on them if they are perceived too differently in terms of roles and service. Part-time communication managers, for example, may work closely with local senior management but will have varying abilities in terms of discussing business issues with them or identifying business needs and appropriate communication solutions.

This can be a greater problem when the agenda of the local client differs from that of the business as a whole. It has been known for the local business unit head to instruct his communication manager to steal the best hits from corporate media and insert them into local videos and newsletters prominently, to make him look good.

Whatever the role internal communicators may take at the centre, other communicators in the organization have to adopt complementary roles. It is pointless for the centre to provide strategic frameworks while members of the network are not providing a basic service. This means that a development path for network members has to be put in place.

PROFESSIONAL LEADERSHIP

Internal communication is still evolving as a discipline, and communicators' networks need professional leadership to bring them to maturity. That leadership has to include equipping, coaching, developing and evaluating internal communicators. Corporate communication departments should be helping communicators grow professionally and encouraging internal clients to value and use them.

Internal communication functions are facing the challenge other functions have faced. Finance has had to reinvent itself from bean counters to decision supporters. Human Resources had to shift from being payroll processors and body shoppers to being business partners. IT has had to reduce radically the total cost of IT, and provide leading edge technology. Internal communication departments that don't examine the value they add will find themselves being examined by the Finance function who, while they may not understand communication, do understand cost and value.

Successful internal communication departments know that communication is a means to an end, and so establish a clear link between the business's desired ends and the means of communication. They start with defining what value they should be adding, then organize themselves to deliver that value.

To deliver their strategy successfully, internal communication departments have to balance four crucial areas – customers, channels, capacity and capability.

Customers

Internal communication teams have to make sure they are providing the service that internal customers expect. Often, confused expectations mean that internal communication departments are forever busy, but not seen as particularly valuable.

Channels

Internal communication teams have to ensure they are investing their money in channels with clear and demonstrable return on investment. Internal communication teams often operate a full range of communication channels which duplicate coverage, use inappropriate content and compete with each other and with other channels in the organization. Internal communication teams need to understand which channels are used by employees for what different types of information and where, therefore, they should be investing time, money and effort.

Capacity

Internal communication teams have to make sure they are putting their time and energies into areas of strategic importance to the business, as defined by the leadership team – otherwise they will always be stretched, usually putting most work into areas of relatively low value – endlessly redrafting leaders' e-mails, and scheduling events.

The greatest amount of communicators' time often goes into the lowest value activity. This is driven by the fact that internal customers expect high degrees of support in areas of tactics and execution but do not expect or welcome support in the higher value areas such as planning, coaching and message articulation.

Capability

Internal communication teams have to develop their skills. The business needs a range of skills from the basic requirements of writing, crafting and drafting, to advice, message creation and challenging and coaching of leaders.

CASE STUDY: ERICSSON

Ericsson provides a good example of an internal communication department that set out to re-examine where it was delivering value for the business. It successfully created a clear internal communication strategy directly linked to the business strategy, then re-examined where it was investing its time, effort and money, and finally refocused on what skills were needed by internal communicators.

Ericsson's internal communication function wanted to add greater value today, while building a more sophisticated approach to internal communication for tomorrow.

Ericsson as a company has traditionally been very positive and supportive of internal communication. The company has a history of allocating a fair amount of resources for internal communication, but the majority of that money was spent on editorial products in printed and electronic form. While the internal communication function had effectively established sound foundations, these no longer met Ericsson's ambitions for global best practice in all areas of its business.

In an environment where the CEO was driving the whole business to focus on 'true world leadership', the same requirement was being made of internal communication. The drive therefore in Ericsson was to make sure that the talent and resources spent on internal communication were focused on making the most difference for the business.

The internal communication department believed that they could add more value by supporting the leadership in the company to be more active as communicators, since research showed that leadership accounted for two-thirds of the impact on employees' attitudes and behaviour. The formal channels – where internal communication by tradition spends most of its efforts – accounted for less than 10 per cent of the impact, but took up the majority of the budget spent.

As part of reassessing the value of their internal communication, Ericsson outsourced all the editorial resources, including 20 journalists, to an external agency. The outsourcing was intended to establish better governance and processes for the internal news flow, reduce costs and provide better career opportunities for the in-house journalists. This allowed the internal communication team to free resources to support the leaders in the company, rather than being occupied with the writing and distribution of text.

The change in Ericsson's approach to internal communication was driven by three basic questions:

1. How should internal communication be adding value for the business and where should we be focusing for the future?

2. How well are our communication channels working and how best can we give people the information they need?

3. What do we need to do better as a professional community, how should our roles develop and what skills do we need?

As a first step, internal communicators from across the organization came together for a 'value proposition' workshop. Using data from past employee surveys, they focused on answering a number of key questions:

*   What was the business strategy of Ericsson, and what was its desired position in the market place?

*   What were the implications for employees – what did Ericsson need from its people in terms of what it wanted them to think, feel and do in order to deliver on the strategy?

*   Where were people now – what did employee survey data tell them about their existing attitudes and behaviours?

*   What was the gap that needed to be closed – how did attitudes, beliefs and behaviours need to be changed in order to get business success?

- What therefore was the job for internal communication – where should internal communication focus its efforts, where could it be most valuable and what were the priorities?

- What were the communication activities that were most needed?

- How did internal communicators have to work with management teams in their businesses?

- What were the performance indicators for success and how would these be measured?

How did they focus on delivering the strategy?

The result of the workshop was an internal communication strategy tying actions to the company's 'Wanted Position'. The strategy was built on four pillars:

- Focus on the customer – and understand the industry from the business perspective.

- Understand strategic and business priorities – so employees can accept strategic business decisions, understand where they fit in, prioritize their daily work and prepare themselves to succeed.

- Feel part of One Ericsson – regain pride following the years of downsizing, feel confident about progress and positive about achievements, and be more motivated to perform.

- Be connected and collaborative – understand how different units connect to serve the customer, and collaborate and cooperate more effectively across units.

The workshop was followed by a thorough re-appraisal of their investment in communication channels. Focus groups and a web-based questionnaire were used to map the views of employees across the global organization. The review identified which channels were preferred for which different sources of information, which channels were performing best for which purpose, and what barriers there were to increasing their impact. Particular emphasis was put on identifying managers' communication performance in comparison to the traditional set of channels (magazines, web, videos and so on.). To no one's surprise the managers came out as the most preferred channel. What was surprising was they were not always the most trusted channel.

The survey provided in-depth information which guided immediate and future actions on individual channels. Video productions with unclear purpose and too few viewers were closed down, while more resources were added to hands-on support to the line managers. The information allowed them to move money out of channels that were no longer effective, and reinvest it where it could be more valuable.

Ericsson then focused on what skills its communicators needed. Identifying these meant making a careful analysis of three things – what the business needed, what the internal communication department was offering as a service and what career aspirations individual communicators had.

These three are routinely out of line in most departments organizations. Businesses are often unclear about what they want, internal communication departments are not clear about the service they are offering, and individuals' aspirations are often disconnected from the job they were expected to do. Providing training in change management, for example, for communicators who should actually be honing their writing skills is a recipe for disaster. Therefore, in Ericsson, individual interviews identified what was expected from each communicator by their business management team, the range of different communication roles they were expected to fill, the range of communication activities they were engaged in and the critical things they had to deliver.

This allowed them to identify a range of different competencies for different communication roles – whether they were at the corporate centre, at a site, in an affiliate or working on a project. By mapping these onto Synopsis' existing internal communication 'role ladder', Ericsson was able to identify what skills were needed to do today's job better, and what skills were needed to allow communicators to develop and provide higher value support.

Ericsson identified the key areas for training and development which were vital to delivering their value proposition, and which would have the greatest impact on business value. Defining the roles and raising skills of internal communicators was also designed to make the job more satisfying. Three main areas were identified for improved development; Facilitation skills, Consulting skills and Message creation.

Special workshops were designed for the internal communication management team – a group of 12 representing the key parts of the business. These were part of a development programme which focused on enabling communicators quickly to adopt the skills and mind-set of global best practice in internal communication.

The internal communication team measured its progress to ensure that its work was focused on the right things. It also worked with Human Resources to ensure all managers had their communication skills measured in Ericsson's yearly employee survey, Dialog, and to include communication skills as part of managers' Leadership Profiles. Internal communication managers then worked with Human Resources to analyze the results and identify how to improve individual communication performance.

Both managers' communication skills and the performance of the internal communicators were measured. Ericsson developed an index of key performance indicators for communicators tied to the company's yearly short-term incentive programme. Communicators were then held accountable for the impact of their communication activities.

Since managers' communication has such a high impact on employees, they also worked closely with Human Resources on managers' training and development. The basic management training was redesigned to help line managers increase the impact of their leadership through better communication with their team members. This training is offered to some 600 line managers each year.

Communication is now one of the core competencies defined in Ericsson's new Leadership framework. The Leadership framework specifies what is important for a manager in Ericsson. The communication skills are defined as an ability to listen, share information and have an impact and influence on others.

Ericsson also worked to make sure that managers were equipped with the necessary tools. A dedicated space was launched on the Ericsson Intranet offering hands-on support to managers, with simple and straightforward content, focusing on tangible advice for successful communication. Local internal communicators then provide additional support to managers needing more in-depth knowledge and advice.

Ericsson's internal communication team has redefined its role and developed a new strategy to support that role. The editorial agenda and planning created a stronger connection to the corporate strategy. The editorial content also shifted to become more outside-in, sharing customer experiences and talking about competitors and trends in the industry. The analysis of its communication channels allowed them to adjust their investment, and their training in critical competencies for internal communicators allowed them to adopt their new roles.

In summary, Ericsson shows how internal communication functions can provide more value to their organizations by clearly identifying their communications strategy, identifying the attitudes and behaviours needed from employees to deliver on the business strategy and, finally, focusing their internal communication on helping to achieve those attitudes and behaviours.

There are a number of lessons that can be learned from this case study, and from the example of other organizations' raising their internal communication game:

Define the value communication should add. Internal communicators need to do internally what their own organizations do externally – define a clear value proposition to advance the business strategy. They must communicate that proposition clearly to manage expectations and then organize themselves and develop the skills to deliver it.

Use communication to solve problems. In order to be convincing, internal communicators must understand the business issues facing the organization and be expert in using communication to help remove barriers to success. Senior managers are interested in their business problems, not communication problems. While they may agree that communication is important, and genuinely feel it ranks among their priorities, they are more likely to be interested in solving their own operational problems – increasing market share or reducing waste. Rather than trying to push communication further up senior management's agenda, the internal communicator should try to link communication with issues that are already at the top of that agenda. Measuring the return on investment can then focus, not on how efficient the distribution of communication has been, but on its effectiveness in helping remove obstacles to the business.

Link communication architecture to the brand, identity and structure. An internal communication strategy should support the business strategy, and should help an organization compete more effectively. Organizations need to structure their communication department to suit their strategy and their organizational structure, their corporate identity and their brands. For better management of communication, to eliminate confusion and to coordinate messages, they will need to reorganize their communication departments. Communication professionals must be networked, coordinated and of a high standard.

Apply process improvement to communication. The drive to identify and improve key processes has forced organizations to re-examine their basic assumptions about the communicating process. Process improvement is based on a continual cycle of planning, doing, checking via feedback and then revising. The same disciplines should be adopted for internal communication – track feedback from employees, and then respond, revise and improve.

Educate the senior managers. Few senior managers have thought through the implications of changing communication internally. Commitment without understanding risks unexpected surprises and recrimination. To bring all the different issues, agendas and values to the surface, debate is necessary. Managers are more likely to enter such a debate if it starts with a business problem than if someone launches into the complaint that 'your communication is poor'.

Agree the remit. To escape from the dilemma of having to be strategic while overloaded with the tactical, communicators need to explicitly agree with the top team where their time and effort can be most valuably spent. This value proposition states how internal communication will add value to the business and frees communicators to deliver against it. This does, however, require the right people with the necessary skills. The structure of the communication network should also mirror that of the organization and how it manages its brands. In addition, clear differentiation of roles and responsibilities between different members of the network must be established to avoid duplication and confusion. If this is not done, local implementers will see themselves as consultants and begin to offer something different. Communicators' roles should be defined to ensure a match of expectations, so that those who are best at organising events are not expected to deliver a culture change. Managing the expectations and demands of local clients should be done through discussion and by establishing a clear service-level agreement.

Build networks and alliances. The internal communication function should connect with human resources, information technology, change management and knowledge management departments, and with the external marketing and public relations functions.

Learn from others in the business. Lessons learned in other areas of the business – that value is created through careful management of assets, efficiencies in supply chain management, applying a customer focus and continuous process improvement – can usefully be applied to internal communication.

CONCLUSION

Repositioning the role of the internal communication department is vital to managing communication for greater value. Departments need to be clear, both for themselves and for the rest of the organization, what they are there for, and what can be expected of them. They have to be able to define the value they add, deliver the value they promise and demonstrate the difference they have made. Good communication must not simply be done, it must be seen to be done.

In the following, and final, chapter we will look at measurement as a way of demonstrating impact.

10 Measuring Impact

In Chapter 1 the advice was to regard internal communication as a process and to manage it as a cycle. The cycle of communication is completed by measuring impact. Make sure that the circuit is unbroken – without measurement, a communication strategy becomes like a computer that is not plugged into the electricity supply.

The bottom line for internal communication is its contribution to the bottom line. This chapter covers the final link in the chain, and makes the connection between investment in internal communication and its pay-off in the changed attitudes and behaviour of people.

Measurement is not new, and there is an accepted management truism that what gets measured gets done. The patchiness of face-to-face communication inside organizations and the frustration among employees and managers alike testifies to the fact that internal communication is not being done well, partly because it is not being measured effectively.

In principle, measurement is attractive to managers, but in practice they are unsure about how best to apply it to communication. Many organizations are moving towards an integrated, balanced approach to measuring their business performance. Using a balanced business scorecard, for example, is an attempt to integrate the different factors against which a business needs to deliver for an 'at a glance' understanding of how a business is performing. Such approaches to business measurement, which acknowledge the importance of employees' contribution, inevitably highlight the need for effective measurement of internal communication. This means that organizations need to understand quickly how best to improve current approaches to measuring communication.

This chapter argues for the need to change the basis for measurement in two ways – first, away from employee satisfaction to successful business outcomes and, second, away from the efficiency of message distribution and creating awareness to testing whether communication has succeeded in converting information into action. Making these changes requires businesses to be clear, at the outset, about desired outcomes. After all, if you do not know where you wanted to go, how do you know if you got there?

The chapter goes on to recommend that research should be used with the intention of changing employee behaviour, and conducted more frequently than the usual 2-yearly survey. Ways of getting greater value from research are given, as well as ways of assessing the impact of communication at a number of levels.

This chapter also argues that, if communication is to improve continuously, information about the whole process – not just the final recipient – has to be gathered. This means measuring impact at each link in the communication supply chain from raw messages, to channel effectiveness through to action and feedback.

Internal communicators need to measure the impact of what they do, and use measurement to drive improvement. To support this, reasons why impact should be measured and a description of some of the barriers to doing it effectively are set out.

Finally, it is proposed that measurement should focus on outcomes and be linked to contribution to the bottom line. This is backed up by some practical advice on how to set standards for communication and how to measure impact.

WHY MEASURE IMPACT?

At the beginning of the 1990s companies began to use employee attitude surveys more extensively to track employees' satisfaction with communication. Then, the concern was to identify employees' needs and improve communication to satisfy them. Companies that have religiously continued measurement ever since have won high ratings both for their communication and for employees' satisfaction. However, what they have often not won are the business results they needed. They could get good survey results but bad business results – a sign that their communication, however satisfactory, lacked impact. Rover Cars, for example, had fabulously high scores for employee satisfaction and pride in the company. However, that very pride contributed to employees' resistance to change, and their subsequent difficulties.

To get the impact they want, organizations need to shift their focus. Communicators readily agree that communication is a means to an end. Yet all too often that end is either ill-defined or unmeasured. Rather than measuring how many people boarded the train and got off at the right stop, communication measurement too often limits itself to whether or not people like the colour of the engine and found the ticket easy to read.

Communicators can be vague about what specific changes in attitudes and behaviour their communication is designed to achieve, or about measuring its effectiveness in achieving those changes. Nor are their internal customers any better. If they see the role of internal communication as simply delivering their messages, they are likely to define success as the arrival of the message at its destination. Being asked what their communication is designed to achieve would be as alien as being asked by the postman what objective their postcard is designed to achieve.

Effective research into the impact of communication brings a range of benefits. The value of conducting internal research is that it often brings senior managers to awareness of the problems without triggering their defences – it gives an opportunity for education not accusation.

Companies need to know what their people's concerns are and how they get their communication. Without this information they might as well be broadcasting into outer space. Internal research allows you to target your communication more effectively, to set benchmarks and to measure performance and return on investment. *PR Week* advises that 15 per cent of any communication budget should be allocated to measuring impact and effectiveness.

Measurement helps replace opinion with fact, tracks progress towards objectives and changes behaviour by focusing people's attention on what they need to do differently. It signals what is important to the business and shows that management is serious about change – especially when leaders offer to be measured and accountable first. It also forces both the management team and employees to clarify their expectations and helps keep communication visible and on the management radar screen.

The results of measurement can be used to acknowledge good performers, demonstrate the value that internal communication is adding to the business and improve the communication process by highlighting inefficiencies.

Measurement can provide the good practice of assessing whether communication achieves the desired outcome. Where organizations like data – 'In God we trust, everyone else brings data' – they like to see metrics, especially for an area such as communication which they may regard as abstract, pink and fluffy. Measurement helps internal communicators to demonstrate they are providing value in a language that the business understands.

Internal communicators want to get senior management's buy-in by demonstrating the value of communication. They want to get the necessary budgets and they want to demonstrate the return on investment of company resources.

They usually want to identify the value of activity that has cost them time, effort and money, and calibrate the degree of success their efforts have had. All this is useful both to justify and support budget requests, but, as importantly, to understand where to focus efforts to improve.

BARRIERS TO EFFECTIVE IMPACT MEASUREMENT

If the benefits of measurement are so manifold, why do businesses experience so few of them? There are a number of obstacles – namely:

- measuring efficiency, not effectiveness;
- not measuring at all, or too infrequently;
- not using feedback to change attitudes and behaviour;
- measuring only part of the process;
- not using measurement to drive improvement;
- not connecting measurement to outcomes which benefit the business.

The following sections expand on these obstacles.

Measuring efficiency, not effectiveness

Because organizations are spending time and money on communication – whether on formal communication or on informal conversations and rumour mongering – they usually want to know whether their communication is effective. Each time there is an off-site meeting or a senior manager has lunch with employees, poor communication will inevitably be a subject for discussion. However, it is almost impossible to answer the question, 'What is the company gaining from its communication budget?' without pulling back and looking at the wider issues that have an impact on communication. Without doing this, organizations will only be able to look at whether their communication activities are efficient – for example, how much it costs to produce briefing packs, how well the newspaper is distributed, what is its readership, whether employees have the opportunity to view a video and whether they attended and liked the town hall meeting.

It is quite possible to get high scores for all of these measures of communication efficiency and yet see no sign of effectiveness in helping the business succeed. Indeed communicators often seem more focused on the communication vehicle, not the destination. This is like measuring the efficiency of a car engine, without ever discovering whether the engine is taking the vehicle any distance in the right direction.

Not measuring at all, or too infrequently

Measurement provides feedback on progress towards a goal. Regular measurement is important to keeping efforts on track. A person who weighs himself on New Year's Day and resolves to diet, but does not weigh himself until the next New Year's Eve is unlikely to achieve the goal. Regular measurement against the intended target is the only way to ensure that what is planned actually happens.

Not using feedback to change attitudes and behaviour

Without feedback, an organization is likely to keep on doing what it traditionally believed was important. Managers may feel that communication is valuable but, short of time, it may be something they never quite get round to. Guilty though they may feel about this, it does not improve their priorities or their performance. Publishing the results of research is more likely to embarrass them into improving their performance. Unless they use research to change managers' behaviour in this way, organizations face a long road of well intentioned surveys that fail to deliver the necessary changes that they want.

Measuring only part of the process

You cannot measure the effectiveness of a process if the outcome is not clear, if the process is disconnected or if expectations of it are undefined and conflicting. Communication involves a chain of interconnected activities, from the person who writes information, to the person who distributes it, to the person who receives, interprets and explains it. Any one of these can fail, and measuring only the final link in the chain does not help identify where the problem lies.

Not using measurement to drive improvement

Research into communication effectiveness has shown that, although many senior managers in the UK now have specific communication targets and are measured against them, the measure is mostly private to the individual being assessed. Performance against standards is rarely published internally.

In measuring how communication is performing, there are two options; keep the measurement private – only the guilty managers know how they have done – or make it public by publishing scores. Embarrassment is more effective than guilt in motivating managers to change. Good companies do regular surveys and measurement, include communication competencies in appraisals, track managers' performance and publish the results.

Not connecting measurement to outcomes which benefit the business

Although senior management may believe that effective communication is fundamental to effective change they do not routinely put that belief to a practical test.

The Jensen Group asked over 70 companies in the US to show how they tracked the connection between communication and successful change. They found almost no benchmarks or measures specifically linking communication effectiveness to change effectiveness. Although most of these companies tracked precisely the impact of training on plant safety, the impact of advertising on sales and the impact of investment on growth, they relied on intuition to track the success of their change communication.

HOW TO GET VALUE FROM RESEARCH

If the above are some of the barriers to effective measurement, what are some of the ways of getting value from research?

Research is more than simply a backward-looking 'How did we do?' assessment. It is a feedback mechanism for those setting strategy, enabling them to change tack and respond to changing situations. Effective communication comprises three elements. First, it is based on business objectives. Second, it is based on a clear set of expectations about what will change as a result of communicating. Third, it is focused on the conversion of information into understanding and then into action. Measurement has to reflect all three of these elements.

The following subsections describe the key elements of successful research and provide guidelines on using internal research effectively.

Successful impact measurement:

- assesses the impact of communication at a range of levels;

- measures the communication process from start to finish;

- measures outcomes – changed attitudes and behaviours;

- measures drivers – things that contribute to successful change;

- links to accountability and measurement systems;

- measures success and makes a link to the bottom line;

- is based on a clear set of communication standards.

Assessing communication impact

Typical measures of communication are based on one of two approaches – checking whether employees are satisfied with what they get, or checking whether they received the messages. Both of these are hangovers from an outmoded model of internal communication that is based on delivering messages to employees in a way they like.

In training and development, organizations have moved further forward in measuring the return on investment of their training budgets.

Donald Kirkpatrick (1994) developed a model for assessing training effectiveness. He recommended measurement on 4 levels:

- Reactions – how did participants respond to the training programme

- Learning – advances in skills, knowledge or attitude

- Transfer – are new skills, knowledge and attitude being applied back on the job

- Whole organization result – the business benefits, such as increased production, fewer accidents, improved quality

Trainers who receive post-course evaluations call them 'happy sheets' because they can only test trainees' immediate reactions to a training event. Even where these are ecstatic, companies have learned that a good course experience is only the first step to successful training. The other, more important, issues are whether the skills that are taught actually transfer back to day-to-day work, whether they meet the needs identified by the business and whether they cause a measurable change in key business outcomes, such as sales or customer service. Achieving a return on the investment depends on whether the training need was correctly identified, whether the training addressed the need and whether the learning was transferred to on-the-job practice.

A similar set of issues applies to communication. Like training managers, internal communicators have options about the level at which they measure communication. They can use surveys as 'happy sheets' which may allow them to test employees' satisfaction with the efficiency of their communication channels. After all, without a sound foundation of communication channels, communication is unlikely to achieve anything. However, when finance directors raise questions about the return on investment in communication, they are not asking about its efficiency, they are questioning its value – what does internal communication actually do for the business, and is it not effectively a corporate tax – an unfortunate necessity, like the statutory audit, with no real value in itself?

If communicators intend to fulfil a strategic role, they have to be able to measure at two levels; first, the communication foundation – how healthy are the communication channels and processes – and, second, communication outcomes – how is communication adding value by contributing to the business's success?

Measuring the process

The first step consists of measuring the process – the communication supply chain – tracking the efficiency of channels and evaluating the distribution of information and messages.

Questions about the communication channels might include:

- How effective are these media in getting the message across?
- What is their cost-effectiveness?
- What is the take-up of new channels – for example, websites and help lines?

Measures applying to messages and information could include:

- How relevant were the messages being distributed?
- Were they targeted at the right audience?
- Were messages received?
- Did people understand and believe them?

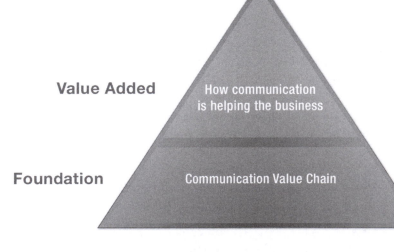

Figure 10.1   Measuring foundations and value

By focusing on the communication process, these measures can demonstrate the value of internal communication to the business. They can identify, for example, the percentage of employees who know and understand the corporate direction and objectives, the frequency with which employees are updated on progress, or the speed with which important information can get to employees.

However, these measures all concern the efficiency of communication processes and channels. While they are important indicators of the health of the communication circulatory system, they say nothing about whether or not the body is moving in the right direction. Efficient processes are needed to distribute information, and channels need to be used effectively. But these are only means to an end, and the end is some shift in understanding, attitude or behaviour that benefits the business.

Figure 10.2 shows how efficient and effective communication processes are the vital foundations of successful communication. However, the added value to the business comes from using these processes to change understanding, attitudes and behaviour.

Communicators can demonstrate the value they add through such measures as the percentage of employees who say they are motivated by what they read, or who believe management to be a credible and trustworthy source of information. Other measures might be the percentage of people who feel that they can identify with the company's vision and values, and who feel that their suggestions are listened to and valued, as well as the extent to which they respect and trust their leaders. Questions might explore whether the target audiences have a greater understanding of the business priorities as a result of communication and whether they modified their opinions or behaviour as a result. Did enough people take action such as signing up for a specific programme, taking voluntary redundancy or relocating, or joining

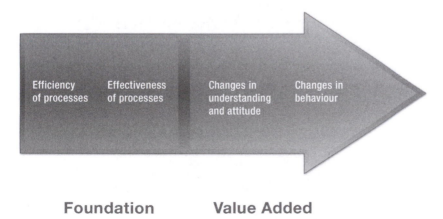

Efficiency of processes Effectiveness of processes Changes in understanding and attitude Changes in behaviour

Foundation   Value Added

Figure 10.2   Using communication means to get to business ends

the voluntary Employee Share Save scheme? Have employees identified improvements to provide better customer care or service quality, and have they identified savings as part of a cost reduction exercise?

The key is to specify the outcome you desire. For example, one morning you wake up with spots and you do not want them. You go to the doctor, he gives you a prescription, you take the medicine and the spots disappear. You are happy with the outcome. If the spots do not disappear, no matter how well the doctor dealt with you, or how legible his handwriting, how courteous the pharmacist or how tasty the medicine, if you do not get the desired outcome you will not be satisfied.

First, you need to identify the behaviours and attitudes which you require of people if your business is to be successful. Second, you need to assess the effectiveness of different communication vehicles in causing those attitudes and behaviours to come about. This should include identifying how people select and prioritize information, the length of time it takes them to assimilate information, and the recall of key messages compared to the cost of messages and the credibility of the message source. Barclays Bank, for example, calculates that it costs £65 000 in employees' time to watch a 12-minute video. Any communicator wanting to use a video therefore has to demonstrate a return on investment not just on the video's production cost, but also on its 'consumption cost'. Rolls-Royce, for example, has built into its online planning tool the ability to calculate the 'consumption' cost of any planned communication.

Matching research to communication objectives

Communication can be seen as a process of conversion of information into meaning and then into action. If the channels and processes are efficient, and the messages are clear and well crafted, but the outcomes are not as intended, the conversion process has broken down. Somewhere, links in the communication chain have become disconnected. Measurement should therefore track the process of conversion as well as the final outcome.

Measurement at each stage of the communication process (see Figure 10.3) allows you to find where the process breaks down and why. Different questions are needed for each stage of the process.

- Content
    - How effective are communication channels?
    - How well is information distributed?
    - Do the intended recipients actually receive it?
    - How accessible is the format in which information is presented?
    - How clear is the language?

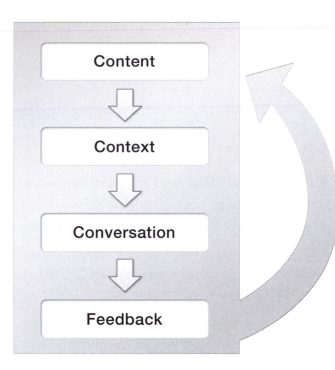

Figure 10.3   Stages of the communication process

  – How relevant is the information?

  – How well are key messages recalled?

• Context

  – How well was the team leader able to make the link between the general business context and specific commercial issues?

  – How clear was the relationship between general points and local implications?

  – How well were the issues presented?

• Conversation

  – How well did the leader stimulate conversation?

  – How involved did people feel in the conversation?

  – How safe did they feel to raise difficult questions?

  – How well did they feel they understood the rationales for decisions?

  – What opportunities were there to contribute?

  – What channels exist to put forward comments and get feedback on suggestions?

- Feedback

  - Were questions raised?

  - Were questions answered?

  - How long did it take to get responses?

  - How credible were the replies?

  - What action was taken?

Linking to accountability and measurement systems

If communication is about making change happen, then changes need to be reinforced so that they take root. A powerful way of reinforcing is to link reward systems with desired behaviours.

Competency frameworks, appraisal systems and 360-degree feedback all provide ways to make this link. Where human resource departments are responsible for both management development and employee research, they should ensure that the communication competencies are included in appraisals, and that the competencies being measured via appraisal are the same as those tracked by employee surveys. Surprisingly, they are often different.

Measuring success and making a link to the bottom line

To demonstrate value, communicators need to make their communication objectives specific. One company had a key goal of improving its Return On Net Assets (RONA). To most staff, RONA meant nothing. Communication would only help improve RONA if people could understand what it was, why it was important and how they could affect it. The communication department set itself the objectives of helping:

- reduce costs by 5 per cent by eliminating scrap;

- reduce cycle time by a factor of 4.

Within 18 months, these outcomes were achieved. These had only been achieved because people understood specifically what management was trying to do. While the communication department was only expected to communicate the new RONA initiative it opted as well to 'gain a 10 per cent increase in demonstrated employee understanding of the new approach'. It educated employees about what RONA meant, why it was important, how it affected them locally and what action they could take to improve matters. Their follow-up research determined what actions employees took once the message was understood, and so measured the contribution of the communications to reduction in cycle time and costs.

Making a direct link between communication and the bottom line is the Holy Grail of most communicators, perhaps because it is so difficult to do.

While it is difficult to demonstrate the direct return on investment in communication, it is possible to show the links between communication and any improvement in the business. This is easier when communication is treated as a process that begins with creating awareness and ends in action being taken.

Business goals and measures need to be broken down for employees so that functions, departments and teams are clear about what they need to do to contribute to business success.

One example is a telecoms organization that was suffering from excessive customer loss and wanted higher levels of retention. Simply communicating the urgent need to employees to reverse the trend might have alarmed employees but would not help them do much about the problem. However, once they had been alerted to the issue, employees were asked to identify those 'moments of truth' that often determined whether a customer stayed or left. One of these was how well the customer service department was able to resolve billing queries. This, in turn, depended on how quickly the finance department responded to customer service's calls and provided relevant information. Employees in each department were able to identify how they could work better together, which in turn improved the level of service to customers, reducing the irritation that caused some customers to leave.

While internal communication could be measured initially on how aware it made employees of the issue of retention, its real contribution was in educating employees to identify moments of truth and then concentrate on those they could affect. Improvements in the level of service between finance and customer service could be measured, demonstrating a strong link between internal communication and customer retention. However, did this show a direct cause-and-effect relationship between communication and retention? No, but it did reveal a chain of consequences that linked the two. In other words, it demonstrated a correlation.

SHOWING CORRELATIONS

Correlations show a relationship between two factors. A strong correlation does not necessarily show that one thing causes another. There is a strong correlation between having tattoos and having a criminal record, but that does not mean having a tattoo makes you commit crime. However, correlations do enable those in communication to demonstrate a relationship between effective communication and better business performance.

A survey by the Institute of Work Psychology at Sheffield University (1998) showed a strong correlation of job satisfaction and feeling committed to one's employer with higher profit and greater productivity. So, if communicators can show that they have helped raise job satisfaction and loyalty, then they can make a link to improving bottom-line performance.

This conversation is backed up by a Gallup Poll (Caffman and Harter, 1998) which indicated that four staff attitudes correlate with high profits:

1.   staff feel they can do their best every day;

2.   staff believe their opinions count;

3.   staff see a commitment to quality;

4.   staff see that their teamwork clearly links to the company mission.

These correlations formed the basis of Gallup's Q12 survey designed to measure employee engagement. Similar correlations were identified by a computer organization which analyzed results of its staff opinion survey against measures of productivity and staff retention. It found that employees who rated communication positively and were satisfied with how their supervisor communicated with them were more likely to be highly productive and less likely to be looking for a new job. The opposite was also true: employees who rated communication as poor had low productivity and were often actively looking for another job.

Similarly, analysis of their staff attitude survey found that those sites where employees rated communication highly were the most profitable, and employees there experienced high job satisfaction. They were therefore able to identify a strong correlation between good communication, higher job satisfaction and higher profitability.

BEWARE BENCHMARKS

Because correlations are so important, it is vital to avoid confusion in measuring communication's impact. Some organizations have regular surveys which include broad comparisons with other companies, against benchmarks. These benchmarks provide a useful starting point for investigating areas that could be improved. However, using benchmarks brings its own problems. Using a survey benchmark with other organizations demands that survey questions are sufficiently general to be comparable. This works against a company asking specific enough questions to identify what its unique problems are. There is also a danger in companies comparing themselves to others, instead of focusing on what they need for their own future. Some benchmarks are not that high, and some organizations will need to exceed the norm to meet their business aims, regardless of how they compare to other organizations.

Those companies which set the benchmarks, and are leaders in their internal communication, are usually the first to declare they have not yet got it right. They caution other companies against believing that equalling their scores means that their business problems are over.

Internal communication needs to be aligned to business strategy, and different companies in the same industry can have different strategies. It is useful to benchmark not just against companies in the same industry but also against companies with similar strategies from different industries. For example, internal communication in a customer service call centre in a financial services business could usefully compare itself to one in the water utility business.

MEASUREMENT IS VITAL, BUT SURVEYS ARE DECEPTIVE

Surveys are a useful tool, but they need to be used carefully. Results should be scrutinized, rather than taken at face value. Surveys contain questions which are usually answered by employees in the same way, no matter which company is being surveyed. For example, working relationships within an organization are almost always rated as very positive. Job satisfaction scores are also typically fairly high. Questions about pay usually prompt employees to say that they are unhappy since they quickly realize that it is not in their best interest to tell their employer otherwise.

Reactions to one's immediate boss are usually more favourable than reactions to company management. This favourability is driven by visibility. Where an employee is more familiar with his boss, and has a relationship, the rating is likely to be positive. The bosses may not be rated highly in terms of power or ability to actually get anything done, but they are seen to be nice and sympathetic.

First-level supervisors tend to be rated more highly because they are seen to take their people's side. When times are hard, and when the management message is likely to be an unpopular one, reactions to the immediate boss are artificially favourable. This is often because it is the immediate boss who denies responsibility by allowing the company to be seen as more of the 'villain'. When the company fails to equip managers to put bad news in context, managers protect their relationship with their team by disowning the message and saying 'don't shoot the messenger'.

Employee attitudes are affected by the national climate. ISR, a leading company in employee surveys, noted that employees in the UK are the most negative in Europe (International Survey Research Ltd, 1998). UK employees have the lowest or second lowest favourable response in ten out of 15 categories in the survey among countries across Europe. They also show the most marked decline in satisfaction levels since 1994. Feelings of employment security and company identification among UK employees have also deteriorated since 1994, and UK management are now rated less favourably by their people than management in any other European country.

Employee attitudes change over time, and also fluctuate with changes in the national economy, and economic cycles. The period 1977–87, for example, saw a sustained improvement in the employees' perception of the competence, credibility and caring qualities of management. This was based on the optimistic expectation that all the de-layering and redundancies had been completed once and for all, and the future would now be leaner but rosier. Organizations surveying employees during this period would have seen continuing change which was perceived positively at the time.

Since 1987 there has been a dramatic decline in these areas, together with a decline in perception of employment security – downsizing and de-layering are a way of life, not a passing phase. Organizations surveying employees since 1987 would have done well if their employees' perceptions of management had simply remained constant, with no deterioration.

If you are benchmarking with other organizations, you need to take into account their ratio of males to females in the workforce, as well as the proportion of managers to non-managers. Female employees respond towards most issues significantly more favourably than the national average. Managers are almost always more positive than non-managers. Similarly, length of service affects satisfaction levels. The two groups often with the highest morale are those who have been in the company for the shortest period of time, and those who have been there the longest. This may be because for the short service employee reality has not yet set in, and for the long stayers, they have either found their niche or have adapted themselves to the organization. Those with lengths of service between these two extremes have lower levels of satisfaction.

Communication is usually rated somewhat unfavourably. Employees rarely feel that they receive all the information they require in a form and at a time which meets their needs. The more employees are told, the more they realise what they previously did not know, and therefore the more they presume that there is still more to learn.

The rating of communication is profoundly affected by expectations – the UK's employees are least satisfied with communication, whereas those in Mexico, South Africa and Brazil are most satisfied. This does not imply that Mexico is proficient at communication and the UK is poor. It is more likely that Mexican employees expect less and are more grateful for what they receive.

This means that we have to be very clear about what we are promising employees in terms of communication, since their satisfaction is so directly linked to their expectations.

Communication standards

Employee dissatisfaction with communication is inevitable unless the promise the company is making is clear. Without an agreed set of expectations, people will judge effectiveness against their own set of criteria, and it will be impossible to satisfy everyone's needs. A further risk is that, without clear standards, employees' expectations grow as internal communication improves. Meeting expectations actually raises them, since the better internal communication becomes, the better employees expect it to be.

This is one of the reasons that communication surveys almost always report that communication is poor inside a company. Those companies that run regular surveys can find that the poor scores their communication receives in the first year's survey improve in the second year as employees see the fruits of managers' commitment to communication. Employees' expectations then rise and, in the third year's survey, scores go down. This is not because the communication improvements have disappeared, but rather because employees are now applying different criteria. Internal communication is poor, they say, but now for a different reason.

Some organizations have asked whether chasing employees' expectations is like trying to reach an ever receding horizon. If employees are never going to be happy with communication, why waste time and energy trying to improve it? The answer is that internal communication has to be improved for the business's success, not for employees' happiness. Customers are equally demanding, and their expectations – particularly of levels of service – keep rising. However tempting it is to stop raising the company's game to meet their expectations, most companies know that they have no other option.

Measurement should be based on what the business needs, not what the employee wants. Setting clear standards and objectives for communication reduces the risk of dissatisfaction and lets employees know what will, and will not, be available.

The senior management team have to agree among themselves what their standards are, so that performance against them can be measured and tracked. The key is to identify what is realistic and acceptable and what senior management are willing to back. It is pointless for the top team to declare that their communication will be open and honest if they then clam up when times become tough. The top team needs to make clear what standards they will actually hold themselves accountable to deliver. This will itself demonstrate their importance and will, in turn, increase their effectiveness.

Since meeting employees' expectations for communication raises those expectations, communicators will need periodically to revisit and clarify standards. Regular reviews, either quarterly or 6-monthly, will be required to monitor and assess how well these standards are being met. The most time-efficient way of doing this is to survey a sample of the workforce with a combination of questionnaires and focus groups. Some organizations, like Shell and Oracle, use regular web-based surveys continually to monitor performance.

Measures should closely reflect standards. If one of the standards is that team meetings will be held regularly to improve face-to-face communication, then it is not enough to measure whether they actually happen; their quality also has to be checked.

When companies set standards for their communication they effectively make a promise to their people. To increase the chances of keeping that promise, organizations must look ahead over the next 2 years and anticipate the impact of upcoming changes on staff attitudes. In the light of these, communicators can then identify which issues they can affect, what promises they can realistically make and what measures they should therefore be applying. For example, if a significant restructuring is likely, a company might be well aware that its communication can do little to make employees' feel safe and secure. While the company cannot promise good news, it can promise early warning and clear information. This means that communication standards would be based on a promise of speed and clarity, for example:

- employees hear about decisions well before they are implemented;
- employees hear about future plans and management explains why they are making changes;
- the rationale behind reorganizations is clearly explained to employees.

By setting clear standards, companies avoid simply asking staff to assess communication, while leaving each employee to apply different criteria. Instead, a company should specify which criteria staff should apply.

Figure 10.4 shows a number of communication standards together with the means by which each is measured. This provides a communication scorecard against which performance can be monitored and regularly reported.

The results from tracking performance should be broken down by grade and level, and data should be analyzed on length of service, grade and location to identify which issues are critical for which groups of employees and for which functions of the business. This allows greater targeting of solutions to specific problems – for example, clerical and secretarial staff may want better distilled information, while middle management may want more context to decisions.

MEASURING IMPACT IN PRACTICE

One problem that besets effective measurement is the proliferation of questionnaires, with every department using them to gather responses. If the

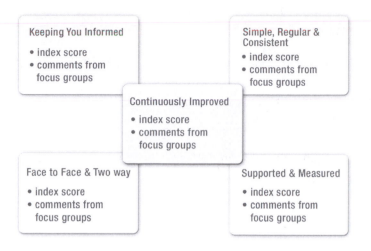

Keeping You Informed
• index score
• comments from
  focus groups

Simple, Regular &
Consistent
• index score
• comments from
  focus groups

Continuously Improved
• index score
• comments from
  focus groups

Face to Face & Two way
• index score
• comments from
  focus groups

Supported & Measured
• index score
• comments from
  focus groups

Figure 10.4   Example of a communication scorecard

knee-jerk solution to a communication problem is a newsletter, the knee-jerk
reaction to wanting feedback is a questionnaire. As waves of questionnaires
pester employees they become devalued as tools, and response rates drop as
employees tire of filling them in.

This problem is compounded by poorly designed and confusing questions.
These create problems for interpretation and, worse, difficulty in defending
any interpretation to senior managers who suddenly become statistical
experts when the survey results are presented.

For example, employees are typically asked to respond to a statement:
'The Company does an excellent job of keeping us informed about matters
affecting us.' This question combines three different issues – the excellence
of the company's job, the degree of keeping staff informed and whether or
not the information is about relevant matters. Another statement frequently
used in surveys is, 'My manager communicates effectively.' Responding to this
depends on how you believe your manager is supposed to be communicating,
and what you believe constitutes effectiveness.

This kind of question produces few clear indications of what action needs
to be taken to improve. Managers often lack the ability, time or inclination
to make sense of survey data, so there's less chance of converting unclear
survey results into appropriate action. However, this does not mean no action
will be taken. Usually, organizations invest heavily in feedback and action
planning. What it does mean is that the action taken may not solve the
company's communication problems, effort will be wasted and frustration on
all sides will increase. This frustration can be avoided by approaching surveys
differently.

Figure 10.5 outlines the typical steps in conducting research via a questionnaire survey.

There are a number of simple steps which can improve how communication is typically measured. These are detailed under the following headings:

- flexibility and responsiveness;

- methods of measurement;

- coordinating different measurement systems;

- matching research to business strategy;

- assessing the appetite for research;

- understanding the context;

- managing expectations;

- managing your response rate.

Flexibility and responsiveness

Traditionally, the employee research survey has been seen primarily as a means of letting employees 'have their say'. Now, internal research is more often used to track how employees are delivering the organization's strategy.

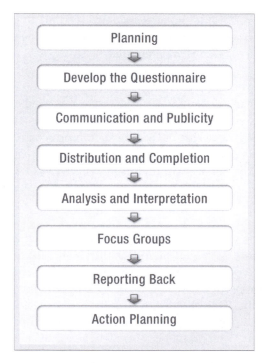

Figure 10.5   Typical steps in a questionnaire survey

Traditional research into communication channels, commissioned every 2 years as a way of keeping a finger on the pulse, may be useful for an organization in a stable market. Any organization in a changing market, however, cannot afford to check communication only every 2 years. Organizations navigating shifting currents have to check the compass more frequently, if they want to stay on course.

Organizations want more frequent and less cumbersome ways of keeping their finger on their employees' pulses using more flexible ways of assessment than the questionnaire survey. Research is no longer seen as the biennial inspection of the dipstick, but as an instrument on the corporate dashboard, providing continual feedback that allows greater responsiveness.

One approach is to use user groups as feedback channels, much as market research companies maintain focus groups to track changes in consumer attitudes. Xerox, for example, uses three tools to assess communications impact:

- their employee motivation and satisfaction survey;

- a leadership survey;

- a communication needs analysis.

Methods of measurement

There are roughly two routes in research – quantitative and qualitative.

Quantitative means getting numbers – what percentage of people say what, how many people say the same thing and how many people differ. Quantitative is about finding out what people think, how many people think it and where they think it. Getting these numbers means surveying representative numbers of an employee population.

Qualitative research is more about whats and whys – finding out what people think and why they think it. Quantitative research includes surveys, whether in print or online, awareness testing and telephone surveys.

Quantitative research tends to ask structured questions, repeats them to significant numbers of people and enables comparisons to be made both within the organization, and benchmarked with external organizations.

Qualitative research involves focus groups and one-to-one interviews, using topic guides for consistency and comparability, but allowing greater freedom in where the conversation might lead.

The purpose of these sessions is to probe beneath the surface of responses, to understand why people think the way they do and to get a greater depth of understanding of complexity and interconnections.

Running focus groups, for example, is a useful way of identifying issues as a first step to identifying questions that can be asked in a broader survey. Similarly, following the results of a quantitative survey, focus groups and interviews are useful ways of digging beneath the numbers, and understanding why people have said what they have and what they meant by it.

If quantitative survey findings show different issues for different employees, in different work groups and locations, focus groups are a good way of digging to find out why these differences have occurred, and what lies beneath apparent differences in perceptions and attitude.

However, qualitative research depends very much on the skill of the interviewer or the focus group facilitators. They need to be adept at leading discussion and uncovering issues, not leading participants towards confirming their own preconceptions.

Census or sample   Quantitative surveys demand well designed questions. Misinterpretation of questions by respondents, or just badly drafted questions, can cause confusion both for the person filling in the survey and for those trying to interpret the data. That is why piloting survey questionnaires is important to flush out any possible problems of misconception or misunderstanding.

Organizations tend to debate whether they should run census surveys – that is for everybody – or sample surveys – that means selecting a representative sample of the population.

There are different arguments for each. Census sends a signal that all employees' views are welcomed, and while not having to select and define a representative sample reduces the workload, the volume of responses makes the job slightly bigger to handle. However, higher volumes do tend to give more information, and there is less chance of a low response rate in some parts of the organizations robbing you of representative data that managers will want for their area.

On the other hand, a sample survey places less burden on the business since not everyone is asked to participate, and a good selection of a representative sample means that everyone has the same chance of being selected. Sample surveys tend to be favoured by organizations that are doing continual waves of research – such as quarterly or 6-monthly – since they can be used to avoid giving employees questionnaire fatigue from being asked to fill in too many questionnaires.

Using personnel lists to select a good representative sample usually means that a smaller survey will still give a good indication of the organizations issues. However, a low response rate can be a problem in a sample survey.

Surveys are not the only tool   One problem with surveys is doing them too infrequently. If you weighed yourself only once every 2 years it would be unlikely that you would be using the information to help you lose weight. The other problem is of course running them too frequently. Since online surveys are a fairly cheap option for workforces with access to computers, the danger is often that employees are over-surveyed, and tire of questionnaires.

Asking employees for their opinions, whether in focus groups or in an online survey, implies that you are going to do something about the results. Some organizations have found that running quarterly surveys does not give them the chance to feed back results, take action and demonstrate progress before the next round of surveying starts.

However, if you are simply looking to track shifts in attitudes, penetration of messages and shifts in beliefs – without needing to action plan to address opinions and attitudes – quarterly surveys allow you to keep the finger on the pulse.

Surveys are not the only tool. Some organizations have employees they use as 'listening posts' – either nominated employees that are brought together to give reactions; act as a sounding board and feed back penetration of messages and understanding of corporate issues. Others simply do random telephone follow-ups after waves of communication.

Another approach to measurement is the 'inbox' exercise – where you set up dummy employees, or dummy managers, and track and record all the communication they receive over a given period – say a month.

In one such exercise, a Pharma company's sales and marketing organization and discovers that 30 per cent of their e-mail traffic was misdirected. In another, the communication director gathered all the print materials which were sent to a tier of managers, and then had the full month's quota of materials delivered to a senior management meeting on a forklift truck, to demonstrate the problem of information overload.

Coordinating different measurement systems

There are often a range of different and discrete measurement activities within an organization, each owned by a different department and measuring different aspects of the business. For example, the marketing department may be measuring the health of the brand, the human resources department may be using appraisals to track management competency and the internal communication department may be running a staff attitude survey.

In a world where employees are bombarded by questionnaires seeking their views on everything from the company's strategic direction to the usefulness of the vending machine, consolidating research is vital. If different types of research, run by different departments, use complementary measures they can provide different pieces of the jigsaw that fit together to give a clearer picture. Marketing, for example, can still track the health of the brand, while the internal communication survey measures how well brand values are conveyed and understood. Finally, the human resources department can appraise managers' ability to open and lead discussion about converting brand values into appropriate action.

Matching research to business strategy

In delivering business strategy, different things are needed from different people. For example, customer-facing staff may need a deep understanding of customer preferences and profiles, a wide knowledge of a range of different products and knowledge of cross-selling opportunities. Research should therefore be targeted on assessing how well communication is equipping different audiences with, for example, knowledge of customers and familiarity with the product range.

If your strategy is to differentiate yourself through excellent customer service, it is not enough to measure whether employees are aware of the strategy – you have to test for knowledge of the customer. Questions should reflect the company's competitive differentiation, testing, for example, the understanding of different customer types and whether some are more important than others. Questions could also test knowledge of product range, typical customer needs and knowledge of the competition.

Assessing the appetite for research

Because conducting any form of research raises employees' expectations that things will change, you have to be certain that managers have the will to make changes. Researchers often advise only asking questions you intend to actually address. One issue to consider, therefore, is how managers might react to the results.

It is worth thinking through how bad the results might be, as managers rarely come out of surveys covered in glory. Therefore, imagine a poor set of results and consider how managers might respond. Talk through with them what the results might be and consider how to move things forward should your predictions come true.

Understanding the context

Research findings in themselves tell you almost nothing about the organization's state of health. You need to understand the context in which the survey has been undertaken and in which your business is operating.

For example, one organization's survey results showed that employees were highly satisfied with the benefits they received and generally very satisfied with their jobs. They believed they received enough information, and were very proud of being part of the company. Out of context, these responses suggested a highly satisfied and aligned workforce. However, the organization was about to enter a period of rapid change which would generate high levels of uncertainty among the workforce. Their working patterns would change significantly, as they were required to move from long to short production runs, requiring much greater flexibility. The survey results showed therefore a 'fat and happy' workforce which was not well placed to respond to the challenges of change that it was about to face.

Managing expectations

Since conducting research raises expectations that you will do something with the answers, only ask about issues you are willing to change. Ask if people are satisfied with their pay or their physical working environments if you have the budget and desire to do something if they say they are not. Otherwise, direct the research questions on to issues about which you can do something, and on which you can afford to take action.

A good way to uncover managers' expectations is to ask them to predict likely employee responses and to consider what actions they would take if their predictions proved correct.

Managing your response rate

There are a range of factors which can encourage a high response rate to a questionnaire survey.

Ensure confidentiality and reassure employees that their responses will remain anonymous by guaranteeing that no results will be broken down for subgroups of less than ten people. If confidentiality has been broken on previous surveys, this will inevitably reduce the response rate.

Use advance publicity to let people know what is going to happen and when. They need to know why the survey is being undertaken, what they need to do and why they should take part. Questionnaires tend to end up in the bottoms of in-trays, so publicize it by means of e-mail reminders, articles on the Intranet, in the staff newsletter or posters on the notice board to keep it at the front of people's minds.

Inevitably staff will ask their managers whether it is worth taking part, so make sure that line managers are briefed to answer any questions that their staff have. Getting line managers bought into the survey process goes a long way to ensuring its success.

In times of turbulence and uncertainty people may well read sinister motives into being asked their views. You therefore need to have a compelling reason for why the survey is happening and a sound business rationale for conducting it.

Inevitably, any survey has its minor problems. You can minimize these by piloting the survey on a small group of people. This allows you to debug it, check that the language is appropriate and find out how long it takes to complete. Piloting helps you put the survey into the respondents' own language, therefore making it easier for them to complete it.

People need to be given the time to complete a survey, and that time should not be too long. People are busy at work, and are probably aware of the importance of productivity. Sending them a questionnaire that will take 40 minutes to complete will therefore ensure it goes straight into the waste bin. Anything much longer than 20 minutes is stretching people's goodwill too far. A survey that takes much longer than 30 minutes probably means that your aim is too wide and that you do not really know why you are doing it.

One of the key factors in getting people to complete a questionnaire is an easy-to-use design and layout. The question flow should be clearly signposted, the ordering of questions should be logical and there should be plenty of white space between questions so that it does not look too lengthy. You should aim for consistency in question layout, but have some variation to prevent the appearance of monotony. You may want to conclude the questionnaire by asking people to write their own additional comments. The value of these 'open ended' questions varies, but it does give people the opportunity to 'have their say'. When respondents fill all the space available, and then continue their comments on additional space, you know that the company has problems.

REVISITING THE CIRCLE

Impact measurement has to be continuous for two reasons: first, because its purpose is to help keep communication aligned with business needs and, second, because people and their expectations keep changing. John Lennon said, 'Life is what happens when you're busy making plans.' If you have reached the end of this book and carefully thought through how each link in the communication chain should work for your organization, life has probably moved on again while you were reading.

One of the key lessons that this book has emphasized is that good communication is a means to an end. That end is often receding. Good communication is a vehicle, not a destination. Once businesses raise their communication game, the market's goalposts usually move and the rules are rewritten. As John F. Kennedy said, 'The only unchangeable certainty is that nothing is certain or unchangeable.' As the business context shifts, business issues and strategy will change. Communication strategy will need to be realigned, and a new wave of measurement and tracking put in place. When I was growing up I measured my height; now as I grow out I measure my weight.

The requirement for business success is good communication, and the price of good communication is, if not eternal vigilance, then regular revisiting and review. A final word from George Bernard Shaw that increasingly appears on the pin boards of communication directors makes the point, 'The greatest problem with communication is the illusion that it has been accomplished.'

REFERENCES AND FURTHER READING

Caffman, C. and Harter, J. (1998), *A Hard Look at Soft Numbers* (London: Gallup Organization).

Institute of Work Psychology (1998), (Sheffield: University of Sheffield)

International Survey Research Limited (1998), *The Rise and Fall of Employee Morale: Attitudes of UK Employees*.

Kirkpatrick, D. L. (1994), *Evaluating Training Programs*, American Society for Training and Development.

The Jensen Group (2000), *Changing the Way We Work: The Search for a Simpler Way* (London: The Jensen Group).

Index

Figures are indicated by bold page numbers, tables by *italics*.